Programming the
Network with
Perl

Programming the Network with Perl

Paul Barry
Institute of Technology, Carlow, Ireland

JOHN WILEY & SONS, LTD

Copyright ©2002   John Wiley & Sons Ltd
Baffins Lane, Chichester,
West Sussex PO19 1UD, England

National   01243 779777
International (+44) 1243 779777

e-mail (for orders and customer service enquiries): cs-books@wiley.co.uk

Visit our Home Page on http://www.wileyeurope.com or http://www.wiley.com

Library of Congress Cataloging-in-Publication Data

(applied for)

British Library Cataloguing in Publication Data

A catalogue record for this book is available from the British Library

ISBN 0 471 48670 1

Typeset in 9.5/12.5pt Lucida Bright by T&T Productions Ltd, London.

This book is printed on acid-free paper responsibly manufactured from sustainable forestry in which at least two trees are planted for each one used for paper production.

Dedicated to Deirdre,
for continuing to put her ambitions on hold
while I pursue mine.

Contents

Preface

The study of Computer Networking, long considered an adjunct to traditional third-level computing programmes, has moved into the mainstream. The Institute of Technology, Carlow, where I lecture, was the first third-level college in Ireland to develop an advanced four-year degree programme devoted entirely to the study of Computer Networking. Students learn computing from a networking perspective, and are trained in traditional programming technologies such as C, C++ and Java. In addition, the established degree programmes have been periodically reviewed to include new mainstream technologies, with recent emphasis on including the technologies associated with computer networks, concentrating, from a programming perspective, on network sockets.

Using a traditional programming language to program network sockets (and networks in general) is a well-established practice. Unfortunately, some students have difficulty grasping the details of these languages, and, consequently, struggle with the complexities of programming network sockets. However, when a higher-level language like Perl is used, students are more comfortable with it and enjoy greater programming success.

Of course, there is more to programming the network than programming network sockets. The modern network programmer needs to be able to analyse the network traffic programs generate, interact with standard network protocols, and manage complex networked systems.

What is in this book

This book supports the study of computer networking through the medium of Perl programming.

Following an introduction to Perl (in Chapter 1, *Meet Perl*), the focus is on debugging. Programmers know how to debug programs. When it comes to the network, they need to know how to *debug communications*. In Chapter 2, *Snooping*, some simple Perl programs are built to capture and analyse the traffic network applications generate. In the absence of any custom network applications, these simple programs are used to analyse the traffic generated by some standard network technologies.

With the analysis tools in place, Chapter 3, *Sockets*, details the creation of a collection of custom network applications using the Socket application programmer interface. These are then developed to add increasing levels of sophistication.

The experience of building networked applications is good preparation for interaction with the standard protocols of the Internet, the biggest computer network of all. In Chapter 4, *Protocols*, the standard and add-on facilities of Perl are used to interact with a selection of standard protocols and applications.

It is important to build robust custom network applications. It is also important to be able to manage the networked environment within which these applications operate. The Internet provides a standard mechanism to do this, and Perl is used to program it in Chapter 5, *Management*.

Programming the Network with Perl concludes with Chapter 6, *Mobile Agents*, which explores an area of computer networking that is generating considerable research. Many believe *Mobile-Agent Technology* to be one of the 'next big things' on the Internet.

At the end of each chapter, a list of *Print* and *Web Resources* is provided to facilitate further study. All chapters conclude with a set of programming exercises.

Who should read this book?

Programming the Network with Perl evolved from my involvement in teaching a 30 week computer networking module to a group of final-year undergraduate software engineers. The material presented here is derived from the practical material developed for the course. Since there is a high practical content related to the study of computer networking, *Programming the Network with Perl* is highly complementary to such a course. In addition, any course on programming Perl will benefit from the real-world examples illustrated. The professional Perl programmer should also find the material interesting, as it is no longer enough to program the computer – *the modern programmer needs to know how to program the network*.

Platform notes

The Linux platform provides a host for our work. Not only is Linux a modern, feature-rich operating system, it is also available free of charge, and is, therefore, readily available. Linux provides excellent support to the Perl programmer. All the code in *Programming the Network with Perl* should run unaltered on any Linux platform, regardless of the underlying hardware technology. Users of UNIX or BSD derived systems should experience no real problems running the code. When working on Windows or Mac OS (prior to release X), getting the code in Chapter 2 to work will cause the most difficulty, although most of the code in the other chapters should run unaltered on these non-UNIX operating systems. For readers new to Linux, two appendixes provide quick references to the most frequently used Linux commands and to the vi text editor.

The network used during the development of *Programming the Network with Perl* is built from Ethernet hardware and TCP/IP software. The Ethernet network is connected to the global Internet via a *cisco* router and an ATM connection. The *Network Employed* appendix provides additional details on the network used (see the diagram on p. 316).

Unless otherwise stated, use of at least release 5.6.0 of the Perl programming language is assumed.

Accompanying website

Details of the mailing-list, source code, errata and other material related to *Programming the Network with Perl* can be found on the book's website, located at `http://glasnost.itcarlow.ie/~pnb/index.html`.

Your comments are welcome

I welcome all comments (good and bad) about *Programming the Network with Perl*. Contact me via email at `paul.barry@itcarlow.ie`. Alternatively, write to me care of the publisher.

Acknowledgments

Thanks to Mark T. Sebastian for providing a detailed technical review of the manuscript, and to Greg McCarroll for his constructive criticism. My father, Jim Barry, thoroughly proof-read the entire manuscript and suggested many improvements to my writing style. A big thank-you to the team (Robert Hambrook, Jill Jeffries and Karen Mosman) at *John Wiley & Sons, Ltd.* Thanks to Michael Baker, John Hegarty, Austin Kinsella and Colm O'Connor at *The Institute of Technology, Carlow*. Thanks, too, to the students of CW082-4 for helping to debug many of the example programs. And hats off to Sam Clark (of T&T Productions Ltd) for turning my amateur LaTeX into that which you see before you now.

I would like to acknowledge a small group of inventors for their inventions: Linus Torvalds for Linux, Bill Joy for vi, Leslie Lamport for LaTeX and, *of course*, Larry Wall for Perl. This book was inspired by the last invention, and produced with the first three.

Programming the Network with Perl would never have been written without the continued support of my wife, Deirdre. While I worked on the manuscript, Deirdre looked after everything else. And with three little ones (all under 6 years of age), everything else was oftentimes quite a handful. Thanks, Deirdre.

1

Meet Perl

This chapter introduces Perl to the non-Perl programmer. Competent Perl programmers need only skim through this material.

The main objective of this chapter is to provide sufficient Perl to allow readers to comfortably work through the rest of *Programming the Network with Perl*. Another is to show that Perl is a rather special programming technology: interesting, powerful, useful and fun.

Newcomers to Perl are advised to work through a good introductory Perl text. See the *Print Resources* section at the end of this chapter for suggestions.

For the purposes of this chapter, it is assumed that the reader is already a programmer. Veterans of the 'C type' languages may find much of Perl familiar. However, although Perl may *look* a lot like C, its behaviour is oftentimes a little strange, and can consequently be quite unlike C. Fans of other programming languages will, initially, just find Perl to be strange. Perl does not set out to be strange, but it is sometimes so unlike the mainstream programming languages that the differences are seen as strangeness in the eyes of 'traditional' programming folk. Which leads into the first bit of Perl strangeness: *default behaviour*.

1.1 Perl's Default Behaviour

Unlike other programming languages, Perl assumes a lot. It does a lot of things by default, and unless told otherwise, a Perl program will inherit this default behaviour. Think of this as Perl's way of giving programmers something for nothing. This is unlike the vast majority of programming languages, which generally assume nothing, and where nothing is free.

1.1.1 Our first Perl program

A simple example[1] will help to illustrate this default behaviour:

```
#! /usr/bin/perl -w

while (<>)
{
    print;
}
```

The first line (all that #! stuff) looks a little strange, so let us conveniently ignore it, for now. The core of this program is the `while` loop, which is printing something with a `print` statement. Just what is getting printed is not clear, but as the `print` statement is in a loop, the assumption is that the printing is happening over and over again (as long as the condition of the `while` loop is true). But, what is getting printed?

The answer lies in the bit of code that has not been explained yet. No, not the strange first line – that is still too strange to discuss – it is the other bit, the `<>` bit. If you are reading this and saying 'that cannot do much', then welcome to the wonderful world of Perl!

The `<>` is a Perl operator which, unless Perl is told otherwise, hooks a program up to standard input and, when it appears in code, returns a line from standard input to the program. Magically, the line of input comes into the program at the top of the `while` loop, then makes its way (magically, again) to the `print` statement and gets printed!

Now, if a selection of lines is fed to this program, they will all get printed one after the other (remember: the `print` statement is within a loop, so the code keeps executing while some condition is true). In this case, the program keeps going while there are input lines to process. To get lines into the program, pass them in from the keyboard (the *hard* way), or from a file (the *easy* way).

Use the `vi` editor to create a file containing the Perl code as shown above. For want of a better name (and a distinct lack of imagination), let us call this program `first`. At the Linux command prompt, enter the following command to test the program's functionality:

```
perl first /etc/passwd
```

The program should print each line from the `/etc/passwd` system file to the screen, one line at a time, until it runs out of lines.

If something other than the content of the file appears, check to see if the Perl code has been typed in correctly. You can ask Perl to check code for syntax errors using the -c command-line switch. That is, typing `perl -c first` will check the `first` program for errors, but *not* run it.

---

[1] Borrowed rather shamelessly from Chapter 2 of Nigel Chapman's book: *Perl: The Programmer's Companion*. See the *Print Resources* section at the end of this chapter.

So, this program will, by default, use the filename from the command-line as standard input to the program. Perl finds the file, opens it, keeps reading from the file one line at a time until there are no more lines to read, then closes the file when the program ends. And all this *behaviour* happens by *default*.

As if that were not enough, the program actually does more. If it is provided with more than one filename on the command-line, as follows:

```
perl first /etc/passwd /etc/inittab .bash_profile
```

it not only prints all the lines from /etc/passwd but, when it is done, moves onto /etc/inittab and prints all the lines in that file, before moving onto .bash_profile and printing any lines contained therein. Again, all this occurs by default, free of charge, no questions asked!

A good question to ask at this point is: while the program is running, just where does Perl put the line that it reads in with <> and then prints out with print? We can answer this question after introducing another bit of Perl strangeness: *the default variable*.

1.1.2 Perl's default variable

Meet the default variable $_, the most used and abused variable in all of Perl.

The general rule-of-thumb is this: if a piece of Perl code expects a variable to be used and one is not provided, 9 out of 10 pieces of code will use $_.

This is exactly what happens with <> and print in the first program. The code could have been written as follows:

```
#! /usr/bin/perl -w

while ($_ = <>)
{
    print $_;
}
```

To re-emphasize, this code is *functionally identical* to the code in the first program (albeit, somewhat more explicit).

1.1.3 The strange first line explained

All that remains of the first program is an explanation of the strange #! line. This line is actually doing two things. As the # symbol in Perl indicates the start of a comment that extends to the end of the current line, the strange line is, first and foremost, a comment that is ignored by the Perl interpreter. Secondly, if the very first character of a file is # followed by a !, then the line takes on special meaning on Linux (and UNIX-like) systems. The #! combination tells the command processor to run the command identified by the rest of the line (in this case, it is the /usr/bin/perl -w part), and then send the rest of the file to it as standard input. So, make the first program executable on Linux using the following command:

```
chmod +x first
```

and then invoke the program as follows:

```
./first /etc/passwd /etc/inittab .bash_profile
```

Linux will find the Perl interpreter (rather conveniently called perl) located in the /usr/bin directory and run the contents of the first file through it. This is a cool feature of Linux (and UNIX), but of lesser importance if running on Mac OS (prior to X) or one of the Windows varieties.

The -w part of the Perl command is a *switch* asking Perl to compile the code with extra warnings enabled. Until you know what you are doing, the advice is to always run Perl with the -w switch.

Oh, by the way (and in case you hadn't noticed), Perl statements end with the ; character, and blocks of code are enclosed in curly braces, { and }. Note, too, that Perl is case sensitive (so be careful). And Perl is an *interpreter*, which means that each time a program is run through Perl, the interpreter scans the code for errors, converts the code to Perl's internal bytecode format, optimizes the bytecode, then runs it. If this all sounds slow, do not worry, in the big scheme of things, it really is not. Once a Perl program is actually running *inside* the interpreter, its performance compares favourably with the traditional compiled languages.

Whew! We are finally done with the first program. Which just goes to show that it is sometimes much easier (and shorter) to write a few lines of Perl code than it is to explain them!

1.2   Using Variables in Perl

So far, the only variable seen and used is $_, the default variable. Creating containers for variables in Perl is easy. Give the container a name (which is made up of a combination of the letters A-Z, a-z, the digits 0-9 and the underscore character), then precede the name with one of Perl's special variable naming characters, depending on what the variable will be used for:

$ – a *scalar* variable (one of something);

@ – an *array* variable (a collection of somethings, a list);

% – a *hash* variable (a collection of name/value pairs); and

\ – a *referenced* variable (a 'pointer' to something else, *usually* another variable).

1.2.1   One of something: scalars

When looking for a place to put one copy of something within a Perl program, use a scalar. Here are some examples:

```
$greeting = "Welcome to Perl!";
$score = 20;
$score = "Goal!";
$next = <>;
$_the_answer = 42;
$WhoWantsToBeA = 1_000_000;
```

Some readers may be looking at the $greeting variable and saying 'that's not one of something, that's three words', but they would only be half right. Yes, it is three words, but they are contained within *one single string*, and Perl refers to this single string with a scalar variable container.

Other readers may find it interesting (even strange) that the variable $score is being set to two different types of values – one a number (20) and the other a string ('Goal!'). Assuming that these six lines were in fact a little Perl program, surely the Perl interpreter would complain that the second usage of $score causes an error, as $score was initially used within a numeric context? On the contrary, Perl does not care what value is assigned to a scalar[2], because Perl has *no real notion of variable types*, at least not like that which readers might be used to in C, C++, Pascal, or Java. So, it is OK (with Perl) to assign seemingly different typed values to the same scalar variable.

Note that variable names can start with and include the underscore character, which can also be used to make literal numbers easier to read – simply place an underscore where it is usual to expect a comma. So:

```
$WhoWantsToBeA = 1_000_000;
```

is equivalent to:

```
$WhoWantsToBeA = 1000000;
```

whereas:

```
$WhoWantsToBeA = 1,000,000;
```

sets the variable $WhoWantsToBeA to 1, but readers will have to wait until lists are covered to find out why.

In the code, the $next variable is assigned the result of Perl processing the <> operator. What happens is that a line of text from standard input is read into the program and assigned to the $next variable. Note that <> on a line by itself within a program does not take a line from standard input and put it into the $_ variable, as this behaviour only works within loops, as was the case with the

---

[2]Well, just so long as it is one of something.

first program. Be warned: if the <> operator appears on a line by itself within a Perl program, a line *is* read in from standard input, but, as Perl has nowhere to put the contents of the line, it is discarded, never to be seen again (unless read again from standard input). Hence, the use of the $next variable in the above example.

1.2.2   A collection of somethings: arrays and lists

Here is an example that shows a relatively standard usage of arrays and lists in Perl:

```
@networks = ('Ethernet', 'Token-Ring', 'Frame-Relay', 'ATM');
```

On the left of the assignment operator (the = symbol), there is an array called @networks. Note the prefixed @ character, which indicates that this is an array variable. On the right, there are four network names in the form of a Perl list. The four names are surrounded by single quotes, enclosed in parentheses, and separated by commas. The elements of the list are all 'one of something' scalar values (in this case, *strings*). This single line of code takes the four network names and assigns them to the first four elements of the @networks array.

In Perl, array indices start counting from zero, and the first element is actually referred to as element 0. So, @networks is a four-element array with elements numbered 0, 1, 2 and 3.

The current size of an array can be determined in one of two ways. Add one to the value of the largest index (using $#), or assign the array to a scalar variable:

```
print "The size of the array is: ", ( $#networks + 1 ), "\n";
$size = @networks;
print "The size of the array is: $size\n";
```

will print the following:

```
The size of the array is: 4
The size of the array is: 4
```

Looking at the code, the $size scalar value is substituted into the part of the double quoted string that gets printed. This process is called *variable interpolation*, and it will be returned to later on in this chapter. The first print statement is actually printing a list, made up of a string, an expression, and another string[3].

Arrays in Perl are automatically dynamic, so it is possible to add elements to the array without first having to reserve space for them. Here is how to add more network names into the array:

```
@networks = ( @networks, ( 'FDDI', 'Arcnet' ) );
```

---

[3]Did you notice this?

The `$#networks` variable now has the value 5, which means there are *six* elements in the array.

Accessing a single, specific array element is accomplished using the standard square bracket notation. The code which follows prints the word Token-Ring (followed by the newline character):

```
print "$networks[1]\n";
```

When accessing a single, specific element of an array, we are no longer referring to a collection of somethings, we are instead referring to the single, scalar element located within the array (i.e. one of something). Hence, the use of the $ prefix in the previous example as opposed to the @ prefix, which would refer to the entire array.

Surprisingly (or strangely), Perl does not complain when code refers to a single array element with the @ prefix. The following code will also print the word Token-Ring (followed by the newline character):

```
print "@networks[1]\n";
```

Technically, this is a single element *array slice*, and should be avoided in situations like this. Strange? Most definitely. Something to worry about? Probably not. Just be sure to prefix single-element array accesses with $ and everything will be OK.

When used in a *scalar context*, arrays and lists have a value. An array has a numeric value equal to the number of elements in the array, whereas a list has a value equal to the first element in the list. This helps explain why the following sets $WhoWantsToBeA to 1 and not 1,000,000 as might initially be expected:

```
$WhoWantsToBeA = 1,000,000;
```

Scalar context can be forced on an array by use of the inbuilt `scalar` subroutine. This code tells Perl to treat the array as a scalar, even though it really still is an array:

```
print "The size of the array is: ", scalar @networks, "\n";
```

An experienced Perl programmer may frown at the initial technique used when creating the first version of the @networks array, which is repeated here:

```
@networks = ('Ethernet', 'Token-Ring', 'Frame-Relay', 'ATM');
```

and could be rewritten as follows:

```
@networks = qw(Ethernet Token-Ring Frame-Relay ATM);
```

This has exactly the same meaning as the initial code, and many Perl programmers prefer it (mainly due to the fact that the latter requires less typing). The qw is called the *quoting operator* and is shorthand for 'quote words'.

1.2.3 Hashes

The third Perl variable container is the hash, more formally known as the *associative array*. Hashes are somewhat like arrays, in that they hold a collection of scalar somethings. However, whereas arrays are indexed using numeric values, hashes are indexed using string values (which are also called 'keys' or 'names'). Each string value index has associated with it a scalar value. These associations are often referred to as *name/value pairs*.

Hashes in Perl are prefixed with a % character. Here is a hash which will hold data on the maximum frame size for a collection of popular networking technologies:

```
%net_mtus;
```

To refer to the entire hash, use the % prefixed name. To refer to an individual element, prefix the hash name with the $ character (just as was done when referring to individual array elements). Here is how to add an element (which is referred to as a 'hash entry') into the newly created hash:

```
$net_mtus{'Ethernet'} = 1500;
```

The name (or key) is the word Ethernet and has the value 1500 associated with it. Lists can be used to initialize a hash:

```
%net_mtus = ( 'Token-Ring', 4464, 'PPP', 1500, 'ATM', 53 );
```

The list (which should have an even number of elements) is taken to contain a set of name/value pairs. Note that this line of code refers to the entire hash using the % prefix. This is shorthand for the following functionally identical code:

```
$net_mtus{'Token-Ring'} = 4464;
$net_mtus{'PPP'} = 1500;
$net_mtus{'ATM'} = 53;
```

Yet another version of this code takes advantage of the Perl feature which aliases the => symbol with the comma. Additional (entirely optional) white space adds to the readability of this code, and helps to highlight the name/value pairs:

```
%net_mtus = ( 'Token-Ring' => 4464,
              'PPP'        => 1500,
              'ATM'        => 53 );
```

It is often useful to think of => as meaning 'has the value' when working with hashes.

Of note here is that, just like arrays, hashes grow dynamically and automatically in Perl. Also important is the fact that hash keys are (and must be) unique[4].

---

[4]The same restriction applies to array indices, although there tends to be much less fuss made of this fact.

When a hash entry is created, a value part does not need to be initially specified. The special value `undef` can be used to set a hash entry (or any variable) to the undefined value:

```
$net_mtus{'SMDS'} = undef;
```

The above code is identical to:

```
$net_mtus{SMDS} = undef;
```

the only difference being that the single quotes are missing around the SMDS. In 'Perl-speak', this is referred to as a *bareword*. If a hash name contains no white-space, the single quotes are generally not required.

A convenient way to clear an entire hash is to set it equal to an empty list:

```
%net_mtus = ();
```

Hashes (and arrays, for that matter) are very useful 'right out-of-the-box'. For the vast majority of the programs in *Programming the Network with Perl*, these inbuilt variable containers are all that is needed. However, on occasion, more complicated data structures help to simplify a solution. The problem with arrays and hashes is that they can only store scalar values. This restriction, on first glance, seems limiting in that it appears no method exists to provide for, say, storing an array in a hash entry, or storing a hash in an array element. This restriction is overcome by the use of references.

1.2.4 References

A reference is a Perl scalar variable container that *refers to* something else. The 'something else' can be one of a number of things, including another scalar, array, hash, subroutine, or Perl object. In this subsection, references to scalars, arrays and hashes are described. References to subroutines and objects will be discussed in later sections.

If a scalar reference refers to an array, the scalar reference can then be, for example, added to an existing hash, creating a hash entry that refers to an array. The entry in the hash is still a scalar value (satisfying the restriction placed on hash values), but as a reference, it now refers to something more complicated than a scalar – in this case, an array.

Creating a reference is very easy. Simply place a \ before the thing to be referenced. Here is code which creates a reference to an existing array, then adds the reference into an existing hash:

```
%networks = ();
@ethernets = qw( Ethernet-II IEEE802.3 IEEE802.3-SNAP );

$e_ref = \@ethernets;

$networks{'Ethernet Standards'} = $e_ref;
```

The 'Ethernet Standards' hash entry now refers to the @ethernets array. It is important to realize that the @ethernets array and the $e_ref scalar both refer to *the same data*. If the array is changed, then what the scalar refers to also changes. Think of the scalar reference as an *alias* to the array's memory location.

To access the array (referred to in the hash), *dereference* the hash entry:

```
print "The Ethernet standards are: ";
print "@{$networks{'Ethernet Standards'}}\n";
```

As it is known that the $networks{'Ethernet Standards'} entry is a reference to an array, prefix the use of the hash entry with the @ symbol. (The hash entry is also enclosed in an extra pair of curly braces, although this is not strictly required.) Read this code as: 'access the array referred to by the hash entry'.

In the earlier code, the use of the $e_ref scalar is redundant. It is equally valid to write the code this way:

```
%networks = ();
@ethernets = qw( Ethernet-II IEEE802.3 IEEE802.3-SNAP );

$networks{'Ethernet Standards'} = \@ethernets;
```

Even this can be shortened, if the sole purpose of having the @ethernets array is to create a reference to it within a hash entry. Here is another, equally valid, way to code this:

```
%networks = ();

$networks{'Ethernet Standards'} =
        [ 'Ethernet-II', 'IEEE802.3', 'IEEE802.3-SNAP' ];
```

By enclosing the list of array elements in square brackets, this code creates an *anonymous array* (i.e. one that has no name). The array is then assigned to a hash entry, and Perl is smart enough to use a reference.

Here is some code which shows the creation and use of references to scalars and hashes:

```
$scalar = 42;
$refs = \$scalar;
print 'Both $scalar and $refs have the value: ', ${$refs}, ".\n";

%hash = ( 'Name' => "Paul Barry",
          'Book' => "Programming the Network with Perl",
          'Year' => 2002 );

$array_of_hashes[0] = \%hash;

print "There's a great book called ";
print "${$array_of_hashes[0]}{'Book'} by\n";
print "${$array_of_hashes[0]}{'Name'}, published in ";
print "${$array_of_hashes[0]}{'Year'}.\n";
```

Unfortunately, as shown in this piece of code, the syntax for accessing an individual hash entry within an array of hashes is complex. To yield the string 'Paul Barry' from the array of hashes, the code referred to it as:

```
${$array_of_hashes[0]}{'Name'}
```

which reads (from the inside out): 'take whatever is at element zero of the @array_of_hashes array, treat it as a hash, then access the value paired with the Name key'. Thankfully, Perl provides an alternative syntax, which can reduce this level of complexity. It is possible to yield 'Paul Barry' like this:

```
$array_of_hashes[0]->{'Name'}
```

or like this:

```
$array_of_hashes[0]{'Name'}
```

When the -> appears between a right and left bracket pair - either]{, }[, }{, or][- its use is not required.

It is also possible to create and use anonymous hashes by enclosing the hash entries in curly braces. Here is another (equally valid) way to populate the first. element of the $array_of_hashes array:

```
$array_of_hashes[0] =
    { 'Name' => "Paul Barry",
      'Book' => "Programming the Network with Perl",
      'Year' => 2002 };
```

Or, this code would also do:

```
%hash = ( 'Name' => "Paul Barry",
          'Book' => "Programming the Network with Perl",
          'Year' => 2002 );

$array_of_hashes[0] = { %hash };
```

When working with the %networks hash of arrays (from earlier), either of the following work, yielding the string 'IEEE802.3':

```
${$networks{'Ethernet Standards'}}[1];
$networks{'Ethernet Standards'}->[1];
$networks{'Ethernet Standards'}[1];
```

Which technique to use is a programmer preference, but be aware that many Perl programmers freely mix their use of each, so it is important to be able to recognize all of them.

To check if some variable is a reference, use the inbuilt ref subroutine, which returns the type of reference as a string.

1.2.5   Built-in variables

The Perl interpreter defines (and uses) a large collection of built-in variables. The default variable ($_) has already been described. A full list of built-ins can be viewed in the perlvar manual page. Type this command at the Linux command-line to page through the material:

```
man perlvar
```

Here is a list of frequently used built-in variables (examples of their use – with explanations – appear throughout *Programming the Network with Perl*).

$! – contains the operating system error code after some operation has failed.

$| – the auto-flush variable, which when set to 1 switches off buffering when Perl writes to an output filehandle (such as standard output). With auto-flushing off, the output buffer will typically not get flushed until a newline character is written.

$1, $2, etc. – the pattern-match variables, created as the result of successful pattern matches and regular expressions.

$a, $b – used by the inbuilt sort subroutine when doing comparisons.

$@ – when eval is used, $@ is set upon the return from eval.

@_ – the *default array*, used when processing parameters inside Perl subroutines.

@ARGV – contains the list of command-line parameters sent to a program.

@INC – lists the series of directories Perl searches when loading (and looking for) add-on modules.

%ENV – a hash containing the current contents of the operating systems environment.

%SIG – a hash of operating system signals and signal handlers.

1.2.6   Scoping with local, my and our

Variable containers in Perl need not be declared prior to their first use. Perl will automatically create them as needed. As a direct result of this behaviour, all variable containers in Perl are *global* in scope.

It is possible to localize a global variable container to a block of code using the inbuilt local subroutine. When local is used in a block, at the end of the block the variable will revert to the value it had prior to entering the block within which it appears. Within the block, the variable can be used in any which way. If the block of code invokes a subroutine, the local value is visible (not the global) within the invoked subroutine. Due to its strange behaviour, use of local tends to be frowned upon nowadays. Consequently, none of the code in *Programming the Network with Perl* uses local.

The inbuilt my subroutine can be used to give a variable container *lexical scope.* The variable is not globally visible, nor is it visible by any invoked subroutine. It is only visible within the block that declares it. When the use strict compiler directive is used at the top of a Perl program, global variables are forbidden, and my must be used. That is, of course, assuming the variable containers have not been declared with our.

The inbuilt our subroutine is new as of release 5.6.0 of Perl. When our is used, the variable container can be used as if it is global, even though it really is not. This allows a program to use the use strict compiler directive, and still use global variable containers when it is convenient (or necessary) to do so.

1.3   Controlling Flow

Perl has the usual collection of flow control statements: if, while and for. Perl also has some of its own: unless, until and foreach. In addition, two built-in subroutines (do and eval) can impact on a program's flow of control. In this section, we will look at each of these constructs in turn.

1.3.1   if

To decide on one or more courses of action, use the if statement. Assuming the $net scalar is set to an appropriate value, a simple if statement might be:

```
if ( $net eq 'Token-Ring' )
{
    print "The network is of the token passing variety.\n";
}
```

This code prints the message if the condition-part (i.e. the first line) of the if statement is true. Veterans of the C-type programming languages need to note that the use of curly braces *is required* by Perl. Two-way decisions are accommodated by the use of an else statement:

```
if ( $net eq 'Token-Ring' )
{
    print "The network is of the token passing variety.\n";
}
else
{
    print "The network is NOT a token passer.\n";
}
```

Multi-way decisions are also possible (note the strange spelling of elsif):

```
if ( $net eq 'Token-Ring' )
{
    print "Your network is of the token-passing variety.\n";
}
elsif ( $net eq 'Ethernet' )
{
    print "Your network is of the CSMA/CD variety.\n";
}
elsif ( $net eq 'Frame-Relay' )
{
    print "Your network is of the ISDN variety.\n";
}
else    #  Assuming a value of 'ATM' ...
{
    print "Your network is of the cell-switching variety.\n";
}
```

This is the only way to perform a multi-way decision in Perl. C and Java programmers may miss the convenience of the switch statement, just as Pascal programmers may miss their case statement. To such programmers, Perl offers nothing more than a shrug of apology (and a nod in the direction of code similar to that shown above).

1.3.2   The ternary conditional operator

Perl supports the *ternary conditional operator*. The following if statement sets the value of $do depending on the current value of $today:

```
if ( ($today eq 'Sat') or ($today eq 'Sun') )
{
    $do = "Play";
}
else
{
    $do = "Work";
}
```

and is functionally identical to this (somewhat more compact) code:

```
$do = ( ($today eq 'Sat') or ($today eq 'Sun') ) ? "Play" : "Work";
```

The condition-part of the if statement comes before the ? symbol. If the condition-part is true, the value Play results, otherwise the value Work results (with the : symbol separating the two possible results). The variable $do is, therefore, assigned an appropriate value.

1.3.3 `while`

The `while` statement was part of the `first` program written at the start of this chapter. Like the `if`, curly braces are required with `while` statements.

Code inside the loop (i.e. within the curly braces) keeps executing while the condition-part of the `while` statement is true. A loop can optionally include a `continue` block which will execute at the end of each loop (or iteration).

Three statements provide programmers with the ability to fine tune the behaviour of loops:

next - jump immediately to the bottom of the loop and execute the `continue` block (if one exists), then start a new iteration if the condition-part evaluates to true;

last - exit the loop, bypassing any `continue` block, and resume execution at the first statement immediately following the loop;

redo - abandon the current iteration of the loop, jump to the first statement of the loop, and re-execute the loop statements.

Example uses (with explanations where required) of these statements appear throughout *Programming the Network with Perl*.

The `while` statement is often used to iterate through a hash, as follows:

```
while ( ($name, $value) = each %net_mtus )
{
    print "$name has the value: $value\n";
}
```

The inbuilt `each` subroutine returns a name/value pair from the specified hash, and with each iteration, the next name/value pair is returned until no more pairs are left. Of note is that the name/value pairs come out of the hash in no particular order (and most definitely not in the order that they were inserted).

1.3.4 `for`

The `for` statement iterates a fixed number of times over code, and is typically used to process arrays. Here is how to print each element of the @networks array on its own line:

```
for ($i = 0; $i <= $#networks; $i++)
{
    print "$networks[$i]\n";
}
```

This code initializes `$i` to zero *before* the loop starts to iterate, then checks to see if the value of `$i` is less than or equal to the largest index of the array (`$#networks`). If it is, the loop iterates, then the value of `$i` is incremented *after* the iteration completes, and prior to the test against $#networks is performed again. The loop iterates until the entire array has been printed.

1.3.5 unless

In Perl, the unless statement is the opposite of if. This code prints the line for values of $net other than Token-Ring:

```
unless ( $net eq 'Token-Ring' )
{
    print "The network is NOT of the token passing variety.\n";
}
```

The unless statement *can* have an else part, but no elsifs.

1.3.6 until

The while statement also has an opposite, the until statement. Rather than iterating *while* a condition is true, this statement iterates *until* some condition is true.

1.3.7 foreach

The for statement described earlier is used so often to process arrays that a special shorthand version exists, the foreach statement. This code is identical to the example used with for above:

```
foreach $i (@networks)
{
    print "$i\n";
}
```

But be careful: while inside the loop, the $i variable is an *alias* to the actual element within the @networks array. If $i is changed, so is the corresponding array element.

The foreach statement can also be used to iterate over a hash:

```
foreach $name ( keys %net_mtus )
{
    print "$name has the value: $net_mtus{$name}\n";
}
```

Another inbuilt subroutine, keys, returns a list of all the name-parts of the named hash. This list (array) is then used normally by the foreach. The keys subroutine can also be used, in conjunction with scalar to calculate the number of elements in any hash:

```
$size = scalar keys %net_mtus;

print "The size of the hash is: $size\n";
```

A common extension to the above hash traversal code is to call the sort or reverse inbuilt subroutine to force an ordering on the hash name-parts:

```
foreach $name ( sort ( keys %net_mtus ) )
{
    print "$name has the value: $net_mtus{$name}\n";
}
```

1.3.8 do

The do subroutine takes a block of code as its sole parameter, and executes the block of code, returning the value of the last line of the code as the result of the do.

The following example sets the value of $res to 15, then prints the value to the screen, and illustrates the basic mechanism:

```
$res = do
        {
            $a = 5;
            $b = 3;
            $a * $b;
        };
print $res;
```

A second form of do takes the name of a file as its sole parameter and executes the contents of the file as a Perl program. Assuming a file called es1 exists in the current working directory, this code opens the file from within the current program and runs any Perl code contained therein:

```
do 'es1';
```

1.3.9 eval

The eval subroutine takes a string as its sole parameter and executes the string as a Perl program (or fragment thereof). This code does the same thing as the do example:

```
$some_code = '$a = 5; $b = 3; $res = $a * $b; print $res;';
eval { $some_code };
```

What makes this eval code different[5] from the equivalent do code is that a certain amount of protection is provided by eval. Specifically, if the code within the eval

---

[5] Some would say 'better'.

block causes a fatal error (which would normally cause the Perl interpreter to exit immediately from a program), `eval` catches the fatal error and provides a way to recover from the error. The built-in variable $@ will be set by `eval` on exit from the code block. If the value of $@ is set to the empty string, no fatal error occurred. However, if the value of $@ contains a non-empty string, a fatal error occurred and a description of the error is in $@. This, therefore, provides a simple, yet highly useful, exception-handling mechanism.

In the code which follows, a call to the inbuilt `die` subroutine causes the generation of a fatal error (and message). When called outside an `eval` block, the program would end immediately. When called inside an `eval` block, the evaluated code ends and the $@ variable is set to the message from `die`.

Here is an `eval` example:

```
eval
{
    print "This is Apollo 13.  Mission Log.\n";
    print "We are half-way to the Moon.\n";

    die "Houston, we have a problem!\n";
};
if ($@)
{
    print "Message from Apollo 13 - $@";
    print "Let's bring them home safely ... ";
}
else
{
    print "Maybe 13 is not that unlucky after-all ... ";
}
```

Due to the fact that the call to `die` is within the `eval` block, the program can recover gracefully from what would otherwise be a fatal error (and go on to save the astronauts). The `else` part of the `if` statement will never execute in this code, but is included here for illustration only.

1.3.10   Statement modifiers

In addition to the control flow mechanisms which enclose blocks of code, Perl also provides support for *statement modifiers*. With these, individual statements can be qualified. A series of examples will help to illustrate.

This code prints the words 'Hello World' if the value of $should_we has some value (i.e. if it is *defined*):

```
print "Hello World" if defined( $should_we );
```

This code prints the words 'Hello World' unless the value of $today is Saturday:

```
print "Hello World" unless $today eq 'Saturday';
```

This single line of code is another way of writing the `first` program from the start of the chapter. The code takes lines of input from standard input (one at a time) and prints them. It keeps going until there is no more input lines to process:

```
print while (<>);
```

It is possible to use `until` anywhere that `while` is used, and this is also true of statement modifiers. When combined with `do`, statement modifiers provide for loops that will iterate at least once, as the condition-part of the loop comes at the end of the block. Here is the general form of the `do...while` construct:

```
do
{
    # Do something ...
}
while  # some condition is true;
```

and here's the general form of a `do...until`:

```
do
{
    # Do something ...
}
until  # some condition is true;
```

1.4 Boolean in Perl

Strangely, Perl has no inbuilt Boolean type[6]. Instead, any Perl expression can be used as a condition, and can be evaluated to be either true or false. A number of rules help determine whether something is true or false as follows.

Strings – a string is true, unless it contains "0" or the empty string. (Strangely, "00" and "0.00" are true.)

Numbers – a number is true, unless it evaluates to zero. (Strangely, this means −42 is true.)

References – all references are true. (This is initially quite strange until one considers what a reference contains.)

Undefs – anything with the *undefined* value is false. (This is *not* strange – how can anything that is undefined possibly be true?)

Lists – empty lists are false, lists with any number of elements are true. (Like `undef`, this is *not* at all strange.)

---

[6]Are you not getting used to all this Perl strangeness yet? After a while, it all becomes quite normal. Strange, but true.

1.5 Perl Operators

In a number of the code examples seen so far, various code snippets have relied on condition tests that have used comparison operators. They have been rather sneakily used, without providing any detailed description. Nobody likes a sneak, so here is the entire list of Perl operators (with brief explanations) in precedence order, starting with those with the highest precedence.

-> - the infix dereference arrow operator, used when working with references (and objects).

++ and -- - the increment and decrement operators.

** - the exponential operator.

!, ˜, \, + and - - the logical negation (!), bit-wise negation (˜), reference (\), numeric affirmation (+) and arithmetic negation (-) operators.

=˜ and !˜ - the binding operators (used when working with regular expressions and pattern matches).

*, /, % and x - the multiply, divide, modulus (%) and repetition (x) operators.

+, - and . - the addition, subtraction and concatenation (.) operators.

<< and >> - the left and right bit shifting operators.

<, >, <=, >=, lt, gt, le and ge - the relational operators. There are two of each, one for working with numbers and the other for working with strings. Be careful to use <, >, <= and >= when comparing numbers, and use lt, gt, le and ge when comparing strings.

==, !=, <=>, eq, ne and cmp - the equality operators. As with the relational operators, different versions exist for use with numbers and for strings. The <=> and cmp operators are used for comparison, and are typically used in conjunction with the inbuilt sort subroutine.

& - the bit-wise AND operator.

| and ˆ - the bit-wise OR and eXclusive OR operators.

&& - the logical AND operator.

|| - the logical OR operator.

.. and ... - the range operators.

?: - the ternary conditional operator.

=, **=, +=, *=, &= and so on - the assignment operators.

, and => - the comma operator (typically used to separate list items).

not - a lower precedence alternative to !.

and - a lower precedence alternative to &&.

or and xor – lower precedence alternatives to || and a logical eXclusive OR operator.

1.6   Subroutines

Perl supports the creation of named, user-defined blocks of code, which go by the generic name of 'subroutine'[7]. Creating subroutines could not be easier: give the subroutine a name, pass the name to the inbuilt `sub` subroutine together with the block of code. Here is a simple example:

```
sub simple {
    print "Hello from the simple subroutine!\n";
}
```

The subroutine can now be invoked (from within the program that defined it) in one of four ways:

```
simple;
simple();
&simple;
&simple();
```

It rarely matters which of these techniques is used, as they all do the same thing, i.e. invoke `simple`. When Perl gets picky about a particular style of invocation, the interpreter will tell you.

1.6.1   Processing parameters

Every user-defined Perl subroutine can take any number of parameters. If `simple` was invoked as:

```
simple( "Hey!  Print this!\n" );
```

it would simply ignore the parameter, and Perl would not complain. Any parameters that are sent to a subroutine become available within the *default array*, which is called @_. Here is another version of `simple` that can process parameters:

```
sub simple {
    $print_what = $_[0];

    print $print_what;
}
```

where $_[0] refers to the first element of the @_ array. To print the entire array contents, use this code:

---

[7]Also known as 'function', 'procedure', 'routine' and/or 'method', depending on your programming background.

```
sub simple {
    print "@_";
}
```

If more than one parameter is passed, each becomes available within the subroutine as a separately accessible array element. Let us assume that another version of simple supports calls like this:

```
simple( "On line one", "On line two" );
```

To access each 'line' within simple, the subroutine could be rewritten to access each element of the default array:

```
sub simple {
    print $_[0], "\n";
    print $_[1], "\n";
}
```

This technique is rarely seen, as most seasoned Perl programmers prefer to take advantage of the inbuilt shift subroutine, which removes *and returns* the first element from a named array, or the first element from the default array if no array is specified. Once again, a rewritten simple illustrates this technique:

```
sub simple {
    print shift, "\n";
    print shift, "\n";
}
```

It is important to realize that when parameters are passed to any user-defined subroutine, they are 'flattened' into a list. So, if a subroutine is written to expect as parameters a hash, followed by an array, and then a scalar, the three parameters will enter the subroutine as one long, flattened list (which is rarely what was wanted). Pass the hash, array, and scalar as references to ensure they arrive in the subroutine in the correct format. In this case, the @_ default array will contain three elements: a hash reference, an array reference, and a scalar reference. Note, too, that when accessed inside the subroutine, the references refer to the original variable containers, so if they are changed within the subroutine, they will be changed elsewhere. By default, all parameters are passed *by value*.

1.6.2   Returning results

A subroutine can return a value, and unless explicitly stated, this will be the value of the last statement in the subroutine. The simple subroutine would therefore return a true value (assuming the call to print was successful). To control what value is returned, use the inbuilt return subroutine:

```
sub simple {
    my $count = 0;
    print shift, "\n";
    $count++;
    print shift, "\n";
    $count++;

    return( $count );
}
```

This code will (always) return the value 2.

1.6.3   I want an array

Perl subroutines can be written to return either a scalar or a list. Consider the inbuilt keys subroutine introduced during the discussion of hashes. When called in what is known as *list context*, keys returns a list of hash name-values. When called in *scalar context*, keys returns the number of elements in the hash.

By employing the services of the inbuilt wantarray subroutine, it is possible to write a user-defined subroutine that works in a similar fashion:

```
sub return_hash_keys {
    %a_hash = @_;

    return ( wantarray ? keys %a_hash : scalar keys %a_hash );
}

%net_mtus = ( 'Token-Ring' => 4464,
              'PPP'        => 1500,
              'ATM'        => 53 );

@keys = return_hash_keys( %net_mtus );
print "Hash keys: @keys\n";

$size = return_hash_keys( %net_mtus );
print "Hash size: $size\n";
```

The wantarray subroutine knows whether the user-defined subroutine has been called in list or scalar context. If called in list context, wantarray evaluates to true.

1.6.4   In-built subroutines

Perl has a large collection of inbuilt subroutines. The entire collection is documented in the perlfunc online documentation. Use this command to view the manpage:

```
man perlfunc
```

Alternatively, use the `perldoc` program (which comes with Perl) to search the `perlfunc` manpage for documentation on a specific subroutine. For instance, to view the documentation for the inbuilt `print` subroutine, use this command:

```
perldoc -f print
```

The inbuilt subroutines take a varying number of parameters. Check the documentation for specifics. Be aware that some inbuilt subroutines can do different things based on how they are invoked and used. The code in this chapter has already used some of the more popular inbuilt subroutines. Here is an abbreviated list[8]:

alarm – signal an alarm to occur a number of seconds in the future;

chomp – deletes the trailing newline character from a scalar;

chop – deletes the last character from a scalar;

close – close a previously opened filehandle;

defined – returns true if a variable has a value associated with it;

delete – delete elements/entries from an array/hash;

die – exit the current program after displaying a user-specified message;

do – execute a block of statements as one, or read in a collection of statements from another file and execute them;

each – used to iterate over a hash;

eof – test for the end-of-file condition;

eval – evaluate a block of code, and provide exception handling;

exists – returns true if a specific array element or hash entry exists;

exit – exit the current program;

fork – create a child process which is a clone of the current process;

gmtime – return the date and time relative to GMT;

goto – jump to a labelled location within a program[9];

join – join a list of strings together;

keys – returns a list of keys for a specified hash;

last – exit from the current loop;

length – return the length of a scalar variable;

local – localize a variable;

localtime – return the date and time relative to the local time zone;

my – mark a variable as being lexically scoped;

---

[8]Subroutines of specific interest to network programmers are not presented here, as they are the subject of Chapter 3.

[9]But *real* programmers never use goto, do they?

next – start the next iteration of the current loop;

open – open a file, and associate a filehandle with it;

our – declare a global variable;

pack – convert a collection of variables into a string of bytes;

package – declare a new namespace;

pop – treat an array like a stack, and pop the last element off the end of the array;

print – print something (to a named output handle);

printf – print to a particular format;

push – treat an array like a stack, then push an element onto the end of the array;

read – read a specified number of bytes from a filehandle;

redo – restart the current loop iteration;

ref – check to see whether a scalar is a reference, and if it is, return the type of reference as a string;

return – return a value from a subroutine;

scalar – force a list to be treated as if it were a scalar;

shift – treat an array like a stack, and pop the first element off the start of the array;

sleep – pause execution for a specified number of seconds;

sort – sort a list using string comparison order (by default), or by using some user-specified ordering;

splice – remove specified elements from an array;

split – split a delimited string into a list of individual elements;

sprintf – like `printf`, except the result is assigned to a scalar;

sub – declare a subroutine;

substr – extract a substring from a string;

system – call an operating system command, and return its exit status to the calling program;

time – returns the number of non-leap seconds since the operating system's 'epoch'[10];

undef – take a previously defined variable, and undefine it;

unpack – the reverse of `pack`: extract a list of values from a string of bytes;

unshift – treat an array like a stack, and push an element onto the start of the array;

wait – wait for a previously created child process to terminate;

---

[10]What the operating system thinks is the start of time. It varies from system to system.

wantarray – return true if a subroutine was called within a list context, false otherwise;

warn – sends output to standard error;

write – write a specified number of bytes to a filehandle.

Example uses of these inbuilt subroutines appear throughput *Programming the Network with Perl*. If their meaning is not clear from the context in which they are used, further description is provided.

1.6.5   References to subroutines

Perl allows references to subroutines.

Here is a preview of a code snippet from the end of Chapter 2 which assigns a subroutine reference to a scalar called $packet_handler based on the value of another scalar called $opt_u:

```
if ($opt_u)
{
    $packet_handler = \&udp_both_packet;
}
else
{
    $packet_handler = \&tcp_both_packet;
}
```

Note the use of the \ character which turns the call to the subroutine into a reference to the subroutine. Later in the code, the previously selected subroutine can be invoked as follows:

```
&$packet_handler;
```

1.7   Perl I/O

Performing input and output (I/O) in Perl is as simple as it gets. Disk files have associated *filehandles*, and each time some input and output is performed, the code need only reference the correct filehandle to work. Filehandles can be opened to read from, write to, or read/write to/from.

Four filehandles are automatically opened for every Perl program: STDIN, STDOUT, STDERR, and DATA. These correspond to standard input (usually the keyboard), standard output (usually the screen), standard error (usually the screen, but sometimes a system log file), and the thoroughly strange 'standard data'. The DATA filehandle is associated with anything that comes after the __END__ symbol at the end of a source code file, and is generally useful when testing code prior to deployment.

To read from a filehandle, enclose the filehandle in the <> angle brackets. This code reads a line from standard input:

```
$line = <STDIN>;
```

which is longhand for:

```
$line = <>;
```

as Perl will assume standard input by default. Writing to output filehandles usually involves the use of the inbuilt `print` subroutine. Here is how to write to standard output:

```
print STDOUT "Writing to standard output, usually the screen.\n";
```

which is longhand for:

```
print "Writing to standard output, usually the screen.\n";
```

as Perl will assume standard output by default. To write to standard error, use code similar to this:

```
print STDERR "Writing to standard error.\n";
```

or use the inbuilt `warn` subroutine which will always write to STDERR:

```
warn "Writing to standard error.\n";
```

To create filehandles, give them a name and associate them with a file. By convention, filehandle names are specified in uppercase, although Perl does not enforce this as a rule. To open a file for reading, use code similar to the following:

```
open MYINFILE, "readme.txt" or die "Could not open: $!";
```

This code will open `readme.txt` and associate it with the MYINFILE filehandle, or if something goes wrong, exit with an appropriate error message.

Once a filehandle is opened, read from it using the <> operator:

```
$a_line = <MYINFILE>;
@entire_file = <MYINFILE>;
```

Here the <> operator is used in both scalar and list context. Be careful when using <> in list context, as reading a large file in one go can result in memory problems.

To close a filehandle, call `close` on the filehandle name:

```
close MYINFILE;
```

which Perl will do anyway when your program ends.

To write to a file, use code like this:

```
open MYOUTFILE, ">readme.txt" or die "Could not open: $!";

print MYOUTFILE "Writing to readme.txt\n";

close MYOUTFILE;
```

Note the > symbol before the name of the file to open for writing. To append to a file, replace the first line above with this line (note the use of the >> symbol):

```
open MYOUTFILE, ">>readme.txt" or die "Could not append: $!";
```

To open a file for reading and writing, use this line:

```
open MYOUTFILE, "+<readme.txt" or die "Could not read/write: $!";
```

To open a file for writing then reading, use this line:

```
open MYOUTFILE, "+>readme.txt" or die "Could not write/read: $!";
```

But be careful with this, as the +> form will first delete the file if it already exists[11], then allow the program to write to the *newly emptied* file and read from it.

1.7.1 Variable interpolation

Some readers may have noticed two differing uses of the inbuilt `print` subroutine. Here are some lines of code repeated from an earlier example:

```
print 'Both $scalar and $refs have the value: ', ${$refs}, ".\n";
```

```
            .
            .
            .


print "There's a great book called ";
print "${$array_of_hashes[0]}{'Book'} by\n";
```

On occasion, the string that gets printed by `print` is enclosed in single quotes, and at other times is enclosed in double quotes. The reason for the two styles has to do with what happens to variable containers when used within each quote type. The usage rule is very straightforward: when you want to print something literally, use single quotes, when you want to include actual variable container values in the output, use double quotes. The process of including variable containers in double quoted strings is called *interpolation*. A short example will illustrate the difference:

---

[11]Known, rather affectionately, as 'clobbering'.

```
$mynet = "Ethernet";
$yournet = "Token-Ring";

print '$mynet is incompatible with $yournet\n';
print "\n$mynet is incompatible with $yournet\n";
```

will print the following:

```
$mynet is incompatible with $yournet\n
Ethernet is incompatible with Token-Ring
```

The first `print` statement outputs the string in its literal form, including the new-line *escape code* at the end of the line. The second `print` statement interpolates the $mynet and $yournet scalars, as well as the newlines at the start and end of the string.

1.8   Packages, Modules and Objects

Perl supports the creation and use of *namespaces*, which are nothing more than a place to put, group and organize a program's variable containers and subroutines. If no namespace is specified in a program, all the variables belong to the *default namespace*, which is called `main`. Use `package` to create namespaces:

```
$ns = 30;

package MyNameSpace;

$ns = 100;
print 'The value of $ns is: ', $ns, "\n";

package main;

print 'The value of $ns is: ', $ns, "\n";

package MyNameSpace;

print 'The value of $ns is: ', $ns, "\n";
```

which produces the following results:

```
The value of $ns is: 100
The value of $ns is: 30
The value of $ns is: 100
```

As each namespace has its own place to put things, this code actually has two different variable containers called $ns, one in each of the namespaces. The *fully qualified name* of each container is $main::ns and $MyNameSpace::ns.

1.8.1 Modules

When a `package` statement, together with whatever code goes with it, is placed in a separate file, it becomes a *module* that can be used by other programs. If the `MyNameSpace` package from above was in a separate file (called `MyNameSpace.pm`), the following code would import its variables and code into the current program:

```
use MyNameSpace;
```

1.8.2 Objects

Modules form the basis of Perl's object-oriented capabilities (as well as being Perl's main code-reuse technology). The code for a Perl *class* is, by convention, placed in a module file. Objects in Perl are, surprisingly, no more than a special type of reference (in effect, a reference that has been marked as containing an object by an inbuilt subroutine called `bless`). It is beyond the scope of this chapter to describe the mechanics employed in creating Perl classes[12]. However, every Perl programmer needs to know how to use objects created from the use of object-oriented modules.

Let us pretend that some friendly programmer has created a truly useful module for use with Perl, and that the module uses an object-oriented interface. Here is how code might `use` the module then access its variable containers and subroutines (which are known as 'methods' in OO speak):

```
use ReallyDead;

$my_cool = ReallyDead->new( First => 'Elvis', Last => 'Presley' );

print "$my_cool->{First} $my_cool->{Last} really is dead.\n";
```

The code uses the `ReallyDead` module, then calls the modules *constructor*, which in this case is called `new` (but could just as easily have been called anything, as using `new` is a convention). The constructor creates a new `ReallyDead` object (passing two named arguments), which will then be referred to by the `$my_cool` variable container. Remember, objects in Perl are a type of reference, so objects are stored in scalars.

To access the data encapsulated within the object and call any subroutines associated with the object, the infix dereference arrow operator is used to refer to the *instance data* and methods. The code above, assuming the `ReallyDead` module actually existed, would print the following:

```
Elvis Presley really is dead.
```

---

[12]However, we will learn a little about creating Perl objects in Chapter 6, *Mobile Agents*.

An alternative invocation technique exists when working with Perl objects, and is known as the *indirect object syntax*. The call to the new constructor above could have been written as:

```
$my_cool = new ReallyDead First => 'Elvis', Last => 'Presley';
```

and some Perl programmers prefer this technique.

1.8.3 The joy of CPAN

The module and object creation technology in Perl is useful. So useful, in fact, that a large collection of third-party add-on modules have been developed for use with Perl. Some of these modules come with Perl and are part of the Perl distribution. These are the *standard modules*. Others are not part of the standard distribution, but are instead made freely available on a central website to anyone with a use for them. This central website[13], is known as CPAN, the Comprehensive Perl Archive Network.

CPAN is a truly wonderful place (if you are a Perl programmer, that is). It is a large software repository of reusable Perl modules, of the object-oriented and functional kind. On CPAN, the modules are organized by category, and cover every conceivable programming activity, from working with database systems to processing digital images. Of particular interest are the modules which provide support to the network programmer.

In addition to the standard networking modules (which come with Perl), a growing collection of third-party networking modules can be found in the following CPAN categories.

- Networking, Device Control and Inter-process Communication.
- Authentication, Security and Encryption.
- World Wide Web, HTML, HTTP, CGI and MIME.
- Server and Daemon Utilities.
- Mail and Usenet News.

When creating modules for use with Perl, one simple rule needs to be adhered to: *do not reinvent the wheel, check CPAN!* If the exact module required does not already exist, a close match may. Take a copy of the close match, make it perform the required way, then resubmit the newly modified module back to CPAN. The entire Perl community benefits as a result of this practice.

Throughout *Programming the Network with Perl*, numerous third-party modules from CPAN are used. Installation instructions are supplied for each third-party module employed. Refer to the *Web Resources* section at the end of this chapter for more information on the CPAN website.

---

[13]Which is actually mirrored extensively on the Internet.

1.9 More Perl

There is an awful lot more to Perl than is presented in this chapter. The intent in this chapter has been to cover only the essentials necessary to support the program code in the remainder of *Programming the Network with Perl*. Of the pieces of Perl not covered, the integrated *regular expression* technology is by far the most important[14]. This technology is often referred to as *pattern matching*, and is thought of by many as Perl's programming language within a programming language.

All of the code in this chapter can be classified as being *functional* in nature. The code specifies *how* Perl is to solve the problem, stating exactly what Perl should do. With regular expressions, Perl can also be programmed in a *declarative* way. The code specifies *what* is required, then leaves it to Perl to work out how to do things. Perl's regular expression technology is very powerful, and is one of the main reasons for Perl's popularity. It is especially useful when working with text data.

A treatment of Perl's regular expression technology is not appropriate for an introductory chapter. However, at some stage, every Perl programmer needs to master its capabilities. Refer to the *Print Resources* section at the end of this chapter for suggested texts. Certain regular expressions are used in later chapters, and when they are, they are accompanied by appropriate explanation.

1.10 Where To From Here?

Trying to cover all of Perl in just one chapter was never going to be easy. The classic Perl text, *Programming Perl*, runs to well over one thousand pages! The great thing about Perl is that any level of proficiency is acceptable within its programming community. There is more than enough material in this chapter to allow the reader to understand the rest of the programs in *Programming the Network with Perl*. And, of course, there is plenty of additional material available elsewhere, should it be required. Refer to the *Print Resources* and *Web Resources* sections below for some guidelines on where to start your search.

As the authors of *Programming Perl* advise at the end of their first chapter: *have the appropriate amount of fun.*

1.11 Print Resources

As a rule, I recommend the following book to programmers wishing to make the move to Perl: *Perl: The Programmer's Companion* by Nigel Chapman (Wiley,

---

[14]And totally *strange*, if regular expressions are new to you.

1997)[15]. This book contains an excellent and highly readable treatment of Perl's regular expression technology.

Additionally, every Perl programmer should have the following books in their collection.

Programming Perl, 3rd edn, by Larry Wall, Tom Christiansen and Jon Orwant (O'Reilly, 2000). This book is known among all Perl programmers as *The Camel*, and is the ultimate reference text for Perl.

Perl Cookbook, by Tom Christiansen & Nathan Torkington (O'Reilly, 1998). The title speaks for itself. The signal-handling code used at the end of Chapter 2 is based on a technique described in *Perl Cookbook*, and many other code snippets draw on material from this book.

Finally, when developing large-scale applications in Perl, it is advisable to master the object-oriented capabilities of the language. The following book is another must have: *Object-Oriented Perl*, by Damian Conway (Manning, 1999).

1.12   Web Resources

`http://www.perl.com` – The home of the Perl community, the Perl website. Always start here when looking for something Perl related.

`http://use.perl.org` – The Perl gossip site.

`http://www.perl.org` – The Perl advocacy site. This is also the home of the *Perl Mongers*.

`http://www.cpan.org` – The official location of CPAN, although nearly every Perl website has a link to it. Also useful is the `http://search.cpan.org` website.

`http://www.perldoc.com` – The Perl 5.6 online documentation as a searchable website.

`http://www.tpj.com` – The quarterly magazine of the Perl community, *The Perl Journal*, maintains a Web presence at this address.

---

[15]The fact that Chapman's book is published by the same publisher as *Programming the Network with Perl* is purely coincidental. Honest.

Exercises

1. If you have not done so already, run all of the code examples from this chapter through Perl in order to convince yourself that they work the way you expect them to.

2. Run the `first` program through the `Deparse` module with the following command: `perl -MO=Deparse first`. Can you explain the output generated? If not, type `man B::Deparse` at the Linux command-line to learn about this module. Remember this module's existence when debugging your Perl programs.

3. Type `man perldebug` to learn about the inbuilt Perl debugger. Run the `first` program through the debugger.

4. Use any Web browser to surf to your nearest CPAN archive and download the `Devel::Coverage` module[16]. Read any documentation associated with the module, then install `Devel::Coverage` into Perl. Use the facilities of this module to perform a *coverage analysis* on a Perl program of your choosing, preferably one that you have written.

---

[16]You may have to search for the module first. Start at `http://search.cpan.org`.

2

Snooping

In order to program the network with any degree of certainty, a mechanism is required to check that the data *sent* is the data *received*. Most programmers are already familiar with using interactive debuggers to monitor and inspect their program code while it runs. What is needed is an equivalent technology for network communications.

In this chapter, Perl is used to develop a series of network analysis tools. These simple, yet powerful, tools can be used to debug network communications on Ethernet networks.

Such tools are known by a number of names: analyser, sniffer, peeker, traffic monitor and (of course) snooper.

Writing a network analyser from scratch is not easy. Luckily, Perl's CPAN repository provides a series of modules that provide a high-level programming interface to the libpcap library, which was initially developed by the Network Research Group at Lawrence Berkeley National Laboratory. This library is a system-independent programming interface (written in C) that provides for Ethernet packet capturing.

Most Linux distributions include the libpcap library. Check to see if it is installed on a Linux system with the following command:

```
find / -name libpcap* -print 2> /dev/null
```

If this command finds nothing, the library is not installed and it needs to be downloaded from the Internet. See the *Web Resources* section at the end of this chapter for details.

2.1   Thank You, Tim Potter

CPAN contains a series of modules, developed by Tim Potter[1], that can be used to build a network analyser. These are as follows.

NetPacket::* - a collection of modules that can assemble/disassemble a number of popular network protocols (most notably, the popular Internet protocols).

Net::Pcap - a Perl interface to the `libpcap` library.

Net::PcapUtils - a small set of utilities designed to make using the `Net::Pcap` module convenient.

At the time of writing, the versions of these modules are 0.03 for `NetPacket::*`, 0.04 for `Net::Pcap` and 0.01 for `Net::PcapUtils`. In addition to the ability to *encode* packets in each of the protocol types, the `NetPacket` modules can *decode* packets, which is the exact functionality required when writing a network analyser.

The `NetPacket::*` collection includes modules for working with Ethernet frames, ARP packets, IP datagrams (including ICMP and IGMP datagrams), UDP datagrams and TCP segments.

When studying computer networking, it is usual to have the discussion structured around the study of a layered reference model (RM). The classic model is the Open Systems Interconnect seven-layer model from the International Standards Organization, commonly referred to as the OSI-RM. Increasingly, the model employed by the standard Internet technologies – the TCP/IP-RM – is replacing the OSI-RM as the basis of study (due in no small part to the fact that the vast majority of the world's computer networks now run TCP/IP). The TCP/IP-RM is simpler than the OSI-RM, and has only four layers, structured (from top to bottom) as follows.

Application – protocols for providing application-level services to user programs (also referred to as 'user-agents'). An example user program is a Web browser, which implements the Hyper-Text Transfer Protocol (HTTP).

Transport – protocols for providing end-to-end data transportation services to application protocols. With TCP/IP networks, two transport protocols exist: the Transmission Control Protocol (TCP) for providing connection-oriented, reliable service, and the User Datagram Protocol (UDP) for providing connectionless, unreliable service.

Network – protocols for moving data from host to host and from network to network. The Internet Protocol (IP) provides this service for TCP/IP networks. Additional protocols provide support for primitive network management (using ICMP, the Internet Control Message Protocol) and network multicasting (using IGMP, the Internet Group Management Protocol).

---

[1]With help from Stephanie Wehner.

Host-To-Network – the underlying network technology (whatever that might be), and the protocols associated with physically moving bits of data 'across the wire'. On TCP/IP networks, a technology called ARP (the Address Resolution Protocol) helps IP to run on top of the underlying network hardware (which in *Programming the Network with Perl* is Ethernet).

The TCP/IP-RM and the `NetPacket::*` protocols are an almost perfect match, except for the protocols at the application layer (which have no `NetPacket` equivalent).

The `NetPacket::*` modules provide a simple interface. A method called `decode` takes a raw packet and returns a reference to a 'packet-object' for the particular protocol. The packet-object returned from `decode` provides access to a collection of instance data associated with the protocol being processed. Additionally, a subroutine called `strip` allows a raw packet to be *stripped* of any protocol header information, i.e. just the data part of the packet (its payload) is returned by each module's `strip` subroutine.

The `Net::PcapUtils` module provides a simple interface to the `Net::Pcap` library by providing just three subroutines to the programmer: `loop`, `open` and `next` (discussed in Section 2.3, p. 41).

2.2 Preparing To Snoop

With `libpcap` installed, the next task is to install each of the Perl CPAN modules introduced in the last section. See the *Web Resources* section at the end of this chapter for information on downloading the required modules from the CPAN directory maintained by Tim Potter.

2.2.1 Installing NetPacket::*

The process of installing a third-party add-on module into an existing Perl installation has been standardized.

To begin, decompress and unpack the downloaded file:

```
gunzip NetPacket-0.03.tar.gz
tar xvf NetPacket-0.03.tar
```

This creates a directory called `NetPacket-0.03` within which all of the files needed to install `NetPacket` are located. To prepare for the install, change into this directory and use Perl to create the required `makefile`:

```
cd NetPacket-0.03
perl Makefile.PL
```

It should now be possible to build and test `NetPacket` using the standard Linux `make` command:

```
make
make test
```

If things go well, the module is now ready to install. For the next command to succeed, superuser privilege is required. If not already logged in as `root`, temporarily become the superuser as follows:

```
su
```

The `root` password will be required.

As the superuser, finish the install as follows:

```
make install
<ctrl-D>
```

Note the use of the `<ctrl-D>` key combination after the `make install` command. This logs out the superuser. As a general rule, only work in superuser mode (i.e. as `root`) for as long as is needed. It is generally a bad idea to do regular work logged in as `root`. Trust me when I tell you that if you spend a lot of time logged in as `root`, sooner or later, bad things will happen.

Test the installation using these two commands:

```
man NetPacket::Ethernet
perl -e 'use NetPacket::Ethernet'
```

The documentation for `NetPacket::Ethernet` should be displayed by the first command here. The second command should display *nothing*; the Linux command prompt should reappear after a short delay. If the second command displays a message something along the lines of the following:

```
# Can't locate NetPacket/Ethernet.pm in @INC.
# BEGIN failed--compilation aborted at -e line 1.
```

this means that the module has been installed incorrectly. If the online documentation is missing, this too means that the module has been installed incorrectly. Check that the above instructions have been followed correctly. If they have, check any README and INSTALL files that came with the module for additional installation instructions to follow. If problems continue, ask your local Linux guru for assistance[2]. If *you* are the local Linux guru, *panic*.

2.2.2 Installing Net::Pcap

The process of installing and testing the `Net::Pcap` module closely resembles that for `NetPacket`. Here are the Linux commands to use:

---

[2]Remember to ask nicely.

```
gunzip Net-Pcap-0.04.tar.gz
tar xvf Net-Pcap-0.04.tar
cd Net-Pcap-0.04
perl Makefile.PL
make
su
make test
make install
<ctrl-D>
man Net::Pcap
perl -e 'use Net::Pcap'
```

2.2.3   Installing Net::PcapUtils

The process of installing and testing Net::PcapUtils closely resembles that for Net::Pcap. Here are the Linux commands to use:

```
gunzip Net-PcapUtils-0.01.tar.gz
tar xvf Net-PcapUtils-0.01.tar
cd Net-PcapUtils-0.01
perl Makefile.PL
make
su
make test
make install
<ctrl-D>
man Net::PcapUtils
perl -e 'use Net::PcapUtils'
```

2.2.4   Online documentation

To view the documentation for any NetPacket module, simply issue a man command at the Linux command prompt. This command displays the documentation for the TCP module:

```
man NetPacket::TCP
```

The Net::Pcap module provides a subroutine-for-subroutine Perl mapping to the libpcap library. Once the library is installed on a Linux system, you can learn about the library by accessing its man-page, as follows:

```
man pcap
```

This command will display a long, complicated list of subroutines and options. The same is true of the Net::Pcap man-page, which helps explain the existence of Net::PcapUtils.

The online man-page, which is quite short, can be viewed with the following command:

```
man Net::PcapUtils
```

2.2.5 Configuring your network interface

On Ethernet networks, the network interface card (NIC) operates in one of two modes. In *normal mode*, the NIC will accept packets from the network if they are addressed to the globally unique 48 bit Ethernet address associated with the NIC. If the NIC is part of an Ethernet multicasting group (which will have its own unique 48 bit address), these packets will also be accepted from the network. The NIC accepts the packet and passes it onto the operating system for ultimate delivery to some application that will process the packet's data.

When an NIC is in normal mode, the computer within which it is installed cannot be used for network snooping. The only network traffic that can be monitored is that sent directly to/from the NIC's 48 bit address, or its multicasting addresses (if any). What is needed is a mechanism to allow a normal mode NIC to accept all packets travelling on the network that it is connected to. On Ethernet networks, this mechanism is called *promiscuous mode*. By setting an Ethernet NIC into promiscuous mode, it is possible to accept all the traffic on a network segment and analyse it.

The process of putting an NIC into promiscuous mode is operating system dependent, and on Linux systems the /sbin/ifconfig command can be used. Here is a typical output from /sbin/ifconfig (with no parameters):

```
eth0      Link encap:Ethernet  HWaddr 00:05:02:97:50:F2
          inet addr:149.153.100.67 Bcast:149.153.100.255 Mask:255.255.255.0
          UP BROADCAST RUNNING MULTICAST  MTU:1500  Metric:1
          RX packets:357231 errors:5 dropped:0 overruns:0 frame:0
          TX packets:85 errors:0 dropped:0 overruns:0 carrier:0
          collisions:0 txqueuelen:100
          Interrupt:42

lo        Link encap:Local Loopback
          inet addr:127.0.0.1  Mask:255.0.0.0
          UP LOOPBACK RUNNING  MTU:3924  Metric:1
          RX packets:0 errors:0 dropped:0 overruns:0 frame:0
          TX packets:0 errors:0 dropped:0 overruns:0 carrier:0
          collisions:0 txqueuelen:0
```

Two interfaces exist on this network device: 'eth0' refers to the Ethernet hardware, and 'lo' refers to the loopback address (typically referred to as *localhost*). Assuming the Linux system is connected to an Ethernet network using a single NIC, commands similar to the following should switch on promiscuous mode:

```
su
/sbin/ifconfig eth0 promisc
<ctrl-D>
```

Note the change to the third line of the output from /sbin/ifconfig after promiscuous mode is switched 'on':

```
eth0      Link encap:Ethernet  HWaddr 00:05:02:97:50:F2
          inet addr:149.153.100.67 Bcast:149.153.100.255 Mask:255.255.255.0
          UP BROADCAST RUNNING PROMISC MULTICAST  MTU:1500  Metric:1
          RX packets:357231 errors:5 dropped:0 overruns:0 frame:0
          TX packets:85 errors:0 dropped:0 overruns:0 carrier:0
          collisions:0 txqueuelen:100
          Interrupt:42

lo        Link encap:Local Loopback
          inet addr:127.0.0.1  Mask:255.0.0.0
          UP LOOPBACK RUNNING  MTU:3924  Metric:1
          RX packets:0 errors:0 dropped:0 overruns:0 frame:0
          TX packets:0 errors:0 dropped:0 overruns:0 carrier:0
          collisions:0 txqueuelen:0
```

The following commands switch off promiscuous mode and return the NIC to normal mode:

```
su
/sbin/ifconfig eth0 -promisc
<ctrl-D>
```

Setting an NIC into promiscuous mode is serious business. For these commands to succeed, they need to be performed by the superuser.

2.3 Building Low-Level Snooping Tools

As discussed earlier, the Net::PcapUtils module provides three subroutines: loop, open and next. By far the most convenient is loop, and it can be used to build a very basic snooping tool:

```
#! /usr/bin/perl -w

use strict;
use Net::PcapUtils;

sub got_a_packet {
    print "Got a packet!\n";
}

my $status = Net::PcapUtils::loop( \&got_a_packet );

if ( $status )
{
    print "Net::PcapUtils::loop returned: $status\n";
}
```

This program, once started, will run forever or until it is *killed* by the operating system. Every time a network packet is accepted from the NIC, the program prints out the words 'Got a packet!' (followed by the newline character) to standard output (usually the screen). Granted, this is not too exciting, but the structure of this small program will form the basis of everything else built in this chapter.

This code begins with the standard (strange) first line which identifies where the underlying operating system can find the Perl interpreter. The -w switch tells Perl to compile the code with warnings enabled. This switch, together with the use strict compiler directive, forces programmers to write Perl code as cleanly and clearly as possible. It is probably overkill at this stage to be this paranoid with such a small amount of code, but, as Perl programs get bigger, these restrictions will more than justify their use.

Perl is then told that the program intends to use the services provided by the Net::PcapUtils module. Next comes a very simple subroutine that, when invoked, prints the words Got a packet! followed by the newline character.

The really useful line is the next one. Here it is again:

```
my $status = Net::PcapUtils::loop( \&got_a_packet );
```

This line calls the loop subroutine within the Net::PcapUtils module, passing a reference to a subroutine as the only parameter. In this case, the subroutine is got_a_packet. The loop subroutine will now arrange to call got_a_packet every time a packet is accepted by the NIC. The got_a_packet subroutine, when used in this manner, is referred to as a *callback function*. The call to loop is a fully qualified name (i.e. Net::PcapUtils::loop) due to the fact that we are using the use strict compiler directive.

The result of the call to Net::PcapUtils::loop is assigned to the scalar variable $status. If the call to Net::PcapUtils::loop is OK, the value returned will be the empty string. If an error has occurred, an error string is returned and placed in $status. The code tests for this, and prints an appropriate error message if necessary.

On its own, this program is not very useful. In the remainder of this chapter, this program will be extended to do much more. Working upwards from the bottom of the TCP/IP-RM, the extensions provide for a collection of tools that can be used to snoop any TCP/IP Ethernet-based network.

2.3.1   loop = open + next

Before building the extensions, let us talk a little bit about the other subroutines the Net::PcapUtils module provides, open and next. These subroutines provide for the manual opening of an NIC (using open) and the manual fetching of an accepted packet from the NIC (using next).

Here is the simple snooper from the previous section rewritten to use open and next instead of loop:

```
#! /usr/bin/perl -w

use strict;
use Net::PcapUtils;

sub got_a_packet {
    print "Got a packet!\n";
}

my $pkt_descriptor = Net::PcapUtils::open;

if ( !ref( $pkt_descriptor ) )
{
    print "Net::PcapUtils::open returned: $pkt_descriptor\n";
    exit;
}

while( 1 )    # i.e. forever, or until "killed" ...
{
    Net::PcapUtils::next( $pkt_descriptor );
    got_a_packet;
}
```

In this code, the call to Net::PcapUtils::open will return a valid reference to a *packet descriptor* upon success, otherwise an error string is returned. The code checks for a valid reference, and prints an error message if a valid reference is not returned. Each time Net::PcapUtils::next is called, the packet descriptor returned from Net::PcapUtils::open is passed to it.

For simple snoopers, this may seem like far too much trouble. However, as our analysis requirements increase, the finer control provided by the use of open and next will become increasingly important.

What is not shown here is that the Net::PcapUtils::next subroutine returns a list containing two values: a scalar packet and a hash header. Typically, the call to next would look like this:

```
my ( $packet, %header ) = Net::PcapUtils::next( $pkt_descriptor );
```

Further processing of the packet and header information is then possible.

2.3.2 Optional parameters: loop and open

The loop and open subroutines can take a list of additional, optional parameters when invoked. The list of parameters is the same and has the same meaning for *both* loop and open.

Let us look at each of them.

SNAPLEN – Default value: 100. The maximum number of bytes to capture for each accepted packet. On Ethernet networks, the maximum value of **SNAPLEN** cannot exceed 1500.

PROMISC – Default value: 1. Set to 0 to capture packets in normal mode, to 1 to capture packets in promiscuous mode.

TIMEOUT – Default value: 1000. The number of milliseconds of read timeout.

NUMPACKETS – Default value: −1. The number of packets to capture, with −1 meaning 'loop forever'.

FILTER – Default value: ' '. Apply a filter to the packets captured and accepted from the NIC. Initially, all packets are accepted, regardless of type (i.e. there is *no* filter). Useful filters include: 'ip', 'udp' and 'tcp'.

USERDATA – Default value: ' '. This is the value to be passed as the first argument to the callback function.

SAVEFILE – Default value: ' '. The name of the file to read *previously saved* packet data from. This data will be processed instead of the packet data arriving at the NIC.

DEV – Default value: ' '. The name of the network interface to open (as a string), for example: 'eth0'.

Throughout this chapter, a number of examples will make use of these parameters. The default parameterless `Net::PcapUtils::loop`, using `got_a_packet` as a callback function, is exactly the same as this *explicit* call:

```
Net::PcapUtils::loop(
    \&got_a_packet,
    SNAPLEN => 100,
    PROMISC => 1,
    TIMEOUT => 1000,
    NUMPACKETS => -1,
    FILTER => '',
    USERDATA => '',
    SAVEFILE => '',
    DEV => ''
);
```

As another example (and without getting too ahead of ourselves), here is a call to `loop` that captures 1000 IP datagrams, and calls the `got_a_packet` subroutine for each of them:

```
Net::PcapUtils::loop(
    \&got_a_packet,
    NUMPACKETS => 1000,
    FILTER => 'ip'
);
```

2.3.3 Optional parameters: the callback function

The `Net::PcapUtils::loop` subroutine will pass a set of parameters to the callback function when it is invoked. Processing of these parameters is entirely optional (as can be seen from the above snoopers where nothing is processed). An array of values is passed into the callback function and the array is assigned to three individual scalar variables to provide for further processing. The second array element is in actual fact a reference to a hash (and the `got_a_packet` subroutine needs to take this into consideration).

Let us rewrite `got_a_packet` to process the parameters:

```
sub got_a_packet {
    my ( $user_arg, $header, $packet ) = @_;

    print "Got a packet!\n\n";
    print "The user argument is: ", $user_arg, "\n";
    print "The header data is:\n";
    foreach my $name (sort keys %{$header})
    {
        print "    $name -> ${header}{$name}\n";
    }
    print "The packet data is:    ", $packet, "\n\n";
}
```

For now, the further processing simply involves printing out the 'raw' values of the parameters. In the subsections which follow, the services provided by the `NetPacket::*` modules will be used to add *meaning* to the raw values. When this version of the simple snooper is executed, do not expect the output to have any real meaning (in fact, most of the output will look like garbage). It is necessary to further process the Ethernet packet data (its payload) to understand what it contains. More on this later.

2.3.4 Ethernet Analysis

The `NetPacket::Ethernet` module provides a subroutine called decode that, when called with an Ethernet frame as its sole parameter, returns an object which provides access to the instance data from the frame.

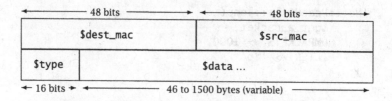

Figure 2.1   The NetPacket::Ethernet frame format.

Within a `NetPacket::Ethernet` object, the instance data for Ethernet frames has the following fields (refer to Figure 2.1 on p. 46):

dest_mac – the 48 bit address for the destination host (the network device destined to receive the Ethernet frame);

src_mac – the 48 bit address for the source host (the network device sending the Ethernet frame);

type – the type of data being sent in the frame;

data – the actual data contained in the Ethernet frame (its payload).

The **type** field is interesting, as it is used to uniquely identify the traffic being carried within the payload of the Ethernet frame[3]. The `NetPacket::Ethernet` module provides a small list of frame types (as Perl constants) that can be imported into a Perl program, as follows:

```
use NetPacket::Ethernet qw( :types );
```

Here is the list of defined constants.

ETH_TYPE_IP – Internet Protocol version 4 datagrams.

ETH_TYPE_ARP – Address Resolution Protocol packets.

ETH_TYPE_RARP – Reverse Address Resolution Protocol packets.

ETH_TYPE_APPLETALK – Apple Computer's AppleTalk packets.

ETH_TYPE_SNMP – Simple Network Management Protocol packets.

ETH_TYPE_IPv6 – Internet Protocol version 6 datagrams.

ETH_TYPE_PPP – Point-To-Point Protocol packets.

Compared with the entire list of Ethernet frame types, this is a very small subset indeed (see the *Web Resources* section at the end of this chapter on how to obtain the complete list).

To work with other frame types, simply define more Perl constants at the top of a program. As the constants are something that will be used in a number of programs, it is worthwhile creating a small Perl module to hold them:

---

[3] Although Ethernet technology rarely cares about the type of traffic being carried.

```
package XtraType;

#
# XtraType.pm - Some additional Ethernet frame types.
#

use 5.6.0;

require Exporter;

our @ISA          = qw( Exporter );

# We export all the symbols declared in this module by
# default.
our @EXPORT       = qw(
                        ETH_TYPE_NOVELL1
                        ETH_TYPE_NOVELL2
                        ETH_TYPE_TCP_IP_COMPRESSION
                      );

our @EXPORT_OK    = qw(
                      );

our %EXPORT_TAGS = (
                      );

our $VERSION      = 0.01;

use constant ETH_TYPE_NOVELL1              => 0x8137;
use constant ETH_TYPE_NOVELL2              => 0x8138;
use constant ETH_TYPE_TCP_IP_COMPRESSION   => 0x876B;

1;
```

Call this module XtraType.pm and place it in the same directory as the programs that will use it, which is accomplished with the following statement near the top of a program:

```
use XtraType;
```

In the rest of the code in this chapter, the individual frame types are referred to using their fully qualified names, for example:

```
XtraType::ETH_TYPE_TCP_IP_COMPRESSION;
```

This is not syntactically necessary, but, for the sake of clarity, will be the preferred technique employed within *Programming the Network with Perl*.

2.3.5 EtherSnooper (v0.01)

The start of the first Ethernet snooper contains these statements:

```
#! /usr/bin/perl -w

use 5.6.0;

use strict;
use Net::PcapUtils;
use NetPacket::Ethernet qw( :types );
use XtraType;
```

The program, which is called *EtherSnooper*, gives total counts for each Ethernet frame type captured as part of the analysis. Two versions of the snooper will be developed, one to capture 1000 packets, and another to capture three minutes worth of network traffic.

Two hashes are used to store information within *EtherSnooper*. The first, %type_totals, maintains a count for each frame type captured, and is initially empty. The second, %type_desc, is used to provide descriptive text when displaying any results. The programs also keep a count of the total number of packets accepted in a scalar called $num_packets.

Initialize the two hashes and the scalar as follows:

```
our %type_totals = ();

our %type_desc = (
        0x0800 => 'IPv4',
        0x0806 => 'ARP',
        0x809B => 'AppleTalk',
        0x814C => 'SNMP',
        0x86DD => 'IPv6',
        0x880B => 'PPP',
        0x8137 => 'NOVELL1',
        0x8138 => 'NOVELL2',
        0x8035 => 'RARP',
        0x876B => 'TCP/IPc'
);

our $num_packets = 0;
```

Declaring these hashes as our allows them to be used as global variables, while still satisfying the restrictions placed upon the program by the use strict compiler directive.

The %type_totals hash is populated by yet another version of the got_a_ packet subroutine:

```
sub got_a_packet {
    my ( $user_arg, $header, $packet ) = @_;

    my $frame = NetPacket::Ethernet->decode( $packet );

    $type_totals{ $frame->{type} }++;

    $num_packets++;
}
```

In this version of the packet-processing callback function, the packet is passed as a parameter and decoded as an Ethernet frame. What is returned is an object of type NetPacket::Ethernet. It is then possible to access the instance data for the frame type value using standard object instance accessing syntax (using $frame->{type} in the above code).

Once the frame type is known, it is used to increment the %type_totals value part associated with the frame type value. The code takes advantage of Perl's ability to dynamically grow a hash as required, as well as ensure that hash names (or keys) are always unique. This may seem like a trick, but it is actually a much-used Perl programming idiom.

The got_a_packet subroutine concludes by incrementing the $num_packets scalar for each processed frame.

The rest of the program is similar to the first snooper developed earlier in this chapter, except that the number of packets to accept is explicitly stated and a call to display_results is made:

```
my $status = Net::PcapUtils::loop(
                \&got_a_packet,
                NUMPACKETS => 1000
            );

if ( $status )
{
    print "Net::PcapUtils::loop returned: $status\n";
}
else
{
    display_results;
}
```

To display meaningful results, the program processes the hashes, using another standard Perl idiom. Worry if the value of $num_packets is something other than 1000:

```
sub display_results {
    print "$num_packets frames processed.\n\n";

    foreach my $etype ( sort keys %type_desc )
```

```
    {
        print "$type_desc{$etype} generated ";
        if ( exists $type_totals{$etype} )
        {
            print "$type_totals{$etype} packets.\n";
        }
        else
        {
            print "no packets.\n";
        }
    }
}
```

And there you have it: a relatively useful Ethernet snooper, which displays information on captured packets by frame type. Here are some results generated (during a standard working day) on the network used during the writing of *Programming the Network with Perl*:

```
1000 frames processed.

IPv4 generated 481 packets.
ARP generated 51 packets.
RARP generated no packets.
AppleTalk generated no packets.
NOVELL1 generated 2 packets.
NOVELL2 generated no packets.
SNMP generated no packets.
IPv6 generated no packets.
TCP/IPc generated no packets.
PPP generated no packets.
```

Oh dear, over 40% of the packets captured are not categorized.

To see what is happening, add the following lines of code to the very bottom of the `display_results` subroutine:

```
print "\n\nRaw statistics:\n\n";
print "frame-type -> frequency\n\n";
foreach my $e_total ( sort keys %type_totals )
{
    printf "%lx -> %d\n", $e_total, $type_totals{$e_total};
}
```

In addition to the output generated above, *EtherSnooper* now displays output similar to the following:

```
Raw statistics:

frame-type -> frequency

64 -> 296
```

```
66 -> 5
a3 -> 2
aa -> 1
800 -> 481
806 -> 51
d9 -> 1
dc -> 2
6002 -> 1
8137 -> 2
22 -> 1
163 -> 2
25 -> 1
26 -> 29
28 -> 1
2a -> 1
2b -> 4
2c -> 68
238 -> 2
5a -> 1
5d -> 1
60 -> 14
62 -> 1
63 -> 32
```

The extra code prints out the Ethernet frame type value in HEX, then indicates (to the right of the -> symbol) how many frames of that type were captured. HEX 800 is the Ethernet frame type for IP, and HEX 806 corresponds to ARP, and these totals match. But, look at all those other frame types! A quick look at the IANA Ethernet frame type file does not help solve this puzzle, as none of these frame type values match with an assigned type in the file.

It turns out that the values are *not* Ethernet frame types at all, but are instead IEEE 802.3 length values. Ethernet hardware can carry frames with different frame formats. When used by technology that generates Ethernet II (or DIX) frames, the two bytes in the header which follow the 48 bit destination and source addresses correspond to the Ethernet frame type value. When used by technology that generates Ethernet frames based on the IEEE 802.3 standards, the same two bytes correspond to the length of the frame. It just so happens that the network used during the development of *Programming the Network with Perl* carries more than one Ethernet frame format: Ethernet II frames (which carry mostly TCP/IP traffic) and the IEEE 802.3 frame format (which is used by *Novell NetWare*).

Having agreed to disagree on the format of Ethernet frames, the Ethernet II and IEEE 802.3 standards developers agreed (thankfully) that no Ethernet II frame type would have a value less than HEX 05DC (which is decimal 1500). So, when a snooper sees a frame type less than 1501, it is OK to assume that the frame is formatted as a variation of the IEEE 802.3 format, and that the frame type value is actually a length value.

To take this into consideration, change the `got_a_packet` subroutine to check the value of the frame type field prior to updating the hash:

```
if ($frame->{type} < 1501)
{
    $type_totals{ 1500 }++;
}
else
{
    $type_totals{ $frame->{type} }++;
}
```

and add these lines to the bottom of `display_results`:

```
print "\nNon Ethernet II (DIX) frames generated";
print " $type_totals{1500} packets.\n";
```

Here is the output generated by this updated version of *EtherSnooper*:

```
1000 frames processed.

IPv4 generated 484 packets.
ARP generated 15 packets.
RARP generated no packets.
AppleTalk generated no packets.
NOVELL1 generated 3 packets.
NOVELL2 generated no packets.
SNMP generated no packets.
IPv6 generated no packets.
TCP/IPc generated no packets.
PPP generated no packets.

Non Ethernet II (DIX) frames generated 498 packets.
```

2.3.6 EtherSnooper (v0.02)

The second version of the *EtherSnooper* captures packets for three minutes (as opposed to stopping after 1000 accepted packets). To do something for a number of minutes in Perl, use code similar to this:

```
my $minute = 3;
my $now = time;
my $then = $now + (60 * $minute);

while ( ($now = time) < $then )
{
    ; # Do whatever you want to do here.
}
```

Calling Perl's inbuilt `time` subroutine returns the number of seconds since the operating systems epoch. The value returned is assigned to $now. Adding 180 seconds to $now turns it into $then. The loop iterates as long as $now is less than $then, and $now is updated each time (no pun intended) the loop iterates.

It is tempting to try and integrate this timing code into *EtherSnooper* (v0.01), as follows:

```
my $minute = 3;
my $now = time;
my $then = $now + (60 * $minute);

while ( ($now = time) < $then )
{
    my $status = Net::PcapUtils::loop(
                    \&got_a_packet,
                    NUMPACKETS => 1
                 );
}
```

The call to `Net::PcapUtils::loop` only captures a single packet each time it is called. Each time `Net::PcapUtils::loop` executes it opens the NIC, configures the NIC using the provided parameters, then calls the callback function for each packet accepted by the NIC (which is only ever going to be one). As this will happen each time the `while` loop iterates, this code ends up opening and configuring the NIC far too often. In short, the code is wasteful. It may also exhibit resource problems when executed over long periods of time.

To overcome this problem, rewrite *EtherSnooper* to use open and next to create v0.02. Here is the entire program:

```
#! /usr/bin/perl -w

use 5.6.0;

use strict;
use Net::PcapUtils;
use NetPacket::Ethernet qw( :types );
use XtraType;

our %type_totals = ();

our %type_desc = (
        0x0800 => 'IPv4',
        0x0806 => 'ARP',
        0x809B => 'AppleTalk',
        0x814C => 'SNMP',
        0x86DD => 'IPv6',
        0x880B => 'PPP',
        0x8137 => 'NOVELL1',
```

```perl
                0x8138 => 'NOVELL2',
                0x8035 => 'RARP',
                0x876B => 'TCP/IPc'
        );

    our $num_packets = 0;

    sub got_a_packet {
        my $packet = shift;

        my $frame = NetPacket::Ethernet->decode( $packet );

        if ( $frame->{type} < 1501 )
        {
            $type_totals{ 1500 }++;
        }
        else
        {
            $type_totals{ $frame->{type} }++;
        }

        $num_packets++;
    }

    sub display_results {
        print "$num_packets processed.\n\n";

        foreach my $etype ( sort keys %type_desc )
        {
            print "$type_desc{$etype} generated ";
            if ( exists $type_totals{$etype} )
            {
                print "$type_totals{$etype} packets.\n";
            }
            else
            {
                print "no packets.\n";
            }
        }
        print "\nNon Ethernet II (DIX) frames generated";
        print " $type_totals{1500} packets.\n";
    }

    my $pkt_descriptor = Net::PcapUtils::open;

    if ( !ref( $pkt_descriptor ) )
    {
        print "Net::PcapUtils::open returned: $pkt_descriptor\n";
        exit;
    }
```

```
my $minute = 3;
my $now = time;
my $then = $now + (60 * $minute);

my ( $next_packet, %next_header );

while ( ($now = time) < $then )
{
    ( $next_packet, %next_header ) =
        Net::PcapUtils::next( $pkt_descriptor );
    got_a_packet( $next_packet );
}

display_results;
```

Working down through the v0.02 code, changes were made to the got_a_packet subroutine as there is now a single parameter which contains the packet contents. Nearer the bottom of the code the call to Net::PcapUtils::loop has been replaced by an equivalent call to Net::PcapUtils::open. The code to run for three minutes controls the loop which calls Net::PcapUtils::next on each iteration. The got_a_packet subroutine is now called explicitly, as opposed to relying on the callback function mechanism from v0.01. At the end, the same display_results subroutine is invoked after a successful run.

Even though more code had to be written, v0.02 of *EtherSnooper* is not only less wasteful than v0.01, it is also more extendable. Here are some results generated by this program:

```
4431 frames processed.

IPv4 generated 2074 packets.
ARP generated 148 packets.
RARP generated no packets.
AppleTalk generated no packets.
NOVELL1 generated 139 packets.
NOVELL2 generated no packets.
SNMP generated no packets.
IPv6 generated no packets.
TCP/IPc generated no packets.
PPP generated no packets.

Non Ethernet II (DIX) frames generated 2070 packets.
```

2.3.7 EtherSnooper (v0.03)

EtherSnooper is now easy to extend. Let us add code to determine the busiest hosts on the network, where 'busiest' is defined as the host that receives the most

Ethernet frames and the host that sends the most Ethernet frames. All that is required is a mechanism to count the number of occurrences of each address captured.

Just as a hash exists to record details of the frame types (`%type_totals`), define two more hashes to record details of the source and destination addresses, which are both initially empty:

```
our %src_hosts = ();
our %dest_hosts = ();
```

With the hashes in existence, make changes to the `got_a_packet` subroutine to count the occurrences of each address captured. Here is the new version of the subroutine:

```
sub got_a_packet {
    my $packet = shift;

    my $frame = NetPacket::Ethernet->decode( $packet );

    if ( $frame->{type} < 1501 )
    {
        $type_totals{ 1500 }++;
    }
    else
    {
        $type_totals{ $frame->{type} }++;
    }

    $src_hosts{ $frame->{src_mac} }++;
    $dest_hosts{ $frame->{dest_mac} }++;

    $num_packets++;
}
```

The same programming idiom used to update `%type_totals` is used to update the `%src_hosts` and `%dest_hosts` hashes. With the data acquired, change the `display_results` subroutine to print the busiest hosts:

```
sub display_results {
    print "$num_packets frames processed.\n\n";

    my $busiest_mac = 0;
    my $busiest_count = 0;

    print "The busiest hosts were:\n\n";

    while ( my ( $host, $count ) = each %src_hosts )
    {
        if ( $count > $busiest_count )
        {
```

```
            $busiest_mac = $host;
            $busiest_count = $count;
        }
    }

    print "Source: $busiest_mac with ";
    print "$busiest_count frames\n";

    $busiest_mac = 0;
    $busiest_count = 0;

    while ( my ( $host, $count ) = each %dest_hosts )
    {
        if ( $count > $busiest_count )
        {
            $busiest_mac = $host;
            $busiest_count = $count;
        }
    }
    print "Destination: $busiest_mac with ";
    print "$busiest_count frames\n";
}
```

Using hash traversal code, `display_results` works through `%src_hosts` and `%dest_hosts` and determines the address of the busiest sending and receiving hosts.

Here are some results generated by *EtherSnooper* (v0.03):

```
3905 frames processed.

The busiest hosts were:

Source: 00d0d3a50002 with 136 frames
Destination: ffffffffffff with 3405 frames
```

The busiest destination address is the Ethernet broadcast address (all-Fs). On LANs running *Novell NetWare*, a certain amount of broadcast traffic is quite common, although this amount appears to be surprisingly high. (In actual fact, it turned out that a large number of misconfigured workstations had been recently installed onto the network used during the writing of *Programming the Network with Perl*. Every one of the workstations were busy broadcasting their existence, and it was not until the entire network's performance suffered that the problem was discovered and, ultimately, diagnosed.)

Use this version of `display_results` to see the statistics for all of the captured hosts:

```
sub display_results {
    print "$num_packets frames processed.\n\n";
```

```
foreach my $etype ( sort keys %type_desc )
{
    print "$type_desc{$etype} generated ";
    if ( exists $type_totals{$etype} )
    {
        print "$type_totals{$etype} packets.\n";
    }
    else
    {
        print "no packets.\n";
    }
}

print "The host statistics are:\n\nSources:\n\n";

foreach my $host (sort keys %src_hosts )
{
    print "Host: $host, Count: $src_hosts{$host}.\n";
}

print "\nDestinations:\n\n";

foreach my $host (sort keys %dest_hosts )
{
    print "Host: $host, Count: $dest_hosts{$host}.\n";
}
}
```

The foreach statements traverse each hash and print the results ordered by address.

2.3.8 Displaying IP addresses

When addresses are displayed by *EtherSnooper* (v0.03), they appear as HEX strings, representing the 48 bits of an Ethernet address. On a TCP/IP network, Ethernet frames used by the Internet have an associated IP address (which is 32 bits long).

If the Ethernet frame contains an IP datagram, the frame type will be set to NetPacket::Ethernet::ETH_TYPE_IP. If this is the case, the facilities of the NetPacket::IP module can be used to decode the IP datagram and determine the IP addresses in use. *EtherSnooper* (v0.04) will display an IP address with its associated Ethernet address when printing results.

Another hash is required to store the Ethernet address to IP address mappings, which can be declared near the top of the program, as follows:

```
our %e2ip = ();
```

The %e2ip hash is keyed by Ethernet address, with an IP address associated with each key. As usual, populate the hash in (yet another) version of got_a_packet:

```
sub got_a_packet {
    my $packet = shift;

    my $frame = NetPacket::Ethernet->decode( $packet );

    if ($frame->{type} < 1501 )
    {
        $type_totals{ 1500 }++;
    }
    else
    {
        $type_totals{ $frame->{type} }++;
    }

    $src_hosts{ $frame->{src_mac} }++;
    $dest_hosts{ $frame->{dest_mac} }++;

    if ( $frame->{type} == NetPacket::Ethernet::ETH_TYPE_IP )
    {
        my $ip_datagram = NetPacket::IP->decode(
                NetPacket::Ethernet::eth_strip( $packet ) );

        $e2ip{ $frame->{src_mac} } = $ip_datagram->{src_ip};
        $e2ip{ $frame->{dest_mac} } = $ip_datagram->{dest_ip};
    }

    $num_packets++;
}
```

With the Ethernet frame decoded and the statistics recorded, the code checks to see if the frame type is NetPacket::Ethernet::ETH_TYPE_IP. If it is, *Ether-Snooper* takes the frame and strips off the Ethernet header information using the NetPacket::Ethernet::eth_strip subroutine, producing the frames payload. The payload is then passed to the decode method of the NetPacket::IP module, which creates an IP datagram object from it.

This method of encapsulating IP datagrams in the payload of Ethernet frames clearly demonstrates the computer networking layered architecture at work. As data moves down through the 'stack' of layers, each protocol adds header information to the payload. The frame is then moved from the source host to the destination host 'across the wire', where the data then moves up through the layers, with each protocol removing its header information before *passing up* the payload to the layer above. As the *EtherSnooper* program pulls the frame *directly off the wire*, it needs to do its own processing of the frame in order to remove any header information that is not required (see Figure 2.2 on p. 60).

The object – called $ip_datagram in the code – has associated with it a collection of IP instance data (refer to Figure 2.3 on p. 64). Of particular interest are the fields containing the source and destination IP addresses, stored in

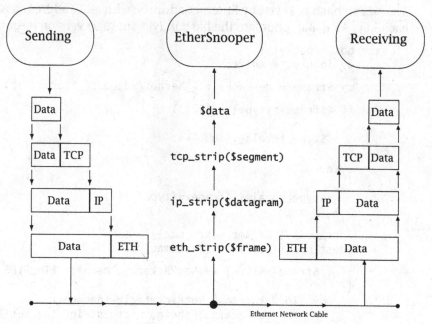

Figure 2.2   How *EtherSnooper* works.

$ip_datagram->{src_ip} and $ip_datagram->{dest_ip} fields. The values in these fields are used to update the %e2ip hash every time got_a_packet is called.

For this code to work, we need to use the modules as follows (at the top of the program):

```
use NetPacket::Ethernet qw( :types :strip );
use NetPacket::IP;
```

The program indicates its intention to use the NetPacket::Ethernet module with particular reference to the predefined frame types as well as the stripping subroutine, which in this case is eth_strip. The program also uses the NetPacket::IP module.

A small change is required to the display_results subroutine to display the IP addresses:

```
sub display_results {
    print "$num_packets frames processed.\n\n";

    foreach my $etype ( sort keys %type_desc )
    {
        print "$type_desc{$etype} generated ";
        if ( exists $type_totals{$etype} )
        {
            print "$type_totals{$etype} packets.\n";
        }
```

```
        else
        {
            print "no packets.\n";
        }
}
print "\nNon Ethernet II (DIX) frames generated";
print " $type_totals{1500} packets.\n";

print "\nThe host statistics are:\n\nSources:\n\n";

foreach my $host (sort keys %src_hosts )
{
    if ( exists $e2ip{$host} )
    {
        print "Host: $host ($e2ip{$host}), ";
        print "Count: $src_hosts{$host}.\n";
    }
    else
    {
        print "Host: $host, Count: $src_hosts{$host}.\n";
    }
}

print "\nDestinations:\n\n";

foreach my $host (sort keys %dest_hosts )
{
    if ( exists $e2ip{$host} )
    {
        print "Host: $host ($e2ip{$host}), ";
        print "Count: $dest_hosts{$host}.\n";
    }
    else
    {
        print "Host: $host, Count: $dest_hosts{$host}.\n";
    }
}
}
```

Prior to printing out the results line for each source and destination, the code checks to see if an entry exists in %e2ip, and if it does, prints out the IP address associated with the Ethernet address. If no entry exists, no IP address is printed. In the next chapter, code is provided to turn IP addresses into IP names.

Here is an extract from results generated by *EtherSnooper* (v0.04). The actual results were several hundred lines long:

```
4945 frames processed.

IPv4 generated 2961 packets.
```

ARP generated 278 packets.
RARP generated no packets.
AppleTalk generated no packets.
NOVELL1 generated 7 packets.
NOVELL2 generated no packets.
SNMP generated no packets.
IPv6 generated no packets.
TCP/IPc generated no packets.
PPP generated no packets.

Non Ethernet II (DIX) frames generated 1699 packets.

The host statistics are:

Sources:

Host: 0002fd06ebed, Count: 2.
Host: 00036bd95d58, Count: 93.
Host: 0005025796a2 (149.153.100.65), Count: 257.
Host: 0005027148a0 (149.153.100.106), Count: 6.
      .
      .
      .

Host: 00105a42187a (149.153.100.20), Count: 4.
Host: 00105af5bdde, Count: 3.
Host: 00b0d065878c (149.153.134.2), Count: 20.
Host: 00b0d065878d (149.153.130.33), Count: 4.
Host: 00b0d0658790, Count: 3.
      .
      .

Host: 00b0d06587ba, Count: 3.
Host: 00d0d3a53f7d (149.153.50.104), Count: 10.
Host: 08000228826f (149.153.100.7), Count: 2.
Host: 0800090fe547, Count: 4.
Host: 080009f9fdf4, Count: 3.

Destinations:

Host: 0005025796a2 (149.153.100.65), Count: 846.
Host: 0080192d295c (149.153.100.23), Count: 223.
Host: 00d0d3a50002 (149.153.1.5), Count: 32.
Host: 01000ccccccc, Count: 3.
Host: 01000cdddddd, Count: 116.
Host: 01005e000001 (224.0.0.1), Count: 4.
Host: 01005e000002 (224.0.0.2), Count: 4.
Host: 01005e00000d (224.0.0.13), Count: 6.
Host: 01005e000116 (224.0.1.22), Count: 307.
Host: 01005e000123 (224.0.1.35), Count: 8.

```
Host: 01005e00013c (224.0.1.60), Count: 25.
Host: 01005e3796d0 (229.55.150.208), Count: 18.
Host: 0180c2000000, Count: 90.
Host: 030000000001, Count: 2.
Host: ffffffffffff (149.153.113.255), Count: 3261.
```

This extract shows IP addresses for those Ethernet frames that are carrying IP traffic. The most used destination address is the broadcast address
149.153.113.255 (which has associated with it the all-Fs Ethernet address). The
reason for all the broadcast traffic is attributed, once again, to the collection of
misconfigured workstations on the LAN, as discussed previously on p. 57, § 2.3.7.
By including the IP address mappings in the results, this version of *EtherSnooper*
has further isolated the problem to those machines on the 149.153.113.0 sub-
network.

Here is the *EtherSnooper* (v0.04) call to open the NIC:

```
my $pkt_descriptor = Net::PcapUtils::open;
```

It is tempting to apply a filter to this call, as follows:

```
my $pkt_descriptor =
        Net::PcapUtils::open( FILTER => 'ip' );
```

This has the effect of only accepting Ethernet frames carrying IP datagrams in
their payload. On a network that carries traffic for more than one network technology (such as the Internet, NetWare and AppleTalk), this would have the effect
of skewing the displayed results, as only IP traffic would be accepted and counted.
If filters are used, be sure that this is what is required.

2.4   Snooping IP Datagrams

The strategy employed while building the first four versions of *EtherSnooper* can
be used to snoop any of the protocols the NetPacket::* modules support. The
technique is always the same.

1. Use the Correct Modules: at the top of the program, specify the modules and
   options that the program will use.

2. Create the Hashes: decide on the statistics that will be gathered, and define
   the required number of hashes to store the information.

3. Modify got_a_packet: populate the hashes every time a frame is accepted
   by the NIC.

4. Modify display_results: post-process the hashes to display meaningful
   results.

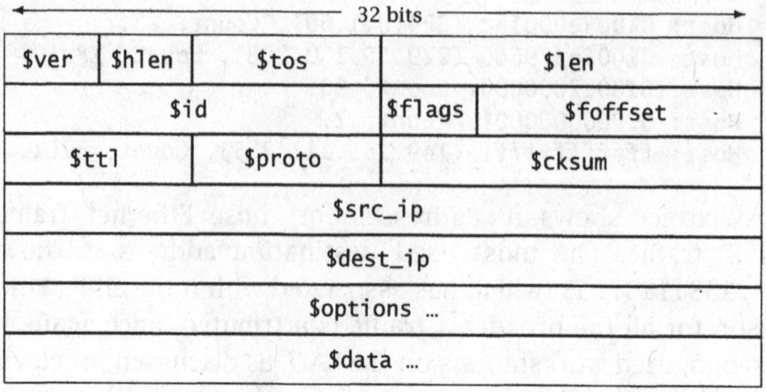

```
← ————————————— 32 bits ————————————— →
```

$ver	$hlen	$tos	$len
$id		$flags	$foffset
$ttl	$proto		$cksum
$src_ip			
$dest_ip			
$options ...			
$data ...			

Figure 2.3   The NetPacket::IP datagram format.

Two additional versions of *EtherSnooper* will now be developed. *EtherSnooper* (v0.05) snoops IP datagrams and collects data on the Time-To-Live (TTL) field. The results of this version of the program display the average TTL value for the IP datagrams captured, as well as the minimum and maximum TTL values.

EtherSnooper (v0.06) snoops IP datagrams and collects data on the different protocols being carried by IP. This functionality is very similar to *EtherSnooper* (v0.02), except that the snooper is capturing statistics at a higher layer (as opposed to the Host-To-Network Layer).

To learn more about the instance fields for the datagram object created by the decode subroutine from `NetPacket::IP`, refer to the online documentation for the `NetPacket::IP` module and to Figure 2.3 on p. 64.

2.4.1   EtherSnooper (v0.05)

Here is the code to *EtherSnooper* (v0.05), which processes each IP datagram's TTL value:

```perl
#! /usr/bin/perl -w

use 5.6.0;
use integer;
use strict;

use Net::PcapUtils;
use NetPacket::Ethernet qw( :strip );
use NetPacket::IP;

our %ttl_totals = ();

our $num_datagrams = 0;
```

```perl
sub got_a_packet {
    my $packet = shift;

    my $ip_datagram = NetPacket::IP->decode(
            NetPacket::Ethernet::eth_strip( $packet ) );

    $ttl_totals{ $ip_datagram->{ttl} }++;
    $num_datagrams++;
}

sub display_results {
    print "$num_datagrams datagrams processed.\n\n";

    my $min_ttl = 256;
    my $max_ttl = 0;
    my $average_ttl = 0;

    while ( my ( $ttl_key, $ttl_value ) = each %ttl_totals )
    {
        if ( $ttl_key < $min_ttl )
        {
            $min_ttl = $ttl_key;
        }
        if ( $ttl_key > $max_ttl )
        {
            $max_ttl = $ttl_key;
        }
        $average_ttl =
                $average_ttl + ( $ttl_key * $ttl_value );
    }

    $average_ttl = ( $average_ttl / $num_datagrams );

    print "Minimum TTL value: $min_ttl\n";
    print "Maximum TTL value: $max_ttl\n";
    print "Average TTL value: $average_ttl\n\n";

    print "TTL distribution analysis:\n\n";

    foreach my $ttlkey ( sort {$a <=> $b} keys %ttl_totals )
    {
        print "TTL: $ttlkey, ";
        print "frequency: $ttl_totals{$ttlkey}.\n";
    }
}

my $pkt_descriptor =
        Net::PcapUtils::open( FILTER => 'ip' );
```

```
if ( !ref( $pkt_descriptor ) )
{
    print "Net::PcapUtils::open returned: $pkt_descriptor\n";
    exit;
}

my $minute = 3;
my $now = time;
my $then = $now + (60 * $minute);

my ( $next_packet, %next_header );

while ( ($now = time) < $then )
{
    ( $next_packet, %next_header ) =
            Net::PcapUtils::next( $pkt_descriptor );
    got_a_packet( $next_packet );
}

display_results;
```

The code uses both the `NetPacket::Ethernet` and `NetPacket::IP` modules. A hash called `%ttl_totals` is created to store the captured TTL values, and is populated each time `got_a_packet` is invoked.

The `display_results` subroutine processes the `%ttl_totals` hash to determine the smallest, largest and average TTL values, before printing the results to the screen. The distribution of TTL values is then printed using a simple `foreach` construct.

IPv4 TTL values are 8 bits long, which means they can contain values in the range 1–255 (which explains the initial values of the `$min_ttl` and `$max_ttl` scalars in the code). The recommended default value for TTL is 60, although some IP software vendors disregard this recommendation.

The code for v0.05 includes the `use integer` compiler directive at the top of the program. This turns on integer arithmetic, as opposed to floating point (which is the default), and helps keep the printed output tidy.

Here are some results produced by *EtherSnooper* (v0.05):

```
2022 datagrams processed.

Minimum TTL value: 1
Maximum TTL value: 255
Average TTL value: 91

TTL distribution analysis:

TTL: 1, frequency: 499.
TTL: 2, frequency: 6.
TTL: 4, frequency: 1.
```

```
TTL: 10, frequency: 18.
TTL: 32, frequency: 72.
TTL: 64, frequency: 2.
TTL: 128, frequency: 1423.
TTL: 255, frequency: 1.
```

As the code filters on the IP protocol, the non-Ethernet II frames have no bearing on the statistics gathered.

A small or large average TTL value may indicate problems on a network. When the TTL value reaches zero, the router processing the datagram will discard it and class it as undeliverable. Each time a router sees an IP datagram, the TTL value is reduced by one. In this way, an undeliverable IP datagram will eventually be discarded.

A large average TTL may result in undeliverable IP datagrams surviving for too long on the network, which could result in wasted network resources and (possibly) congestion. A small average TTL value may result in IP datagrams being discarded too soon, which could result in IP datagram retransmission (assuming some higher-level protocol is monitoring for such occurrences and performing the retransmission – IP as a technology is *unreliable* and does not care when a datagram is discarded).

2.4.2   EtherSnooper (v0.06)

Here is the code to *EtherSnooper* (v0.06), which processes the higher-level protocols carried by IP:

```perl
#! /usr/bin/perl -w

use 5.6.0;

use strict;
use Net::PcapUtils;
use NetPacket::Ethernet qw( :strip );
use NetPacket::IP qw( :protos );

our %ip_type_totals = ();

our %ip_type_desc = {
        0   => 'IP',
        1   => 'ICMP',
        2   => 'IGMP',
        4   => 'IP/IP',
        6   => 'TCP',
        17  => 'UDP'
    };

our $num_datagrams = 0;
```

```perl
sub got_a_packet {
    my $packet = shift;

    my $ip_datagram = NetPacket::IP->decode(
            NetPacket::Ethernet::eth_strip( $packet ) );

    $ip_type_totals{ $ip_datagram->{proto} }++;

    $num_datagrams++;
}
sub display_results {
    print "$num_datagrams processed.\n\n";

    foreach my $iptype ( sort keys %ip_type_desc )
    {
        print "$ip_type_desc{$iptype} generated ";
        if ( exists $ip_type_totals{$iptype} )
        {
            print "$ip_type_totals{$iptype} datagrams.\n";
        }
        else
        {
            print "no datagrams.\n";
        }
    }
}

my $pkt_descriptor =
        Net::PcapUtils::open( FILTER => 'ip' );

if ( !ref( $pkt_descriptor ) )
{
    print "Net::PcapUtils::open returned: $pkt_descriptor\n";
    exit;
}

my $minute = 3;
my $now = time;
my $then = $now + (60 * $minute);

my ( $next_packet, %next_header );

while ( ($now = time) < $then )
{
    ( $next_packet, %next_header ) =
            Net::PcapUtils::next( $pkt_descriptor );
    got_a_packet( $next_packet );
}

display_results;
```

This code is so close to *EtherSnooper* (v0.02), that there is not much to say about it.

The capturing is happening at the network layer, so the code filters on the IP protocol. Statistics are captured by `got_a_packet` and then processed by `display_results`.

Here are some results produced by *EtherSnooper* (v0.06):

```
2102 datagrams processed.

IP generated no datagrams.
ICMP generated 9 datagrams.
UDP generated 1659 datagrams.
IGMP generated 47 datagrams.
IP/IP generated no datagrams.
TCP generated 381 datagrams.
```

As with *EtherSnooper* (v0.05), non-Ethernet II frames have no bearing on the statistics gathered. The statistics gathered are quite surprising: look at all that UDP traffic! Nearly every computer networking text describing TCP/IP short-shifts UDP as a protocol that is used by few applications (when compared with the number employing TCP). So, if applications are not using UDP to transport data, what is?

Returning to the problem of the misconfigured, broadcasting workstations from earlier, it transpired that they were broadcasting UDP datagrams. This fact alone accounts for the large number of UDP datagrams captured by this version of *EtherSnooper*.

2.5 Transport Snoopers

The versions of *EtherSnooper* seen thus far have concerned themselves with producing results generated from the header fields of the analysed frames. No attention has been paid to the *data* being carried in the frames. To get to the stage where the data can be analysed (where 'analysed' means 'debugged'), the data need to be processed. In fact, it *only* makes real sense to process the data at the application layer, where the data have real meaning.

In addition, the *EtherSnoopers* have all operated at the Host-To-Network or Network layers. Before getting to the application layer, an understanding of how application data is handled by the Transport Layer is required.

On TCP/IP networks, data is transported by one of two technologies. If the application can withstand some data loss, the lightweight, unreliable User Datagram Protocol (UDP) is used. If data loss is intolerable, the reliable, highly monitored Transport Control Protocol (TCP) is used. Support for analysing both technologies is available in the `NetPacket::TCP` and `NetPacket::UDP` modules.

The technique for interacting with each module is as seen earlier: `use` the correct module, define hashes, modify `got_a_packet` and modify `display_results`.

2.5.1 Preparing to snoop UDP

The fields associated with the UDP datagram, as defined in `NetPacket::UDP`, are as shown in Figure 2.4 on p. 72. To process UDP datagrams, start the program as follows:

```perl
#! /usr/bin/perl -w

use 5.6.0;

use strict;
use Net::PcapUtils;
use NetPacket::Ethernet qw( :strip );
use NetPacket::IP qw( :strip );
use NetPacket::UDP;
```

Within `got_a_packet`, extract the UDP datagram as follows:

```perl
my $udp_datagram = NetPacket::UDP->decode(
        NetPacket::IP::ip_strip(
                NetPacket::Ethernet::eth_strip( $packet ) ) );
```

The call to the `decode` subroutine returns a UDP object (which is called `$udp_datagram` in this code) which provides access to the instance data associated with the UDP datagram. To get the UDP datagram, the code takes the Ethernet frame, strips off the Et hernet header, leaving the IP datagram. The call to `ip_strip` then removes the IP headers from the datagram and passes the payload to the UDP `decode` subroutine.

When opening the NIC, request a filter on UDP datagrams:

```perl
my $pkt_descriptor = Net::PcapUtils::open(
                        FILTER => 'udp',
                        SNAPLEN => 1500
                     );
```

The call to `Net::PcapUtils::open` specifies that the SNAPLEN parameter should be set to 1500 bytes, the maximum frame size for Ethernet. The snooper is interested in getting at the data contained in the frame, so it captures all of it, as opposed to only capturing the first 100 bytes (which would only capture some of the header information).

2.5.2 Preparing to snoop TCP

To process TCP segments (refer to Figure 2.5 on p. 72), start the program as follows:

```perl
#! /usr/bin/perl -w

use 5.6.0;
```

```
use strict;
use Net::PcapUtils;
use NetPacket::Ethernet qw( :strip );
use NetPacket::IP qw( :strip );
use NetPacket::TCP;
```

Within `got_a_packet`, extract the TCP segment as follows:

```
my $tcp_segment = NetPacket::TCP->decode(
        NetPacket::IP::ip_strip(
                NetPacket::Ethernet::eth_strip( $packet ) ) );
```

The call to the `decode` subroutine returns a TCP object (which is called `$tcp_segment` in this code) which provides access to the instance data associated with the TCP segment. To get the TCP segment, the code takes the Ethernet frame, strips off the Ethernet headers, leaving the IP datagram. The call to `ip_strip` then removes the IP headers from the datagram and passes the payload to the TCP `decode` subroutine.

When opening the NIC, request a filter on TCP segments:

```
my $pkt_descriptor = Net::PcapUtils::open(
                            FILTER => 'tcp',
                            SNAPLEN => 1500
                        );
```

As with UDP data capturing, this code sets SNAPLEN to 1500 to ensure the entire Ethernet frame (header and data) is captured.

Figure 2.2 (on p. 60) shows *EtherSnooper* 'stripping' as it relates to each of the layers of the network 'stack'. By successive calls to each layer's `strip` subroutine, a snooping program (running its NIC in promiscuous mode) can eventually determine the data originally created by the sending user-agent. *The program can then do with the data whatever it pleases.* It is important to realize that neither the sending nor the receiving user-agent has any knowledge that snooping has occurred. The snooper simply takes a *copy* of the data transmitted on the wire.

2.5.3 The TCP and UDP gotcha!

When discussing snooping UDP and TCP traffic above, the code filtered on the protocol of interest when invoking `Net::PcapUtils::open`. This has the effect of ensuring that when the 'protocol packet' (either a UDP datagram or TCP segment) makes it as far as the `got_a_packet` subroutine, the code can invoke the correct `decode` subroutine, because it already knows the 'type' of packet to expect.

However, when it comes to UDP, this does *not* guarantee that an entire UDP datagram is decoded. The reason for this has to do with the way UDP datagrams are created and handled by the network.

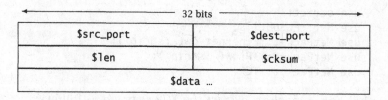

Figure 2.4   The NetPacket::UDP datagram format.

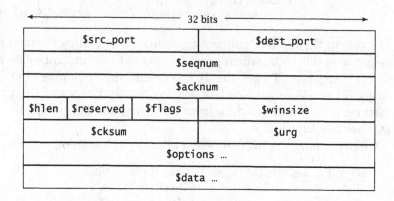

Figure 2.5   The NetPacket::TCP segment format.

When a UDP datagram is created, the UDP technology hands the *entire* datagram to IP for delivery. If the UDP datagram is larger than the Maximum Transmission Unit (MTU) supported by the underlying networking technology[4], the IP technology will break the large UDP datagram into as many smaller parts as are required to send the UDP datagram across the network. This process is referred to as IP fragmentation. When the parts (or fragments) arrive at their destination, the IP technology rebuilds the large UDP datagram before passing it to UDP for further processing. This process is referred to as IP re-assembly.

Figure 2.6 (on p. 73) illustrates this mechanism on an Ethernet network. A 3000 byte UDP datagram is passed to IP for delivery. IP then creates three separate 1000 byte IP datagrams prior to transmission. Of the three IP datagrams created, only the first IP datagram will contain the UDP header information. (In reality, the possibility of IP breaking the 3000 byte datagram into three even 1000 byte fragments is unlikely. Typically, IP will stuff as much data as it can into an IP datagram. But, to illustrate the point, let us keep the mathematics simple.)

With this in mind, a problem surfaces when *EtherSnooper* snoops a packet designated as carrying UDP data. The Ethernet header will indicate that IP traffic is being carried in its payload. The IP header will indicate that UDP traffic is being carried in its payload. However, without processing the 'fragmentation options'

---

[4]1500 bytes for Ethernet, and 4464 bytes for Token-Ring (the 4 megabyte variety).

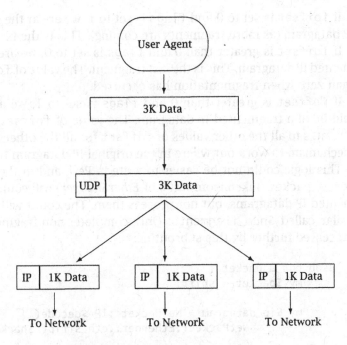

Figure 2.6   UDP/IP fragmentation.

associated with the IP datagram, it is not possible to determine if the IP payload is an entire UDP datagram or just part of one (and if it is part of one, just where in the entire UDP datagram the part belongs).

So, to work with UDP data within *EtherSnooper*, additional code is required to make sense of the (possibly fragmented) IP datagrams.

The instance fields $ip_datagram->{flags} and $ip_datagram->{foffset} contained in the IP datagram object hold the information needed to determine if fragmentation has occurred.

Possible values for the $ip_datagram->{flags} field are as follows.

000 – (decimal 0) this datagram may be fragmented, or this is the last and/or only fragment.

001 – (decimal 1) this datagram may be fragmented, and more fragments are coming.

010 – (decimal 2) do not fragment this datagram.

Used in combination with the value of $ip_datagram->{foffset}, these values determine if an IP datagram is part of a fragmented one or not, as the foffset value identifies where in the datagram the fragment belongs.

Obviously, if flags is set to 2, then this is a non-fragmented IP datagram, because the network device that created the datagram set this flag, forbidding fragmentation to occur.

If foffset is set to 0 and flags is set to 1, we are at the start of a fragmented IP datagram (as more fragments are coming). This is the first fragment.

If foffset is greater than 0 and flags is set to 0, we are at the end of a fragmented IP datagram. This is the last fragment. The value of foffset will be greater than zero when fragmentation has occurred.

If foffset is greater than 0 and flags is set to 1, we are somewhere in the middle of a fragmented IP datagram. The value of foffset for this fragment as it relates to all the other values of foffset for all the other fragments provides a mechanism to work out where in the original IP datagram the fragment belongs.

This logic could not be easier to write in Perl, and in the code which follows, got_a_packet (taken from v0.06 of *EtherSnooper*) will count the number of fragmented IP datagrams, but not process them. The count will be stored in a global scalar called $num_fragments. Only complete, non-fragmented datagrams are processed further by this subroutine:

```perl
sub got_a_packet {
    my $packet = shift;

    my $ip_datagram = NetPacket::IP->decode(
            NetPacket::Ethernet::eth_strip( $packet ) );

    $num_datagrams++;

    if ($ip_datagram->{foffset} > 0)
    {
        $num_fragments++;
        exit;
    }

    $ip_type_totals{ $ip_datagram->{proto} }++;
}
```

Reassembling a fragmented IP datagram is complicated by the fact that there is no guarantee all the fragments will arrive, that they will arrive in the correct order, that they will arrive without error, and that they will not be duplicated. IP is, after all, an unreliable, best-effort technology. It was *designed* that way.

Out-of-order arrivals and duplicates are easily dealt with by the choice of the correct data structure. By using a Perl hash keyed on foffset (with the value part containing the fragments data), code can ensure that duplicates are dealt with, as the key values in hashes are automatically unique. If duplicate fragments do arrive, they will simply update the already existing hash entry, and uniqueness will be maintained. By keying on foffset – and once all the fragments have arrived – the code can sort on the keys to produce the correct data order. But, what if a fragment is lost? And what if another fragmented IP datagram starts to arrive before the code is finished dealing with the current one?

One possible solution is to use another hash keyed on the value of the *fragment identifier*, which is stored in the $ip_datagram->{id}$ field. Each fragment associated with a fragmented IP datagram will have the same value for id. To complete the solution, the value part of this hash will contain a reference to the hash which contains the fragments (as discussed in the last paragraph). As the program runs, this hash-of-hashes will contain any number of fragmented IP datagrams *in the process* of being reassembled.

Code can be added to got_a_packet to update the hash-of-hashes each time the subroutine is invoked. The code can also check to see if the latest fragment completes the IP datagram and take any appropriate action.

Of course, the program still has to deal with the problem of lost fragments. How long should the code wait before determining any particular IP datagram cannot be reassembled? Coming up with a reasonable answer – and implementation – is a suggested exercise (see the end of this chapter).

With TCP traffic, the situation discussed above as it relates to UDP is very different. TCP will endeavour to ensure the successful transmission of any data entrusted to it. To this end, TCP tries to ensure that IP fragmentation never happens to the traffic it generates. Figure 2.7 (on p. 76) illustrates TCP's behaviour. The 3000 bytes of data are 'fragmented' by TCP before being handed off to IP for delivery. Each IP datagram created will carry in its payload a chunk of TCP data and the appropriate TCP header information.

However, fragmentation will occur when TCP traffic has to travel through a network segment that has a smaller MTU than the sending and receiving networks MTU values. For example, data created on a Token-Ring network and destined for a FDDI network can create TCP segments as large as 4352 bytes[5]. However, if the Token-Ring and FDDI networks are connected by an Ethernet segment, then the large TCP segments will be fragmented (by IP) in order to allow for their transmission over Ethernet. So, it is quite possible to snoop TCP data and experience the same fragmentation difficulties associated with UDP snooping.

Additional code is therefore required to take this possibility into consideration when snooping TCP.

2.5.4 Application traffic monitoring

It is possible to snoop user-agent data using the techniques from the last section. What is missing is a mechanism to determine what application the data is associated with. Does the captured data belong to a standard Web browser, email client, file transfer, or terminal emulation application? Or does the data belong to some non-standard or custom network application?

To learn more about the data, *EtherSnooper* needs to examine the protocol port-numbers associated with the data. Both UDP and TCP use protocol port-numbers

---

[5]FDDI's MTU is 4352 bytes, whereas Token-Ring's is 4464 bytes.

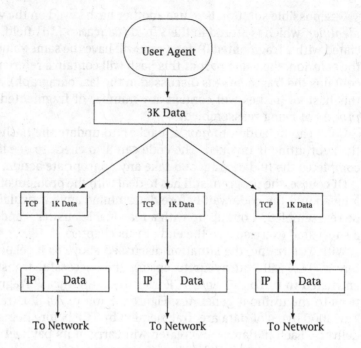

Figure 2.7 TCP/IP fragmentation.

to multiplex application traffic onto a single network connection. And network programmers use protocol port-numbers to associate network traffic with applications.

The protocol port-number information is available in both the UDP and TCP header (and is available to *EtherSnooper* as instance fields of the decoded UDP and TCP objects – refer to Figures 2.4 and 2.5 on p. 72). Within the appropriate `got_a_packet` subroutine, refer to the source and destination protocol port-numbers as follows (for UDP traffic):

```
$udp_datagram->{src_port}
$udp_datagram->{dest_port}
```

and as follows (for TCP traffic):

```
$tcp_segment->{src_port}
$tcp_segment->{dest_port}
```

The meaning of a large number of protocol port-numbers (both for UDP and TCP) has been standardized by the Internet Assigned Numbers Authority (IANA). Refer to the *Web Resources* section at the end of this chapter for the location from which to download the current list of assignments. Protocol port-numbers operate within a 16 bit range, so they start at 0 and go up to 65 535. Within this range, the IANA reserves the first 1024 ports as *well-known* port-numbers (i.e. 0–1023).

Located in the range 1024–49 151 are the *registered* ports, and the rest (49 152–65 535) are referred to as *dynamic* or *private* ports. In practice, these ranges mandate that only standard, agreed-to, well-known services should be allocated a protocol port-number below 1024. Above 1023, a custom application can choose any port-number, with the assumption that on shared computers, a clash may occur with an already existing, custom service[6].

A quick look at the downloaded `port-numbers` file confirms that a lot of assignments have been made. Here is a small extract:

```
.
.
.
```

```
To the extent possible, these same port assignments
are used with the UDP [RFC768].

The range for assigned ports managed by the IANA is 0-1023.
```

```
.
.
.
```

```
vettcp          78/tcp    vettcp
vettcp          78/udp    vettcp
#                         Christopher Leong <leong@kolmod.mlo.dec.com>
finger          79/tcp    Finger
finger          79/udp    Finger
#                         David Zimmerman <dpz@RUTGERS.EDU>
http            80/tcp    World Wide Web HTTP
http            80/udp    World Wide Web HTTP
www             80/tcp    World Wide Web HTTP
www             80/udp    World Wide Web HTTP
www-http        80/tcp    World Wide Web HTTP
www-http        80/udp    World Wide Web HTTP
#                         Tim Berners-Lee <timbl@W3.org>
hosts2-ns       81/tcp    HOSTS2 Name Server
hosts2-ns       81/udp    HOSTS2 Name Server
```

```
.
.
.
```

The version of the `port-numbers` file this extract is taken from is 9487 lines long (close to 160 pages). Despite its length, the file conforms to a reasonably standard format. Paragraphs of text introduce the three types of assignments, comments start with a # character, and the actual assignment entry lines detail: a descriptive

---

[6]However, in reality, this is quite rare.

keyword, a port-number/protocol designation, and a protocol description (which may also include a contact email address or reference). Note how the UDP and TCP assignments are 'mixed' in the one file.

To produce a version of *EtherSnooper* to capture statistics based on the protocol port-number assignments would be madness – populating a hash with upwards of 9000 entries (generated from the `port-numbers` file) is not something to do on a whim. So, let us just worry about the *well-known* ports.

Here is a small Perl program that will take the downloaded `port-numbers` file and create two new files: `well-known-udp`, which will contain the well-known UDP port-number assignments; and `well-known-tcp`, which will contain the well-known TCP port-number assignments:

```perl
#! /usr/bin/perl

# Process the IANA 'port-numbers' file so that we just
# have the well-known ports (i.e. < 1024) for the TCP
# and UDP protocols.  Two new files are created:
#
#     well-known-udp  - well-known ports for TCP.
#     well-known-tcp  - well-known ports for UDP.

open PORTNUMS, 'port-numbers' or die "Ooops: $!";

open PROCESSED_TCP, '>well-known-tcp' or die "Ooops: $!";
open PROCESSED_UDP, '>well-known-udp' or die "Ooops: $!";

while ($_ = <PORTNUMS>)
{
    next if /Unassigned/;
    next if /Reserved/;
    next if /^#/;

    next unless m[/(udp|tcp)];

    m[(\d+)/(udp|tcp)];

    print PROCESSED_TCP $_ if ($1 < 1024) and m[/tcp];
    print PROCESSED_UDP $_ if ($1 < 1024) and m[/udp];
}

close PROCESSED_TCP;
close PROCESSED_UDP;

close PORTNUMS;
```

This is the first time the code in *Programming the Network with Perl* has made use of Perl's regular expression, pattern-matching technology. For this reason, let us go through the code in some detail.

After the standard first line, and a comment as to the program's purpose, three files are opened:

```
open PORTNUMS, 'port-numbers' or die "Ooops: $!";

open PROCESSED_TCP, '>well-known-tcp' or die "Ooops: $!";
open PROCESSED_UDP, '>well-known-udp' or die "Ooops: $!";
```

The `port-numbers` disk-file is opened for reading, and subsequently the `well-known-tcp` and `well-known-udp` disk-files are created for writing. The code then loops through the `port-numbers` disk-file one line at a time and executes the code within the `while` for each line (which is stored in the `$_` default variable):

```
while ($_ = <PORTNUMS>)
  {
```

Three `next` `if` statements come next:

```
    next if /Unassigned/;
    next if /Reserved/;
    next if /^#/;
```

Within a loop, `next` will cause the current loop iteration to end, returning control to the top of the loop prior to starting the next iteration. By appending an `if` to the `next`, the code only performs the `next` if the conditional part is true. The conditionals are all pattern matches, which (in order) search the current line from the `port-numbers` disk-file for the word 'Unassigned', the word 'Reserved', and the # character at the start of the line. The code has no interest in lines that contain these 'patterns', so it ignores them (thanks to the use of `next`).

A fourth `next` statement follows:

```
    next unless m[/(udp|tcp)];
```

This statement searches the line for the string '/udp' or '/tcp', and discards the line if neither of these strings appear in the file. This has the effect of discarding the paragraphs of text that introduce each section of the file.

The `while` loop ends with a further pattern match, followed by two conditional `print` statements:

```
    m[(\d+)/(udp|tcp)];

    print PROCESSED_TCP $_ if ($1 < 1024) and m[/tcp];
    print PROCESSED_UDP $_ if ($1 < 1024) and m[/udp];
  }
```

The pattern match has the effect of matching a number ((\d+)), followed by a slash character (/), followed by the string 'udp' or the string 'tcp' ((udp|tcp)). Refer to the extract from the `port-numbers` file above to see where the matches occur for this pattern.

If a match on the number occurs (i.e. if a number is found on the line), Perl automatically arranges to put the match into a variable called $1. The conditional part of the print statements use the value of $1 (together with one final string match) to decide which of the two output files to write to.

When the while loop terminates, the three opened files are then closed (although Perl will do this automatically if the explicit close statements are missing):

```
close PROCESSED_TCP;
close PROCESSED_UDP;

close PORTNUMS;
```

After a successful execution of this program, two new files are produced, called well-known-udp and well-known-tcp.

These files are a more reasonable size, with 681 lines for the UDP well-known port assignments, and 683 lines for the TCP well-known port assignments.

It is now reasonable to use the values from these files to populate hashes that can then be referred to in a version of *EtherSnooper*.

Here is code to process the well-known TCP port assignments:

```
my %tcp_desc = ();

open WELLKNOWN_TCP, 'well-known-tcp' or die "Ooops: $!";

while ($_ = <WELLKNOWN_TCP>)
{
    chomp;

    m[(\d+)/tcp];

    $tcp_desc{$1} = $_;
}

close WELLKNOWN_TCP;
```

The code defines a hash called %tcp_desc to contain the information. This hash is keyed on the protocol port-number, and has as its value part the entire line from the file.

Having built the hash, reference its data as follows:

```
print "$tcp_desc{69}\n";
print "$tcp_desc{80}\n";
print "$tcp_desc{110}\n";
print "$tcp_desc{434}\n";
```

The above lines of code produce the following output:

```
tftp            69/tcp     Trivial File Transfer
www-http        80/tcp     World Wide Web HTTP
pop3            110/tcp    Post Office Protocol - Version 3
mobileip-agent  434/tcp    MobileIP-Agent
```

2.5.5 EtherSnooper (v0.07)

Let us create a new version of *EtherSnooper* to gather statistics on the TCP traffic being carried on the network. Here is the code:

```perl
#! /usr/bin/perl -w

use 5.6.0;

use strict;
use Net::PcapUtils;
use NetPacket::Ethernet qw( :strip );
use NetPacket::IP qw( :strip );
use NetPacket::TCP;

our %tcp_proto_totals = ();

our $num_datagrams = 0;

sub got_a_packet {
    my $packet = shift;

    my $tcp_segment = NetPacket::TCP->decode(
            NetPacket::IP::ip_strip(
                    NetPacket::Ethernet::eth_strip( $packet ) ) );

    if ($tcp_segment->{src_port} < 1024)
    {
        $tcp_proto_totals{ $tcp_segment->{src_port} }++;
    }
    if ($tcp_segment->{dest_port} < 1024)
    {
        $tcp_proto_totals{ $tcp_segment->{dest_port} }++;
    }

    $num_datagrams++;
}

sub display_results {
    print "$num_datagrams segments processed.\n\n";

    my %tcp_desc = ();

    open WELLKNOWN_TCP, 'well-known-tcp' or die "Ooops: $!";

    while ($_ = <WELLKNOWN_TCP>)
    {
        chomp;

        m[(\d+)/tcp];

        $tcp_desc{$1} = $_;
    }
```

```
        close WELLKNOWN_TCP;

        foreach my $port (sort keys %tcp_proto_totals)
        {
            print "Port: $port, ";
            print "generated $tcp_proto_totals{$port} segments.\n";
            print "Protocol-port: $tcp_desc{$port}.";
            print "\n\n";
        }
    }

    my $pkt_descriptor = Net::PcapUtils::open(
                            FILTER => 'tcp',
                            SNAPLEN => 120
                        );

    if ( !ref( $pkt_descriptor ) )
    {
        print "Net::PcapUtils::open returned: $pkt_descriptor\n";
        exit;
    }

    my $minute = 3;
    my $now = time;
    my $then = $now + (60 * $minute);

    my ( $next_packet, %next_header );

    while ( ($now = time) < $then )
    {
        ( $next_packet, %next_header ) =
                Net::PcapUtils::next( $pkt_descriptor );
        got_a_packet( $next_packet );
    }

    display_results;
```

This version of *EtherSnooper* conforms closely to the model used to produce all the previous versions. When opening the NIC, the code sets the value of SNAPLEN to 120, which ensures that we capture the IP and TCP header information, which is required to produce statistics[7]. Statistics are only gathered for the well-known ports (i.e. those that are less than 1024).

Here are some self-explanatory results generated by this code:

```
2302 segments processed.

Port: 110, generated 36 segments.
Protocol-port: pop3       110/tcp    Post Office Protocol Version 3.
```

---

[7]TCP/IP reserves up to 60 bytes for the IP header, and up to a further 60 bytes for the TCP header.

```
Port: 119, generated 55 segments.
Protocol-port: nntp      119/tcp     Network News Transfer Protocol.

Port: 80, generated 2211 segments.
Protocol-port: www-http 80/tcp     World Wide Web HTTP.
```

It is a rather trivial exercise to change *EtherSnooper* (v0.07) to gather statistics on UDP traffic, as opposed to TCP. So trivial, in fact, that it is left as an exercise to the reader.

It is also trivial to further filter the capturing to a specific IP address. Create a scalar to hold the IP address of interest:

```
my $filter_address = '149.153.100.23';
```

When calling got_a_packet include an additional parameter:

```
got_a_packet( $filter_address, $next_packet );
```

Then adjust got_a_packet to filter on the IP address:

```
sub got_a_packet {
    my ($ip_addr, $packet) = @_;

    my $ip_datagram = NetPacket::IP->decode(
            NetPacket::Ethernet::eth_strip( $packet ) );

    if ( ($ip_datagram->{src_ip} eq $ip_addr) or
            ($ip_datagram->{dest_ip} eq $ip_addr)
    {
        my $tcp_segment =
                NetPacket::TCP->decode( $ip_datagram->{data} );

        $tcp_proto_totals{ $tcp_segment->{src_port} }++;
        $tcp_proto_totals{ $tcp_segment->{dest_port} }++;

        $num_datagrams++;
    }
}
```

This version of got_a_packet creates an IP datagram object, then checks to see if it has a match on either the source or destination IP address (as carried in the IP datagram). If there is a match, the payload from the IP datagram is used to create a TCP segment object, which is then used to provide access to the TCP protocol port-number data. The $num_datagrams scalar is only updated if the IP address matches.

2.6 The Network Debugger

It is now possible to snoop at each of the network layers described at the start of this chapter. And it is not going to take much to turn *EtherSnooper* into a network debugger, which can be used to both analyse and test applications running on a TCP/IP network.

A requirement exists to make the debugger (which will be called *NetDebug*) as generic as possible, as it would be too unwieldy to have to make changes to the source code every time we wanted to do something different. A number of command-line parameters will be defined to provide a simple mechanism to turn the generic into the specific, as follows.

-c *count* – specifies the number of packets to capture and, if specified, overrides any value set for the **-m** parameter (see the **-m** parameter, below).

-d *ip-addr* – specifies a destination IP address to filter on, which is used in conjunction with the **-s** parameter. (The *ip-addr* value is specified in standard dotted-decimal notation.)

-m – specifies the number of minutes to capture for, with a default value of 1 minute (see the **-c** parameter, above).

-n – a Boolean that, when specified, puts the NIC into *normal mode*. The default is *promiscuous mode.*

-p *protocol port-number* – specifies the decimal *protocol port-number* to filter on. If not specified, traffic for every protocol port-number is captured.

-s *ip-addr* – specifies a single (or source) IP address to filter on, which can be used on its own, or in combination with the **-d** parameter. If not specified, all IP sources are debugged. (The *ip-addr* value is specified in standard dotted-decimal notation.)

-u – a Boolean that, when specified, captures UDP traffic as opposed to TCP traffic (which is the default).

-v – a Boolean that, when specified, switches on verbose mode. When 'on', *Net-Debug* will log considerably more detail about each packet captured. The default setting for this switch is 'off'.

For example, the following command-line runs the network debugger, capturing HTTP Web traffic (using protocol port-number 80) from the 149.153.100.67 network device to/from the 149.153.100.23 network device:

```
./netdb -s149.153.100.67 -d149.153.100.23 -p80
```

Whereas this command-line captures 250 UDP datagrams (using verbose mode) to and from the networking segment *NetDebug* is running on:

```
./netdb -c250 -uv
```

2.6.1   Processing command-line parameters

The technology for processing command-line parameters in Perl is well established, and the standard module `Getopt::Std` makes things very convenient.

The following code fragment initializes a series of scalar variables to hold the values of each of the command-line parameters:

```perl
use Getopt::Std;

our ($opt_c, $opt_d, $opt_m, $opt_n);
our ($opt_p, $opt_s, $opt_u, $opt_v);

getopts( 'c:d:nm:p:s:uv' );
```

After using the standard module, the code declares eight scalar variables to hold the value of each command-line parameter (the names of the variables must conform to that shown, namely `$opt_` followed by the letter associated with the parameter). A call to `getopts` extracts any command-line parameters from the operating system and sets the appropriate variable. The string sent to the `getopts` subroutine indicates which parameters are Boolean switches, and which are not. If a `:` is appended to the letter, the parameter is not a Boolean switch.

The above `getopts` call sets `$opt_n`, `$opt_u` and `$opt_v` as Boolean values, whereas `$opt_c`, `$opt_d`, `$opt_m`, `$opt_p` and `$opt_s` will have values associated with them.

2.6.2   Storing captured results

NetDebug will not display any results on the screen, for two reasons.

Firstly, by avoiding direct screen I/O, *NetDebug* can be executed to operate as a background process on Linux (and UNIX-like) systems using the standard 'trailing-ampersand' notation. For example, this command-line will run *NetDebug* as a background process for five minutes, returning the user to the command-line immediately (to enter more interactive commands) as opposed to forcing the user to wait five minutes to issue another command:

```
./netdb -m5 &
```

Secondly, screen I/O tends to be relatively slow (compared with writes to memory or secondary storage). If *NetDebug* takes too long writing results to the screen, a potential problem may arise: if *NetDebug* is busy writing to the screen, it may miss packets arriving at the NIC. So, *NetDebug* tries to avoid this problem before it occurs, by not using screen I/O. Results will be written to secondary storage instead. This has the added advantage of producing a record of every execution of *NetDebug*.

The results will be stored in a disk-file called `netdb.log`. Standard file handling code will be used to open, write to and close the file:

```
open NETDEBUG, ">>netdb.log" or
    die "NETDEBUG: Could not open log file: $!";
        .
        .
        .
print NETDEBUG "Log something useful.\n";
        .
        .
        .
close NETDEBUG;
```

The log file is opened in append mode, so as not to destroy any previously existing results. Delete the log file if starting afresh. Note, too, that the log file will grow large very quickly.

2.6.3   The NetDebug source code

The code for *NetDebug* starts with the now familiar collection of use statements:

```
#! /usr/bin/perl -w

use 5.6.0;

use strict;

use Net::PcapUtils;

use NetPacket::Ethernet qw( :strip );
use NetPacket::IP qw( :strip );
use NetPacket::UDP;
use NetPacket::TCP;

use Getopt::Std;
```

Next, a collection of global variables are declared as our variables, as they will be used later in the program, as well as within *NetDebug*'s subroutines:

```
our $num_datagrams = 0;

our ($opt_c, $opt_d, $opt_m, $opt_n);
our ($opt_p, $opt_s, $opt_u, $opt_v);

our $packet_handler;
```

The *NetDebug* subroutines appear near the top of the source code file. In Perl, there is no real requirement to define subroutines before they are used[8], but,

---

[8]Well, when code uses use strict, the rules change.

to keep things nice and orderly, they are all defined together, at the top of the *NetDebug* source code file.

First up, three subroutines log details about the packets captured. The first logs details about an IP datagram, the second logs details about a UDP datagram, and finally, the third subroutine logs details about a TCP segment. The IP logging subroutine is called for each packet captured, and it is here that the $num_datagrams counter is incremented, whereas the UDP and TCP logging subroutines log valid UDP and TCP traffic, respectively.

The code in each subroutine is straightforward. An object of the appropriate protocol is passed as a parameter, then this object is used to print details about the 'protocol packet' to the log file. Note the effect of $opt_v:

```
sub display_ip_details  {
    my $ip_obj = shift;

    print NETDEBUG '- ' x 36, "\n";
    print NETDEBUG "$ip_obj->{src_ip} -> $ip_obj->{dest_ip}";
    print NETDEBUG " (id: $ip_obj->{id}, ttl: $ip_obj->{ttl})\n\n";

    $num_datagrams++;
}

sub display_udp_details {
    my $udp_obj = shift;

    print NETDEBUG "UDP Source: $udp_obj->{src_port} -> ";
    print NETDEBUG "UDP Destination: $udp_obj->{dest_port}\n";
    if ($opt_v)
    {
      print NETDEBUG "UDP Length: $udp_obj->{len}, ";
      print NETDEBUG "UDP Checksum: $udp_obj->{cksum}\n";
    }
    print NETDEBUG "UDP Data:\n\n$udp_obj->{data}\n";
}

sub display_tcp_details {
    my $tcp_obj = shift;

    print NETDEBUG "TCP Source: $tcp_obj->{src_port} -> ";
    print NETDEBUG "TCP Destination: $tcp_obj->{dest_port}\n";
    print NETDEBUG "TCP Header Length: $tcp_obj->{hlen}, ";
    print NETDEBUG "TCP Checksum: $tcp_obj->{cksum}\n";
    if ($opt_v)
    {
      print NETDEBUG "TCP Sequence Number: $tcp_obj->{seqnum}\n";
      print NETDEBUG "TCP Ack Number:      $tcp_obj->{acknum}\n";
      print NETDEBUG "TCP Flags:           $tcp_obj->{flags}\n";
      print NETDEBUG "TCP Window Size:     $tcp_obj->{winsize}\n";
```

```
        print NETDEBUG "TCP Urgent Pointer:   $tcp_obj->{urg}\n";
        print NETDEBUG "TCP Options:          $tcp_obj->{options}\n";
        print NETDEBUG "TCP Reserved:         $tcp_obj->{reserved}\n";
    }
    print NETDEBUG "TCP Data:\n\n$tcp_obj->{data}\n";
}
```

The `display_udp_details` and `display_tcp_details` subroutines are called
by one of two subroutines, one called `udp` and another called `tcp`. These subroutines take an object of the appropriate protocol, then check to see if the -p
command-line parameter was specified. If it was, the code checks for a match on
the protocol port-number before processing the object further (with no match
resulting in an ignored object). If no -p command-line parameter was specified,
the code processes the object anyway:

```
sub udp {
    my $udp_datagram_obj = shift;

    if (defined( $opt_p ))
    {
        if (($udp_datagram_obj->{src_port} == $opt_p) or
                ($udp_datagram_obj->{dest_port} == $opt_p))
        {
            display_udp_details( $udp_datagram_obj );
        }
    }
    else
    {
        display_udp_details( $udp_datagram_obj );
    }
}

sub tcp {
    my $tcp_segment_obj = shift;

    if (defined( $opt_p ))
    {
        if (($tcp_segment_obj->{src_port} == $opt_p) or
                ($tcp_segment_obj->{dest_port} == $opt_p))
        {
            display_tcp_details( $tcp_segment_obj );
        }
    }
    else
    {
        display_tcp_details( $tcp_segment_obj );
    }
}
```

The -s and -d command-line parameters can be used to specify source and destination IP addresses to filter on. The user either specifies both parameters, a single (source) parameter, or no IP address parameters on the command-line. To handle each of these three cases, three subroutines handle UDP datagrams and a further three subroutines handle TCP segments:

```perl
sub udp_both_packet {
    my $ip_obj = shift;

    my $udp_datagram =
            NetPacket::UDP->decode( $ip_obj->{data} );

    if ( (($ip_obj->{src_ip} eq $opt_s) and
                ($ip_obj->{dest_ip} eq $opt_d)) or
         (($ip_obj->{src_ip} eq $opt_d) and
                ($ip_obj->{dest_ip} eq $opt_s)) )
    {
        display_ip_details( $ip_obj );
        udp( $udp_datagram );
    }
}

sub tcp_both_packet {
    my $ip_obj = shift;

    my $tcp_segment =
            NetPacket::TCP->decode( $ip_obj->{data} );

    if ( (($ip_obj->{src_ip} eq $opt_s) and
                ($ip_obj->{dest_ip} eq $opt_d)) or
         (($ip_obj->{src_ip} eq $opt_d) and
                ($ip_obj->{dest_ip} eq $opt_s)) )
    {
        display_ip_details( $ip_obj );
        tcp( $tcp_segment );
    }
}

sub udp_single_packet {
    my $ip_obj = shift;

    my $udp_datagram =
            NetPacket::UDP->decode( $ip_obj->{data} );

    if ( ($ip_obj->{src_ip} eq $opt_s) or
                ($ip_obj->{dest_ip} eq $opt_s) )
    {
        display_ip_details( $ip_obj );
        udp( $udp_datagram );
    }
}
```

```perl
sub tcp_single_packet {
    my $ip_obj = shift;

    my $tcp_segment =
            NetPacket::TCP->decode( $ip_obj->{data} );

    if ( ($ip_obj->{src_ip} eq $opt_s) or
                ($ip_obj->{dest_ip} eq $opt_s) )
    {
        display_ip_details( $ip_obj );
        tcp( $tcp_segment );
    }
}
sub udp_packet {
    my $ip_obj = shift;

    my $udp_datagram =
            NetPacket::UDP->decode( $ip_obj->{data} );

    display_ip_details( $ip_obj );
    udp( $udp_datagram );
}

sub tcp_packet {
    my $ip_obj = shift;

    my $tcp_segment =
            NetPacket::TCP->decode( $ip_obj->{data} );

    display_ip_details( $ip_obj );
    tcp( $tcp_segment );
}
```

For *NetDebug*, the got_a_packet subroutine takes the captured Ethernet frame and decodes it as an IP datagram. The IP object is passed to the appropriate 'packet handler' subroutine for processing[9]:

```perl
sub got_a_packet {
    my $packet = shift;

    my $ip_datagram = NetPacket::IP->decode(
            NetPacket::Ethernet::eth_strip( $packet ) );

    &$packet_handler( $ip_datagram );
}
```

The display_results subroutine has very little to do, as most of the 'displaying' is performed by one of the aforementioned logging subroutines. The

---

[9]The code to set up the packet handler will be explained shortly.

`display_results` subroutine logs the number of datagrams processed, then time-stamps the file:

```
sub display_results {
    print NETDEBUG '- ' x 36, "\n";
    print NETDEBUG "$num_datagrams datagrams processed.\n\n";
    print NETDEBUG scalar localtime, " - netdebug END run.\n\n";
}
```

With the subroutines defined, it is now time to look at the program code used by *NetDebug*. Any command-line parameters are processed by a call to the `getopts` subroutine, then the log file is opened and time-stamped:

```
getopts( 'c:d:nm:p:s:uv' );

my $minutes = defined( $opt_m ) ? $opt_m : 1;
my $promisc = defined( $opt_n ) ? 0 : 1;

open NETDEBUG, ">>netdb.log" or
    die "NETDEBUG: Could not open log file: $!";

print NETDEBUG scalar localtime, " - netdebug BEGIN run.\n\n";
```

During the call to `got_a_packet`, the code makes a call to a referenced subroutine (`&$packet_handler`). The reference to this subroutine is set depending on the value of the `-s`, `-d` and `-u` command-line parameters:

```
if ( defined( $opt_s ) and defined( $opt_d ) )
{
    if ($opt_u)
    {
        $packet_handler = \&udp_both_packet;
    }
    else
    {
        $packet_handler = \&tcp_both_packet;
    }
}
elsif ( defined( $opt_s ) or defined( $opt_d ) )
{
    if ($opt_u)
    {
        $packet_handler = \&udp_single_packet;
    }
    else
    {
        $packet_handler = \&tcp_single_packet;
    }
}
else
```

```
        {
            if ($opt_u)
            {
                $packet_handler = \&udp_packet;
            }
            else
            {
                $packet_handler = \&tcp_packet;
            }
        }
```

The value of the `$filter` scalar is set depending on the value of the -u command-line parameter, then `$filter` is used when calling `Net::PcapUtils::open`. The SNAPLEN value is set to 1500 to ensure that the entire datagram is captured (header and payload). The rest of the program is similar to that developed for each version of *EtherSnooper*:

```
        my $filter = ($opt_u) ? 'udp' : 'tcp';

        my $pkt_descriptor = Net::PcapUtils::open(
                            FILTER   => $filter,
                            SNAPLEN  => 1500,
                            PROMISC  => $promisc
                    );

        if ( !ref( $pkt_descriptor ) )
        {
            print "Net::PcapUtils::open returned: $pkt_descriptor\n";
            exit;
        }
```

Prior to calling `Net::PcapUtils::next`, a check is made to determine if the -c command-line parameter was specified. If it was, *NetDebug* iterates the required number of times until the packet count is exhausted. Otherwise, *NetDebug* iterates for a specified number of minutes (as set by the value assigned to the -m command-line parameter):

```
        my ( $next_packet, %next_header );

        if ( defined( $opt_c ) )
        {
            while ( $num_datagrams <= $opt_c )
            {
                ( $next_packet, %next_header ) =
                        Net::PcapUtils::next( $pkt_descriptor );
                got_a_packet( $next_packet );
            }
        }
        else
        {
```

```
    my $now = time;
    my $then = $now + (60 * $minutes);

    while ( ($now = time) < $then )
    {
        ( $next_packet, %next_header ) =
                Net::PcapUtils::next( $pkt_descriptor );
        got_a_packet( $next_packet );
    }
}

display_results;

close NETDEBUG;
```

A subtle problem surfaces when *NetDebug* is used to capture traffic on a quiet network for a specified period of time. To illustrate the problem, let us assume that *NetDebug* is invoked from the command-line as follows:

```
./netdb -m3
```

Here, *NetDebug* is being asked to capture three minutes worth of TCP-based traffic using any protocol port-number. Now, let us assume that the network is very quiet, and that there are currently very few TCP segments being generated and sent. When the code arrives at the call to Net::PcapUtils::next, *NetDebug* will sit and wait (block) for a TCP segment to arrive, prior to proceeding. If no TCP segment arrives for ten minutes, *NetDebug* waits *for ten minutes*. The segment is processed, then *NetDebug* immediately exits as the three minute timer will have expired[10]. The problem is that *NetDebug* should have finished after three minutes, somehow noticing when the three minutes was up, and acted on the timer expiration.

Perl provides support for this type of behaviour. By calling the inbuilt alarm subroutine, it is possible to generate an ALRM signal, which *NetDebug* can then catch and process, even if it is sitting waiting for a packet to arrive as a result of a call to Net::PcapUtils::next. Rewrite the timer loop as follows:

```
$SIG{ALRM} = sub { die; };

eval
{
    alarm( ( 60 * $minutes ) + 1 );

    my $now = time;
    my $then = $now + (60 * $opt_m);

    while ( ($now = time) < $then )
    {
```

---

[10]This problem can also occur with *EtherSnooper*.

```
        ( $next_packet, %next_header ) =
              Net::PcapUtils::next( $pkt_descriptor );
        got_a_packet( $next_packet );
    }

    alarm(0);
};
alarm(0);
```

The alarm is set to go off one second after the number of minutes to capture.

At over 300 lines long, this is the longest Perl program yet seen in *Programming the Network with Perl*. However, despite its length, the code is straightforward and easy to follow. This is how it should be, and it is a testament to the power of Perl and the CPAN repository.

Here is a small, edited extract from some results generated by an early version of *NetDebug* which was pressed into active service when trying to determine why the misconfigured workstations (identified earlier in this chapter) were generating so many UDP broadcasts:

```
Wed Jan 24 16:21:36 2001 - netdebug BEGIN run.

- - - - - - - - - - - - - - - - - - - - - - - - - - - - - - - - - - - -
149.153.134.27 -> 149.153.134.255 (id: 12388, ttl: 128)
UDP Source: 137 -> UDP Destination: 137
- - - - - - - - - - - - - - - - - - - - - - - - - - - - - - - - - - - -
149.153.130.14 -> 149.153.130.255 (id: 64027, ttl: 128)
UDP Source: 137 -> UDP Destination: 137
- - - - - - - - - - - - - - - - - - - - - - - - - - - - - - - - - - - -
149.153.112.2 -> 149.153.112.255 (id: 7271, ttl: 128)
UDP Source: 138 -> UDP Destination: 138
- - - - - - - - - - - - - - - - - - - - - - - - - - - - - - - - - - - -
149.153.112.11 -> 149.153.112.255 (id: 34816, ttl: 128)
UDP Source: 137 -> UDP Destination: 137
- - - - - - - - - - - - - - - - - - - - - - - - - - - - - - - - - - - -
149.153.112.11 -> 149.153.112.255 (id: 35328, ttl: 128)
UDP Source: 137 -> UDP Destination: 137
- - - - - - - - - - - - - - - - - - - - - - - - - - - - - - - - - - - -
149.153.112.11 -> 149.153.112.255 (id: 35584, ttl: 128)
UDP Source: 137 -> UDP Destination: 137
- - - - - - - - - - - - - - - - - - - - - - - - - - - - - - - - - - - -
149.153.124.14 -> 149.153.124.255 (id: 22727, ttl: 128)
UDP Source: 138 -> UDP Destination: 138
- - - - - - - - - - - - - - - - - - - - - - - - - - - - - - - - - - - -
149.153.130.108 -> 149.153.130.255 (id: 5633, ttl: 128)
UDP Source: 137 -> UDP Destination: 137
- - - - - - - - - - - - - - - - - - - - - - - - - - - - - - - - - - - -
149.153.112.16 -> 149.153.112.255 (id: 25513, ttl: 128)
UDP Source: 137 -> UDP Destination: 137
```

```
- - - - - - - - - - - - - - - - - - - - - - - - - - - - - - - -
149.153.20.131 -> 149.153.20.255 (id: 9504, ttl: 128)
UDP Source: 137 -> UDP Destination: 137
- - - - - - - - - - - - - - - - - - - - - - - - - - - - - - - -
149.153.112.16 -> 149.153.112.255 (id: 25769, ttl: 128)
UDP Source: 137 -> UDP Destination: 137
- - - - - - - - - - - - - - - - - - - - - - - - - - - - - - - -
371 datagrams/segments processed.

Wed Jan 24 16:27:05 2001 - netdebug END run.
```

The UDP 137 and 138 well-known protocol port-numbers, as assigned by IANA, correspond to the *NETBIOS Name Service* and the *NETBIOS Datagram Service*. The workstations are convinced they are actually servers and are broadcasting their existence to all and sundry. The problem is that no one is listening, nor responding, so the workstations keep trying and the network is suffering a *broadcast storm*. This is not good.

The results produced by the 'production' *NetDebug* tend to be quite long (especially if verbose mode is 'on'). Rather than present the results here (and risk doubling the size of this chapter), refer to Appendix D, *Sample NetDebug Results*, for sample invocations of *NetDebug*, together with the logged results and a brief commentary.

Each set of results in the appendix show the logged application-level protocol data. It is therefore possible to use the contents of the log file to *debug* the communications between network devices. This capability will be most useful when writing and debugging custom network applications, which is the topic of the next chapter.

2.7 Where To From Here?

In this chapter, the interface provided by Net::PcapUtils was used to build a set of simple, yet highly useful, snooping tools, as well as *The Network Debugger*. This may be all most programmers ever need to know. To learn and do more, graduate from using Net::PcapUtils to working directly with the Net::Pcap module. Tim Potter provides a series of Perl scripts located in the t directory of the Net::Pcap installation directory to get you started. Have fun.

Another Perl module that may be of interest is Net::RawIP by Sergey Kolychev. This is an alternative interface to the libpcap library. Find Net::RawIP at any CPAN repository.

2.8 Print Resources

An excellent companion text to this chapter is: *Internet Core Protocols: The Definitive Guide*, by Eric A. Hall (O'Reilly, 2000). This book covers the following protocols in considerable depth: IP, ARP, ICMP, IGMP, UDP and TCP. The discussion is considerably enhanced by the authors use of screenshots from a commercial network analyser – *Surveyor Lite* by Shomiti Systems.

An excellent treatment of networking technology is *Computer Networks*, 3rd edn, by Andrew S. Tanenbaum (Prentice-Hall, 1996). This is one of the classic textbooks in this area, and is written by a highly respected author. Chapter 4 includes a description and commentary on the various Ethernet standards.

2.9   Web Resources

The most recent release of the libpcap library (in C source code form) can be downloaded from http://www.tcpdump.org. Once downloaded, unpack the contents of the file using the following commands:

```
uncompress libpcap.tar.Z
tar xvf libpcap.tar
```

Change into the newly created libpcap directory and read the README and INSTALL files for instructions on building and installing the library. Note: *root* privileges may be required to install the library. Check the documentation. Alternatively, search the website for the Linux distribution being used on your computer, as some vendors provide optional, prebuilt library packages for download. This is particularly convenient if the distribution uses RPM (the RedHat Package Manager), and an RPM for libpcap is available.

http://www.cpan.org/modules/by-module/Net/TIMPOTTER/ – the CPAN directory of Tim Potter.

Commercial network analysers are available for most platforms.

Surveyor Lite from Shomiti Systems operates on the Windows platform and is available from http://www.shomiti.com.

Macintosh users can download a demo of *EtherPeek* from WildPackets (formerly 'The AG Group'), which is available online at http://www.wildpackets.com. *EtherPeek* is also available for Windows.

A number of full-featured analysers exist for the Linux platform (most of them available for free). The best-known technology is tcpdump.

http://www.iana.org/assignments/ethernet-numbers – a relatively complete list of Ethernet types.

http://www.iana.org/assignments/port-numbers – the current list of assigned protocol port-numbers.

Exercises

1. Study the rest of the NetPacket::* modules and create versions of *EtherSnooper* capable for capturing statistics on ICMP, IGMP and ARP traffic. Are you surprised by the amount of traffic these protocols generate on your network?

2. Create a new version of *EtherSnooper* (v0.07) that gathers statistics on UDP traffic as opposed to TCP.

3. Expand on the version of *EtherSnooper* from the last exercise to take into consideration fragmented UDP datagrams (as fragmented by IP, that is). Use the hash-of-hashes technique described in this chapter to implement IP fragment reassembly. [Questions to consider include: how will your code deal with lost fragments? What is the downside of putting too much functionality into the got_a_packet subroutine (if any)?]

4. Can you improve on *NetDebug*, with 'improve' meaning 'do the same with less code'?

5. Using an appropriate reference text, research the meaning of the 'options' field contained within each TCP header, then develop a version of *EtherSnooper* to capture and interpret options 1–8.

6. Following on from the last exercise, research the meaning of the 'flags' field contained within each TCP header, then develop a version of *EtherSnooper* to capture and interpret the 'flags' used during TCP connection establishment and tear-down.

7. Ask your local network administrator to identify the format of the Ethernet frames carried on your LAN. If the IEEE 802.3 SNAP format is used, develop a version of *EtherSnooper* to process the Ethernet frame type information contained within the SNAP header.

8. Download the tcpdump program from http://www.tcpdump.org and install it on your Linux computer. Read the supplied documentation to learn how to use this advanced packet-sniffing technology, then configure tcpdump to emulate the functionality provided by *NetDebug*.

3

Sockets

In this chapter a series of custom network applications are built using Perl.

The techniques used to build custom network applications have been standardized for quite some time. Two types of application programmer interface (API) have gained favour among network programmers: the *XTI API*, initially developed by AT&T Bell Laboratories (where it is known as TLI), and the *Socket API*, developed at the University of California, Berkeley. Of the two, the Socket API has the largest following, and has been ported to most operating systems. Consequently, the Socket API is the *de facto* standard.

On the Windows platform, the Socket API is referred to as *WinSock*, whereas programmers using Mac OS (prior to X) know it as *Gusi*. Slight platform-specific variations to the API exist on these non-UNIX platforms. However, the Socket API built into Linux closely matches the original API, which was initially developed on the UNIX operating system.·

The Socket API is designed to provide programmers with a platform-independent interface to the functionality of the network. By abstracting the details of the physical network, the API allows programmers to concentrate on the details of an application, as opposed to the details of a network.

The standard distribution of Perl provides direct support for the Socket API as built into the underlying operating system. Two programming interfaces to the API exist within Perl, a functional interface and an object-oriented one. The functional interface is described and used first. The latter part of this chapter describes the object-oriented interface.

3.1 Clients and Servers

The Socket API provides support for the *mechanics* of network programming. Although this is an important aspect of network programming, programmers also need to concern themselves with the proper *design* of the applications they build. Consequently, a number of design models have been developed.

The *distributed model* provides for the different parts of a custom network application to be located on a collection of geographically dispersed network devices. When working within this model, programmers need not concern themselves with the physical network location of the resources they use (i.e. where the various parts are to be found). Instead, the application is developed in the traditional way, as if it were executing on a single computer. Special tools are employed to break the application into its different parts, prior to distribution on the network. Examples of this model include the Remote Procedure Call (RPC) technology developed at Sun MicroSystems, and the Common Object Request Broker Architecture (CORBA) as promoted by The Object Management Group. Any further discussion of this model is beyond the scope of this book.

The *mobile-agent model* provides an operating environment within which custom network applications can transport themselves from one networking device to another *while they are executing*. This interesting technology is the topic of Chapter 6.

The *client/server model*, by far the most common, splits an application into two major components. Each component is in effect a separate program, and the two communicate across the network by way of *standard messages*.

As an example of the client/server model, consider how the World Wide Web works. The Web browser provides for the viewing of hyperlinked, text documents. These documents are stored at a large collection of remote websites, connected to the global Internet. Based on the actions of the user, the Web browser sends a *request message* to a website asking for the delivery of a particular document. The website finds the document, and sends a *response message* containing the document to the Web browser. The Web browser receives the document, and renders its contents on the screen. In this example, the Web browser is the *client* and the website is the *server*.

Within the client/server model, the local client typically requests some service from the remote server. The server responds to the client with the results generated as a consequence of satisfying the service request. In addition to the World Wide Web, most of the applications used daily by millions on the Internet conform to the client/server model, and these include electronic mail, file transfer, terminal emulation and network news.

3.1.1 Client characteristics

The client application (or user-agent), regardless of the application domain, conforms to a set of characteristics, as follows.

Active – the client actively initiates the communication by contacting the remote server and requesting some service.

Interactive – the client provides access to the services of the remote server to some interactive user, as the client is integrated into an application-level software program.

Temporary – the client is started by a user when needed, interacts with a remote server, and, when finished, is shut down by the user. It is very rare indeed for a client to execute for an extended period of time.

The client application *temporarily becomes a client* to the server, sends a request message and waits for a response. When not interacting with the remote server, the client is interacting with the user. Clients do not necessarily contact the same server each time they are invoked (just think about how the World Wide Web works). They can run on any network device, but are typically found on user computers: PCs, Macs and workstations.

3.1.2   Server characteristics

The remote server application (or daemon) also conforms to a set of characteristics, as follows.

Passive – the server waits passively for a client to initiate contact prior to performing some service.

Non-Interactive – the server typically executes as a *background process* and, therefore, does not directly support interactions with a user of the network device it is executing on (other than perhaps logging error and status messages to a disk-file or system log).

Permanent – once started, the server runs continuously until it is shutdown by the operating system administrator.

When a client contacts a server, the server springs into life and services the client's request. A response message is sent to the client, after which the server waits, passively again, for another client to contact it. If no client ever contacts the server, the server does nothing but wait.

Servers can execute on any network device. However, it is customary to find them installed as a privileged process on large, centralized computer systems, although this is not a hard-and-fast rule. For instance, it is common when testing custom network applications to execute the client and server on the same network device.

3.2   Transport Services

The Socket API supports the mechanics of network programming, and the client/server model provides a workable design. The last consideration is the selection of an appropriate *transport service*.

A transport service arranges to send application data from one end-system network device to another end-system network device. The transport service does not concern itself with how this is accomplished by the underlying networking technology. It is concerned only that the services provided by the network layer allow it to send its data through the network.

Within TCP/IP networks, two transport service protocols are available to the network programmer, the User Datagram Protocol (UDP) and the Transmission Control Protocol (TCP). Based on the characteristics of the custom network application being designed, one or other of these transport service protocols is selected to build the application.

3.2.1   Unreliable transport

UDP, the User Datagram Protocol, is a lightweight, unreliable transport service protocol. It is 'lightweight' because it provides very little additional functionality over and above that provided by the TCP/IP Network Layer Protocol, the Internet Protocol (IP). Indeed, only the provision of support for the protocol port-number is required of UDP. It is 'unreliable' in that it does not concern itself with trying to ensure that the application data arrives at the destination end-system, that it arrives without error, that it is not duplicated, nor that it arrives in the order in which it was sent (one or more UDP datagrams within the data stream may have been delayed). UDP is a *best-effort* transport service.

Another important transport-level technology is the provision of flow control services. Without flow control, a fast sender can easily swamp a slow receiver with data. UDP provides no flow control mechanism to the network programmer. UDP does not even check that a remote system is ready to receive data or that it is operational. UDP sends the data to the network and, rather optimistically, hopes for the best.

So, when is it appropriate to use UDP, if ever? When the custom network application can withstand some data loss, UDP may be appropriate, especially if the application does not want to incur large overhead when communicating. An example application might be the provision of a video-feed over a wide-area network (WAN). Typically, it is more important to get a steady stream of data through the network than it is to ensure every single bit of data is delivered. If the odd packet goes astray (or becomes corrupt), it should not impact the viewing pleasure of the user, especially if 'odd' works out at 1 packet in every 10 000 delivered. The show must go on, after all.

Another important use of UDP occurs on the local-area network (LAN). LAN technology is designed to conform to best-effort data delivery principles, and is, therefore, classed as unreliable. However, as LANs are typically implemented in hardware, they tend to operate in a highly reliable manner. This contradiction in terms can be exploited by the unreliable UDP when operating on a LAN. By piggybacking UDP on top of the 'reliable' LAN, a custom network application may not suffer data loss, *but only when operating on the LAN*. Move the application from the LAN to a wide-area network (WAN) and the lack of any inherent reliability in the underlying network has the potential to exhibit unreliable results.

The classic example of using UDP on LANs occurs with the Domain Name System (DNS), used to translate Internet names (`glasnost.itcarlow.ie`) into Internet numbers (`149.153.100.67`). As each Internet site maintains a DNS server on its LAN, it makes sense to configure the network devices attached to the LAN to use UDP to contact the DNS, and keep the communication overhead associated with this service to a minimum.

UDP can, of course, be made more reliable by the addition of program logic to deal with its shortcomings. However, program logic has to be added to the application using UDP. Adding additional program logic to handle the unreliable nature of UDP is very rarely justified. If more reliable communications are required, TCP should be considered.

3.2.2   Reliable transport

TCP, the Transport Control Protocol, is a highly monitored, reliable transport service protocol. TCP monitors the communication between two end-systems to ensure that reliable communication is maintained. TCP will ensure that all data sent are received. Data will arrive without error, will not be duplicated and will maintain the order in which they were sent (even if one or more of the TCP segments within the stream are delayed). TCP accomplishes this by using a variety of technologies. Any further discussion of these is beyond the scope of *Programming the Network with Perl*. Please refer to the *Print Resources* section at the end of this chapter for suggested further reading.

Flow control services are central to the design of TCP. A fast sender will never swamp a slow receiver with data, as TCP will always arrange to *throttle back* the fast sender so that it sends data at a speed which the receiver can handle. This helps to ensure that TCP connections remain reliable. TCP also ensures that the remote system is both operational and willing to receive data before commencing any data transfer.

The vast majority of custom network applications on TCP/IP networks use TCP as their transport service protocol, as they cannot tolerate *any* level of data loss. What use would a file transfer program be if its users could not depend on the entire file being transferred in an error-free manner? The same goes for terminal emulation programs and Web applications. From the network programmers point of view, TCP is very useful precisely because it provides this reliable service as a standard feature. The programmer specifies that TCP is the transport service protocol to use, then builds the custom network application confident that any communication will be reliable.

Of course, there are occasions when it is not appropriate to use TCP, since inbuilt reliability comes at a price. Typically, TCP carries with it considerable overhead. Connections need to be established before communication can occur, and this can be time consuming. Once established, the connection needs to be constantly monitored to ensure it is performing as required, i.e. in a reliable manner. If data is lost, becomes corrupted or is duplicated, TCP employs a number of techniques to recover from these errors. Retransmission of previously sent data can occur frequently, and TCP must maintain a considerable amount of *state information* about each communication. If the custom network application can tolerate this overhead, TCP should be used. However, not all applications need this level of reliability. Returning to the example of the video-feed application from the discussion of UDP, it is clear that TCP would be a poor choice for this type of application. Losing one packet in every ten thousand is not a problem for the video-feed application when using UDP, but, if TCP is employed, the delivery of data to their destination application is delayed while TCP tries to deliver the complete data stream. TCP identifies and locates the missing segment, retransmits the segment, and reorders the data on the receiving system, prior to making it available for delivery. This inevitably leads to noticeable delays on the receiving end-system. Not quite the movie-going experience most people are used to, nor willing to accept.

3.3   Introducing the Perl Socket API

In this section, the Perl Socket API is introduced. Subsequent sections use the API to develop UDP and TCP custom network applications.

The Perl Socket API arranges for a network connection (called a *socket*) to appear to the program in the form of a standard *input/output handle*. When working with files, the input/output handle is a *filehandle*, were the <> operator and inbuilt `print` subroutine can be used to read from and write to the opened disk-file. When the input/output handle is a *sockethandle*, <> and `print` can be used to read from and write to the opened network connection (when TCP is used).

When working with sockets, put the following lines of code at the top of each custom network application:

```
#! /usr/bin/perl -w

use strict;
use Socket;
```

As usual, the strange first line (with warnings enabled) is followed by a `use strict` compiler directive which gently forces the programmer to write more structured Perl code. The code then uses the standard `Socket` module which comes with Perl. This module provides access to the Socket API as implemented by the underlying operating system. It is assumed that these lines of code appear before each of the code snippets in the remainder of this chapter.

3.4   Socket Support Subroutines

Before considering writing custom network applications, let us look at a collection of *support subroutines* provided to the network programmer, which are themselves part of the Perl Socket API.

3.4.1   `inet_aton` and `inet_ntoa`

On TCP/IP networks, every network device is assigned at least one unique 32 bit address, known as an *IP Address*. Although computing devices are designed to process bits, human beings tend not to be. When referring to an IP address, humans describe the 32 bits in dotted-decimal notation. So, instead of referring to 01111111000000000000000000000001, the dotted-decimal equivalent can be used, which is 127.0.0.1. The problem this creates is that the relatively low-level Socket API expects IP addresses in 32 bit format.

To keep things convenient for humans *and* computers, the `inet_aton` subroutine provides for the translation of any given dotted-decimal notation to the equivalent binary form. The `inet_ntoa` subroutine translates from any given binary form to dotted-decimal notation. The binary form is often referred to as a *packed binary address*. Here is how to use these subroutines:

```
my $ip = '127.0.0.1';
my $binary = inet_aton( $ip );
my $dotted_decimal = inet_ntoa( $binary );
```

which results in the scalar `$dotted_decimal` having the value 127.0.0.1. These subroutines are often combined with another subroutine called `sockaddr_in` to create a *socket address*.

3.4.2   Socket addresses

A socket address is the combination of a packed binary address and a protocol port-number, and socket addresses are manipulated with the `sockaddr_in` subroutine. In Perl, `sockaddr_in` is actually two subroutines in one[1]. When used in scalar context, the subroutine creates a socket address from a combination of a packed binary address and protocol port-number. When used in list context, the subroutine takes a socket address as its sole parameter, and returns the protocol port-number and packed binary address (which can then be passed to `inet_ntoa` to determine the dotted-decimal notation). Another code snippet demonstrates the standard usage of `sockaddr_in`:

```
my $ip = '127.0.0.1';
my $port = 80;
```

---

[1] Perl strangeness strikes again!

```
my $binary = inet_aton( $ip );
my $socket_addr = sockaddr_in( $port, $binary );
my ( $socket_port, $socket_binary ) = sockaddr_in( $socket_addr );
my $socket_dotted_decimal = inet_ntoa( $socket_binary );
```

The first invocation of sockaddr_in creates a socket address from the supplied protocol port-number and the packed binary address, and places the socket address into the scalar $socket_addr. The second invocation of sockaddr_in takes the socket address and extracts the original protocol port-number (80, the well-known port for the HTTP) and packed binary address, which is then passed to inet_ntoa to determine the original IP address, 127.0.0.1.

The use of the *hard-coded* value of 80 in the above code is often discouraged, since it is better practice not to rely on hard-coded numeric values.

3.4.3   getservbyname and getservbyport

The Socket API provides a subroutine that allows the programmer to look up the correct numeric value for a well-known application service. It is perhaps safer to replace:

```
my $port = 80;
```

with the following:

```
my $port = getservbyname( 'http', 'tcp' );
```

The two parameters passed to the getservbyname subroutine specify the application service to look up, as well as the transport service protocol. The second parameter is needed, since some application services can use both UDP and TCP (for example, DNS). When used in list context, getservbyname returns considerably more port information on the application level service. See the perlfunc manpage for additional details.

Another related subroutine is getservbyport, which takes a protocol port-number and returns the service name. Like getservbyname, the behaviour of this subroutine varies depending on whether it is called in scalar or list context.

3.4.4   getprotobyname and getprotobynumber

The need for getservbyname and getservbyport helps explain the existence of a few more utility subroutines. Rather than litter the API (and the program code that uses it) with numeric constants, the designers of the Socket API decided to leave the choice of numeric constants as an implementation detail. For example, rather than dictate the use of 17 as the internal identifier for the UDP protocol, code can determine the correct identifier to use, as follows:

```
my $trans_service_id = getprotobyname( 'udp' );
```

This sets `$trans_service_id` to whatever numeric constant decided upon by the Socket API implementers on the operating system being used[2]. Again, invoking `getprotobyname` in list context will produce more information. As will be seen in the code examples later in this chapter, `getprotobyname` is used extensively to identify the transport service associated with the socket being used.

If the numeric constant is known, the `getprotobynumber` subroutine can be used to determine the protocol name associated with the constant. However, this subroutine is not often used (or needed).

3.4.5   `gethostbyname` and `gethostbyaddr`

Two additional subroutines provide for the translation of Internet names into packed binary form, and vice versa.

The `gethostbyname` subroutine takes an Internet name as its sole parameter and, in scalar context, returns a packed binary address. In list context, it returns additional information on the Internet name (or *hostname*).

The `gethostbyaddr` subroutine takes two parameters, a packed binary address and an *address family identifier*. As the initial intent of the Socket API designers was to provide a networking API that could be adapted to any networking technology (not just TCP/IP), the second parameter is required, and should be set to `AF_INET` when working with TCP/IP. Like `gethostbyname`, the behaviour of this subroutine differs in scalar and list context. In scalar context (the most used and useful form), `gethostbyaddr` returns the Internet name associated with an IP address.

Some code will help to demonstrate the standard usage of these subroutines:

```
my $packed_binary_addr = gethostbyname( 'tyndall.itcarlow.ie' );
my $ip_addr = inet_ntoa( $packed_binary_addr );
print "tyndall's IP address is: $ip_addr\n";
my $ip_name = gethostbyaddr( $packed_binary_addr, AF_INET );
print "$ip_addr has the following name: $ip_name\n";
```

This code will produce the following output:

```
tyndall's IP address is: 149.153.1.5
149.153.1.5 has the following name: ns.itcarlow.ie
```

Note how the name associated with `149.153.1.5` is not, as might be expected, `tyndall.itcarlow.ie`. The administrator of the DNS server running on the `itcarlow.ie` network has associated more than one name with `149.153.1.5`. The `ns.itcarlow.ie` name is referred to as the *canonical* name for this network device, and this is what `gethostbyaddr` returns.

---

[2]Which will more than likely be 17, but it may not be.

3.5   Simple UDP Clients and Servers

It is now time to build some simple custom network applications.

The specification for the first UDP client and server is straightforward. The server will wait for a client to send data to it at a predetermined protocol port-number. When data arrives on the port, the server prints the received data on the screen, and then returns to a waiting status. No acknowledgment of successful receipt is sent to the client. The server repeats this behaviour until terminated by the operating system (which can be accomplished interactively on Linux by pressing Ctrl-C).

The client, when invoked, will send a string to the server at a predetermined protocol port-number, then exit. The client does not concern itself with whether or not the data arrives. Note that the client does not check that the server is up and operating prior to sending data. Remember, this is UDP, and as a transport service it is one shot, best effort and unreliable.

3.5.1   Testing with localhost

When developing custom network applications, it is often inappropriate to build and test the application on a live network, for the same reasons that it is inappropriate to build and test a new non-networked application on a production system. Within TCP/IP networks, a hostname/IP address combination is reserved for testing new applications. The IP address is 127.0.0.1 and the hostname is localhost. When used by network applications, either of these arrange for network-bound traffic to *loopback* within a networked device, which has the effect of keeping the traffic off the live network. It is therefore possible to execute the client and server parts of the custom network application on the same network device while they are being developed, then, when their behaviour is deemed acceptable, move the parts to their *deployment hosts*.

When using Linux, it is convenient within the *X Window System* graphical environment to open two terminal windows (called xterms), one for the client and another for the server. If the X Window environment is not running, use two virtual console screens to achieve the same result. Using the Alt key in combination with the <- or -> key moves from one virtual console to the next.

3.5.2   The first UDP server

The code for the server starts as follows:

```
#! /usr/bin/perl -w

use strict;
use Socket;
```

```
use constant SIMPLE_UDP_PORT => 4001;
use constant MAX_RECV_LEN    => 1500;
use constant LOCAL_INETNAME  => 'localhost';

my $trans_serv = getprotobyname( 'udp' );

my $local_host = gethostbyname( LOCAL_INETNAME );
my $local_port = SIMPLE_UDP_PORT;
my $local_addr = sockaddr_in( $local_port, $local_host );
```

After the standard first line and required **use** statements, three constants are defined as follows.

SIMPLE_UDP_PORT – the protocol port-number of the service, which is set to 4001 so as not to conflict with any well-known UDP service.

MAX_RECV_LEN – the maximum number of bytes to receive at any one time from the network. This is set to 1500, which is a reasonable value, since it is the maximum frame size on Ethernet networks.

LOCAL_INETNAME – the name of the network device on which the server will run.

The $trans_serv scalar is then initialized to the internal protocol identifier for UDP. The hostname and protocol port-number are then used to create a socket address, called $local_addr in this code. The $trans_serv value is used by the next line of code, which creates a sockethandle for the server to use:

```
socket( UDP_SOCK, PF_INET, SOCK_DGRAM, $trans_serv );
```

The **socket** subroutine creates a sockethandle, or returns **undef** if it fails. The code really should check for this, but let us keep things simple for now (later versions of the client and the server will include error-handling code). The **socket** subroutine takes four parameters as follows.

Sockethandle name – the user-defined name of the sockethandle to create, typically specified in uppercase. This is similar to the handles given to disk-files as shown in Chapter 1. Each disk-file within Perl has an associated user-defined filehandle, typically specified in uppercase. In this server, the UDP_SOCK sockethandle is created.

Protocol family name – this specifies the networking protocol family being used by the application, and a series of constants are defined in the Socket module. The PF_INET constant states that the Internet Protocol Family will be used by this code (as the network is built on TCP/IP). This parameter is often referred to as the *domain*.

Transport type name – this will be set to the constant SOCK_STREAM for reliable transport, or SOCK_DGRAM for unreliable transport. Other types exist, but, as they are rarely used, further discussion of them is not considered here.

Transport service identifier – the internal numeric constant used to identify the transport service protocol to use. This value should always be the result of a successful call to `getprotobyname`.

From the description of the parameters to `socket`, it should now be clear that the UDP server will use a sockethandle called UDP_SOCK, will operate on a TCP/IP network, will be of an unreliable type, and will communicate using the UDP protocol.

However, creating a sockethandle is not enough to enable communication. The socket address and the sockethandle need to be associated with each other, so that the operating system can arrange to deliver data sent to an IP address and protocol port-number combination to a waiting sockethandle. This is the function of the `bind` subroutine, which takes as parameters the sockethandle and socket address:

```
bind( UDP_SOCK, $local_addr );
```

Communication can now occur. Here is the rest of the code for the first UDP server:

```
my $data;

while( 1 )
{
    my $from_who = recv( UDP_SOCK, $data, MAX_RECV_LEN, 0 );

    if ( $from_who )
    {
        my ( $the_port, $the_ip ) = sockaddr_in( $from_who );

        warn 'Received from ', inet_ntoa( $the_ip ), ": $data\n";
    }
    else
    {
        warn "Problem with recv: $!\n";
    }
}
```

After creating a scalar to hold any data received ($data), the server enters an infinite loop. Within the loop, the code calls `recv` to receive any data arriving on the UDP_SOCK sockethandle. If the receive is successful, `recv` returns the socket address of the network device that sent the data, or `undef` if things go wrong. The result is stored in the $from_who scalar. This is then used to print an appropriate message to the screen.

The call to `recv` requires further explanation. Here is the line of code again:

```
my $from_who = recv( UDP_SOCK, $data, MAX_RECV_LEN, 0 );
```

Given the explanation above, it should be possible to work out what the first three parameters to `recv` are, but what about that zero at the end of the parameter list?

The fourth parameter is reserved for a set of *flags*, which can impact the behaviour of recv. In reality, the flags are rarely used, and specifying zero indicates that the default behaviour should be assumed. Consequently, no further explanation of the use of the flags field will appear in *Programming the Network with Perl*.

Obviously, the UDP_SOCK parameter tells receive to look for data on the UDP_SOCK sockethandle, and put any data received into the $data scalar, up to and including MAX_RECV_LEN bytes. The actual number of bytes received (if less than MAX_RECV_LEN) can be determined by taking the length of $data with the inbuilt length subroutine.

If the first UDP server code is placed in a file called udp_s1, it can be made executable and executed as follows:

```
chmod +x udp_s1
./udp_s1
```

And, of course, nothing will happen. The first UDP server is sitting, waiting passively for a client to contact it. Let us look at some client code which, when executed, will put the server out of its misery.

3.5.3 The first UDP client

Surprisingly, the code for the client is quite simple:

```perl
#! /usr/bin/perl -w

use strict;
use Socket;

use constant SIMPLE_UDP_PORT => 4001;
use constant REMOTE_HOST      => 'localhost';

my $trans_serv  = getprotobyname( 'udp' );
my $remote_host = gethostbyname( REMOTE_HOST );
my $remote_port = SIMPLE_UDP_PORT;
my $destination = sockaddr_in( $remote_port, $remote_host );

socket( UDP_SOCK, PF_INET, SOCK_DGRAM, $trans_serv );

my $data = "This is a simple UDP message";

send( UDP_SOCK, $data, 0, $destination );

close UDP_SOCK;
```

In essence, the code is similar to that used by the server. The sockethandle is created as it was in the server to be one shot, best effort and unreliable. The $data scalar is set to an appropriate message, then it is sent to the server. The sockethandle is then closed and the client exits.

The call to send takes four parameters: the name of the sockethandle, the data to send, a value for flags (similar to that seen with recv), and the socket address where data are to be sent. This is stored in a scalar called $destination.

Place the first UDP client code in a file called udp_c1, make it executable and execute it, as follows:

```
chmod +x udp_c1
./udp_c1
```

Again, nothing will happen, other than the operating system command-line prompt reappearing. However, something should have happened at the server. The server, if running, should have displayed this message on screen:

```
Received from 127.0.0.1: This is a simple UDP message
```

The client successfully sent a small message to the server.

3.6 Genericity and Robustness

Now that the code has been tested on localhost, the client and server can be moved to the deployment hosts and tested on a live network. The client (udp_c1) will run on glasnost.itcarlow.ie, and the server (udp_s1) will run on the pblinux.itcarlow.ie network device, both of which are on the same LAN segment (refer to the network diagram on p. 316).

As they are written, the client and server both expect to run on localhost. They can be adapted to be more generic by providing for command-line parameters. For the client, the parameters will identify the IP name of the server, as well as the protocol port-number. For the server, the command-line parameter will identify the protocol port-number to use.

The line which sets the value of $local_port on the server can be changed to this:

```
my $local_port = shift || SIMPLE_UDP_PORT;
```

which has the effect of setting the port to the command-line supplied protocol port-number, or to the value of SIMPLE_UDP_PORT (the default value) if no parameters are supplied. The second version of the server (called udp_s2) can now be invoked in one of two ways:

```
./udp_s2
./udp_s2 20000
```

The first invocation uses the default value of 4001 for the protocol port-number, whereas the second uses 20000. Note that the server can bind to a well-known UDP protocol port-number only if executed with superuser privilege (as root).

In addition to providing for a command-line parameter for the protocol port-number, it is necessary to deal with the use of localhost on the server. Ideally, the server should bind to the IP address currently in use on the network device executing the server code.

Rather than have the IP address hard-coded in the server code (which would be inflexible), the Socket API defines a constant (INADDR_ANY) that, when specified, arranges for any IP address currently in use on the network device to be used. Here is how to use the constant:

```
my $local_addr = sockaddr_in( $local_port, INADDR_ANY );
```

Note that this use of INADDR_ANY removes the requirement to call gethostbyname as was necessary in the first version of the UDP server.

The client code will process up to two command-line parameters, as follows:

```
my $remote = shift || REMOTE_HOST;
my $remote_port = shift || SIMPLE_UDP_PORT;
    .

    .

    .
my $remote_host = gethostbyname( $remote )
```

If the name of the remote server to contact is provided, it is used to initialize the $remote scalar, otherwise the value of the REMOTE_HOST constant is used. Additionally, the protocol port-number of the remote server can be provided and will be used to initialize the $remote_port scalar. Again, a default value of SIMPLE_UDP_PORT is assumed if no protocol port-number is provided. The second version of the client (called udp_c2) can now be invoked in one of three ways:

```
./udp_c2
./udp_c2 pblinux.itcarlow.ie
./udp_c2 pblinux.itcarlow.ie 20000
```

The first invocation uses localhost and 4001 as the location and protocol port-number for the server. The second uses pblinux.itcarlow.ie as the server name, and 4001 as the protocol port-number. The third invocation uses pblinux as the name of the remote server, and 20000 as the protocol port-number.

In addition to genericity, the client and server can be made more robust by including error-handling code for the calls to the Socket API subroutines. The standard strategy is to check the value returned from each call, and if an error is detected, warn the user and exit. Here are error-checked invocations of socket and bind on the server (the code already checks the return status of the call to recv):

```
socket( UDP_SOCK, PF_INET, SOCK_DGRAM, $trans_serv )
    or die "udp_s2: socket creation failed: $!\n";

bind( UDP_SOCK, $local_addr )
    or die "udp_s2: bind to address failed: $!\n";
```

On the client, each of the Socket API calls are error checked, as follows:

```
my $remote_host = gethostbyname( $remote )
    or die "udp_c2: name lookup failed: $remote\n";

socket( UDP_SOCK, PF_INET, SOCK_DGRAM, $trans_serv )
    or die "udp_c2: socket creation failed: $!\n";

send( UDP_SOCK, $data, 0, $destination )
    or warn "udp_c2: send to socket failed.\n";

close UDP_SOCK
    or die "udp_c2: close socket failed: $!\n";
```

The call to send does not die on failure, but rather sends a warning message to standard output, and soldiers on regardless.

The only other improvement (on the server) is to replace the call to inet_ntoa with a call to gethostbyaddr. This allows the server to report the IP name as opposed to the IP address when connections are made from clients:

```
if ( $from_who )
{
    my ( $the_port, $the_ip ) = sockaddr_in( $from_who );

    my $remote_name = gethostbyaddr( $the_ip, AF_INET );

    warn "Received from $remote_name: $data\n";
}
```

The server now produces more meaningful output, such as:

```
Received from localhost: This is a simple UDP message
Received from glasnost.itcarlow.ie: This is a simple UDP message
Received from localhost: This is a simple UDP message
Received from glasnost.itcarlow.ie: This is a simple UDP message
Received from localhost: This is a simple UDP message
Received from localhost: This is a simple UDP message
Received from localhost: This is a simple UDP message
Received from glasnost.itcarlow.ie: This is a simple UDP message
Received from localhost: This is a simple UDP message
Received from glasnost.itcarlow.ie: This is a simple UDP message
Received from localhost: This is a simple UDP message
Received from localhost: This is a simple UDP message
Received from glasnost.itcarlow.ie: This is a simple UDP message
Received from localhost: This is a simple UDP message
            .
            .
            .
```

Note how a client on localhost and another on glasnost.itcarlow.ie are communicating with the server. The client and server have been made more generic and they can now operate as expected on the deployment hosts.

Here is an extract from the log file created by an invocation of *NetDebug* which was snooping UDP traffic to and from the pblinux.itcarlow.ie computer:

```
Thu Mar  1 12:40:42 2001 - netdebug BEGIN run.


- - - - - - - - - - - - - - - - - - - - - - - - - - - - - -
149.153.100.67 -> 149.153.100.66 (id: 50788, ttl: 64)

UDP Source: 2064 -> UDP Destination: 4001
UDP Data:

This is a simple UDP message
- - - - - - - - - - - - - - - - - - - - - - - - - - - - - -
149.153.100.66 -> 149.153.1.5 (id: 3086, ttl: 64)

UDP Source: 1027 -> UDP Destination: 53
UDP Data:

    .
    .
    .

- - - - - - - - - - - - - - - - - - - - - - - - - - - - - -
149.153.1.5 -> 149.153.100.66 (id: 3591, ttl: 63)

UDP Source: 53 -> UDP Destination: 1027
UDP Data:
```

The 149.153.100.67 address corresponds to glasnost.itcarlow.ie, and 149.153.100.66 corresponds to pblinux.itcarlow.ie.

The log file clearly shows glasnost sending the UDP message to pblinux, with a destination protocol port-number of 4001. The source protocol port-number is 2064, which was automatically allocated by the operating system executing the client.

Immediately upon receiving the UDP data, pblinux sends a different UDP message to 149.153.1.5, which corresponds to the IP address of the DNS server on the local subnet. The message is being sent to protocol port-number 53, the well-known UDP port-number for the DNS service. This message is created by the server as a direct result of the call within the server code to gethostbyaddr.

The next datagram snooped by *NetDebug* shows the DNS response generated as a consequence of the DNS query[3].

This short interaction highlights an interesting characteristic of some network applications. The UDP server is very much a server when interacting with the UDP client. However, when necessary, the UDP server can *temporarily become a client* to some other server (in this case, the DNS server), before returning to its role as server, passively waiting for its next client.

3.7   UDP Is Unreliable

Let us extend the UDP client to send five numbered messages to the UDP server in quick succession. Replace the last three lines of code in udp_c2 with these:

```
my $msg_count = 1;

while ( $msg_count < 6 )
{
    my $data = "This is a simple UDP message, number $msg_count";

    send( UDP_SOCK, $data, 0, $destination )
        or warn "udp_c3: send to socket failed: $msg_count\n";

    $msg_count++;
}

close UDP_SOCK
    or die "udp_c3: close socket failed: $!\n";
```

This new version of the UDP client is called udp_c3. When the client is executed, the server displays the following:

```
Received from localhost: This is a simple UDP message, number 1
Received from localhost: This is a simple UDP message, number 2
Received from localhost: This is a simple UDP message, number 3
Received from localhost: This is a simple UDP message, number 4
Received from localhost: This is a simple UDP message, number 5
```

Remember, the UDP client and the UDP server are running on the same LAN[4], so it appears as if the communication is occurring in a reliable manner. Shutdown the server, then execute udp_c3 again. With no server to send to, the UDP client displays the following messages:

```
udp_c3: send to socket failed: 2
udp_c3: send to socket failed: 4
```

[3]The details of these DNS messages are not shown, as the captured data contained a number of 'binary unprintables'.
[4]The same machine, in this case.

The client code has indicated that messages 2 and 4 could not be sent, but, strangely, it did not complain about messages 1, 3 and 5! As far as the UDP client is concerned, the odd-numbered messages appear to have been sent without error. However, sending data is not the same as receiving it, and the client is still unsure as to the server's operational status. UDP is, after all, unreliable.

3.7.1 No flow control

Rather than attempting to find a fast sender and a slow receiver, let us simulate the required behaviour by creating another version of the UDP client and the UDP server.

The new version of the server (udp_s3) needs to be slowed down, so after every recv, the server will sleep for three seconds:

```
warn "Received from $remote_name: $data\n";

sleep(3);
```

The changes to the client (udp_c4) involve creating a large UDP datagram, which is then sent to the server ten times, pausing for one second between each send. This makes the client three times faster than the server:

```
my $big_chunk = 'x' x 65000;

while ( $msg_count < 11 )
{
    my $data = $msg_count . ' -> ' . $big_chunk;

    send( UDP_SOCK, $data, 0, $destination )
        or warn "udp_c4: send to socket failed: $msg_count\n";

    sleep(1);

    $msg_count++;
}
```

The $big_chunk of data is required because the operating system running the server may employ some type of UDP buffering, which could result in ten small UDP datagrams being queued prior to their ultimate delivery to a slow server. However, when ten large UDP datagrams arrive, the impact of buffering has no impact, because the UDP *receive buffer* is unlikely to buffer more than 64 kb[5]. On some systems, the UDP implementation may restrict the size of UDP datagrams further. For example, glasnost, which is running a BSD-UNIX derived system, failed to create UDP datagrams larger than 8 kb.

---

[5]No single UDP datagram can be greater than 65 536 bytes.

When executed, the client sends the ten large UDP datagrams onto the network successfully (which can be verified by running *NetDebug*). Here is an edited copy of the output generated by the UDP server:

```
Received from localhost: 1448 -> 1 -> xxxxxxxxxxxxxxxxxxxxxxxxxxx
Received from localhost: 1448 -> 2 -> xxxxxxxxxxxxxxxxxxxxxxxxxxx
Received from localhost: 1448 -> 4 -> xxxxxxxxxxxxxxxxxxxxxxxxxxx
Received from localhost: 1448 -> 7 -> xxxxxxxxxxxxxxxxxxxxxxxxxxx
Received from localhost: 1448 -> 10 -> xxxxxxxxxxxxxxxxxxxxxxxxxxx
```

Not all the large UDP datagrams arrived, only five out of ten made it to the server (datagrams 1, 2, 4, 7 and 10). Worse still is the fact that only a portion of each datagram was received, the first 1500 bytes. This is due to the fact that the value of MAX_RECV_LEN is currently set to 1500, so the server cannot possibly receive anything larger than this value in a single recv. This deficiency can be easily overcome by setting MAX_RECV_LEN to 65536 within the server code. A new version of the UDP server (udp_s4) implements this fix. Change the value of MAX_RECV_LEN as follows:

```
use constant MAX_RECV_LEN    => 65536;
```

The code which displays the received data is also changed to print out the number of bytes received on the socket, together with the first 40 bytes received. This is preferable to waiting for the large datagram to be displayed on screen:

```
warn "Received from $remote_name: ", length( $data ),
    ' -> ', substr( $data, 0, 39 ), "\n";
```

Now that the server can receive large datagrams, the datagrams that do arrive are complete. As regards datagrams 3, 5, 6, 8 and 9, it is still unclear what has become of them, except that they are gone, and gone for good.

Now, let us all say it out loud: *UDP is unreliable.*

3.8   Sending and Receiving with UDP

The UDP client has only concerned itself with sending a message to the UDP server. The client and server will be extended one last time to provide for messages to flow in both directions, to and from the server. The changes to the code are not extensive. To keep things interesting, the code that slows the server will remain active.

On the server (udp_s5), this code can be placed after the invocation of sleep:

```
send( UDP_SOCK, $data, 0, $from_who )
    or warn "udp_s5: send to socket failed.\n";
```

Once a 'big chunk' of data arrives at the server, it is immediately sent back to the client. The client borrows a few lines of code from the server to receive the

UDP datagram being sent back, and this code is also placed after the call to sleep within the client code:

```
my $from_who = recv( UDP_SOCK, $data, MAX_RECV_LEN, 0 );

my ( $the_port, $the_ip ) = sockaddr_in( $from_who );

my $remote_name = gethostbyaddr( $the_ip, AF_INET );

warn "Received from $remote_name: ", length( $data ),
     ' -> ', substr( $data, 0, 39 ), "\n";
```

This produces some interesting results. Here is a copy of the messages received on both the server and on the client when executed on localhost:

```
Received from localhost: 65005 -> 1 -> xxxxxxxxxxxxxxxxxxxxxxxxxx
Received from localhost: 65005 -> 2 -> xxxxxxxxxxxxxxxxxxxxxxxxxx
Received from localhost: 65005 -> 3 -> xxxxxxxxxxxxxxxxxxxxxxxxxx
Received from localhost: 65005 -> 4 -> xxxxxxxxxxxxxxxxxxxxxxxxxx
Received from localhost: 65005 -> 5 -> xxxxxxxxxxxxxxxxxxxxxxxxxx
Received from localhost: 65005 -> 6 -> xxxxxxxxxxxxxxxxxxxxxxxxxx
Received from localhost: 65005 -> 7 -> xxxxxxxxxxxxxxxxxxxxxxxxxx
Received from localhost: 65005 -> 8 -> xxxxxxxxxxxxxxxxxxxxxxxxxx
Received from localhost: 65005 -> 9 -> xxxxxxxxxxxxxxxxxxxxxxxxxx
Received from localhost: 65006 -> 10 -> xxxxxxxxxxxxxxxxxxxxxxxxxx
```

What is interesting[6] is that all ten datagrams were received by the server, sent back to the client and received there. Although being essentially identical to both the previous versions of the client and server, the 'missing datagram problem' has not affected these programs. What is going on?

The answer has to do with localhost. The use of the *loopback* address in this code is affecting the behaviour of these programs, and lulling the network programmer into a false sense of security. To demonstrate what can actually happen, the udp_c5 client and the udp_s5 server will be moved to their deployment hosts: linux303.itcarlow.ie and pblinux.itcarlow.ie. These network devices are on separate LAN segments, and are connected via a campus router (see the diagram on p. 316).

To further illustrate the behaviour of these programs, the following 'debugging' line needs to be added to the server just before its call to send:

```
warn "Sending back to client ... \n";
```

and the following line is added to the client before its call to send:

```
warn "Sending $msg_count to server ...\n";
```

The server is started on pblinux.itcarlow.ie with this command:

```
./udp_s5
```

---

[6]Strange, alarming, confusing and just plain weird.

and the client is started on linux303.itcarlow.ie with this command:

```
./udp_c5 pblinux.itcarlow.ie
```

Once the client starts to send large datagrams to the server, the 'conversation' begins, and the server displays the following messages:

```
Server starting up on port: 4001.
Received from linux303.itcarlow.ie: 65005 -> 1 -> xxxxxxxxxxxxxxx
Sending back to client ...
Received from linux303.itcarlow.ie: 65005 -> 2 -> xxxxxxxxxxxxxxx
Sending back to client ...
```

On the linux303 network device, the client displays this:

```
Sending 1 to server ...
Received from pblinux.itcarlow.ie: 65005 -> 1 -> xxxxxxxxxxxxxxx
Sending 2 to server ...
```

At this point, both the client and the server have stopped displaying messages. The client has not yet received datagram 2, even though it has been received and sent back by the server. The client is *blocking* on its call to recv, and it will not continue until some data arrive on the socket. Unfortunately, the datagram that was successfully sent by the server has (somehow) become lost. What is worse is that the server – thinking all is well – has called recv and is waiting for the next datagram to arrive from the client. The server is *also* blocking on its call to recv. The two sides of the conversation are waiting to receive data, but neither side is sending. They will now wait forever (or until some friendly individual kills them with Ctrl-C). This is a rather classic and catastrophic example of *network deadlock*[7].

3.9 Dealing with Deadlock

To avoid deadlock, it is necessary to somehow prevent the call to recv within the UDP client from blocking forever. The blocking behaviour of the call to recv within the UDP server code will remain, as the server is designed to wait forever. To avoid deadlock, a number of strategies can be followed, and three which are regularly employed, in order of increasing complexity, are as follows.

Specify a time-out – the technique employed by the *Network Debugger* in Chapter 2 to specify an alarm can be used to abort the call to recv after a set amount of time.

---

[7]Also known by the more imaginative name of *Deadly Embrace*.

Checking for data – the inbuilt `select` subroutine can be used to check if there are data to receive on the sockethandle prior to invoking `recv`.

Spawning a subprocess – a subprocess can be created on the client to process the `recv`. This allows the UDP client, the main process, to continue sending independently of the requirement to receive. Of course, if no data arrive, the subprocess's call to `recv` will block forever, and a strategy for dealing with this eventuality is also required.

As a reminder, here is the current version of the code (from `udp_c5`) that has to be 'fixed':

```
my $from_who = recv( UDP_SOCK, $data, MAX_RECV_LEN, 0 );

if ( $from_who )
{
    my ( $the_port, $the_ip ) = sockaddr_in( $from_who );

    my $remote_name = gethostbyaddr( $the_ip, AF_INET );

    warn "Received from $remote_name: ", length( $data ),
        ' -> ', substr( $data, 0, 39 ), "\n";
}
else
{
    warn "Problem with recv: $!\n";
}
```

Let us take a detailed look at the code required to implement each of the three *deadlock-avoidance* strategies.

3.9.1 Specifying a time-out

The technique used here, which has already been used at the end of the last chapter, is to set an alarm, then `eval` the block of code which will contain the blocking call to `recv`. If the timer expires before any data are received on the sockethandle, this version of the UDP client (called `udp_c6`) effectively cancels the `recv` and allows the client to send another large datagram to the server, before trying to `recv` again:

```
$SIG{ALRM} = sub { die "recv timeout\n"; };

alarm( 5 );

eval {
    my $from_who = recv( UDP_SOCK, $data, MAX_RECV_LEN, 0 );

    if ( $from_who )
```

```
    {
        my ( $the_port, $the_ip ) = sockaddr_in( $from_who );

        my $remote_name = gethostbyaddr( $the_ip, AF_INET );

        warn "Received from $remote_name: ", length( $data ),
            ' -> ', substr( $data, 0, 39 ), "\n";
    }
    else
    {
        warn "Problem with recv: $!\n";
    }
    alarm( 0 );
};

if ($@)
{
    die "udp_c6: $@\n" unless $@ =~ /recv timeout/;

    warn "udp_c6: recv timed out, canceling ...\n";
}
```

This code is similar to that from Chapter 2, except that we explicitly check to see if the alarm was signalled due to the five second timer expiring on the call to recv.

Here is the output generated on the server now that udp_c6 is running as the client:

```
Server starting up on port: 4001.
Received from linux303.itcarlow.ie: 65005 -> 1 -> xxxxxxxxxxxxxx
Sending back to client ...
Received from linux303.itcarlow.ie: 65005 -> 2 -> xxxxxxxxxxxxxx
Sending back to client ...
Received from linux303.itcarlow.ie: 65005 -> 3 -> xxxxxxxxxxxxxx
Sending back to client ...
Received from linux303.itcarlow.ie: 65005 -> 4 -> xxxxxxxxxxxxxx
Sending back to client ...
Received from linux303.itcarlow.ie: 65005 -> 5 -> xxxxxxxxxxxxxx
Sending back to client ...
Received from linux303.itcarlow.ie: 65005 -> 6 -> xxxxxxxxxxxxxx
Sending back to client ...
Received from linux303.itcarlow.ie: 65005 -> 7 -> xxxxxxxxxxxxxx
Sending back to client ...
Received from linux303.itcarlow.ie: 65005 -> 8 -> xxxxxxxxxxxxxx
Sending back to client ...
Received from linux303.itcarlow.ie: 65005 -> 9 -> xxxxxxxxxxxxxx
Sending back to client ...
Received from linux303.itcarlow.ie: 65006 -> 10 -> xxxxxxxxxxxxxx
Sending back to client ...
```

Look at this! All ten messages have been successfully received by the server and sent back to the client[8]. On the client, the following output was generated:

```
Sending 1 to server ...
Received from pblinux.itcarlow.ie: 65005 -> 1 -> xxxxxxxxxxxxx
Sending 2 to server ...
Received from pblinux.itcarlow.ie: 65005 -> 2 -> xxxxxxxxxxxxx
Sending 3 to server ...
udp_c6: recv timed out, canceling ...
Sending 4 to server ...
Received from pblinux.itcarlow.ie: 65005 -> 4 -> xxxxxxxxxxxxx
Sending 5 to server ...
Received from pblinux.itcarlow.ie: 65005 -> 5 -> xxxxxxxxxxxxx
Sending 6 to server ...
udp_c6: recv timed out, canceling ...
Sending 7 to server ...
Received from pblinux.itcarlow.ie: 65005 -> 7 -> xxxxxxxxxxxxx
Sending 8 to server ...
Received from pblinux.itcarlow.ie: 65005 -> 8 -> xxxxxxxxxxxxx
Sending 9 to server ...
Received from pblinux.itcarlow.ie: 65005 -> 9 -> xxxxxxxxxxxxx
Sending 10 to server ...
Received from pblinux.itcarlow.ie: 65006 -> 10 -> xxxxxxxxxxxxx
```

Datagrams 3 and 6 did not arrive at the client, even though they were received and sent back by the server. Note how this version of the client has timed out the receipt of these missing messages. Critically, the client and server no longer deadlock. However, the entire conversation is slowed down by all those 5 second delays.

3.9.2 Checking for data

The four-argument version of the inbuilt `select` subroutine can be used to check the sockethandle for any waiting data. If data are waiting to be read, this version of the UDP client (called `udp_c7`) will call `recv` to get the data, otherwise the call to `recv` is skipped and the UDP client proceeds to send another large datagram to the remote server:

```
my $read_bits = '';

vec( $read_bits, fileno( UDP_SOCK ), 1 ) = 1;

my $recv_ok = select( $read_bits, undef, undef, 0 );

if ( $recv_ok )
```

---

[8]This has more to do with luck than with this version of the UDP client including timeout code. When I executed the client about 30 seconds later, *no* messages arrived at the server!

```
    {
        my $from_who = recv( UDP_SOCK, $data, MAX_RECV_LEN, 0 );

        if ( $from_who )
        {
            my ( $the_port, $the_ip ) = sockaddr_in( $from_who );

            my $remote_name = gethostbyaddr( $the_ip, AF_INET );

            warn "Received from $remote_name: ", length( $data ),
                ' -> ', substr( $data, 0, 39 ), "\n";
        }
        else
        {
            warn "Problem with recv: $!\n";
        }
    }
    else
    {
        warn "udp_c7: recv skipped, no data waiting.\n";
    }
```

The inbuilt vec subroutine creates a *packed integer* which represents the input
and output handle(s) to check for data. The inbuilt fileno subroutine returns the
internal numeric value of the input/output handle of interest, which is passed to
vec. The packed integer (stored in $read_bits) is then passed to select which,
when invoked, checks the indicated input/output handle for data. In this version
of the UDP client, the UDP_SOCK sockethandle is checked, and if data are waiting
to be read from the socket, the $recv_ok scalar will be set to true. Obviously, a
true value results in an invocation of recv, safe in the knowledge that data are
waiting to be read.

The server produced this output as a result of interacting with udp_c7:

```
Server starting up on port: 4001.
Received from linux303.itcarlow.ie: 65005 -> 1 -> xxxxxxxxxxxxxxxx
Sending back to client ...
Received from linux303.itcarlow.ie: 65005 -> 2 -> xxxxxxxxxxxxxxxx
Sending back to client ...
Received from linux303.itcarlow.ie: 65005 -> 5 -> xxxxxxxxxxxxxxxx
Sending back to client ...
Received from linux303.itcarlow.ie: 65005 -> 8 -> xxxxxxxxxxxxxxxx
Sending back to client ...
```

Datagrams 3, 4, 6, 7, 9 and 10 did not arrive at the server and, obviously, will not
be making their way back to the client ever. The output generated by the client
was:

```
Sending 1 to server ...
udp_c7: recv skipped, no data waiting.
Sending 2 to server ...
udp_c7: recv skipped, no data waiting.
Sending 3 to server ...
udp_c7: recv skipped, no data waiting.
Sending 4 to server ...
udp_c7: recv skipped, no data waiting.
Sending 5 to server ...
udp_c7: recv skipped, no data waiting.
Sending 6 to server ...
udp_c7: recv skipped, no data waiting.
Sending 7 to server ...
Received from pblinux.itcarlow.ie: 65005 -> 2 -> xxxxxxxxxxxxxxx
Sending 8 to server ...
udp_c7: recv skipped, no data waiting.
Sending 9 to server ...
udp_c7: recv skipped, no data waiting.
Sending 10 to server ...
udp_c7: recv skipped, no data waiting.
```

Only datagram 2 was successfully received by the client. More importantly, the client and server no longer deadlock. The use of vec, fileno and select is quite complex, and increases in complexity as more input/output handles need to be checked.

3.9.3 Spawning a subprocess

The inbuilt fork subroutine can be used on Linux (and UNIX-like) systems to spawn a subprocess. When fork is successfully invoked, it clones an exact copy of the current program, which then proceeds to execute independently of the program that called fork.

The call to fork, which is parameterless, returns a scalar value. If the scalar value is undef, the call to fork failed and the subprocess was not created. If the scalar is zero, the fork was successful, and the clone is executing. The clone is referred to as the *child process*. If the scalar is a positive integer, the fork was also successful, and the original program is continuing to execute. The original program is referred to as the *parent process*, and the positive integer is the *process identifier* of the child process which was successfully spawned.

Here is some code which demonstrates the standard forking technique:

```
my $child_pid = fork;

if ( $child_pid )
{
    continue_as_parent( $child_pid );
}
```

```
elsif ( defined( $child_pid ) )
{
    continue_as_child;
    exit;
}
else
{
    warn "fork failed: $!\n";
}
```

Two subroutines (which are not shown) contain the code that the parent process executes (in `continue_as_parent`) and the code that the child process executes (in `continue_as_child`). The `continue_as_parent` subroutine takes a single parameter, the process identifier of the child process, which will be used later. Immediately after the call to `continue_as_child`, the code invokes the inbuilt `exit` subroutine which ensures the child process terminates properly.

What can be confusing – when `fork` is used – is that the parent and child code are in the same file. Once `fork` is called, two separate copies of the source code file come into existence, each with their own copy of Perl to continue processing the remaining code.

The other important side effect of calling `exit` when the child process completes is that the child sends the parent process a signal, specifically the CHLD signal. When the parent process acknowledges receipt of the signal, all evidence of the child process is destroyed by the host operating system. Until then, the child is referred to as being in a *zombied* state – it has stopped executing, but it is still registered as existing in the operating system's *process table*. Typically, only the parent process can remove the non-executing process table entry (or zombie), which is why the parent is sent the CHLD signal. The removal process, as performed by the parent process, is known as *reaping*. Here is the standard idiom for reaping child processes[9]:

```
use POSIX ":sys_wait_h";

sub zombie_reaper {
    while ( waitpid( -1, WNOHANG ) > 0 )
    { }
    $SIG{CHLD} = \&zombie_reaper;
}

$SIG{CHLD} = \&zombie_reaper;
```

This code imports a set of constants from the standard POSIX module, after which the reaping subroutine is defined. Within `zombie_reaper`, an empty loop is defined that calls the inbuilt `waitpid` subroutine, which does the reaping. As

---

[9]Apologies if you find this use of language distasteful, but this is the standard nomenclature used when discussing this facility.

there may be more than one child waiting to be reaped, the code repeatedly calls `waitpid` until it returns -1, which indicates that there are no more zombies for this parent. The two parameters tell `waitpid` to look for any zombied child process to reap (-1) and not to block if there are no zombies (WNOHANG). If the second parameter was not specified, `zombie_reaper` would block and wait for some child process to exit, which is rarely the required functionality, especially if the creation of the child process occurs as a direct result of trying to avoid blocking.

The final piece of the puzzle is the line of code which sets the CHLD signal handler to refer to the `zombie_reaper` subroutine. When the parent process receives a CHLD signal from any child process, the `zombie_reaper` subroutine will now execute.

Of course, there is no absolute requirement to reap child processes. However, if this is not done, the process table may well become clogged with zombies, and if the process table is full, no more processes can be created and the system administrator will come looking for the culprit, and she/he will not be happy. Of course, if you are your own system administrator, be prepared to slap yourself on the wrist!

When working with child processes, it can be useful (within the parent process) to check to see if a child is still executing. In the final version of the UDP client (udp_c8), only one child process need exist at any one time, so a mechanism is needed to check for this situation before creating another child. This is accomplished by signalling the most recently created child process with the inbuilt `kill` subroutine. Here is the code:

```
if ( kill 0 => $child_pid )
{
    warn "udp_c8: some child is already executing.\n";
}
else
{
    warn "udp_c8: the child is dead, zombied or " .
        "now belongs to some other user.\n";
}
```

Remember that the => symbol in Perl is an alias for comma. We `kill` the process identified by `$child_pid` with the value of zero. This has the effect of not killing the child process at all, but instead returns true if it is still running.

And now, after all that, here is the code to add to the child-spawning version of the UDP client (udp_c8):

```
no strict 'vars';
if ( defined( $child_pid ) )
{
    if ( kill 0 => $child_pid )
    {
        next;
```

```
        }
    }

    $child_pid = fork;

    if ( $child_pid )
    {
        next;
    }
    elsif ( defined( $child_pid ) )
    {
        my $from_who = recv( UDP_SOCK, $data, MAX_RECV_LEN, 0 );

        if ( $from_who )
        {
            my ( $the_port, $the_ip ) = sockaddr_in( $from_who );

            my $remote_name = gethostbyaddr( $the_ip, AF_INET );

            warn "Received from $remote_name: ", length( $data ),
                ' -> ', substr( $data, 0, 39 ), "\n";
        }
        else
        {
            warn "Problem with recv: $!\n";
        }

        exit;
    }
    else
    {
        warn "udp_c8: fork failed: $!\n";
    }
    use strict 'vars';
```

Note that the `continue_as_parent` and `continue_as_child` subroutines are not defined in this code as the amount of code executed by the (continuing) parent and child processes is no more than a few lines. The parent simply calls `next` to signal its intention to start another loop iteration. The child executes the standard blocking `recv` call, before calling `exit`. If the child process could not be forked, the code simply moves onto another iteration, after displaying an appropriate warning message.

The code begins by checking to see if the child process is executing, first by checking the `$child_pid` for a defined value, then by sending zero to the child process (with `kill`). If the child is deemed to be alive, the code calls `next` to avoid creating another blocking child process. Note that the `$child_pid` scalar is checked for 'definedness' prior to its first use. This type of thing is generally OK with Perl, but not when the `use strict` compiler directive is in effect. To get around this problem, the code temporarily switches off strict checking for variables with the no strict 'vars' directive, before switching it back on with use strict 'vars' at the bottom of the code snippet.

At the end of the while loop, add a continue block to increment the $msg_count scalar:

```
continue {
    $msg_count++;
}
```

The udp_c8 version of the UDP client also needs to include the child reaping code from earlier, which is typically placed at the top of the source code file. Also, the code needs to deal with the situation that can result from a child process continuing to block on a call to recv after the ten iterations within the parent process have completed. This code waits a reasonable amount of time (5 seconds), then kills any waiting child process:

```
sleep( 5 );

if ( kill 0 => $child_pid )
{
    kill 9 => $child_pid;
}
```

After starting the server, udp_s5 produced:

```
Server starting up on port: 4001.
Received from linux303.itcarlow.ie: 65005 -> 1 -> xxxxxxxxxxxxxxxx
Sending back to client ...
Received from linux303.itcarlow.ie: 65005 -> 2 -> xxxxxxxxxxxxxxxx
Sending back to client ...
Received from linux303.itcarlow.ie: 65005 -> 5 -> xxxxxxxxxxxxxxxx
Sending back to client ...
Received from linux303.itcarlow.ie: 65005 -> 8 -> xxxxxxxxxxxxxxxx
Sending back to client ...
Problem with recv: Connection refused.
```

As with udp_c7, a number of datagrams did not arrive at the server. The server also reported a strange error with the last recv. The output generated by the child-spawning, zombie-exhuming client (udp_c8) was:

```
Sending 1 to server ...
Sending 2 to server ...
Sending 3 to server ...
Sending 4 to server ...
Sending 5 to server ...
Sending 6 to server ...
Sending 7 to server ...
Received from pblinux.itcarlow.ie: 65005 -> 2 -> xxxxxxxxxxxxx
```

```
Sending 8 to server ...
Sending 9 to server ...
Sending 10 to server ...
Received from pblinux.itcarlow.ie: 65005 -> 5 -> xxxxxxxxxxxxx
```

As this code does not need to wait for recv (or for any timeout to expire), the datagrams are sent in quick succession. Even though a child process is waiting for data, only two of the four received datagrams complete the round-trip from the client to the server, then back to the client.

Once again, this version of the UDP client avoids deadlock. But at what cost? The code is bloated and complex. It is also the least portable, as the use of signals and fork as illustrated above is tied closely to the Linux/UNIX Perl implementation. With the 5.6.0 release of Perl, the Windows version emulates the functionality of fork; however, the most recent version of *MacPerl* does not[10].

Despite all this extra code, the three most recent versions of the UDP client have *only* managed to avoid deadlock. The remaining shortcomings resulting from the use of UDP can still impact the communications between the client and the server. Yet more code would be required to deal with all of those. And when it comes to improving the reliability of UDP, more code leads to increased complexity.

Of course, another strategy exists for dealing with the problems encountered with the UDP client and server, and it is to use an *alternative* transport service. Specifically, a *reliable* one. The UDP client has increased in complexity as a direct result of our attempts to counteract one of the inherent shortcomings of the unreliable UDP. However, when TCP is used, the requirement to add this additional, complex code is nullified.

In the section which follows, the UDP client and the UDP server will be redeveloped to use TCP.

3.10 TCP Clients and Servers

The fifth version of the UDP client (udp_c5) and server (udp_s5) will form the basis of the first TCP client and server. The TCP server will wait at a known IP address and protocol port-number to be contacted by a client, receive any amount of data, then send all data received back to the client. The TCP client will contact the server ten times, each time sending a large TCP segment. The client will wait to receive each segment sent to the server before sending another. As was the case with the UDP code, the TCP client and server both include calls to sleep to keeps things interesting from a flow-control point of view.

---

[10]Note that Mac OS X, which includes and supports Perl 5.6.0, is a modern derivative of BSD-UNIX, *not* a modern derivative of Mac OS 9.

3.10.1   The first TCP server

Here is the code for the TCP server (tcp_s1), which is discussed in detail below:

```perl
#! /usr/bin/perl -w

use strict;
use Socket;

use constant SIMPLE_TCP_PORT => 4001;
use constant MAX_RECV_LEN    => 65536;

my $local_port = shift || SIMPLE_TCP_PORT;

my $trans_serv = getprotobyname( 'tcp' );

my $local_addr = sockaddr_in( $local_port, INADDR_ANY );

socket( TCP_SOCK, PF_INET, SOCK_STREAM, $trans_serv )
    or die "tcp_s1: socket creation failed: $!\n";

setsockopt( TCP_SOCK, SOL_SOCKET, SO_REUSEADDR, 1 )
    or warn "tcp_s1: could not set socket option: $!\n";

bind( TCP_SOCK, $local_addr )
    or die "tcp_s1: bind to address failed: $!\n";

listen( TCP_SOCK, SOMAXCONN )
    or die "tcp_s1: listen couldn't: $!\n";

warn "Server starting up on port: $local_port.\n";

my $from_who;

while ( $from_who = accept( CLIENT_SOCK, TCP_SOCK ) )
{
    my $data;

    $from_who = recv( CLIENT_SOCK, $data, MAX_RECV_LEN, 0 );

    if ( $from_who )
    {
        my ( $the_port, $the_ip ) = sockaddr_in( $from_who );

        my $remote_name = gethostbyaddr( $the_ip, AF_INET );

        warn "Received from $remote_name: ", length( $data ),
            ' -> ', substr( $data, 0, 39 ), "\n";
    }
```

```
        else
        {
            warn "tcp_s1: problem with recv: $!\n";
            next;
        }

        sleep( 3 );

        warn "Sending back to client ... \n";

        send( CLIENT_SOCK, $data, 0 )
            or warn "tcp_s1: problem with send: $!\n";
    }
    continue {
        close CLIENT_SOCK
            or warn "tcp_s1: close failed: $!\n";
    }

    close TCP_SOCK;
```

The TCP server code starts out looking quite similar to the 'equivalent' UDP code. The first few lines are as expected. A default protocol port-number is then defined to be 4001, the same value used by the UDP server. Note that, despite the fact that the protocol port-number is the same for both the UDP server and the TCP server, no conflict will arise, as the port-number in each case is being used with a different transport service protocol, so uniqueness is maintained. The transport service protocol is identified by a call to getprotobyname with the value of tcp as the only parameter, and the result is placed in $trans_serv.

In this code, the sockethandle is referred to as TCP_SOCK and is created with the following call to socket:

```
socket( TCP_SOCK, PF_INET, SOCK_STREAM, $trans_serv )
    or die "tcp_s1: socket creation failed: $!\n";
```

The type of socket is set to SOCK_STREAM, which asks that a reliable, connection-oriented service be provided to this custom network application, and the protocol to use is identified by the value stored in the $trans_serv scalar. The TCP server will now inherit all of the reliability mechanisms built into TCP. Once a connection has been established with the server, any communication which occurs will be reliable: no data will be lost, no data will become corrupt, ordering in the data stream will be maintained and a fast sender will be prohibited from swamping a slow receiver with data. Most importantly, the details of all this reliability are taken care of by TCP, *not* the network programmer.

The setsockopt support subroutine is then called to set a socket-level option (SOL_SOCKET) on the TCP_SOCK sockethandle. A number of options can be set, but the most useful (and used) is the SO_REUSEADDR, which when switched on, tells the operating system to re-allow binding to the server socket address immediately, as opposed to waiting a number of minutes for the operating system to timeout. Although the wait may not seem very long, it *is* when the server is being stopped and restarted continuously during testing:

```
setsockopt( TCP_SOCK, SOL_SOCKET, SO_REUSEADDR, 1 )
    or warn "tcp_s1: could not set socket option: $!\n";
```

After `bind` hooks up the sockethandle to the socket address, the code calls the `listen` subroutine. This tells the operating system that the TCP_SOCK socket-handle will be used to *listen* for connections. If the TCP server is busy servicing a client, the operating system will queue pending connections, up to and including SOMAXCONN connections, an implementation-specific value for the maximum number of allowed pending connections. Any value can be specified, but it is typical for servers to support SOMAXCONN pending connections:

```
listen( TCP_SOCK, SOMAXCONN )
    or die "tcp_s1: listen couldn't: $!\n";
```

When it comes to `listen`, a common misunderstanding is that programmers often think `listen` actually listens for connections (that is, it waits passively for some client to contact the server). It does not. It merely informs the operating system that the sockethandle will be of the 'listening type'.

The sockethandle is now ready for use. From this point on, the code starts to differ from that found in the UDP server. The first major difference is in the condition part of the `while` loop:

```
while ( $from_who = accept( CLIENT_SOCK, TCP_SOCK ) )
```

Within the condition-part, the code calls the `accept` subroutine, which is part of the Socket API. The call to `accept` blocks, waiting passively for a client to contact the server on the listening sockethandle (TCP_SOCK).

Three things happen when the client establishes communication with the server as follows.

The code unblocks – the call to `accept` stops waiting and returns control to the server.

The $from_who scalar is set – `accept` sets the value of $from_who to be the socket address of the client contacting the server.

A new sockethandle is created – the CLIENT_SOCK sockethandle is created, and the remote client is connected to it. Any and all communication from the server to the client will use this new sockethandle, not the listening socket-handle referred to by TCP_SOCK.

If `accept` returns successfully, the code enters the body of the loop. First up is the code to receive any amount of data from the client:

```
my $data;

$from_who = recv( CLIENT_SOCK, $data, MAX_RECV_LEN, 0 );
```

This is very similar to the call to recv from the UDP server.

After using the value of $from_who to determine the IP name of the connected client, the TCP server displays the usual message, sleeps for 3 seconds, then sends the data received back to the client with this code:

```
send( CLIENT_SOCK, $data, 0 )
    or warn "tcp_s1: problem with send: $!\n";

close CLIENT_SOCK
    or warn "tcp_s1: close failed: $!\n";
```

The code calls send as was the case with the UDP server, except that the last argument to send is not required. The server is connected to the client, and as such, does not need to tell send *where* to send the data. When done, the code closes the client sockethandle with a call to close, which means that the sockethandle is closed both for reading and writing. The code then returns to the top of the loop and blocks on another call to accept.

At the bottom of the code, the TCP server ends with a call to close to shutdown the TCP_SOCK sockethandle, before ending. Note that this close is only invoked if the call to accept fails. Otherwise, the TCP server runs forever (or until *killed* by the operating system or by Ctrl-C).

The TCP server accepts the same command-line parameter as the UDP server, and can be made executable and started, as follows:

```
chmod +x tcp_s1
./tcp_s1
```

As with the UDP server, nothing happens. The TCP server is waiting, passively, for some TCP client to contact it.

3.10.2 The first TCP client

With the TCP server up and running, and waiting for clients, it is time to look at the code for the first TCP client (tcp_c1), which will contact the server and communicate reliably. Here is the client source code:

```
#! /usr/bin/perl -w

use strict;
use Socket;

use constant SIMPLE_TCP_PORT => 4001;
use constant REMOTE_HOST      => 'localhost';
```

```perl
use constant MAX_RECV_LEN     => 65536;

my $remote = shift || REMOTE_HOST;
my $remote_port = shift || SIMPLE_TCP_PORT;

my $trans_serv = getprotobyname( 'tcp' );

my $remote_host = gethostbyname( $remote )
    or die "tcp_c1: name lookup failed: $remote\n";

my $destination = sockaddr_in( $remote_port, $remote_host );

my $msg_count = 1;

my $big_chunk = 'x' x 65000;

while ( $msg_count < 11 )
{
    socket( TCP_SOCK, PF_INET, SOCK_STREAM, $trans_serv )
        or die "tcp_c1: socket creation failed: $!\n";

    my $con_ok = connect( TCP_SOCK, $destination )
        or warn "tcp_c1: connect to remote system failed: $!\n";

    next unless $con_ok;

    my $data = $msg_count . ' -> ' . $big_chunk;

    warn "Sending $msg_count to server ...\n";

    send( TCP_SOCK, $data, 0 )
        or warn "tcp_c1: problem with send: $!\n";

    sleep( 1 );

    my $from_who = recv( TCP_SOCK, $data, MAX_RECV_LEN, 0 );
    if ( $from_who )
    {
        my ( $the_port, $the_ip ) = sockaddr_in( $destination );

        my $remote_name = gethostbyaddr( $the_ip, AF_INET );

        warn "Received from $remote_name: ", length( $data ),
            ' -> ', substr( $data, 0, 39 ), "\n";
    }
    else
    {
        warn "tcp_c1: problem with recv: $!\n";
```

```
        }

        close TCP_SOCK
            or warn "tcp_cl: close failed: $!\n";
    }
    continue {
        $msg_count++;
    }
```

The explanation of how the TCP server operates helps to explain the vast majority of the code found in the TCP client. The call to `getprotobyname` returns the internal protocol identifier for TCP, and this is used to create a sockethandle called TCP_SOCK. The call to `socket` is exactly the same in the client as it was in the server – the created sockethandle is one which is reliably built on TCP.

Inside the `while` loop, the code calls the `connect` subroutine, as follows:

```
my $con_ok = connect( TCP_SOCK, $destination )
    or warn "tcp_cl: connect to remote system failed: $!\n";

next unless $con_ok;
```

This is the only piece of code that has not been seen already. The call to the `connect` subroutine takes the TCP_SOCK sockethandle and establishes communication with the remote network device identified by the `$destination` socket address (which in this case is the TCP server). Think of this as the client equivalent of the call to `bind` in the server code, except that the socket address identifies some remote network device, not the device the code is running on, as was the case with the TCP server.

If `connect` is successful, a reliable connection will have been established with the TCP server. On the server, the call to `accept` will have returned successfully as a result of the TCP client successfully calling `connect`.

The `connect` subroutine returns a true value if all is well, false otherwise. The code checks for this (twice). A warning message is displayed if the connection cannot be established[11], then the code calls `next` to start the next loop iteration, after executing any code within the loop's `continue` block. Note that the TCP client does not call `bind`, `listen`, `setsockopt` or `accept`, as the functionality provided by these Socket API subroutines is primarily of interest to servers.

With a successful connection established, the TCP client executes code similar to that executed by the TCP server. The server reads from then writes to the sockethandle, whereas the client writes to then reads from it. The code is exactly the same as that already used by the TCP server, the ordering is simply reversed on the TCP client. Appropriate messages provide a mechanism to watch what is going on.

As with the UDP code, the TCP server will execute on `pblinux.itcarlow.ie`, and the TCP client will operate on the network device `linux303.itcarlow.ie`.

---

[11]Most likely due to the fact that the TCP server is not executing.

These commands can be used to make the client executable, then execute it, on linux303:

```
chmod +x tcp_c1
./tcp_c1 pblinux.itcarlow.ie
```

Here are the messages generated by the TCP server:

```
Server starting up on port: 4001.
Received from linux303.itcarlow.ie: 1448 -> 1 -> xxxxxxxxxxxxxx
Sending back to client ...
Received from linux303.itcarlow.ie: 1448 -> 2 -> xxxxxxxxxxxxxx
Sending back to client ...
Received from linux303.itcarlow.ie: 1448 -> 3 -> xxxxxxxxxxxxxx
Sending back to client ...
Received from linux303.itcarlow.ie: 1448 -> 4 -> xxxxxxxxxxxxxx
Sending back to client ...
Received from linux303.itcarlow.ie: 1448 -> 5 -> xxxxxxxxxxxxxx
Sending back to client ...
Received from linux303.itcarlow.ie: 1448 -> 6 -> xxxxxxxxxxxxxx
Sending back to client ...
Received from linux303.itcarlow.ie: 1448 -> 7 -> xxxxxxxxxxxxxx
Sending back to client ...
Received from linux303.itcarlow.ie: 1448 -> 8 -> xxxxxxxxxxxxxx
Sending back to client ...
Received from linux303.itcarlow.ie: 1448 -> 9 -> xxxxxxxxxxxxxx
Sending back to client ...
Received from linux303.itcarlow.ie: 1448 -> 10 -> xxxxxxxxxxxxxx
Sending back to client ...
```

And here are the messages generated by the TCP client:

```
Sending 1 to server ...
Received from pblinux.itcarlow.ie: 1448 -> 1 -> xxxxxxxxxxxxxx
Sending 2 to server ...
Received from pblinux.itcarlow.ie: 1448 -> 2 -> xxxxxxxxxxxxxx
Sending 3 to server ...
Received from pblinux.itcarlow.ie: 1448 -> 3 -> xxxxxxxxxxxxxx
Sending 4 to server ...
Received from pblinux.itcarlow.ie: 1448 -> 4 -> xxxxxxxxxxxxxx
Sending 5 to server ...
Received from pblinux.itcarlow.ie: 1448 -> 5 -> xxxxxxxxxxxxxx
Sending 6 to server ...
Received from pblinux.itcarlow.ie: 1448 -> 6 -> xxxxxxxxxxxxxx
Sending 7 to server ...
Received from pblinux.itcarlow.ie: 1448 -> 7 -> xxxxxxxxxxxxxx
Sending 8 to server ...
Received from pblinux.itcarlow.ie: 1448 -> 8 -> xxxxxxxxxxxxxx
Sending 9 to server ...
Received from pblinux.itcarlow.ie: 1448 -> 9 -> xxxxxxxxxxxxxx
```

```
Sending 10 to server ...
Received from pblinux.itcarlow.ie: 1448 -> 10 -> xxxxxxxxxxxxxx
```

If the connection was successfully established, the ten large messages are transferred from the client to the server, then back again.

But are they? Look at the size of the datagrams being reported. It appears not all the data are arriving at each end of the connection. Surely this cannot be? The code asked for TCP, so why does there appear to be loss of data?

The problem here is that TCP (as a transport service technology) is arranging to deliver all data entrusted to it. However, the custom network applications (the TCP client and server) are not interacting with TCP in an appropriate manner. The code needs to be amended to keep reading from the network (i.e. from TCP) until there are no more data to receive, as the internal buffering mechanisms employed by TCP may be adjusting the size of the 'chunks' of data being transferred from one end-system to another. In the above case, the chunk is the maximum amount of TCP data that fits inside an Ethernet frame that is carrying IP traffic.

On the server, change the single call to recv to:

```
my ( $chunk, $data );

recv( CLIENT_SOCK, $chunk, MAX_RECV_LEN, 0 );

while ( $chunk )
{
    $data = $data . $chunk;
    recv( CLIENT_SOCK, $chunk, MAX_RECV_LEN, 0 );
}
```

After the initial recv, this code keeps receiving chunks of data from the socket-handle until the value of $chunk contains nothing, which allows the loop to terminate. With each iteration, the chunk is added to $data.

On the client, similar code to that on the server replaces the single invocation of recv, with one major exception, a call to the inbuilt shutdown subroutine:

```
shutdown( TCP_SOCK, 1 );

$data = '';

my $chunk;

recv( TCP_SOCK, $chunk, MAX_RECV_LEN, 0 );

while ( $chunk )
{
    $data = $data . $chunk;
    recv( TCP_SOCK, $chunk, MAX_RECV_LEN, 0 );
}
```

As sockethandles are just like any other input/output handles, they can be closed with a call to the inbuilt `close` subroutine when they are no longer needed. This has the effect of closing the handle for reading and writing. When it comes to network connections, finer control is often required, and the inbuilt `shutdown` subroutine provides for this. By identifying the sockethandle to close, together with an integer value as the second parameter, `shutdown` can be used to close the sockethandle for reading (value 0), for writing (value 1) or for both reading and writing (value 2). When there is nothing more to send to the server, the TCP client closes the sockethandle for writing. In the above code, the client indicates to the server that it has finished writing data by closing the connection for further writes.

Here are the messages generated by the amended TCP server (`tcp_s1b`), running on the `pblinux` network device:

```
Server starting up on port: 4001.
Received from linux303.itcarlow.ie: 65005 -> 1 -> xxxxxxxxxxxxx
Sending 65005 back to client ...
Received from linux303.itcarlow.ie: 65005 -> 2 -> xxxxxxxxxxxxx
Sending 65005 back to client ...
Received from linux303.itcarlow.ie: 65005 -> 3 -> xxxxxxxxxxxxx
Sending 65005 back to client ...
Received from linux303.itcarlow.ie: 65005 -> 4 -> xxxxxxxxxxxxx
Sending 65005 back to client ...
Received from linux303.itcarlow.ie: 65005 -> 5 -> xxxxxxxxxxxxx
Sending 65005 back to client ...
Received from linux303.itcarlow.ie: 65005 -> 6 -> xxxxxxxxxxxxx
Sending 65005 back to client ...
Received from linux303.itcarlow.ie: 65005 -> 7 -> xxxxxxxxxxxxx
Sending 65005 back to client ...
Received from linux303.itcarlow.ie: 65005 -> 8 -> xxxxxxxxxxxxx
Sending 65005 back to client ...
Received from linux303.itcarlow.ie: 65005 -> 9 -> xxxxxxxxxxxxx
Sending 65005 back to client ...
Received from linux303.itcarlow.ie: 65006 -> 10 -> xxxxxxxxxxxxx
Sending 65006 back to client ...
```

And the following messages are those generated by the amended TCP client (`tcp_c1b`), running on the `linux303` network device:

```
Sending 1 65005 to server ...
Received from pblinux.itcarlow.ie: 65005 -> 1 -> xxxxxxxxxxxxx
Sending 2 65005 to server ...
Received from pblinux.itcarlow.ie: 65005 -> 2 -> xxxxxxxxxxxxx
Sending 3 65005 to server ...
Received from pblinux.itcarlow.ie: 65005 -> 3 -> xxxxxxxxxxxxx
Sending 4 65005 to server ...
Received from pblinux.itcarlow.ie: 65005 -> 4 -> xxxxxxxxxxxxx
Sending 5 65005 to server ...
```

```
Received from pblinux.itcarlow.ie: 65005 -> 5 -> xxxxxxxxxxxxxx
Sending 6 65005 to server ...
Received from pblinux.itcarlow.ie: 65005 -> 6 -> xxxxxxxxxxxxxx
Sending 7 65005 to server ...
Received from pblinux.itcarlow.ie: 65005 -> 7 -> xxxxxxxxxxxxxx
Sending 8 65005 to server ...
Received from pblinux.itcarlow.ie: 65005 -> 8 -> xxxxxxxxxxxxxx
Sending 9 65005 to server ...
Received from pblinux.itcarlow.ie: 65005 -> 9 -> xxxxxxxxxxxxxx
Sending 10 65006 to server ...
Received from pblinux.itcarlow.ie: 65006 -> 10 -> xxxxxxxxxxxxxx
```

With the amendments ensuring that all data are received from TCP, the complete messages are being sent/received. The ten messages arrive with no errors, data loss, corruption or flow-control difficulties. TCP has compensated for the fact that the TCP server is three times slower than the TCP client, and deadlock has not occurred.

3.11   A Common TCP Gotcha

Here is another TCP server (tcp_s2) that, when contacted by another TCP client (tcp_c2), sends a message to the client, waits for 10 seconds, sends another message, then closes the connection. The client contacts the server, receives the messages, then exits. Here is the code which executes on the server:

```perl
#! /usr/bin/perl -w

use strict;
use Socket;

use constant SIMPLE_TCP_PORT => 4001;

my $local_port = shift || SIMPLE_TCP_PORT;
my $trans_serv = getprotobyname( 'tcp' );
my $local_addr = sockaddr_in( $local_port, INADDR_ANY );

socket( TCP_SOCK, PF_INET, SOCK_STREAM, $trans_serv )
    or die "tcp_s2: socket creation failed: $!\n";
setsockopt( TCP_SOCK, SOL_SOCKET, SO_REUSEADDR, 1 )
    or warn "tcp_s2: could not set socket option: $!\n";
bind( TCP_SOCK, $local_addr )
    or die "tcp_s2: bind to address failed: $!\n";
listen( TCP_SOCK, SOMAXCONN )
    or die "tcp_s2: listen couldn't: $!\n";

warn "Server starting up on port: $local_port.\n";

while ( accept( CLIENT_SOCK, TCP_SOCK ) )
{
    my $secs = 10;
```

```
        print CLIENT_SOCK "Sleeping for $secs seconds ... \n";
        sleep( $secs );
        print CLIENT_SOCK "I awake, only to die ... \n";

        close( CLIENT_SOCK )
            or warn "tcp_c1: close failed: $!\n";
    }
    close TCP_SOCK;
```

What is different in this code is the fact that this server does not use the Socket API send subroutine to communicate with the client. Instead, the sockethandle is treated like any other input/output handle, and the standard inbuilt `print` subroutine is used to send data.

On the client, the familiar `<>` operator is used to receive data from the server, as opposed to using `recv`. Here is the client code:

```
#! /usr/bin/perl -w

use strict;
use Socket;

use constant SIMPLE_TCP_PORT => 4001;
use constant REMOTE_HOST      => 'localhost';

my $remote = shift || REMOTE_HOST;
my $remote_port = shift || SIMPLE_TCP_PORT;
my $trans_serv  = getprotobyname( 'tcp' );
my $remote_host = gethostbyname( $remote )
        or die "tcp_c2: name lookup failed: $remote\n";
my $destination = sockaddr_in( $remote_port, $remote_host );

socket( TCP_SOCK, PF_INET, SOCK_STREAM, $trans_serv )
        or die "tcp_c2: socket creation failed: $!\n";
connect( TCP_SOCK, $destination )
        or die "tcp_c2: connect to remote system failed: $!\n";

while ( <TCP_SOCK> )
{
    print $_;
}
close( TCP_SOCK );
```

This is all very straightforward. When the server is started and the client is then executed, the client pauses for 10 seconds, then the following messages appear on the screen:

```
Sleeping for 10 seconds ...
I awake, only to die ...
```

But wait, the 10 second wait should have occurred *before* the I awake only to die ... message was printed. What is going on?

The Network Debugger can help to solve the mystery. Here is an extract from the log file created after the above communication was snooped:

```
- - - - - - - - - - - - - - - - - - - - - - - - - - -
149.153.103.5 -> 149.153.100.65 (id: 28377, ttl: 63)

TCP Source: 4001 -> TCP Destination: 1269
TCP Header Length: 8, TCP Checksum: 65123
TCP Data:

Sleeping for 10 seconds ...
I awake, only to die ...
- - - - - - - - - - - - - - - - - - - - - - - - - - -
```

The log file shows that both messages were received as part of a single TCP segment. Two individual segments were expected, so why is this happening?

The answer lies in the fact that sockethandles behave like all other input/output handles, and as such *flushing* is off by default. This means that output will not appear until the buffer is flushed. Usually, flushing occurs when a newline is sent to an input/output handle, but this does not work with sockethandles as the above code includes the newline.

In addition to input/output handle buffering, socket-based applications can also fall foul of the internal buffering mechanism of TCP, which is what is happening here. The first message, the 'Sleeping for 10 seconds ... ' part, gets buffered on the outgoing sockethandle, then this version of the TCP server sleeps for 10 seconds. The second message is then printed to the sockethandle and, as the connection is then closed by the server, the buffer is flushed and this causes the two messages to be sent to the client (as one), where they then get displayed. After making the initial connection, the client waited for 10 seconds for data to arrive due to the fact that the server was having a 10 second nap.

When it comes to enabling auto-flushing on sockethandles, the same technique as used with any other input/output handle can be used, and TCP will honour the request. The following lines of code can be added to the server to turn flushing on, and this allows the amended TCP server (tcp_s3) to behave in the way that it is expected to:

```
my $previous = select CLIENT_SOCK;
$| = 1;
select $previous;
```

Be well warned: this is a different select to the select used in udp_c7. The single-argument version of select returns and sets the currently selected output filehandle. The code above remembers the $previous output filehandle, while setting the output filehandle to be the client sockethandle (CLIENT_SOCK). Flushing is then switched on for CLIENT_SOCK by setting the built-in $| variable to a true value, then the previously selected output filehandle (which we conveniently remembered in $previous) is made current again.

Now, when the client contacts the server, the first message arrives immediately, the client then pauses for 10 seconds while the server sleeps for 10 seconds, then the second message arrives at the client. The client terminates, and the server goes back to waiting for another client to contact it. All is now well with the second TCP server and client.

Another extract from a *Network Debugger* log file proves that the required behaviour is occurring:

```
- - - - - - - - - - - - - - - - - - - - - - - - - - - - - -
149.153.103.5 -> 149.153.100.65 (id: 28389, ttl: 63)

TCP Source: 4001 -> TCP Destination: 1270
TCP Header Length: 8, TCP Checksum: 55511
TCP Data:

Sleeping for 10 seconds ...
- - - - - - - - - - - - - - - - - - - - - - - - - - - - - -
149.153.100.65 -> 149.153.103.5 (id: 14187, ttl: 64)

TCP Source: 1270 -> TCP Destination: 4001
TCP Header Length: 8, TCP Checksum: 28529
TCP Data:
    .
    .
    .
- - - - - - - - - - - - - - - - - - - - - - - - - - - - - -
149.153.103.5 -> 149.153.100.65 (id: 28390, ttl: 63)

TCP Source: 4001 -> TCP Destination: 1270
TCP Header Length: 8, TCP Checksum: 34174
TCP Data:

I awake, only to die ...
- - - - - - - - - - - - - - - - - - - - - - - - - - - - - -
```

The log file confirms that the two messages are being carried in two individual TCP segments. The log file also shows that some other communication is occurring in the reverse direction, and that this traffic separates the two TCP segments of interest. The details of this traffic are not important to this discussion. However, the segments' existence proves that there is some time delay between the receipt of the first and second message.

3.12 More TCP Socket Communication

Let us build a TCP server that does a little more work than those developed thus far. Typically, servers do more than echo large chunks of data sent to them from clients.

The next TCP server accepts a filename from a client, followed immediately by the contents of the same file (from the client's local storage). The server writes the file to its local storage then runs the file through the Perl interpreter, checking the file for syntax errors. Any and all messages generated by the Perl interpreter are captured by this TCP server and returned to the client, then the connection is closed.

3.12.1   The remote syntax checker server

The code for this server (tcp_s4) begins like any other TCP server:

```
#! /usr/bin/perl -w

use strict;
use Socket;

use constant SIMPLE_TCP_PORT => 4001;

my $local_port = shift || SIMPLE_TCP_PORT;
my $trans_serv = getprotobyname( 'tcp' );
my $local_addr = sockaddr_in( $local_port, INADDR_ANY );

socket( TCP_SOCK, PF_INET, SOCK_STREAM, $trans_serv )
    or die "tcp_s4: socket creation failed: $!\n";
setsockopt( TCP_SOCK, SOL_SOCKET, SO_REUSEADDR, 1 )
    or warn "tcp_s4: could not set socket option: $!\n";
bind( TCP_SOCK, $local_addr )
    or die "tcp_s4: bind to address failed: $!\n";
listen( TCP_SOCK, SOMAXCONN )
    or die "tcp_s4: listen couldn't: $!\n";

warn "Server starting up on port: $local_port.\n";
```

The sockethandle is created, the SO_REUSEADDR option is set, then the socket address and port are bound together. The call to listen tells the operating system that this custom network application will listen for and, if needs be, queue connections. The TCP server then loops on a call to accept, waiting for connections:

```
my $from_who;

while ( $from_who = accept( CLIENT_SOCK, TCP_SOCK ) )
{
```

As soon as a client contacts the server, the CLIENT_SOCK sockethandle comes into existence, and the TCP server immediately switches on auto-flushing, prior to receiving the filename from the client with the usual <> operator. Note that the code calls the inbuilt chomp subroutine to remove any trailing newline from the filename (which is stored in the $tmp_fn scalar):

```
my $data = '';

my $previous = select CLIENT_SOCK;
$| = 1;
select $previous;

my $tmp_fn = <CLIENT_SOCK>;

chomp( $tmp_fn );
```

The next line of code is a little bit of Perl magic:

```
$tmp_fn = (split /\//, $tmp_fn)[-1];
```

Although this is a single line of code, there is a lot going on here. The first thing to happen is that the inbuilt `split` subroutine *splits* the `$tmp_fn` scalar based on a provided delimiter. In this case, the delimiter is the / character, which is referred to as \/ in the above code, as `split` expects the delimiter to be surrounded by leading and trailing / characters, so *escaping* is necessary. When used in list context, `split` returns a list of items resulting from the splitting operation. The parentheses around the call to `split` force list context to be in effect. Although the array is anonymous, it is there, and the [-1] accesses the last element of the array returned by the call to `split`. The result of the array access is then assigned to `$tmp_fn`. Using the same scalar on both sides of an assignment (as happens here) is perfectly OK, as Perl evaluates the right-hand side of the assignment *before* performing the assignment operation.

Now that it is known what this line of code does, why is it used here? The answer has to do with the fact that the client can send any file it wishes to the server. The server will create the file (with the same name) on its local storage to temporarily hold the file before it is fed to the Perl interpreter for syntax checking. It would be foolish to simply accept the filename from the client verbatim. Why? Consider if the client sent this file: /etc/passwd. If the TCP server proceeded to use this filename as is, it would try and create the file on its own local storage, overwriting the file if it already exists. Yikes! It would be a case of *Double Yikes and Groans* if the TCP server happened to be executing with superuser privilege (which it should *never* be). The magic line guards against this eventuality, by stripping away the directory-part of the filename passed by the client and setting `$tmp_fn` to contain the filename-part.

A few examples will further illustrate how this line of code works. On the left of the arrow is the original filename as sent by the client, and on the right, the *sanitized* filename as produced by the server's call to `split` is shown:

```
/etc/passwd             ->      passwd
testing.pl              ->      testing.pl
/etc/sysconfig/network  ->      network
/book/chapter2/netdb    ->      netdb
```

After this magic line, the server continues, and loops on the CLIENT_SOCK socket-handle, receiving the contents of the file as sent by the client. The contents are placed in the $data scalar, then the local disk-file is opened for writing, and the contents of the received file are written to it. The server then closes the local disk-file (which is referred to by the FILETOCHECK filehandle):

```
while ( my $chunk = <CLIENT_SOCK> )
{
    $data = $data . $chunk;
}

open FILETOCHECK, ">$tmp_fn";

print FILETOCHECK $data;

close FILETOCHECK;
```

The TCP server then builds a command-line to execute and assigns the command-line to the $cmd scalar:

```
my $cmd = "perl -c $tmp_fn 2>&1 1>/dev/null";
```

Like the call to split earlier, this line looks a little strange. In actual fact, the stuff between the double quotes is not really Perl code, it is a command that will be executed by the operating system shell. The command will execute Perl and pass the syntax check switch and the filename to the interpreter, together with some *output redirections*. The Perl interpreters standard error output (2>) is redirected to standard output (&1), and standard output (1>) is sent to the /dev/null file, which causes it to be discarded. This has the effect of having any STDERR output from the Perl interpreter being sent to STDOUT, which then provides a mechanism for the TCP server to capture the messages generated by the interpreter.

If $tmp_fn contains testing.pl, the command-line produced will be:

```
perl -c testing.pl 2>&1 1>/dev/null
```

The code then determines the IP name (or the IP address) of the client, and assigns the result to $remote_name:

```
my ( $the_port, $the_ip ) = sockaddr_in( $from_who );

my $remote_name = gethostbyaddr( $the_ip, AF_INET )
       || inet_ntoa( $the_ip );
```

Note the call to inet_ntoa if the call to gethostbyaddr fails. Not all IP addresses have associated IP names, and the above code takes this into consideration. The server then displays a message to standard error which shows the command-line it is about to execute, then the command-line is executed by the operating system shell using Perl's *back-tick* operator qx:

```
warn "tcp_s4: executing: [ $cmd ] for $remote_name\n";

my $stderr_output = qx/$cmd/;
```

Any standard error messages generated as a result of the command-line executing are returned to the server and assigned to the $stderr_output scalar. This is then sent to the client sockethandle using a simple call to print:

```
print CLIENT_SOCK $stderr_output;

close CLIENT_SOCK
    or warn "tcp_s4: close failed: $!\n";

unlink $tmp_fn;
}

close TCP_SOCK;
```

The CLIENT_SOCK is closed by the TCP server, and the file is then removed from the server's local storage by calling the inbuilt unlink subroutine. The loop iteration then ends, and the server waits for the next client to contact it by calling accept.

3.12.2   The remote syntax checker client

The code for the client (tcp_c3) is presented below. The standard collection of lines gets things going:

```
#! /usr/bin/perl -w

use strict;
use Socket;

use constant SIMPLE_TCP_PORT => 4001;
use constant REMOTE_HOST     => 'localhost';
```

The client expects at least one but not more than three command-line parameters to be provided by the user. The first parameter is the name of the file to send to the server. The client does not continue if this parameter is not supplied, nor if the file specified cannot be opened. If it can, the contents of the entire file is read into the client and assigned to the @entire_file array:

```
my $filetosend = shift;

die "tcp_c3: you must provide a filename: $!\n"
    unless defined $filetosend;

open TOSEND, "$filetosend"
    or die "tcp_c3: could not open $filetosend: $!\n";
```

```
my @entire_file = <TOSEND>;

close TOSEND;
```

The client then executes code to create the sockethandle and connect it to the remote server. The client switches on auto-flushing for the successfully created sockethandle (TCP_SOCK):

```
my $remote = shift || REMOTE_HOST;
my $remote_port = shift || SIMPLE_TCP_PORT;

my $trans_serv = getprotobyname( 'tcp' );
my $remote_host = gethostbyname( $remote )
    or die "tcp_c3: name lookup failed: $remote\n";
my $destination = sockaddr_in( $remote_port, $remote_host );

socket( TCP_SOCK, PF_INET, SOCK_STREAM, $trans_serv )
    or die "tcp_c3: socket creation failed: $!\n";
connect( TCP_SOCK, $destination )
    or die "tcp_c3: connect to remote system failed: $!\n";

my $previous = select TCP_SOCK;
$| = 1;
select $previous;
```

The remaining client code is, perhaps surprisingly, straightforward. The filename is sent to the server using a simple `print` statement. Note the concatenation of the newline character. The call to `print` is immediately followed by another, and this time the contents of the file are sent to the server, by printing the `@entire_file` array to the sockethandle. The sockethandle is then closed for further writing with a call to `shutdown`:

```
print TCP_SOCK $filetosend . "\n";

print TCP_SOCK @entire_file;

shutdown( TCP_SOCK, 1 );
```

The client then receives all data (the response) from the server, using a simple loop on the <> operator. The client closes the sockethandle before printing the received response to the screen. The client then terminates:

```
my $data = '';

while ( my $chunk = <TCP_SOCK> )
{
    $data = $data . $chunk;
}

close TCP_SOCK
```

```
or warn "tcp_c3: close failed: $!\n";

print "$data";
```

To test this client/server combination, the server (tcp_s4) was deployed on the linux303.itcarlow.ie network device, and the client (tcp_c3) was deployed on pblinux.itcarlow.ie and 149.153.103.15. A campus router separates pblinux from the other deployment hosts.

After being contacted four times, the server's output looked like this:

```
Server starting up on port: 4001.
tcp_s4: executing: [ perl -c hosts 2>&1 1>/dev/null ]
    for 149.153.103.15
tcp_s4: executing: [ perl -c udp_c8 2>&1 1>/dev/null ]
    for 149.153.103.15
tcp_s4: executing: [ perl -c udp_c1 2>&1 1>/dev/null ]
    for pblinux.itcarlow.ie
tcp_s4: executing: [ perl -c tcp_s5 2>&1 1>/dev/null ]
    for pblinux.itcarlow.ie
```

Here we see the command-line that was executed together with the IP name or IP address of the network device that requested the remote syntax check. Note that the 149.153.103.15 network device does not have an associated IP name within the local DNS, and that this TCP server calls inet_ntoa to determine the dotted-decimal notation to report.

The first invocation of the client was performed on the 149.153.103.15 network device as follows, and it generated the response shown:

```
./tcp_c3 /etc/hosts linux303

Bareword found where operator expected at hosts line 1,
near "0.1localhost" (Missing operator before localhost?)
syntax error at hosts line 1, near "0.1 localhostlocalhost"
Number found where operator expected at hosts line 2,
near "149.153" (Missing semicolon on previous line?)
Bareword found where operator expected at hosts line 2,
near "103.15 linux303_15" (Missing operator before linux303_15?)
hosts had compilation errors.
```

This looks like a bit of a mess, and so it should. The /etc/hosts disk-file does not (usually) contain Perl code, so asking the server to syntax check the file produces a barrage of error messages from the Perl interpreter.

When the server is sent a file containing well-formed Perl code, the response is more predictable, as shown here:

```
./tcp_c3 udp_c8 linux303

udp_c8 syntax OK
```

As the server can accept connections from any networked device running the client code, the next invocation occurs on `pblinux`. Again, well-formed Perl code is sent to the server:

```
./tcp_c3 udp_c1 linux303

udp_c1 syntax OK
```

As a final example, an early version of the next TCP server (`tcp_s5`) was sent to the server. This file contained Perl code, but the code is not well formed and contains an error. The server reports the error to the client as follows:

```
./tcp_c3 tcp_s5 linux303

Bareword "CLIENT_SOCK" not allowed while "strict subs" in
use at tcp_s5 line 86.
tcp_s5 had compilation errors.
```

This is all well and good, but imagine that this version of the server was deployed on an Internet-accessible network device, and that its remote syntax checking was widely advertised. Now imagine that the server receives ten thousand hits per day.

At certain times of the day, the server may be swamped with requests from clients and the SOMAXCONN queued connection limit may be reached and exceeded. When this happens, connections are refused by the server. Connections may also be refused by the server if a particularly large file is being checked, resulting in the server waiting for the syntax check to complete. While the server waits, it is not calling accept, which may result in an excessive queueing delay for a client, or – in some cases – connection refusals. A number of strategies for dealing with these eventualities exist, and by far the most widely used is to create a *concurrent TCP server*, which creates a subprocess to handle each successful client connection.

3.13   The Concurrent Syntax Checker

In this section, code will be added to the Remote Syntax Checker Server to support concurrent operation. The technique used is not very different from that employed by the `udp_c8` client from earlier in this chapter.

The code begins by using the appropriate modules, then defining the child reaping subroutine that responds to CHLD signals:

```
#! /usr/bin/perl -w

use strict;
use Socket;

use POSIX ":sys_wait_h";
```

```perl
sub zombie_reaper {
    while ( waitpid( -1, WNOHANG ) > 0 )
    { }
    $SIG{CHLD} = \&zombie_reaper;
}

$SIG{CHLD} = \&zombie_reaper;
```

An additional subroutine, continue_as_child, is then defined. This subroutine
is called by the child process after a successful fork. The subroutine takes two
parameters: the sockethandle to communicate on and the socket address of the
connected client. The actual code is an exact copy of the client sockethandle
processing code from tcp_s4. With auto-flushing switched on, the child process
receives the filename and its contents, a command-line is then constructed, then
the server calls the Perl interpreter to syntax check the received file (using the
just-built command-line). Any and all messages from the Perl interpreter are then
returned to the connected client. When processing is complete, the sockethandle
is closed and the local file is removed from the server's disk storage:

```perl
sub continue_as_child {
    my $handle = shift;
    my $from_who_client = shift;

    my $data = '';

    my $previous = select $handle;
    $| = 1;
    select $previous;

    my $tmp_fn = <$handle>;

    chomp( $tmp_fn );

    $tmp_fn = (split /\//, $tmp_fn)[-1];

    while ( my $chunk = <$handle> )
    {
        $data = $data . $chunk;
    }

    open FILETOCHECK, ">$tmp_fn";

    print FILETOCHECK $data;

    close FILETOCHECK;

    my $cmd = "perl -c $tmp_fn 2>&1 1>/dev/null";

    my ( $the_port, $the_ip ) = sockaddr_in( $from_who_client );

    my $remote_name = gethostbyaddr( $the_ip, AF_INET )
        || inet_ntoa( $the_ip );
```

```
warn "tcp_s5: executing: [ $cmd ] for $remote_name\n";

my $stderr_output = qx( $cmd );

print $handle $stderr_output;

close $handle
    or warn "tcp_s5: close failed: $!\n";

unlink $tmp_fn;
}
```

With the subroutines defined, the code for creating the listening socket is the same as in the non-concurrent Remote Syntax Checker Server (tcp_s4):

```
use constant SIMPLE_TCP_PORT => 4001;

my $local_port = shift || SIMPLE_TCP_PORT;
my $trans_serv = getprotobyname( 'tcp' );
my $local_addr = sockaddr_in( $local_port, INADDR_ANY );

socket( TCP_SOCK, PF_INET, SOCK_STREAM, $trans_serv )
    or die "tcp_s5: socket creation failed: $!\n";
setsockopt( TCP_SOCK, SOL_SOCKET, SO_REUSEADDR, 1 )
    or warn "tcp_s5: could not set socket option: $!\n";
bind( TCP_SOCK, $local_addr )
    or die "tcp_s5: bind to address failed: $!\n";
listen( TCP_SOCK, SOMAXCONN )
    or die "tcp_s5: listen couldn't: $!\n";

warn "Server starting up on port: $local_port.\n";
```

The main loop starts as expected with a blocking call to accept:

```
my $from_who;

while ( $from_who = accept( CLIENT_SOCK, TCP_SOCK ) )
{
```

The server then invokes fork to spawn a subprocess. If this is successful, the server code moves directly to the next loop iteration after executing any code in the continue block, which in this code simply closes the CLIENT_SOCK sockethandle. In the child process, the subprocess first closes the TCP_SOCK sockethandle before calling the continue_as_child subroutine, passing as parameters the CLIENT_SOCK sockethandle and the socket address of the connected client (in $from_who). When the subroutine returns, the child calls the inbuilt exit subroutine, which terminates the child subprocess and sends a CHLD signal to the parent. If the fork is unsuccessful, a warning is displayed, then the continue block is executed prior to starting another loop iteration:

```
    my $child_pid = fork;

    if ( $child_pid )
    {
        next;
    }
    elsif ( defined( $child_pid ) )
    {
        close( TCP_SOCK );
        continue_as_child( *CLIENT_SOCK, $from_who );
        exit;
    }
    else
    {
        warn "tcp_s5: fork failed: $!\n";
    }
}
continue {
    close( CLIENT_SOCK );
}

close TCP_SOCK;
```

The extra `close` statements in the above code are interesting, and require further explanation. When `fork` was introduced earlier in this chapter, it was stated that when the call to `fork` succeeded, the created child process was an *exact copy* of the parent. If the parent has open input/output handles, they will exist in the child process *and* in the parent process. It is necessary, therefore, to close those input/output handles that are not required in each process. Specifically, the listening TCP_SOCK sockethandle is not required in the child process, and the connected clients CLIENT_SOCK sockethandle is not required in the parent process. As they are not needed, these sockethandles are closed.

This version of the Remote Syntax Checker Server (`tcp_s5`) now supports concurrency, which allows it to better support a greater number of clients. The parent process concentrates on accepting connections, while the child process concentrates on servicing them. This model can be easily extended to build any number and type of network servers.

3.14 Object-Oriented Sockets

In addition to the functional interface to the Socket API, Perl provides an object-oriented (OO) interface. Part of the standard Perl distribution, the IO::Socket module provides a mechanism to simplify the creation and use of sockethandles, or *socket objects* to use the correct OO terminology. Once a socket object is created, a set of methods can be called on the object to effect network communication. The method names correspond to the Socket API subroutines introduced earlier in this chapter.

The decision as to which interface to use, whether functional or OO, is primarily a personal one. The functional interface does not incur as high an overhead as the OO interface, and it does provide finer control over what is going on. However, the OO interface can be very convenient.

3.14.1   `IO::Socket`

The `IO::Socket` module (or *class* to use OO speak) is a subclass of Perl's standard `IO::Handle` class, which provides an OO interface to input/output handles. As was seen with sockethandles, all input/output handles share characteristics: for instance, it is possible to use `print` to send data to any input/output handle. It is these shared characteristics that are implemented in `IO::Handle`, creating input/output objects, and expanded upon within its derived classes, of which `IO::Socket` is one.

However, when it comes to creating network socket objects, `IO::Socket` is not enough, as only those methods common to any socket type are implemented in the `IO::Socket` module. Two types of socket subclasses can be created, those that work over a network (type INET) and those that work within a single computing device (type UNIX), which may or may not be networked. The UNIX type will not be discussed here, as it is of lesser interest to the network programmer.

3.14.2   `IO::Socket::INET`

To create a socket object, invoke the new method[12] from the `IO::Socket::INET` class. This method takes a variable number of *named parameters*, as follows.

PeerAddr - the address and (optionally) the protocol port-number of the remote host. The address can be specified as an IP name or a dotted-decimal address. The port can be specified as a decimal port-number, or as a service-name/port-number combination. Examples would be '`pblinux.itcarlow.ie`', '`linux303.itcarlow.ie:80`' and the rather strange looking '`149.153.103.15:mobileip-agent(434)`'. Another name for this parameter is `PeerHost`.

PeerPort - the decimal protocol port-number, or a service-name/port-number combination. Examples are '`110`' and '`pop3(110)`'.

LocalAddr - specifies the address on the local network device to bind with. The format is as with `PeerAddr` above. Another name for this parameter is `LocalHost`.

---

[12]In OO speak, 'method' is the name given to 'subroutine'.

LocalPort - specifies the protocol port-number on the local network device to bind with. The format is as with **PeerPort** above.

Proto - the transport service protocol to use. Typical values would be 'tcp' and 'udp'.

Type - the transport type name for the socket object, typically either SOCK_ STREAM or SOCK_DGRAM.

Listen - the size of the connection queue.

Reuse - set to 1 to enable SO_REUSEADDR.

Timeout - sets a timeout value for operations that require it. It is used most often with connect on clients and accept on servers.

MultiHomed - a Boolean, that when true, arranges for a client to try to contact a server on any of its IP addresses (assuming it has more than one, that is, it is *multihomed*). This is especially useful when the client does not know which of the server's addresses to connect with.

The following call to new will set up a socket object that runs on a server, uses any locally available address, and operates on port 4001. Reliable communication will be used (that is, TCP):

```
my $sock_obj = IO::Socket::INET->new( LocalPort    => 4001,
                                       Proto        => 'tcp',
                                       Listen       => SOMAXCONN )
    or die "Could not create socket object: $!\n";
```

The call to new returns a socket object, which is then assigned to the $sock_obj scalar. Note that, as the parameters are named, the ordering within the parameter list is not important. As one of the parameters is Listen, a server-side, listening socket object is created. No value for LocalAddr is provided, and IO::Socket uses INADDR_ANY by default.

It is now possible to call other methods, inherited from IO::Socket, to interact with and communicate on the socket object. After calling the accept method, the most useful of these are send and recv:

```
my $connected_client_obj = $sock_obj->accept
    or die "Unable to accept a connection: $!\n";

my $data;

$connected_client_obj->recv( $data, MAX_RECV_LEN, 0 );
$connected_client_obj->send( $data, 0 );
```

Here, the calls to send and recv do not need to reference a sockethandle as their first parameter, as is the case with the functional interface. As send and recv are called on a socket object, the use of sockethandles is not required as with the functional interface. Note, too, that the call to `accept` takes no parameters as it *returns* a connected socket object on success.

It is also possible to use the familiar `print` and `<>` mechanism:

```perl
my $data;

$data = <$connected_client_obj>;
print $connected_client_obj $data;
```

As was stated at the start of this section, the OO interface is very convenient.

3.14.3   An object-oriented client and server

As a complete example, the functional versions of `tcp_c2` and `tcp_s3` from earlier will be rewritten to use the OO interface.

Here is server code (`oo_tcp_s3`):

```perl
#! /usr/bin/perl -w

use strict;
use IO::Socket;

use constant SIMPLE_TCP_PORT => 4001;

my $port = shift || SIMPLE_TCP_PORT;

my $sock_obj = IO::Socket::INET->new( LocalPort  => $port,
                                      Proto      => 'tcp',
                                      Reuse      => 1,
                                      Listen     => SOMAXCONN )
    or die "oo_tcp_s3: could not create socket object: $!\n";

warn "OO Server starting up on port: ", $sock_obj->sockport, ".\n";

while ( my $client_obj = $sock_obj->accept )
{
    my $secs = 10;

    print $client_obj "Sleeping for.$secs seconds ... \n";
    sleep( $secs );
    print $client_obj "I awake, only to die ... \n";

    $client_obj->close
        or warn "oo_tcp_s3: close failed: $!\n";
}
$sock_obj->close;
```

Compared with the functional code from earlier, this code is much shorter. Gone are the individual invocations of `socket`, `setsockopt`, `bind` and `listen`. These have been replaced by a single call to the IO::Socket::INET->new method. Note how the Type of the socket object has not been specified, as this can be determined by the use of 'tcp' as the value for Proto. The code calls the sockport method to return the protocol port-number being used by the server socket object, and this value is used during the display of the start-up message. The rest of the code is not too different from the functional version, except that socket objects are used where sockethandles were used before. Of note is the absence of the auto-flushing code from the functional version. With the most recent versions of Perl (release 5.004_4 and later), socket objects are automatically flushed, and auto-flushing is on by default. The autoflush method, inherited from the IO::Handle class, can be used to change this behaviour.

The changes to the code are straightforward. Here is the code (oo_tcp_c2):

```perl
#! /usr/bin/perl -w

use strict;
use IO::Socket;

use constant SIMPLE_TCP_PORT => 4001;
use constant REMOTE_HOST      => 'localhost';

my $remote = shift || REMOTE_HOST;
my $remote_port = shift || SIMPLE_TCP_PORT;

my $sock_obj = IO::Socket::INET->new( PeerAddr => $remote,
                                      PeerPort => $remote_port,
                                      Proto    => 'tcp' )
    or die "oo_tcp_c3: could not create socket object: $!\n";

while ( <$sock_obj> )
{
    print $_;
}
$sock_obj->close;
```

Again, a single call to IO::Socket::INET->new replaces the calls to socket and connect from the functional version of this code. The new method knows to establish a connection to a server due to the fact that 'tcp' is specified as the value for Proto, and that the values of PeerAddr and PeerPort are defined. This default behaviour, that pervades the IO::Socket class, enhances the usefulness and convenience of using this socket interface.

Additional information on the methods available to IO::Socket and IO::Handle derived objects can be found in the Perl online documentation. Issue either of the following commands at the command-line to view the manual page of interest:

```
man IO::Handle
man IO::Socket
```

An excellent treatment of Perl's OO socket technology is Chapter 5 of Lincoln Stein's book (see the *Print Resource* section at the end of this chapter).

3.15   Where To From Here?

In this chapter, the main features of the Perl Socket API were described. Much can be learned from the experience of building some custom network applications. Start with the *Exercises* at the end of this chapter, then explore the documentation included with Perl, in particular the `perlipc` manual page. A number of excellent books (by respected authors) cover the Socket API in great depth – see the *Print Resources* section, below. The Web has an extensive collection of sites which offer primers and tutorials on programming sockets (mostly geared toward the C programmer, although Java is popular too).

CPAN has a small collection of add-on modules to Perl that implement common network server behaviour. These include Jochen Wiedmann's `Net::Daemon` module, Charlie Stross's `NetServer::Generic`, and the `Net::Server` module by Paul Seamons. Each comes with extensive online documentation. Before creating a network server from scratch, take the time to become familiar with the functionality provided by each of these modules. In addition, there is much to be gleaned from reviewing each module's source code.

The techniques described in this chapter can be used to interact with any Internet server, as the vast majority of Internet servers (be they offering Web, email, news or file-transfer services) are typically built on top of the Socket API. However, to do this effectively can involve quite a bit of work (not to mention source code). Thankfully, some great and generous Perl programmers have built add-on modules that allow the Perl network programmer to interact with these standard servers at a higher level of abstraction. The use of a collection of add-on Internet modules forms the basis of the next chapter.

3.16   Print Resources

For a gentle introduction to the Socket API, and computer networking in general, refer to *Computer Networks and Internets, with Internet Applications*, 3rd edn, by Douglas E. Comer (Prentice-Hall, 2001). Dr Comer's work in this area is well known, and this book includes a brief description of RPC and CORBA, as well as sufficient details on the various mechanisms used by TCP to achieve reliability. The client and server characteristics described at the start of this chapter are based on material from Dr Comer's book.

The ultimate reference to the Socket and XTI APIs (for C programmers) is *UNIX Network Programming, Volume 1: Networking APIs: Sockets and XTI*, 2nd edn, by W. Richard Stevens (Prentice-Hall, 1999). Although written for the C programmer, this book is still a very useful reference, as Perl's functional interface to the Socket API is very close to C's.

For Perl programmers, the definitive reference to the Socket API is the excellent and very thorough *Network Programming with Perl*, by Lincoln D. Stein (Addison-

Wesley, 2001). If the treatment of the Perl Socket API in this chapter only served to whet your appetite, then Stein's book will more than satisfy. His book includes additional material on multithreading, broadcasting and multicasting network programming with Perl, and much more besides. The description of the OO technology is especially good. The examples are quite involved, and significantly longer than those found in this chapter. Highly recommended reading.

Chapter 17 of *The Perl Cookbook* contains a good collection of networking clients and servers. Refer to the *Print Resources* section from Chapter 1.

3.17 Web Resources

The `http://www.perl.com` website maintains a short list of links of interest to network programmers.

An excellent resource is maintained at `http://www.sockets.com` for Windows programmers.

Exercises

1. Revisit the *NetDebug* code from the last chapter and amend it to take an IP address or an IP name as the value for the `-s` command-line parameter.

2. Research the threading technology available with Perl 5.6.0 (and higher), then redevelop the child-spawning, zombie-exhuming UDP client to use threads as opposed to `fork` when creating and managing subprocesses.

3. The `connect` subroutine is typically used with TCP, but can also be used with UDP. What are the advantages/disadvantages (if any) of using `connect` with UDP?

4. The `tcp_s4` and `tcp_s5` servers work well, but they are not very robust. For example, if they are sent a single / as the filename, the server gets into difficulty. Additionally, the servers should not accept a file that already exists on the server, as doing so would overwrite the file (rarely the required behaviour). This is a particularly serious problem on network devices executing the concurrent version of this server. Amend both servers to guard against these situations. (Hint: does the `flock` function from the standard `Fcntl` module help?) Can you think of any other amendments that would improve the robustness of these servers?

5. Some authors suggest that production servers should be executed with *tainting* switched on, that is, the `-T` command-line switch should be specified on the strange first line of Perl servers. It is also suggested that the `use sigtrap` compiler directive be enabled. Research the impact that each of these features has on the execution status of servers. Do you agree that they should be used on all servers? Should either feature be used on clients?

6. Create a reliable server that receives any amount of text from a client, spell checks the text received using the `spell` program (included with most versions of Linux and UNIX), then returns the list of suspect words to the connected client. Develop the server to support concurrency using the OO socket interface. The client (which also needs to be developed) should use the functional interface.

4

Protocols

In this chapter, Perl is used to interact with some of the Internet's most popular application-level protocols. Over the last three decades, the Internet has spawned a large and growing collection of these protocols and Perl has a series of add-on modules (some of which come as standard) for interacting with them. These can be used to great effect when working with the standard services of the Internet. Of course, it is also possible to program to the Internet protocol standards using the Socket API. Although effective, using the Socket API in this way can often be a chore.

After dispensing with a common *gotcha*, this chapter begins with a discussion of the most popular application-level protocol, HTTP, the HyperText Transfer Protocol. HTTP powers the World Wide Web, and a simple program is written in Perl's Socket API to illustrate interactions with this protocol. This simple program is then replaced, and expanded-upon, by an 'add-on alternative', which takes advantage of one of the most popular third-party add-on modules, libwww-perl. HTTP server technology is then explored. The remainder of the chapter is given over to working with some other Internet protocols, and included is a brief description of the most popular add-on module library for non-HTTP protocol programming, namely libnet. A brief survey of some additional add-on modules rounds off this chapter.

4.1 Gotcha!

Prior to interacting with some standard Internet protocols, it is necessary to consider one of the biggest network programming gotchas of them all: *an inadequate understanding of newline.*

4.1.1   What's the deal with newline?

Most programming languages have a good understanding of what newline is. Within Perl, the \n escape sequence is used to represent newline. Operating systems also have a good understanding of what newline is. Unfortunately, no two operating systems agree on exactly how the newline should be represented. Personal computers running technology from Microsoft use a different representation for newline than those that run Apple's Mac OS. Yet another value for newline is used on UNIX and Linux systems. Strangely (and this strangeness has *nothing* to do with Perl), under certain circumstances, what some operating systems think of as newline actually changes based on what is going on.

Regardless of the operating system (OS) running, Perl will try to do the *right thing*, so when \n is used, Perl uses the ASCII value for newline expected by the underlying OS. This can be very convenient for the programmer, as it is possible to use \n without worrying about how the underlying OS might interpret it. Unfortunately, this convenience can lead to problems when data are transmitted over a network. This is especially true when the data include embedded newline characters and the data are being sent from a network device running a different OS to that running on the receiving device. What was newline on a device running Mac OS (ASCII value 13) will not be treated as such on a device running Linux, which uses ASCII value 10 to represent newline. On a Microsoft-infected network device, the sequence of ASCII value 13 followed by ASCII value 10 is used to represent the *single* newline character. Simply using \n within a custom network application and hoping for the best is foolhardy, as the meaning associated with the OS-specific value of newline will be lost when communicating with a network device running a different OS.

The solution to this problem is simple: as a rule, do not use \n to represent newline when sending data over a network connection[1]. This rule leads to a rather obvious question: if \n is not used, what is? Well, it depends. The correct value should always be specified and *explicitly* used. If ASCII value 13 is used, then ASCII value 13 should be specified in the code. Instead of writing this line of code:

```
print CLIENT_SOCK "This is a line.\n";
```

use:

```
print CLIENT_SOCK "This is a line.\015";
```

where \015 is the octal representation of ASCII value 13. If ASCII value 10 is used to represent newline, octal \012 can be used. Microsoft's idea of newline can be specified as \015\012. Do not fret if all this octal brings on a migraine. The Socket

---

[1] Eagle-eyed readers will note that this rule was broken (actually, ignored) in the previous chapter. We only got away with this due to the fact that all communication was occurring between Linux and UNIX-derived network devices, which use the same representation for newline.

module provides a small collection of constants that can be used instead, and they are imported into a custom network application with the following statement:

```
use Socket qw( :DEFAULT :crlf );
```

It is now possible to use $CR (or CR) for ASCII value 13, $LF (or LF) for ASCII value 10, and $CRLF (or CRLF) for the ASCII value 13 followed by ASCII value 10 sequence. The line of code from earlier can be written in a more readable way, as follows:

```
print CLIENT_SOCK "This is a line.$CR";
```

So, if the value used to specify newline on one end of a connection is known, it can be used on the other end. And if the newline value has to be converted to the newline value expected by the receiving devices OS, then this becomes an added responsibility of the custom network application. However, what happens when the value of newline is not known? It is not possible to provide a generic mechanism for determining the value of newline used by the other end of a network connection. Consequently, a convention exists on the Internet. The de facto standard representation for newline within the vast majority of Internet protocols is the ASCII value 13 followed by ASCII value 10 sequence[2]. Within custom network applications, the $CRLF constant should be used to represent newline. In order to conform with this standard, the readable line of code from above should now be:

```
print CLIENT_SOCK "This is a line.$CRLF";
```

However, for an application to be classed as *robust*, it is also recommended that it recognize a single ASCII value 10 ($LF) as newline. Aren't de facto standards wonderful? It is relatively easy within Perl to reliably deal with this particular protocol quirk. When data arrive from a connected socket, the receiving application need only convert the protocol's idea of newline into a form that is acceptable to the underlying operating system, as follows:

```
my $line = <TCP_SOCK>;

$line =~ s/$CR?$LF/\n/;

print $line;
```

This code receives a newline-terminated chunk from the TCP_SOCK sockethandle. If the line uses $CRLF or $LF as newline, it is replaced by the \n escape sequence. The second line is an example of the substitution mechanism built into Perl's regular-expression technology. The use of ? between the $CR and $LF constants tells Perl to treat the $CR part as optional, which is exactly what is required to support the recommended robustness. Once the substitution is complete, the substituted line is reassigned to $line before it is printed by the inbuilt print subroutine.

---

[2]It is not just Microsoft that is infected!

4.2   Working with the Web

For most users, the Web *is* the Internet and the Internet *is* the Web. In recent years, the Web browser – in addition to providing its 'bread and butter' service of hypertext browsing – has become the tool used for accessing other standard Internet services, such as electronic mail, network news and file transfer. As multimedia Internet services are becoming increasingly popular, the Web browser (with optional extensions) now provides access to video, television, music, telephony and radio services. The humble Web browser is well on its way to becoming the *universal client platform*.

The protocol used by the Web browser (the client) when communicating with a website (the server) is the HyperText Transfer Protocol (HTTP), and three versions of the standard are in use: 0.9, 1.0 and 1.1. Most new technology is built to support the 1.1 standard which, by and large, provides backward compatibility with the earlier versions.

HTTP is built on top of TCP, which means all Web communication is reliable. This also means that prior to any communication occurring, the HTTP client and HTTP server must establish a TCP connection.

4.2.1   HTTP requests and responses

Once a connection has been established, requests arriving from an HTTP client to an HTTP server begin by specifying a *method* which governs how the server is to respond to the client. As of HTTP 1.1, the standard set of methods are as follows.

OPTIONS – allows a client to request details about a specific server resource, or about the server itself.

GET – allows a client to instruct the server to locate a specified resource, retrieve it, and deliver it to the client. The resource has two parts: a header and a body. The header-part contains data about the contents of the body-part, which contains the *something of interest*, for example, a Web page or graphic. Data about data are often referred to as *metadata*. This is one of the most used HTTP methods.

HEAD – this is identical to the GET method, except that the body-part of the resource is not sent to the client, just the header-part.

POST – allows the client to send data to the server for processing. As an example, consider the data sent from a Web browser displaying an HTML fill-out form. When a user clicks on the Submit button, the client sends (or *posts*) the data to the server. Like GET, this is a heavily used method.

PUT – allows a client to send a resource to the server, updating or creating the resource on the server as needs be. This assumes, of course, that the client is authorized to *write* to the server.

DELETE - allows a client to request that the server remove a specified resource from the server.

TRACE - allows a client to request loopback information for a particular server resource, typically used during testing.

CONNECT - is reserved for use with proxy servers.

In addition to the method, the HTTP request identifies the resource it is interested in. This is typically the path and name of an HTML document, as HTTP was initially designed to support the retrieval and delivery of HTML Web pages. The request concludes with an indication of the version of HTTP being used on the client, together with any required terminating newlines. For example, to retrieve the index.html page from any website, an HTTP client written in Perl would send the following *request string* to a Web server:

```
"GET /index.html HTTP/1.0$CRLF$CRLF"
```

Note that this code identifies itself as a speaker of version 1.0 of HTTP. Note, too, the double newline at the end of the request, as well as the space character separating each part of the request. Within the official HTTP standard document (refer to the *Web Resources* section at the end of this chapter), this request string is referred to as a *Request-Line*.

The response generated by the Web server contains two parts: a header and a body. The header-part is composed of a series of newline-delimited lines of text. The body-part, which comes after the header (and from which it is separated by a blank line), contains the requested resource. Within the HTTP world, resources can be anything, although they are typically an HTML page or graphic file.

Without knowing much more about HTTP, let us write a simple HTTP client using the facilities of Perl's Socket API to interact with any standard Web server.

4.3 The World's Worst Web Browser

The code for the simple HTTP client begins as expected. For convenience, the OO version of Perl's Socket API is used. The code also imports the newline constants from the standard Socket module:

```
#! /usr/bin/perl -w

use strict;
use Socket qw( :DEFAULT :crlf );
use IO::Socket;
```

This client is command-line driven and can take up to three optional parameters: the HTTP request method, the name of the network device running the HTTP server, and the name of the resource. Three lines of code implement this behaviour, with appropriate defaults defined for each parameter:

```
my $http_method = shift || 'GET';
my $http_server = shift || 'localhost';
my $html_page   = shift || '/index.html';
```

Next, the code creates a connected socket object, using TCP and protocol port-number 80 (the well-known TCP port for Web services):

```
my $http_obj = IO::Socket::INET->new( PeerAddr => $http_server,
                                       PeerPort => 80,
                                       Proto    => 'tcp' )
    or die "wwwb: could not create socket object: $!\n";
```

If all is well, the client sends the request to the server using a simple call to the inbuilt print subroutine:

```
print $http_obj "$http_method $html_page HTTP/1.0$CRLF$CRLF";
```

A loop is then entered and, with each iteration, a line is received from the server. Each line's idea of newline is converted to \n prior to the line being written to the client's standard output (most likely the screen). When there are no more lines to be received from the server, the loop terminates, and the socket object is closed. The client then terminates:

```
while ( my $line = <$http_obj> )
{
    $line =~ s/$CR?$LF/\n/;
    print $line;
}
$http_obj->close;
```

And there it is: the world's worst Web browser (wwwb) in just 20 lines of Perl code.

Why 'worst'? Well, as Web browsers go, wwwb is pretty poor. It does not work graphically, so any resource received is displayed as is on the screen – no HTML is rendered, and any embedded graphics are not displayed. It does not allow for the traversal of hypertext links[3]. And it is not exactly user-friendly, requiring the user to specify the HTTP method to use. So wwwb is not going to replace any of the brand-name Web browsers any time soon.

However, what wwwb does allow its users to do is interact with an HTTP server at a lower level than is typically available from within a full-featured Web browser. To get an idea of its capabilities, make wwwb executable and invoke it with the following commands:

```
chmod +x wwwb
./wwwb
```

Note that the parameterless invocation of wwwb is equivalent to this (be warned: the / in front of index.html is *required*):

```
./wwwb GET localhost /index.html
```

---

[3]So we are stretching things somewhat by calling it a browser.

With wwwb installed on `pblinux.itcarlow.ie`, which also has a default installation of the *Apache Web Server* running, the parameterless invocation of wwwb
sends the following (double-newline terminated) request to the server:

```
GET /index.html HTTP/1.0
```

The server responds with the following HTTP response:

```
HTTP/1.1 200 OK
Date: Thu, 19 Apr 2001 16:43:34 GMT
Server: Apache/1.3.19 (Unix)
Content-Location: index.html.en
Vary: negotiate,accept-language,accept-charset
TCN: choice
Last-Modified: Fri, 19 Jan 2001 19:39:47 GMT
ETag: "9e6-51e-3a689803;3adc205d"
Accept-Ranges: bytes
Content-Length: 1310
Connection: close
Content-Type: text/html
Content-Language: en
Expires: Thu, 19 Apr 2001 16:43:34 GMT

<!DOCTYPE HTML PUBLIC "-//W3C//DTD HTML 3.2 Final//EN">
<HTML>
 <HEAD>
  <TITLE>Test Page for Apache Installation</TITLE>
 </HEAD>
<!-- Background white, links blue (unvisited), navy
(visited), red (active) -->
 <BODY BGCOLOR="#FFFFFF" TEXT="#000000" LINK="#0000FF"
  VLINK="#000080" ALINK="#FF0000" >

<p>If you can see this, it means that the installation of
the Apache Web server software on this system was
        .
        .
        .
Web server.  Thanks for using Apache!</p>

<DIV ALIGN="CENTER"><IMG SRC="apache_pb.gif" ALT=""></DIV>

</BODY>
</HTML>
```

Note that (for brevity's sake) not all of the body-part of the HTTP response is
shown here. The body-part is in fact the default HTML test page as supplied with
Apache. The header-part of the response precedes the HTML page. The first line
of the header (response) is the HTTP *Status-Line*:

```
HTTP/1.1 200 OK
```

The *Apache* server is stating that it understands version 1.1 of HTTP, and that the request it is responding to was properly formatted, understood and processed.

After the status line, a collection of name/value pairings appear. The meaning of most of these pairings should be self-explanatory. Among other things, the *Apache* server informs wwwb what time it thinks it is, the version of *Apache* running, the date/time index.html was last modified, the length of the body-part (1310 bytes) and the body-part's type (it is textual, and it is HTML). For an explanation of the other pairings, refer to the HTTP and *Apache* documentation as referenced in the *Web Resources* section at the end of this chapter.

4.3.1 Embedded graphics

The header-part of the response as sent by *Apache* is separated from the body-part by a blank line. Near the bottom of the HTML page, an <IMG> tag includes the 'Powered by Apache' graphic logo, called apache_pb.gif. Note how the initial response from the HTTP server has not sent this embedded graphic, even though it is reasonable to think of the graphic as being *part of the page*. It is the responsibility of the HTTP client to parse the HTML for such graphics tags and send a separate request to the server for each graphic tag found. The client is then required to render the graphic and the HTML page on screen.

As wwwb is the world's worst Web browser, it does not do this for its users, so use the following command-line to tell wwwb to request the delivery of the graphic from the HTTP server:

```
./wwwb GET localhost /apache_pb.gif
```

Apache responds as follows:

```
HTTP/1.1 200 OK
Date: Thu, 19 Apr 2001 16:45:41 GMT
Server: Apache/1.3.19 (Unix)
Last-Modified: Wed, 03 Jul 1996 06:18:15 GMT
ETag: "9df-916-31da10a7"
Accept-Ranges: bytes
Content-Length: 2326
Connection: close
Content-Type: image/gif

GIF89aˆCˆA ˆ@%ˆ@
 .
 .
 .

ZV Cˆ˜A@5ˆ]+ˆPIVo ˜CˆM-5ˆKKUO˜Zo "=ˆH@ˆBˆDˆDˆ@;
```

Again, only a small portion of the body-part is shown here. What is shown looks like garbage, but is, in actual fact, the contents of the GIF file as sent by *Apache*.

Note that the header-part has a different collection of name/value pairings than those associated with the previous HTML page. With this resource, the type of the body-part is identified as an image file conforming to the popular GIF standard.

So, to retrieve a single HTML page containing a single embedded graphic requires two HTTP request/response interactions. Note that each interaction requires the establishment of its own TCP connection from the client network device to the server network device. Even though the HTML page and the graphic are considered to be part of the same page, as far as HTTP is concerned, they are separate resources that must be retrieved separately using separate connections. If the HTML page contains 100 embedded graphics, the HTTP client is required to establish 101 connections with the HTTP server in order to retrieve the entire page. And all those connection establishments and teardowns take time.

That is, of course, if the HTTP client is using version 1.0 of HTTP. If version 1.1 is used instead, the client can take advantage of *persistence*, which allows for a single established connection to retrieve many resources. This, as can be imagined, can have a very positive impact on performance.

4.3.2   A persistent wwwb

In order to use persistence, the client needs to tell the server that it is speaking version 1.1 of HTTP. This is easily accomplished by sending:

```
GET /index.html HTTP/1.1
```

instead of:

```
GET /index.html HTTP/1.0
```

to the server. However, this alone is not enough. Version 1.1 of HTTP is more strict in what it will accept as a valid resource request. To illustrate what happens, a small change to wwwb can be made, so that the request sent to the server now looks like this:

```
print $http_obj "$http_method $html_page HTTP/1.1$CRLF$CRLF";
```

When sent to *Apache*, the following response is returned:

```
HTTP/1.1 400 Bad Request
Date: Tue, 24 Apr 2001 15:11:59 GMT
Server: Apache/1.3.19 (Unix)
Connection: close
Transfer-Encoding: chunked
Content-Type: text/html; charset=iso-8859-1

172
<!DOCTYPE HTML PUBLIC "-//IETF//DTD HTML 2.0//EN">
<HTML><HEAD>
```

```
<TITLE>400 Bad Request</TITLE>
</HEAD><BODY>
<H1>Bad Request</H1>
Your browser sent a request that this server could
not understand.<P>
client sent HTTP/1.1 request without hostname (see
RFC2616 section 14.23): /index.html<P>
<HR>
<ADDRESS>Apache/1.3.19 Server at pblinux. Port 80</ADDRESS>
</BODY></HTML>

0
```

The *Status-Line* informs the client that the request was bad. The body-part of the response contains an HTML page detailing additional information. Note that the name/value pairings in the header-part of the response do not include a Content-Length value. Instead, the header-part identifies the body-part as conforming to the chunked *transfer-encoding*. Here each 'chunk' of information sent from the server is bracketed by two size indicators (in this case 172 and 0). Any number of chunks can be sent, and the last chunk always ends with a size indicator of zero. Obviously, with this response, only one chunk is sent.

The important information is included in the HTML page. *Apache* states that the *client sent HTTP/1.1 request without hostname*, then refers to the relevant section within the standards document. With HTTP (regardless of version), it is possible to send multiple newline separated lines as part of the request. Various pieces of information can be sent, and with HTTP/1.1, it became a requirement to send the Host value. To ensure the client is 1.1 compatible, change the single line request from above to:

```
my $http_request;

$http_request =  "$http_method $html_page HTTP/1.1$CRLF" .
                 "Host: $http_server$CRLF" .
                 "$CRLF";

print $http_obj $http_request;
```

The Host value specifies the name of the HTTP server, which is available to the code in the $http_server scalar. As the request now spans more than one line[4], the code introduces the $http_request scalar to keep things nice and orderly. With this small change, this version of wwwb works as expected.

By default, persistence is *on* when an HTTP/1.1 client and server communicate. To switch off persistence, the Connection: Close line can be included with the request. Otherwise, Connection: Keep-Alive is assumed. These two lines (or *directives*) are the key to using a single connection to request multiple resources.

---

[4]Remember: the '.' in Perl is the concatenation operator.

As long as the `Connection: Close` line is *not* specified, multiple requests can be sent.

Let us assume that a subroutine exists which can take one required parameter and up to four named parameters (which are all optional). This subroutine, called `get_resource`, must specify the HTTP object to send the request to (the required parameter) as well as the following four optional parameters.

METHOD - the HTTP method to use. The default is GET.

RESOURCE - the name of the HTTP resource to request. The default is `/index.html`.

CTYPE - the connection type, either `Close` or `Keep-Alive`. The default is `Close`.

SERVER - the server to specify on the `Host` line. The default is `localhost`.

With such a subroutine available to the code, it is possible to call the subroutine twice, as follows, to request `index.html` and `apache_pb.gif` from the Web server:

```
get_resource( $http_obj, CTYPE => 'Keep-Alive' );
get_resource( $http_obj, RESOURCE => '/apache_pb.gif' );
```

Note how the code explicitly asks for persistence with the first invocation, even though this is HTTP/1.1's default. However, it is not the default for `get_resource`.

Here is a first attempt at the `get_resource` subroutine:

```
sub get_resource {
    my $http_obj = shift;
    my %params = @_;

    my $http_method  = $params{METHOD}   || 'GET';
    my $html_page    = $params{RESOURCE} || '/index.html';
    my $connect_type = $params{CTYPE}    || 'Close';
    my $http_server  = $params{SERVER}   || 'localhost';

    my $http_request = "$http_method $html_page HTTP/1.1$CRLF" .
                       "Host: $http_server$CRLF" .
                       "Connection: $connect_type$CRLF" .
                       "$CRLF";

    print $http_obj $http_request;

    while ( $line = <$http_obj> )
    {
        $line =~ s/$CR?$LF/\n/;
        print $line;
    }
}
```

This code begins by assigning the *required* parameter to the $http_obj scalar. Any other parameters are then assigned to the %params hash. Looking at the above invocations of the get_resource subroutine, and recalling that the => symbol is 'syntactic sugar' for comma in Perl, these invocations send a list of items to the subroutine. The list (@_) is then used to initialize the hash. If the hash values are defined, they are used to initialize four scalars, $http_method, $html_page, $connect_type and $http_server. Note the use of default values for each of these scalars. The HTTP request is then built from the values, and sent to the HTTP server (using a call to print). The rest of the code is as it was from the first version of wwwb.

Unfortunately, this version of get_resource does not work properly. When it is executed, the program successfully receives and displays the file called index.html, then it appears to pause for a number of seconds, before returning to the command-line. The request for the apache_pb.gif resource seems to have somehow disappeared.

What is going on? The problem is that the client code is getting stuck inside the while loop within the get_resource subroutine. The connection type is set to Keep-Alive, so the server is keeping the connection open. However, the client does not know when to stop reading, so it is waiting for something to happen. Eventually, the server times out (after about 15 seconds), closes the connection and then the loop ends. When the client tries to send the next request, it is ignored as the connection is closed.

4.3.3 A better get_resource

What the code needs to do within get_resource is stop reading once the first resource has been received. But how is this done? One technique is to use the Content-Length value from the resource's header-part. The strategy is to determine the Content-Length value while reading the header-part, determine when the header-part ends and the body-part starts, then read the number of bytes indicated by the Content-Length value. Once the body-part is received, the loop can end, and the next request can be processed. Here is a version of get_resource that does this:

```
sub get_resource {
    my $http_obj = shift;
    my %params = @_;

    my $http_method  = $params{METHOD}   || 'GET';
    my $html_page    = $params{RESOURCE} || '/index.html';
    my $connect_type = $params{CTYPE}    || 'Close';
    my $http_server  = $params{SERVER}   || 'localhost';

    my $http_request = "$http_method $html_page HTTP/1.1$CRLF" .
                       "Host: $http_server$CRLF" .
```

```
                              "Connection: $connect_type$CRLF" .
                              "$CRLF";

        print $http_obj $http_request;

        my $body_length = 0;
        my $body_part = "";
        my $line;
        my $in_header = 1;

        while ( $line = <$http_obj> )
        {
            if ( $line =~ /Content-Length: (\d+)/ )
            {
                $body_length = $1;
            }
            if ( $line =~ /^$CRLF$/ )
            {
                $in_header = 0;
            }
            $body_part = $body_part . $line if !$in_header;

            $line =~ s/$CR?$LF/\n/;
            print $line;

            if (!$in_header)
            {
                last if length( $body_part ) >= $body_length;
            }
        }
    }
```

There is a lot of code here, and it relies heavily on Perl's regular-expression technology. After the call to print, which sends the request to the server, four scalars
are declared:

```
my $body_length = 0;
my $body_part = "";
my $line;
my $in_header = 1;
```

The $body_length scalar will hold the determined Content-Length value. The
$body_part will hold the body-part of the resource, which is made up of a collec-
tion of $lines. The $in_header scalar is a Boolean, and is true when the $line
is part of the header, false otherwise. The code to check for the Content-Length
value comes next:

```
if ( $line =~ /Content-Length: (\d+)/ )
{
    $body_length = $1;
}
```

This code checks to see if the $line contains the string 'Content-Length:' followed by a number (\d+). If it does, it remembers the number in $body_length. When the regular-expression engine matches the Content-Length value it places it in the built-in $1 variable.

The code then checks to see if the $line contains only a newline, which is specified by the ^ $CRLF$ regular expression. This states that the pattern begins at the start of a line (^), has a single newline character ($CRLF) which is at the end of a line ($). If this pattern matches, a blank line has been received, which means that the header-part has been received and the body-part is about to arrive. When this happens, the $in_header scalar is set to false, as the header-part has been received.

The next line adds the contents of $line to $body_part if the value of the scalar $in_header is false:

```
$body_part = $body_part . $line if !$in_header;
```

The next two lines convert the protocols idea of newline into the underlying operating systems, then $line is printed out. The subroutine ends by checking to see if the body-part is being processed, and if it is, a check is performed to see if the current length of the $body_part is greater than or equal to the Content-Length value, which is stored in the $body_length scalar. If it is, the inbuilt last subroutine is invoked and the loop ends, allowing the subroutine to end and the next request to be processed, which is the required behaviour:

```
if (!$in_header)
{
    last if length( $body_part ) >= $body_length;
}
```

This version of the world's worst Web browser (wwwb1.1) now behaves as required, and supports persistence. To keep things simple, the code only works with the index.html and apache_pb.gif files as served by *Apache* running on localhost, which means that this 'improved' version of the world's worst Web browser is not *all that* flexible.

The cost of producing this *improved* wwwb has been high. The code is beginning to bloat and will get more complex as additional functionality is added. Note too that the code has no mechanism for dealing with chunked transfer-encoding.

4.4 HTTP Status Codes

Before exploring Perl's HTTP add-on technology, the HTTP *Status-Line* requires further explanation. The lines seen so far have looked like this[5]:

```
HTTP/1.1 200 OK
```

---

[5]The exception was a malformed HTTP/1.1 request sent to the server earlier in this chapter.

The *Status-Line* is made up of three parts as follows.

Version – the *HTTP-Version* understood by the responding server.

Code – the HTTP *Status-Code* returned as a result of the server servicing (or attempting to service) the client's request.

Text – the HTTP *Reason-Phrase* associated with the response code (and designed to be read by a human being, not a machine).

The codes, which are all three digits in length, are categorized by the following number ranges.

100–199 – are *informational* messages. The server is informing the client that the request has been received and some further action is progressing.

200–299 – indicates *success.* The request has been received, the required service has been performed, and the server is sending any results to the client.

300–399 – are *redirection* messages. Further activity on the part of the client is required to complete the request.

400–499 – indicates a *client error.* The server is stating that the client did something wrong and that the request cannot be processed until the client corrects the problem.

500–599 – indicates a *server error.* What would otherwise be considered to be a valid request from a client has resulted in a server error.

Only a handful of codes from each number-range are officially allocated in the HTTP standard. As HTTP/1.1 is designed to be easily extendible, the number-ranges are much larger than they need to be in order to support the addition of codes by extension technologies. Some further invocations of the original wwwb illustrate the use of a selection of these codes.

Here is a request to retrieve the homepage from *Linux Journal* magazine's website:

```
./wwwb GET www.linuxjournal.com
```

which results in this response from the server:

```
HTTP/1.1 302 Found
Date: Thu, 19 Apr 2001 14:58:23 GMT
Server: Apache/1.3.14 (Unix) PHP/4.0.4pl1
        mod_ssl/2.7.1 OpenSSL/0.9.6 AuthMySQL/2.20
Location: http://www3.linuxjournal.com/index.html
Connection: close
Content-Type: text/html; charset=iso-8859-1

<!DOCTYPE HTML PUBLIC "-//IETF//DTD HTML 2.0//EN">
```

```
<HTML><HEAD>
<TITLE>302 Found</TITLE>
</HEAD><BODY>
<H1>Found</H1>
The document has moved
<A HREF="http://www3.linuxjournal.com/index.html">here</A>.<P>
<HR>
<ADDRESS>Apache/1.3.14 Server at linuxjournal.com Port 80</ADDRESS>
</BODY></HTML>
```

A 302 code is sent from the server, informing the client that the requested resource (`index.html`) is temporarily available at some other location. The 'other location' is identified by the value associated with the `Location` header-line. The client should react to this *Status-Line* by retrieving the resource from the identified temporary location.

For those clients that are incapable of doing this[6], the *Linux Journal* Web server (in this case, a relatively recent version of *Apache*) sends a small page of HTML as part of the response.

This next request will attempt to delete the `index.html` resource from the website maintained by *University College Dublin* in Ireland:

```
./wwwb DELETE www.ucd.ie
```

The network administrator at UCD will be pleased to see that wwwb, as an ordinary Web browser with no special privileges, is unable to succeed with this request. Here is the response:

```
HTTP/1.1 405 Method Not Allowed
Date: Mon, 16 Apr 2001 16:12:45 GMT
Server: Apache/1.2.4
Allow: GET, HEAD, OPTIONS, TRACE
Connection: close
Content-Type: text/html

<HTML><HEAD>
<TITLE>405 Method Not Allowed</TITLE>
</HEAD><BODY>
<H1>Method Not Allowed</H1>
The requested method DELETE is not allowed for
the URL /index.html.<P>
</BODY></HTML>
```

Note how the server at UCD (running an old version of *Apache*) indicates with the `Allow` header-line which HTTP methods are allowed.

Even though wwwb is the world's worst Web browser, it can still request the execution of server-side programs, such as Common Gateway Interface (CGI) scripts.

---

[6]The wwwb client falls squarely into this category.

Here is an example invocation of wwwb that requests that the server execute the printenv script (which is usually shipped with *Apache*):

```
./wwwb GET pblinux.itcarlow.ie /cgi-bin/printenv
```

The code to printenv is very straightforward. It iterates through the environment variables available to the script and prints them to standard output. Conveniently, these variables are stored (within Perl) inside the built-in %ENV hash:

```
print "Content-type: text/plain\n\n";

foreach $var (sort(keys(%ENV)))
{
    $val = $ENV{$var};
    $val =~ s|\n|\\n|g;
    $val =~ s|"|\\"|g;

    print "${var}=\"${val}\"\n";
}
```

The above request was sent to pblinux.itcarlow.ie, which has *Apache* installed and operational. Here are the results returned by the above request:

```
HTTP/1.1 200 OK
Date: Sat, 19 May 2001 17:14:22 GMT
Server: Apache/1.3.19 (Unix)
Connection: close
Content-Type: text/plain

DOCUMENT_ROOT="/usr/local/apache/htdocs"
GATEWAY_INTERFACE="CGI/1.1"
PATH="/usr/local/sbin:/usr/sbin:/sbin:/usr/local/sbin:
        /usr/local/bin:/sbin:/bin:/usr/sbin:/usr/bin:
        /usr/X11R6/bin:/root/bin"
QUERY_STRING=""
REMOTE_ADDR="149.153.100.66"
REMOTE_PORT="1031"
REQUEST_METHOD="GET"
REQUEST_URI="/cgi-bin/printenv"
SCRIPT_FILENAME="/usr/local/apache/cgi-bin/printenv"
SCRIPT_NAME="/cgi-bin/printenv"
SERVER_ADDR="149.153.100.66"
SERVER_ADMIN="paul.barryp@itcarlow.ie"
SERVER_NAME="pblinux.itcarlow.ie"
SERVER_PORT="80"
SERVER_PROTOCOL="HTTP/1.0"
SERVER_SIGNATURE="<ADDRESS>Apache/1.3.19 Server at
        pblinux.itcarlow.ie Port 80</ADDRESS>\n"
SERVER_SOFTWARE="Apache/1.3.19 (Unix)"
```

The *Status-Line* reports code 200, so the servicing of this request was a success.

In order to force the server into generating an error, the first line of code from `printenv` is removed from the file, and `printenv` is renamed `broken`. Here is the call to `broken`:

```
./wwwb GET pblinux.itcarlow.ie /cgi-bin/broken
```

This CGI script will cause the server problems due to the missing line of code. Here is the response from the server:

```
HTTP/1.1 500 Internal Server Error
Date: Sat, 19 May 2001 17:17:55 GMT
Server: Apache/1.3.19 (Unix)
Connection: close
Content-Type: text/html; charset=iso-8859-1

<!DOCTYPE HTML PUBLIC "-//IETF//DTD HTML 2.0//EN">
<HTML><HEAD>
<TITLE>500 Internal Server Error</TITLE>
</HEAD><BODY>
<H1>Internal Server Error</H1>
The server encountered an internal error or
misconfiguration and was unable to complete
your request.<P>
Please contact the server administrator,
paul.barryp@itcarlow.ie and inform them of the time
the error occurred, and anything you might have done
that may have caused the error.<P>
More information about this error may be available
in the server error log.<P>
<HR>
<ADDRESS>Apache/1.3.19 Server at pblinux.itcarlow.ie
Port 80</ADDRESS>
</BODY></HTML>
```

The server did not know what to do with the results returned from the `broken` CGI script, and this caused an internal error. The client is told this in no uncertain terms by the 500 code on the *Status-Line*.

It would be nice if `wwwb` handled these status codes in a more meaningful way. Adding the code to do so is not difficult, but it is a chore. And it has definitely been done before. It is time to turn to the Perl programming community for help.

4.5   It's the Gisle and Graham Show!

Of all the networking add-on modules available for Perl, two stand out when it comes to programming standard Internet protocols. They are `libwww-perl` (also known as LWP) and `libnet`. The `libwww-perl` module *primarily* supports the programming of clients using HTTP and related protocols. The `libnet` module supports client programming of the popular non-HTTP protocols. Both modules operate at a higher-level of abstraction than the code seen so far in this chapter, building on the standard IO::Socket::INET module included with the Perl distribution.

Of all the programmers active within the Perl community, two stand out when it comes to programming standard Internet protocols. They are Gisle Aas, the principal author of libwww-perl[7], and Graham Barr, the author of libnet[8]. In fact, both Gisle and Graham are highly active contributors to Perl as a whole.

In the sections which follow, these libraries are introduced. To begin, the facilities of libwww-perl are used to rewrite the world's worst Web browser.

Of course, before working with these modules, it is necessary to install each of them into Perl.

4.5.1 Getting libwww-perl and libnet

The libwww-perl and libnet libraries are available on CPAN (see the *Web Resources* section at the end of this chapter), from where they can be downloaded. The libwww-perl library has a number of prerequisites, one of which is (rather conveniently) libnet. A list of files to download from CPAN to satisfy all of the dependencies follows[9].

MIME-Base64-2.12.tar.gz - provides support for encoding and decoding 'base64 strings', used on the Internet when transmitting arbitrary data formats.

URI-1.12.tar.gz - supports manipulating Uniform Resource Identifiers, used on the Internet to name arbitrary resources.

Digest-MD5-2.13.tar.gz - provides support for using the MD5 Message Digest as defined by *RSA Data Security, Inc.*

HTML-Parser-3.23.tar.gz - supports working with documents which have been marked-up with HTML formatting tags.

These modules can be installed using the standard installation process that was first seen in Chapter 2. Assuming a fictitious module called PJB-3.01.tar.gz, use these commands at a Linux prompt to unpack, install and test release 3.01 of the PJB module:

```
gunzip PJB-3.01.tar.gz
tar xvf PJB-3.01.tar
```

---

[7]Many fine programmers also contribute to this effort.

[8]And the author of the IO::Socket::* modules which are now a standard part of Perl.

[9]Note that by the time of publication some of these modules will have been updated, so the version numbers may not match exactly with those of the modules you download. However, they should be *at least* the versions shown here.

```
cd PJB-3.01
perl Makefile.PL
make
make test
su
make install
<ctrl-D>
man PJB
perl -e 'use PJB'
```

Recall the requirement to issue the `make install` command with superuser privilege.

To install the set of modules required for this chapter, work through the list of prerequisites in the order shown and replace PJB-3.01 with the name and version number of each of the modules. Some of the modules will require some user input during the installation phase. Remember to refer to any README and INSTALL files within each module's distribution directory if necessary.

In order to complete the installation, you will need to download and install `libnet-1.09.tar.gz` and `libwww-perl-5.53_94.tar.gz`.

4.6   The Library for WWW Access in Perl

Although primarily known for its Web technology, the `libwww-perl` add-on technology to Perl is a collection of related modules that provides support for programming Internet protocols. The protocols supported are as follows.

HTTP – version 1.0 of the HTTP standard. The supplied functionality is implemented in the `LWP::Protocol::http` module. A new version of `libwww-perl` called LWPng is under development and will (when released) provide full support for the HTTP/1.1 protocol.

HTTPS – the secure version of HTTP as developed by *Netscape Communications* and incorporating the Secure Sockets Layer (SSL) protocol. Implemented in the `LWP::Protocol::https` module.

GOPHER – a precursor to the web, Gopher provides retrieval of information from 'Gopher Servers' by navigating simple menu systems. This functionality is implemented in the `LWP::Protocol::gopher` module.

FTP – the venerable File Transfer Protocol, used to relocate files from one network-connected device to another, and implemented in the `LWP::Protocol::ftp` module.

NNTP – the Network News Transfer Protocol, which powers the Internet-wide, distributed discussion forum known as *Usenet*. Implemented in the `LWP::Protocol::nntp` module.

In addition, `libwww-perl` provides two other services as follows.

FILE - provides a means to work with files on a local file system within a `libwww-perl` context, and implemented in the `LWP::Protocol::file` module.

MAILTO - provides a simple method of sending Internet email. Implemented in the `LWP::Protocol::mailto` module.

4.6.1   The `libwww-perl` classes

The `libwww-perl` library is entirely object oriented, and the application programmer interface (API) reflects this[10]. A hierarchy of classes (or modules) exist within `libwww-perl`, and these provide support for working with the library's Internet protocols.

There is a lot to `libwww-perl`, and each library component includes excellent online documentation (installed as Linux manual pages). In addition, two additional manual pages are included to help programmers get started with the library. They are as follows.

LWP - the main `libwww-perl` manual page, which contains an overview of the library and the functionality provided.

lwpcook - a selection of 'cookbook recipes' which provide common solutions to common requirements.

Of all the classes (or submodules) provided, those that deal with HTTP requests and responses are of most interest. As expected, `libwww-perl` provides a class to work with requests, and another to work with responses:

HTTP::Request - is used to construct a *request object* which is then sent to a server running any of the above `libwww-perl`-supported protocols;

HTTP::Response - is created as a result of a request object being processed by a server.

To enable interaction with these classes, `libwww-perl` supplies another class, `LWP::UserAgent`, which provides a layer between the application and the network service being programmed. To see how this works, let us rebuild wwwb to use `libwww-perl`.

4.7   The LWPwwwb Program

Here is the entire code to the world's worst Web browser (LWPwwwb), rewritten to use `libwww-perl`:

---

[10]That was a *tiny* white lie. Included with the library is a module called `LWP::Simple` which provides a procedural interface to common `libwww-perl` functionality. Although useful, `LWP::Simple` is not discussed in *Programming the Network with Perl*.

```perl
#! /usr/bin/perl -w

use strict;
use LWP::UserAgent;

my $http_method = shift || 'GET';
my $http_server = shift || 'localhost';
my $html_page   = shift || '/index.html';
my $http_port   = shift || 80;

my $wwwb_useragent = new LWP::UserAgent;

my $wwwb_url = 'http://' . $http_server . ':'
                         . $http_port . $html_page;

my $wwwb_request = new HTTP::Request $http_method => $wwwb_url;

my $wwwb_response = $wwwb_useragent->request( $wwwb_request );

print $wwwb_response->as_string;
```

Let us go through the code in detail. It starts with the usual first line, followed by the inclusion of two modules, strict and LWP::UserAgent. Although this program works with the HTTP::Request and HTTP::Response modules, there is no requirement to specify their use. The fact that LWP::UserAgent is explicitly specified brings in the other classes. Remember: the LWP::UserAgent acts as a layer between the application and the network service being programmed.

The LWPwwwb program can take up to four parameters at the command-line, and these are assigned to four scalars if supplied, or set to default values if not. Note that unlike wwwb, this version of the world's worst Web browser provides a mechanism to specify the protocol port to establish a connection with. The default value for this scalar is 80, the well-known port for Web services. As will be seen in a later section, Web services often operate on a protocol port-number other than 80, and LWPwwwb supports this behaviour.

The next line of code creates a user-agent object, and assigns it to a scalar called $wwwb_useragent:

```perl
my $wwwb_useragent = new LWP::UserAgent;
```

Note the use of the object-oriented syntax for constructing an object of type LWP::UserAgent. Although this looks a little strange, it is nothing more than a call to the subroutine called new included with the LWP::UserAgent class. The invocation of new results in the production of a LWP::UserAgent object, which is then assigned to the $wwwb_useragent scalar. In Perl, objects are stored in scalars and are a special type of reference.

   The URL for the resource is constructed from three of the four scalar values initialized at the start of the program:

```
my $wwwb_url = 'http://' . $http_server . ':'
                          . $http_port . $html_page;
```

With the URL created, an HTTP::Request object is then created:

```
my $wwwb_request = new HTTP::Request $http_method => $wwwb_url;
```

Again, a call to a subroutine called new results in the production of another object, this time of type HTTP::Request. The call to this new takes a named parameter, which is identified by the $http_method scalar (which has a default value of 'GET') and is set to the previously constructed URL, stored in the $wwwb_url scalar. The created object is assigned to the $wwwb_request scalar.

   Now that an HTTP::Request object exists, it can be used with an LWP:: UserAgent object to do something useful:

```
my $wwwb_response = $wwwb_useragent->request( $wwwb_request );
```

The request method associated with the $wwwb_useragent object is invoked. This subroutine sends the request contained in the $wwwb_request object to the server. A response from the server is returned to the program and libwww-perl uses the response to construct an HTTP::Response object, which is assigned to the $wwwb_response scalar. The final line of code prints the contents of the response to the screen in a format that mimics the original wwwb program:

```
print $wwwb_response->as_string;
```

The as_string subroutine (from the HTTP::Response class) prints both the header-part and body-part of the response, which is what the world's worst Web browser does. Use this line of code when the header-part is all that is required:

```
print $wwwb_response->headers_as_string;
```

If only the body-part is of interest, use this line:

```
print $wwwb_response->content;
```

Here is the abridged output generated by LWPwwwb when invoked with no parameters from the Linux command-line:

```
HTTP/1.1 200 OK
Connection: close
Date: Tue, 22 May 2001 16:16:05 GMT
Accept-Ranges: bytes
Server: Apache/1.3.19 (Unix)
Vary: negotiate,accept-language,accept-charset
Content-Language: en
Content-Length: 1310
```

```
Content-Location: index.html.en
Content-Type: text/html
ETag: "848e6-51e-3a689803;3b03acc7"
Expires: Tue, 22 May 2001 16:16:05 GMT
Last-Modified: Fri, 19 Jan 2001 19:39:47 GMT
Client-Date: Tue, 22 May 2001 16:16:05 GMT
Client-Peer: 127.0.0.1:80
TCN: choice
Title: Test Page for Apache Installation

<!DOCTYPE HTML PUBLIC "-//W3C//DTD HTML 3.2 Final//EN">
<HTML>
 <HEAD>
  <TITLE>Test Page for Apache Installation</TITLE>
     .
     .
     .


 <p>You are free to use the image below on an
Apache-powered Web server.  Thanks for using Apache!</p>

<DIV ALIGN="CENTER"><IMG SRC="apache_pb.gif" ALT=""></DIV>

</BODY>
</HTML>
```

Referring back to the output generated by the original wwwb, LWPwwwb's header-part differs slightly.

This has to do with the fact that programs based on libwww-perl provide more information to servers by default, and this results in the server providing a slightly different header-part response. The HTTP::Response class also post-processes the received response and adds some metadata to the header-part. As the header-part is typically only of interest to programmers debugging web-based applications, this particular *strangeness* is not something to worry about.

4.8 Doing More with LWPwwwb

The world's worst Web browser remains the worst due to its inability to intelligently process the response returned from the server (other than printing it to the screen). To spice things up a little, let us extend LWPwwwb to post-process the response received from the server. Specifically, code will be added to parse any HTML received and extract hyperlinks and any associated textual description. To do this, LWPwwwb will take advantage of the facilities provided by the HTML::Parser module, which was one of the modules installed as a result of satisfying libwww-perl's dependencies.

4.8.1   Parsing HTML

The HTML::Parser module provides a framework within which documents written in HTML can be parsed by a Perl program. Although complex, the module is very powerful, and its authors[11] have gone to great pains to ensure it can work with the vast majority of HTML documents. The module itself is *event driven*. By associating certain actions with certain occurrences (or *events*), a program can arrange for specific processing to occur at specific points within an HTML document. For example, a requirement might exist to print a message to the screen when an anchor tag (<A>) is encountered. These event processors are known as *handlers* and are nothing more than programmer-defined subroutines. The HTML::Parser module provides a mechanism to associate subroutines with events, then arranges to call the correct subroutine when the event occurs.

Rather than describe the HTML::Parser module in detail, let us look at a new version of LWPwwwb which incorporates code to identify hyperlinks and any associated textual description within a received HTML resource. This version of the world's worst Web browser is called parsewwwb.

The code starts as with LWPwwwb, but for the fact that the use of HTML::Parser is specified:

```
#! /usr/bin/perl -w

use strict;
use LWP::UserAgent;
use HTML::Parser;
```

Next comes the definition of three subroutines (or *event handlers*, to use the language of HTML::Parser). The first, print_dtext, is invoked whenever the parser encounters some descriptive text associated with an HTML hyperlink. The subroutine receives two parameters: a reference to a parser object and any descriptive text. The text is simply printed to the screen with a short descriptive tag. Just how the handler is set up will become clear in just a moment:

```
sub print_dtext {
    my ( $parser, $text ) = @_;

    print "text -> ", $text, "\n\n";
}
```

The next event handler, called end, is invoked whenever an end-tag is encountered (for example, the </A> end-tag). The parsewwwb program is not interested in what the end-tag actually is, only that the default text and end handlers are *undefined* when an end-tag is encountered. This code stops the text and end event handlers from *over firing*. To see what is meant by this, comment out the

---

[11]Gisle Aas and Michael A. Chase.

two `$parser->handler` lines from this subroutine and compare the resulting output with that generated by this *correct* version of the subroutine:

```perl
sub end {
    my ( $parser ) = @_;

    $parser->handler( text => undef );
    $parser->handler( end  => undef );
}
```

The code to set up `print_dtext` and `end` occurs within the next event handler, called `print_link`.

Here is the code:

```perl
sub print_link {
    my ( $parser, $tag, $attr ) = @_;

    if ( $tag eq 'a' )
    {
        print "link -> ", $attr->{href}, "\n";

        $parser->handler( text => \&print_dtext, 'self,dtext' );
        $parser->handler( end  => \&end, 'self' );
    }
}
```

This subroutine is called for every hyperlink embedded in the retrieved HTML resource. It is invoked with three parameters: a reference to a parser object, an HTML tag and a hash reference to any attributes associated with the HTML tag. If the HTML tag is an anchor tag (i.e. <A>), the code prints the hyperlink stored in the `$attr->{href}` hash entry. The code then calls the `handler` method associated with the `$parser` object to ensure the `print_dtext` subroutine is invoked for any associated descriptive text, and the `end` subroutine for the encountered end-tag. In other words, this code tells the parser to react to these events when they occur by calling the named subroutines.

With the event handlers defined, the program begins with eight lines of code that are identical to those used in the LWPwwwb program. The facilities of `libwww-perl` are used to send a request to a remote HTTP server and receive a response:

```perl
my $http_method = shift || 'GET';
my $http_server = shift || 'localhost';
my $html_page   = shift || '/index.html';
my $http_port   = shift || 80;

my $wwwb_useragent = new LWP::UserAgent;
my $wwwb_url = 'http://' . $http_server . ':'
                        . $http_port . $html_page;
my $wwwb_request = new HTTP::Request $http_method => $wwwb_url;
my $wwwb_response = $wwwb_useragent->request( $wwwb_request );
```

An HTML::Parser object is created, and a reference to the object is stored in the $parser scalar:

```
my $parser = HTML::Parser->new( api_version => 3 );
```

Note that the code requests version 3 of the HTML::Parser API. This is significant. Version 3 of the HTML::Parser API works as described in this section: event handlers are registered with the parser to react to events as they occur. The other version of the API, version 2, works differently[12]. With version 2, the programmer inherits from HTML::Parser and extends its functionality to do the parsing. This tends to be a bit more involved than the version 3 API, and, as such, is somewhat deprecated at this stage.

After displaying a brief message on screen, the code to parsewwwb continues with a call to the handler method associated with the $parser object to invoke the print_link subroutine whenever the parser encounters the start of an HTML tag. Note that a reference to the parser object (self), the tag encountered (tagname) and a hash reference containing the tag attributes (attr) are sent as parameters to the print_link subroutine whenever it is called by the parser:

```
print "Parsing $http_server$html_page on port: $http_port:\n\n";

$parser->handler( start => \&print_link, 'self,tagname,attr' );
```

With the event handlers set up, the code starts the parser on its way by calling its parse method. Passed as a single parameter is the HTTP response object retrieved earlier, and stored in the $wwwb_response scalar. The HTTP response is sent to the parser as a string, which is the entire HTTP response in textual form. The parser takes the content of the response (HTML) and works its way through it, calling print_link for each start tag encountered. When the parser is done, the code calls the parser's eof method to shut down the parser in an orderly manner, and the program ends:

```
$parser->parse( $wwwb_response->content );
$parser->eof;

print "\nDone.\n";
```

4.8.2 Some parsewwwb examples

To see parsewwwb in action, let us use it against a small selection of Web servers. First up, the *Linux Journal* magazine homepage. This Linux command-line:

```
./parsewwwb GET www.linuxjournal.com
```

produces the following output:

---

[12]It is not clear from the HTML::Parser documentation what happened to version 1 of the API.

```
Parsing www.linuxjournal.com/index.html on port: 80:

link -> http://noframes.linuxjournal.com
text -> http://noframes.linuxjournal.com

Done.
```

With all due respect to the good folk at *Linux Journal*, there is nothing too exciting here, other than a single link to a 'no frames' version of their website. Both the link and the descriptive text are identical.

Another 'not too exciting' website[13] belongs to *The Institute of Technology, Carlow* (IT Carlow). Here is the command-line to use:

```
./parsewwwb GET www.itcarlow.ie
```

which results in the following output:

```
Parsing www.itcarlow.ie/index.html on port: 80:

link -> indexRoll.html
link -> index2.html
link -> http://u.extreme-dm.com/?login=itcarlow
text ->

Done.
```

Note the absence of any associated textual description with this Web page's hyperlinks. This is due to the fact that these links are in fact graphic links which have no text associated with them. The third link is of some interest, as no graphic link appears on screen when IT Carlow's homepage is viewed within a standard Web browser. A quick visit to the `http://u.extreme-dm.com` website confirms that this website is used to track visits to sites on the Internet. It is reasonable to assume that IT Carlow is interested in tracking visitors to its website and is using the services of the `http://u.extreme-dm.com` website to do this.

The default *Apache* welcome page (when running on `localhost`) can be parsed with this command-line:

```
./parsewwwb
```

which produces this list of links and descriptive text:

```
Parsing localhost/index.html on port: 80:

link -> manual/
text -> documentation

Done.
```

---

[13]From the perspective of the `parsewwwb` program, that is.

As a follow-on, the *Apache* manual can be parsed with this command-line:

```
./parsewwwb GET pblinux.itcarlow.ie /manual/index.html
```

which produces a long list of links and descriptive text. Here is a small sample of the output:

```
Parsing pblinux.itcarlow.ie/manual/index.html on port: 80:

link -> misc/FAQ.html
text -> FAQ

link -> mod/directives.html
text -> Directives

link -> mod/
text -> Modules

link -> http://www.apache.org/search.html
text -> Search

link -> new_features_1_3.html
text -> New Features in Version 1.3

        .
        .
        .

link -> misc/FAQ.html
text -> Frequently Asked Questions

link -> misc/tutorials.html
text -> Tutorials

link -> misc/
text -> Other Notes

link -> http://httpd.apache.org/docs-project/
text -> Apache HTTP Server Documentation Project

Done.
```

4.8.3 The HTML::Parser examples

The HTML::Parser distribution includes a small set of example programs which are worth studying. These can be found in the eg directory. A brief description of each example program follows.

hanchors – another implementation to the parsing code from the parsewwwb program. Given a file containing HTML, this program displays any hyperlinks and associated textual description.

hrefsub – provides a means of changing every hyperlink within a supplied HTML document. This small program makes good use of Perl's regular-expression technology.

hstrip – provides a mechanism to remove any unwanted tags and attributes from an HTML document.

htext – takes an HTML document and extracts all of the plain text contained therein.

htextsub – provides a means of changing plain text within a supplied HTML document.

htitle – a small program that prints out the title of any supplied HTML document.

4.9   Building a Custom Web Server

The libwww-perl technology is primarily known as a client-side programming library. Despite this, the distribution includes a fully functioning HTTP server module, called HTTP::Daemon, which conforms to RFC 2068, the penultimate official release of the HTTP/1.1 standard document. The HTTP::Daemon module can be put to a number of uses, such as creating a simple, stand-alone HTTP server or embedding an HTTP server in another application[14].

The simplehttpd program is a simple, stand-alone HTTP server written to take advantage of the functionality provided by HTTP::Daemon. This server – the code to which is loosely based on the sample code from the HTTP::Daemon manual page – only supports the GET method.

4.9.1   The custom Web server source code

Before working through the code in detail, here is the entire source:

```
#! /usr/bin/perl -w

use strict;

use POSIX ":sys_wait_h";
```

---

[14]An excellent example of a commercial product that uses this technique is the *InterMapper* network management software. See the *Web Resources* section at the end of this chapter for more information on *InterMapper*.

```perl
use HTTP::Daemon;
use HTTP::Status;

use constant HTML_DEFAULT_PAGE => "index.html";

sub zombie_reaper {
    while ( waitpid( -1, WNOHANG ) > 0 )
    { }
    $SIG{CHLD} = \&zombie_reaper;
}
$SIG{CHLD} = \&zombie_reaper;

sub continue_as_child {
    my $http_client = shift;

    while ( my $service = $http_client->get_request )
    {
        my $request = $service->uri->path;

        print $service->method, ": ", $request, " -> ";

        if ( $service->method eq 'GET' )
        {
            my $resource;

            if ( $request eq "/" )
            {
                $resource = HTML_DEFAULT_PAGE;
            }
            else
            {
                $request =~ m{^[./]*(.*)};
                $resource = $1;
            }
            print $resource, " -> ";
            if ( -e $resource )
            {
                $http_client->send_file_response( $resource );
                print "OK.";
            }
            else
            {
                $http_client->send_error( RC_NOT_FOUND );
                print "NOT FOUND.";
            }
        }
        else
        {
            $http_client->send_error( RC_METHOD_NOT_ALLOWED );
            print "NOT OK.";
        }
```

```
            print " Remote addr: ", $http_client->peerhost, "\n";
    }
}

my $tcp_port = shift || 8080;

my $httpd = HTTP::Daemon->new( LocalPort => $tcp_port,
                               Reuse     => 1 )
    || die "simplehttpd: could not create HTTP daemon.\n";

print "\nListening for clients at: ", $httpd->url, "\n\n";

while ( my $http_client = $httpd->accept )
{
    my $child_pid = fork;

    if ( $child_pid )
    {
        next;
    }
    elsif ( defined( $child_pid ) )
    {
        continue_as_child( $http_client );
        exit;
    }
    else
    {
        print "simplehttpd: fork failed: $!\n";
    }
}
continue
{
    $http_client->close;
    undef( $http_client );
}
```

This program begins with the usual collection of statements. After specifying strictness, the code specifies its intention to use the services of a collection of modules: POSIX (required as this server is of the *forking* kind), HTTP::Daemon and HTTP::Status. The latter module provides for the processing of HTTP status codes:

```
#! /usr/bin/perl -w

use strict;

use POSIX ":sys_wait_h";

use HTTP::Daemon;
use HTTP::Status;
```

This server retrieves and returns a file called index.html if none is specified by the HTTP request. A simple constant definition supports this behaviour:

```
use constant HTML_DEFAULT_PAGE => "index.html";
```

As simplehttpd will support concurrency by forking clones of itself to deal with each client connection, the usual zombie-reaping code is required to ensure the parent process cleans up after itself:

```
sub zombie_reaper {
while ( waitpid( -1, WNOHANG ) > 0 )
{ }
$SIG{CHLD} = \&zombie_reaper;
}
$SIG{CHLD} = \&zombie_reaper;
```

Next comes the code executed by the child process after a successful call to fork. The continue_as_child subroutine starts by placing its single parameter, a reference to an object of type HTTP::Daemon::ClientConn, into the $http_client scalar. The code then loops on a call to this object's get_request method, which creates an HTTP::Request object on the server with each iteration. A reference to the request is stored in the $service scalar, which is then used to initialize the $request scalar. A check is then performed to see if the HTTP request uses the GET method:

```
sub continue_as_child {
    my $http_client = shift;

    while ( my $service = $http_client->get_request )
    {
        my $request = $service->uri->path;

        print $service->method, ": ", $request, " -> ";

        if ( $service->method eq 'GET' )
        {
```

Prior to servicing the request, simplehttpd pre-processes it. If the HTTP request attempts to access root, the server sets the value of the $resource scalar to index.html. Otherwise, the HTTP request is stripped of any leading dots and slashes and is assigned to $resource prior to processing:

```
            my $resource;

            if ( $request eq "/" )
            {
                $resource = HTML_DEFAULT_PAGE;
            }
            else
```

```
    {
        $request =~ m{^[./]*(.*)};
        $resource = $1;
    }
    print $resource, " -> ";
```

The code to strip leading dots and slashes from the request URL requires further explanation.

The stripping is accomplished by the strange looking regular-expression pattern-matching code in the `else` part of the conditional statement. The pattern to match is delimited by the `m{` and `}` tokens. The pattern starts matching at the beginning of the line (`^`), and matches zero or more leading dots and slashes (`[./]*`). If a match is made, the rest of the line (`(.*)`) is remembered by the regular expression engine and placed (by Perl) into the `$1` scalar, which then gets assigned to `$resource`.

The reason for this code becomes clear when it is considered that the HTTP server retrieves a resource (most likely a disk-file) from its local storage and returns it to the connected Web client. If a client was to send /etc/passwd as the requested URL, it is inappropriate for the HTTP server to locate the password file from its local storage and send it to the client. So, `simplehttpd` attempts to sanitize the request by removing leading dots and slashes from the request. If the request is for /etc/passwd, ../../../etc/passwd, ////etc/passwd or ../etc/passwd, the pattern matching code sanitizes the request to etc/passwd, which forces the server to look for the file relative to the directory the program is running from. Although not foolproof, this should thwart most crackers.

The code then checks to see if the sanitized resource actually exists as a disk-file on its local storage. If it does, the `send_file_response` method associated with the `$http_client` object is sent the value of `$resource` and this has the effect of retrieving the disk-file and sending it to the Web client as an HTTP response. If the disk-file does not exist, the code uses the `send_error` method to send the appropriate HTTP status code to the client:

```
    if ( -e $resource )
    {
        $http_client->send_file_response( $resource );
        print "OK.";
    }
    else
    {
        $http_client->send_error( RC_NOT_FOUND );
        print "NOT FOUND.";
    }
```

The `continue_as_child` subroutine concludes with code that executes if the HTTP request method is something other than GET:

```
        }
        else
        {
            $http_client->send_error( RC_METHOD_NOT_ALLOWED );
            print "NOT OK.";
        }
        print " Remote addr: ", $http_client->peerhost, "\n";
    }
}
```

Throughout this subroutine, the inbuilt `print` subroutine is used to incrementally display a descriptive message to the server's screen as a result of `simplehttpd` servicing HTTP requests.

The code to `simplehttpd` proper then starts by assigning a protocol port-number to the `$tcp_port` scalar. If the `simplehttpd` program was invoked with a numeric command-line argument, the value is used to initialize the scalar. Otherwise the protocol port-number if set to 8080, a common alternative (but not well-known) protocol port-number for Web services. Note that a program that attempts to bind to a well-known port-number can only do so if operating with superuser privilege[15]:

```
    my $tcp_port = shift || 8080;
```

The `HTTP::Daemon` class is a subclass of the standard `IO::Socket::INET` class, and is constructed in the familiar way, assigning the resulting socket object to a scalar called `$httpd`:

```
    my $httpd = HTTP::Daemon->new( LocalPort => $tcp_port,
                                   Reuse      => 1 )
        || die "simplehttpd: could not create HTTP daemon.\n";

    print "\nListening for clients at: ", $httpd->url, "\n\n";
```

There is nothing exceptional about the rest of the code, as `simplehttpd` conforms to the standard *forking server model* from the previous chapter. A call is made to the `accept` method associated with the `HTTP::Daemon` object, resulting in the creation of an object of type `HTTP::Daemon::ClientConn`. The code then forks, with the child process invoking `continue_as_child` and the parent process starting another loop iteration by calling `next`. The code runs forever, or until killed by the operating system:

```
    while ( my $http_client = $httpd->accept )
    {
        my $child_pid = fork;
```

---

[15]On Linux and UNIX-like systems, that is. The same restriction does not apply to other popular PC-based operating systems.

```
        if ( $child_pid )
        {
            next;
        }
        elsif ( defined( $child_pid ) )
        {
            continue_as_child( $http_client );
            exit;
        }
        else
        {
            print "simplehttpd: fork failed: $!\n";
        }
    }
    continue
    {
        $http_client->close;
        undef( $http_client );
    }
```

4.9.2   The custom Web server in action

The `simplehttpd` Web server can be started from the command-line as follows:

```
./simplehttpd
```

An optional numeric argument can be provided on the command-line when a requirement exists to operate at a protocol port-number other than the default of 8080. A message will appear on screen similar to the following:

```
Listening for clients at: http://pblinux.itcarlow.ie:8080/
```

For each connection on protocol port-number 8080, the server displays a status line. Here is some sample output:

```
GET: /index.html -> index.html -> OK. Remote addr: 149.153.100.104
GET: /simplehttpd -> simplehttpd -> OK. Remote addr: 149.153.100.65
GET: /etc/passwd -> etc/passwd -> NOT FOUND. Remote addr: 149.153.1.5
POST: /test.html -> NOT OK. Remote addr: 149.153.100.23
GET: /test.html -> test.html -> OK. Remote addr: 149.153.100.23
```

The status line identifies the HTTP method requested, the request URL together with its sanitized equivalent, the request result (OK, NOT OK, etc.) and the IP address of the remote Web client. With the `simplehttpd` server running, any browser (even the world's worst) can be used to interact with it. Here is how to request the server's `index.html` file using the LWPwwwb program:

```
./LWPwwwb GET pblinux.itcarlow.ie /index.html 8080
```

And here is the output displayed by LWPwwwb:

```
HTTP/1.1 200 OK
Date: Tue, 29 May 2001 19:41:37 GMT
Server: libwww-perl-daemon/1.24
Content-Length: 590
Content-Type: text/html
Last-Modified: Tue, 29 May 2001 05:34:04 GMT
Client-Date: Tue, 29 May 2001 19:41:37 GMT
Client-Peer: 149.153.100.66:8080
Title: This is the simplehttpd server

<HTML>
  <HEAD>
    <TITLE>This is the simplehttpd server</TITLE>
  </HEAD>

  <BODY>
    <H1>Welcome</H1>
    This is the <B>simplehttpd</B> test page.
    Not too exciting, but it does the job.
    <H2>More Information</H2>
    To find out more about <B>simplehttpd</B>,
    check out a great book
    <A HREF="http://glasnost.itcarlow.ie/~pnb/index.html">
    at this location</A>.  <BR>You can email the author at this
    <A HREF="mailto:paul.barry@itcarlow.ie">email address</A>.
    <P>There's nothing quite like a little bit
    of self-promotion.  :-) </P>
  </BODY>
</HTML>
```

The header-part of the response identifies the server as libwww-perl-daemon/ 1.24, and not simplehttpd. *Credit where credit's due.*

The simplehttpd server can interact with any of the brand-name commercial Web browsers. When operating at protocol port-number 8080 on network device pbmac.itcarlow.ie, a user of a brand-name Web browser would type 'http://pbmac.itcarlow.ie:8080/' into their browser's location or address box. Refer to the exercises at the end of this chapter for suggestions as to how simplehttpd can be extended with additional features.

4.10 The libnet Library

Graham Barr's libnet library provides solid support for a collection of the most popular pre-Web Internet protocols. The protocols supported in individual modules, and bundled in the library, are as follows.

FTP – the *File Transfer Protocol* as defined in RFC 959 and implemented in the `Net::FTP` module.

SMTP – the *Simple Mail Transfer Protocol* as defined in RFC 821 and implemented in the `Net::SMTP` module.

Daytime/Time – as defined in RFC 867 and RFC 868 and implemented in the `Net::Time` module.

NNTP – the *Network News Transfer Protocol* as defined in RFC 977 and implemented in the `Net::NNTP` module.

POP3 – the *Post Office Protocol, Version 3* as defined in RFC 1939 and implemented in the `Net::POP3` module.

SNPP – the *Simple Network Pager Protocol* as defined in RFC 1861 and implemented in the `Net::SNPP` module.

All of these modules inherit from the `Net::Cmd` module, which is also part of the `libnet` library. `Net::Cmd` is an *abstract base class*. This means that the module cannot be used directly by application programmers, but it can form the basis of another module that turns its abstract functionality into something *concrete*. As all of the other `libnet` modules inherit from `Net::Cmd` (which itself inherits from the standard `IO::Handle` module), they all exhibit a shared set of characteristics and a common API.

To provide a *feel* for how the `libnet` modules work, a small Usenet news reading program will be developed to take advantage of the API provided by the `Net::NNTP` module.

4.10.1 Working with Usenet

The `nws` program provides a simple and quick method for reading Usenet news articles. From the command-line, the user provides the Internet name of the server to contact (and optionally, if required, a valid user-id and password). Once an NNTP connection is established with the remote server, `nws` asks the user to specify a newsgroup to 'read'. If the newsgroup exists, `nws` queries the server to provide the *first* and *last* article numbers currently available on the server for the specified newsgroup. The user then has the option of changing these values if desired, before `nws` starts retrieving and displaying the articles, newest first. With each article, the user has the option of reading the article, skipping to the next article or quitting `nws` and returning to the operating system's command-line prompt.

4.10.2   The news reading source code

As with the discussion of simplehttpd, the entire source code to nws is shown here prior to providing a detailed description of its functionality. Here is the code:

```perl
#! /usr/bin/perl -w

use strict;
use Net::NNTP;

$| = 1;

my $the_server = shift;
my $userid = shift;
my $passwd = shift;

my $server = Net::NNTP->new( $the_server )
    or die "nws: Can't connect to server: $@\n";

$server->authinfo( $userid, $passwd ) if defined( $userid );

my ( $group_to_check, $n, $f, $l, $g );

while ( do {
                print "\nGroup: ";
                $group_to_check = <STDIN>;
                chomp( $group_to_check );
                eval
                {
                    ( $n, $f, $l, $g ) =
                        $server->group( $group_to_check )
                            or die "No group: $group_to_check\n";
                };
                if ( $@ ) { 1; };
        } )
{
    print "\nGroup not found: $group_to_check: try another.";
}

print "\nNumber of articles:\t$n\n";
print "Value of first:\t\t$f\n";
print "Value of last:\t\t$l\n";

print "\nEnter start of range: ";
my $start = <STDIN>;
print "\nEnter end of range: ";
my $end = <STDIN>;
```

```perl
chomp( $start );
chomp( $end );

if ( $start eq '' ) { $start = $f; }
if ( $end eq '' ) { $end = $l; }

print "\nProcessing this range: $end to $start ... \n";

for ( my $i = $end; $i >= $start; --$i )
{
    my $filename = 'art' . $i;

    my ( $header, $bodytext );

    eval
    {
        $header = $server->head( $i )
            or die "Can't get header from article $i in $g\n";
    };
    if ( $@ ) { next; }

    print "\n";
    foreach my $line ( @{$header} )
    {
        print $line if $line =~ /^From/;
        print $line if $line =~ /^Date/;
        print $line if $line =~ /^Lines/;
        print $line if $line =~ /^Subject/;
    }
    print "Get article $i? (y/n/q): ";
    my $yorn = <STDIN>;
    chomp( $yorn );

    if ( $yorn eq 'q' )
    {
        last;
    }

    if ( $yorn eq 'y' )
    {
        eval
        {
            $bodytext = $server->body( $i )
                or die "Can't get body from $i in $g\n";
        };
        if ( $@ ) { next; }

        open OUTARTFILE, ">$filename" or
            die "Could not open $filename: $@\n";
```

```
                print OUTARTFILE @{$bodytext};
                close OUTARTFILE;

                my $cmd = 'less ' . $filename;

                system( $cmd );
            }
        }

        $server->quit;

        print "\nDone.\n";
```

After switching on strictness, the nws program uses the Net::NNTP module, enables autoflushing on standard output by setting $|, then initializes three scalar variables. The name of the NNTP server to establish communication with is stored in the $the_server scalar, and any supplied username and password are stored in $userid and $passwd:

```
#! /usr/bin/perl -w

use strict;
use Net::NNTP;

$| = 1;

my $the_server = shift;
my $userid = shift;
my $passwd = shift;
```

The value of $the_server is passed to the Net::NNTP module's new method. This method will attempt to establish an NNTP connection with the named server and, if successful, return a Net::NNTP server object to the program. The server object is assigned to the $server scalar. If a value for $userid was provided on the command-line, the authinfo method associated with the $server object is invoked, ensuring that authentication is performed as necessary:

```
my $server = Net::NNTP->new( $the_server )
    or die "nws: Can't connect to server: $@\n";

$server->authinfo( $userid, $passwd ) if defined( $userid );
```

Five scalars are then declared to be lexically scoped:

```
my ( $group_to_check, $n, $f, $l, $g );
```

The scalars are as follows.

$group_to_check - the name of the Usenet newsgroup to work with. The user is asked to interactively provide this value.

$n – the number of articles associated with the newsgroup on the server.

$f – the number of the first article associated with the newsgroup available for retrieval from the server.

$l – the number of the last article associated with the newsgroup available for retrieval from the server.

$g – the name of the newsgroup (as reported by the remote server).

With the scalars declared, a `while` loop ensures that nws does not continue until the user enters the name of a valid Usenet newsgroup currently available on the remote server:

```
while ( do {
                print "\nGroup: ";
                $group_to_check = <STDIN>;
                chomp( $group_to_check );
                eval
                {
                    ( $n, $f, $l, $s ) =
                        $server->group( $group_to_check )
                            or die "No group: $group_to_check\n";
                };
                if ( $@ ) { 1; };
            } )
    {
        print "\nGroup not found: $group_to_check: try another.";
    }
```

If this code looks strange, don't worry, *it is*. For starters, the condition-part of the `while` loop is in fact a collection of statements contained within a single do. The do subroutine in Perl allows a group of statements to be treated as one, and arranges for the value of do to be the result of the last executed statement within the block. The last statement in this do block is:

```
if ( $@ ) { 1; };
```

which will return a true value if the $@ built-in variable is defined. The $@ scalar is defined if the most recent invocation of `eval` *failed*. This only happens if the call to the $server object's group method fails. Note that the single parameter to the group method, a scalar called $group_to_check, gets its value as a result of asking the user to enter the name of a newsgroup to check. The call to chomp removes any trailing newline from the $group_to_check scalar. If the call to do returns false, the body of the `while` loop executes and the user is asked to try another newsgroup name. If do returns true, the `while` loop ends, and nws continues safe in the knowledge that the requested newsgroup exists on the remote NNTP server.

The next collection of lines displays the statistics about the newsgroup to the user and provides a means of adjusting the first and last article numbers. If the user decides not to enter values for the start and end of the range of article numbers, two if statements set the $start and $end scalars to $f and $l, respectively. A short message then informs the user that nws is processing the articles in the newsgroup starting with the most recent article and working backwards:

```perl
print "\nNumber of articles:\t$n\n";
print "Value of first:\t\t$f\n";
print "Value of last:\t\t$l\n";

print "\nEnter start of range: ";
my $start = <STDIN>;
print "\nEnter end of range: ";
my $end = <STDIN>;

chomp( $start );
chomp( $end );

if ( $start eq '' ) { $start = $f; }
if ( $end eq '' ) { $end = $l; }

print "\nProcessing this range: $end to $start ... \n";
```

Another loop is entered, this time a for statement, which starts at the article numbered $end and works down to the article numbered $start, decrementing the value of the loop index ($i) with each iteration:

```perl
for ( my $i = $end; $i >= $start; --$i )
{
```

A $filename is created as a concatenation of the string 'art' and the number of the current article being processed (which is stored in the $i loop index). After declaring scalars to hold the article's header-part ($header) and body-part ($bodytext), a call to the head method associated with the $server object is made within an eval block. Note that head has the current article number passed as a single parameter. If the call to head succeeds, the $header scalar contain a reference to an array of *header-lines*. If the call to head fails, the code dies[16], eval sets the $@ built-in variable and the code starts the next loop iteration:

```perl
my $filename = 'art' . $i;

my ( $header, $bodytext );

eval
{
    $header = $server->head( $i )
```

---

[16]Remember: within an eval block, when die is invoked, only the evaluated block of codes dies, not the entire program.

```
                or die "Can't get header from article $i in $g\n";
      };
      if ( $@ ) { next; }
```

After a successful call to the head method, the code loops through the array referred to by the $header scalar. The current header-line is printed to the screen if it contains the word 'From', 'Date', 'Lines' or 'Subject' at the start of the header-line. When the entire array has been processed, a short message asks the user if the current article is to be retrieved, and the user's input is read from the keyboard (<STDIN>) and used to initialize the $yorn scalar (which is then *chomped*):

```
      print "\n";
      foreach my $line ( @{$header} )
      {
          print $line if $line =~ /^From/;
          print $line if $line =~ /^Date/;
          print $line if $line =~ /^Lines/;
          print $line if $line =~ /^Subject/;
      }
      print "Get article $i? (y/n/q): ";
      my $yorn = <STDIN>;
      chomp( $yorn );
```

If the user entered 'q', the program exits from the loop by calling last:

```
      if ( $yorn eq 'q' )
      {
          last;
      }
```

If the user entered 'y', a call to the body method associated with the $server object is made (with the current article number, still stored in $i, as the sole parameter). As with the call to head, the call to body occurs within an eval block. If the call to body succeeds, the $bodytext scalar contain a reference to an array of *body-lines*. If the call to body fails, the code dies, eval sets the $@ built-in variable and the code starts the next loop iteration:

```
      if ( $yorn eq 'y' )
      {
          eval
          {
              $bodytext = $server->body( $i )
                  or die "Can't get body from $i in $g\n";
          };
          if ( $@ ) { next; }
```

The text of the current article, stored in the array referenced by $bodytext is then written to a disk-file. Standard input/output code opens a disk-file called $filename and writes the body-lines to it:

```
        open OUTARTFILE, ">$filename" or
             die "Could not open $filename: $@\n";
        print OUTARTFILE @{$bodytext};
        close OUTARTFILE;
```

The loops ends with the construction of a Linux command-line, concatenating the string 'less' with the value of $filename. The nws program then asks the underlying operating system to execute the command-line by sending it to the inbuilt system subroutine:

```
        my $cmd = 'less ' . $filename;
        system( $cmd );
    }
```

This causes the standard Linux less program to display the contents of the article's body-lines one screen at a time[17].

Once the for loop terminates (as a result of the user either pressing 'q' when prompted or the program running out of articles), a call is made to the quit method associated with the $server object, which ensures the connection to the remote NNTP server is shutdown in an orderly way:

```
    }
    $server->quit;

    print "\nDone.\n";
```

4.11   Email Enabling simplehttpd

Let us extend the simplehttpd Web server to send an email message whenever an invalid HTTP request is received from a browser. As logging methods go, generating an individual email message for every malformed HTTP request received by the server is somewhat excessive behaviour. Typically, such information would be logged to a disk-file for later perusal by the Web server administrator. However, this technique serves your author's purpose in demonstrating how to automatically generate email messages with Perl.

4.11.1   The simple mail transfer protocol

On the Internet, the Simple Mail Transfer Protocol (SMTP) is used to transfer text messages from mail system to mail system. SMTP is defined in RFC 821 and support for programming the protocol with Perl is provided by the Net::SMTP module (which is part of the libnet library).

---

[17]If less is not installed on your Linux system, use the more command instead. If more is not installed on your Linux system, use cat. If cat is not installed on your Linux system, you are not using Linux!

As networking protocols go, SMTP is remarkably straightforward. A sender establishes a reliable connection with a recipient mail system (or an intermediate relay), then converses with the mail system using a small set of SMTP commands. Critically, these commands enable the sender to identify the recipient(s) of the message, as well as transfer the email message as plain 7 bit ASCII text. When the message is transferred to the server, the reliable connection is closed.

Rather than describe the SMTP commands in detail, let us look at extracts from a *NetDebug* packet capture of the traffic generated as a result of an email user-agent and SMTP server communicating.

The user-agent is running on `pbmac.itcarlow.ie`, with an IP address of `149.153.100.65`. The SMTP server is hosted by `pat.itcarlow.ie`, which has an IP address of `149.153.100.8`.

The conversation begins with the user-agent establishing a reliable TCP connection with the SMTP server, to which the server replies:

```
- - - - - - - - - - - - - - - - - - - - - - - - - - - - - - -
149.153.100.8 -> 149.153.100.65 (id: 57624, ttl: 128)

TCP Source: 25 -> TCP Destination: 1128
TCP Header Length: 5, TCP Checksum: 55369
TCP Data:

220 PAT Mercury 1.48 ESMTP server ready.^M
- - - - - - - - - - - - - - - - - - - - - - - - - - - - - - -
```

This extract shows the server using the well-known TCP protocol port-number of 25 for SMTP. The response includes a three-digit *reply-code* (220) together with a human-readable message ('PAT Mercury 1.48 ESMTP server ready.')[18]. With this reply, the server is indicating that it understands the extended services of SMTP, as defined in RFC 1869.

The user-agent introduces itself to the server by sending its Internet domain name as a parameter to the EHLO command:

```
- - - - - - - - - - - - - - - - - - - - - - - - - - - - - - -
149.153.100.65 -> 149.153.100.8 (id: 1871, ttl: 64)

TCP Source: 1128 -> TCP Destination: 25
TCP Header Length: 5, TCP Checksum: 15266
TCP Data:

EHLO itcarlow.ie^M
- - - - - - - - - - - - - - - - - - - - - - - - - - - - - - -
```

The server responds with a 250 reply-code and message, indicating it supports a small number of extended SMTP commands (TIME and HELP):

---

[18]Note that ^M corresponds to the ASCII representation of the captured new-line character.

```
- - - - - - - - - - - - - - - - - - - - - - - - - - - - - -
149.153.100.8 -> 149.153.100.65 (id: 57880, ttl: 128)

TCP Source: 25 -> TCP Destination: 1128
TCP Header Length: 5, TCP Checksum: 62996
TCP Data:

250-PAT Hello itcarlow.ie; ESMTPs are:^M
250-TIME^M
250 HELP^M
- - - - - - - - - - - - - - - - - - - - - - - - - - - - - -
```

The user-agent sends the sender's address (paul.barry@itcarlow.ie) using the MAIL command, and the server responds by accepting the sender (reply-code 250), then asking for a list of recipients:

```
- - - - - - - - - - - - - - - - - - - - - - - - - - - - - -
149.153.100.65 -> 149.153.100.8 (id: 1873, ttl: 64)

TCP Source: 1128 -> TCP Destination: 25
TCP Header Length: 5, TCP Checksum: 7989
TCP Data:

MAIL FROM:<paul.barry@itcarlow.ie>^M
- - - - - - - - - - - - - - - - - - - - - - - - - - - - - -
149.153.100.8 -> 149.153.100.65 (id: 58392, ttl: 128)

TCP Source: 25 -> TCP Destination: 1128
TCP Header Length: 5, TCP Checksum: 36521
TCP Data:

250 Sender OK - send RCPTs.^M
- - - - - - - - - - - - - - - - - - - - - - - - - - - - - -
```

There is only one recipient for this email (test.user@itcarlow.ie), and the user-agent sends this address to the server with the RCPT command. The SMTP server indicates its acceptance of the recipient's email address, again with the 250 reply-code. After accepting the recipient, the server indicates that it is willing to either accept more recipients (if there are any) or the data that make up the email message:

```
- - - - - - - - - - - - - - - - - - - - - - - - - - - - - -
149.153.100.65 -> 149.153.100.8 (id: 1874, ttl: 64)

TCP Source: 1128 -> TCP Destination: 25
TCP Header Length: 5, TCP Checksum: 25389
TCP Data:

RCPT TO:<test.user@itcarlow.ie>^M
```

```
- - - - - - - - - - - - - - - - - - - - - - - - - - - - - - -
149.153.100.8 -> 149.153.100.65 (id: 58648, ttl: 128)

TCP Source: 25 -> TCP Destination: 1128
TCP Header Length: 5, TCP Checksum: 49474
TCP Data:

250 Recipient OK - send RCPT or DATA.^M
+
- - - - - - - - - - - - - - - - - - - - - - - - - - - - - - -
```

To this query, the user-agent responds with a DATA command, indicating that the list of recipients is complete and that it is now ready to send the text of the message:

```
- - - - - - - - - - - - - - - - - - - - - - - - - - - - - - -
149.153.100.65 -> 149.153.100.8 (id: 1875, ttl: 64)

TCP Source: 1128 -> TCP Destination: 25
TCP Header Length: 5, TCP Checksum: 30509
TCP Data:

DATA^M
- - - - - - - - - - - - - - - - - - - - - - - - - - - - - - -
```

The SMTP server responds positively with a 354 reply-code, which indicates to the user-agent that the data can now be sent. Note the server's insistence that the text message end with a single dot character on a line of its own (the CRLF.CRLF sequence):

```
- - - - - - - - - - - - - - - - - - - - - - - - - - - - - - -
149.153.100.8 -> 149.153.100.65 (id: 58904, ttl: 128)

TCP Source: 25 -> TCP Destination: 1128
TCP Header Length: 5, TCP Checksum: 63950
TCP Data:

354 OK, send data, end with CRLF.CRLF^M
- - - - - - - - - - - - - - - - - - - - - - - - - - - - - - -
```

Upon receipt of the 354 reply-code, the user-agent promptly sends the message (which is formatted to comply with RFC 822, the standard format for Internet text messages). Note the inclusion of the dot character on a line of its own at the end of the message:

```
- - - - - - - - - - - - - - - - - - - - - - - - - - - - - - -
149.153.100.65 -> 149.153.100.8 (id: 1877, ttl: 64)

TCP Source: 1128 -> TCP Destination: 25
TCP Header Length: 5, TCP Checksum: 53249
TCP Data:
```

```
Message-ID: <3BE7B5A0.AC5DE93B@itcarlow.ie>^M
Date: Tue, 06 Nov 2001 10:04:16 +0000^M
From: Paul Barry <paul.barry@itcarlow.ie>^M
Reply-To: paul.barry@itcarlow.ie^M
Organization: IT Carlow^M
X-Mailer: Mozilla 4.73 [en] (X11; I; Linux 2.2.18-4hpmac ppc)^M
X-Accept-Language: en^M
MIME-Version: 1.0^M
To: test.user@itcarlow.ie^M
Subject: Capturing SMTP Traffic with NetDebug^M
Content-Type: text/plain; charset=us-ascii^M
Content-Transfer-Encoding: 7bit^M
^M
Hi!^M
^M
Here it is.  A simple test message for NetDebug to capture.^M
This will be used when explaining SMTP in Chapter 4 of^M
Programming the Network with Perl.^M
^M
Paul.^M
--^M
Paul Barry, Lecturer, IT Carlow, Ireland.^M
email: paul.barry@itcarlow.ie^M
.^M
```

Upon receipt of the CRLF.CRLF sequence, the server indicates that the data were properly received (with another 250 reply-code):

```
149.153.100.8 -> 149.153.100.65 (id: 59672, ttl: 128)

TCP Source: 25 -> TCP Destination: 1128
TCP Header Length: 5, TCP Checksum: 4410
TCP Data:

250 Data received OK.^M
```

Satisfied the text message is now sent, the user-agent requests the termination of the reliable connection with the QUIT command. The server responds with a 221 reply-code, and the connection is closed:

```
149.153.100.65 -> 149.153.100.8 (id: 1878, ttl: 64)

TCP Source: 1128 -> TCP Destination: 25
TCP Header Length: 5, TCP Checksum: 29169
TCP Data:

QUIT^M
```

```
- - - - - - - - - - - - - - - - - - - - - - - - - - - - - - - - - - - - -
149.153.100.8 -> 149.153.100.65 (id: 60184, ttl: 128)

TCP Source: 25 -> TCP Destination: 1128
TCP Header Length: 5, TCP Checksum: 36182
TCP Data:

221 PAT Service closing channel.^M
- - - - - - - - - - - - - - - - - - - - - - - - - - - - - - - - - - - - -
```

Although by no means complete, this description of SMTP provides enough details for any competent Sockets programmer to develop a simple Internet mailer. However, for the Perl programmer, the requirement to resort to directly programming the Socket API can be avoided by the use of the Net::SMTP module.

4.11.2   The Net::SMTP module

The Net::SMTP module provides an object-oriented client interface to the SMTP and ESMTP protocols. Once an object of type Net::SMTP is created (by calling its new constructor), a collection of methods (whose names closely match those of the SMTP commands) are invoked to interact with the SMTP server.

Those methods which match the SMTP commands identified as a result of the *NetDebug* packet capture are as follows.

hello – uses EHLO to announce the sender's domain name to the SMTP server. This method is rarely called directly, as Net::SMTP invokes hello automatically upon creation of the object.

mail – uses the MAIL command to send the email address of the sender to the SMTP server.

recipient – uses RCPT to identify the intended recipient(s) of the text message. Other versions of this method (providing similar functionality) are: to, cc and bcc.

data – uses the DATA command to initiate the start of the send of the text message. This method is also used to send the text message to the server. However, it is more common to use the datasend and dataend methods (inherited from the Net::Cmd module) to do this.

quit – sends the QUIT command to the server, effectively closing the connection.

Other Net::SMTP methods include banner, domain, etrn, expand, help, send, send_or_mail, send_and_mail, reset and verify. Refer to the Net::SMTP documentation for more details.

4.11.3   Creating `simplehttp2d`

To add email logging facilities to `simplehttpd`, a subroutine called `email_log` is defined. This subroutine takes three parameters:

$method – the value of the HTTP request method (e.g. GET or POST);

$resource – the name of the resource requested (e.g. a valid URL);

$peerhost – the IP address of the browser making the request (in dotted-decimal format).

This new version of `simplehttpd` (which is called `simplehttp2d`) has code changes in a number of places. Specifically, the code within the `continue_as_child` subroutine that displays the diagnostic messages to the server's screen now needs to call the `email_log` subroutine, as follows:

```
        else
        {
            $http_client->send_error( RC_NOT_FOUND );
            print "NOT FOUND.";
            eval {
                email_log( $service->method,
                           $resource,
                           $http_client->peerhost );
            };
        }
    }
    else
    {
        $http_client->send_error( RC_METHOD_NOT_ALLOWED );
        print "NOT OK.";
        eval {
            email_log( $service->method,
                       $request,
                       $http_client->peerhost );
        };
    }
    print " Remote addr: ", $http_client->peerhost, "\n";
```

The two calls to the `email_log` subroutine include the three required parameters, and are enclosed within `eval` blocks. This is due to the fact that the `email_log` subroutine can result in a call to the inbuilt `die` subroutine, and it is inappropriate for the `simplehttp2d` Web server to `die` whenever there is a problem with its email subsystem. Using `eval` in this way provides a mechanism for `simplehttp2d` to recover from an otherwise fatal error in the `email_log` subroutine.

At the top of the `simplehttp2d` code, the `Net::SMTP` module is used, and three (self-explanatory) constants are defined:

```
use Net::SMTP;

use constant SMTP_SERVER        => 'pat.itcarlow.ie';

use constant SMTP_TO            => 'web.admin@itcarlow.ie';
use constant SMTP_FROM          => 'simplehttp2d@itcarlow.ie';
```

The `email_log` subroutine is then defined, and it begins by assigning the three required parameters to lexical scalars. An object of type `Net::SMTP` is then created. At this point, the SMTP server has been contacted and the sender has been announced to it (with an EHLO command):

```
sub email_log {
    my ( $method, $resource, $peerhost ) = @_;

    my $email = Net::SMTP->new( SMTP_SERVER )
                    or die "Could not create SMTP object.\n";
```

If all is well, a reliable connection now exists between `simplehttp2d` and the SMTP server. If this is not the case, the call to `die` aborts the production of the text message. It is this call to `die` that the `eval` blocks protect against in the `simplehttp2d` code.

Two method invocations follow (`mail` and `to`), resulting in the SMTP server being told the email address of the sender and the recipient. A single call to the `data` method then indicates to the server that the text of the message is about to be sent:

```
$email->mail( SMTP_FROM );
$email->to( SMTP_TO );
$email->data;
```

It is possible to pass a reference to an array containing the text message to be sent to the server (as a parameter to the `data` method). However, it is often more convenient to send smaller chunks of data, and this is possible using the `datasend` method, as follows:

```
$email->datasend( "To: ", SMTP_TO, "\n" );
$email->datasend( "From: ", SMTP_FROM, "\n" );
$email->datasend( "Subject: Message from simplehttp2d\n" );
$email->datasend( "\n" );
$email->datasend( "The following request could not be " );
$email->datasend( "satisfied:\n\n" );
$email->datasend( "    Remote user: $peerhost\n" );
$email->datasend( "    Method:      $method\n" );
$email->datasend( "    Resource:    $resource\n" );
```

Each individual line of this RFC 822-formatted text message is sent to the server by the `datasend` method. Note how the text message has two parts: a *header-part*, consisting of a collection of name/value pairings (the : character separates the name from its associated value), and a *body-part*, consisting of the actual text of the email message. The header-part and body-part are separated by a single blank line. The body-part includes the values of the three scalars passed to the email_log subroutine.

To complete the transfer of the message, simplehttp2d sends the CRLF.CRLF sequence to the server by invoking the dataend method. A call to the quit method informs the server that simplehttp2d is done, and requests that the reliable connection be closed:

```
        $email->dataend;
        $email->quit;
}
```

And that is it. The simplehttp2d Web server now sends an email message to the web.admin@itcarlow.ie email address every time a malformed HTTP request is processed.

The simplehttpd Web server can be further extended in any number of interesting ways. Refer to the *Exercises* at the end of this chapter for some suggestions.

4.12 Other Networking Add-On Modules

The Perl community has its fair share of talented programmers, and some of them have been hard at work writing networking add-on modules for the language. In addition to the add-on modules already discussed in *Programming the Network with Perl*, CPAN contains a large and growing collection of interesting modules. One final example presents a small program written to take advantage of the Net::Telnet module developed by *Jay Rogers*.

As the name suggests, Net::Telnet provides a mechanism to communicate with remote systems using the standard TELNET protocol, as defined in RFC 854. Rather than require the user to interactively operate some terminal emulation software, Net::Telnet allows the programmer to program (or *script*) the interactive session.

4.12.1 Installing Net::Telnet

Download the module from CPAN then issue the following commands at the Linux command-line to install and test Net::Telnet:

```
gunzip Net-Telnet-3.02.tar.gz
tar xvf Net-Telnet-3.02.tar
cd Net-Telnet-3.02
perl Makefile.PL
make
make test
```

```
su
make install
<ctrl-D>
man Net::Telnet
perl -e 'use Net::Telnet'
```

4.12.2   A Net::Telnet example

A requirement exists to quickly and easily determine the names of users currently logged into a collection of computers running the Linux operating system. Rather than require an overworked system administrator to manually connect to each system and issue the who command from the command-line (thus generating a list of users), a small program based on Net::Telnet automates the process. Here is the source code to the program, called multiwho:

```perl
#! /usr/bin/perl -w

use strict;
use Net::Telnet ();

sub do_who {
    my ( $telnet_host, $userid, $passwd ) = @_;

    my $telnet_obj = new Net::Telnet ( );

    $telnet_obj->open( $telnet_host );
    $telnet_obj->login( $userid, $passwd );

    my @who_list = $telnet_obj->cmd( "/usr/bin/who" );

    $telnet_obj->close;

    $#who_list = $#who_list - 1;

    return @who_list;
}

my @list;

@list = do_who( 'linux303', 'barryp', 'passwordhere' );
@list = (@list, do_who( '149.153.103.15',
                        'barryp', 'passwordhere' ));
@list = (@list, do_who( 'glasnost', 'barryp', 'passwordhere' ));

print "@list\n";
```

The program begins in the usual manner: strictness is specified and the required modules are used (in this case, only the Net::Telnet module is needed). Next comes a subroutine, called do_who, which does all the work. Here is the first half of this subroutine:

```
sub do_who {
    my ( $telnet_host, $userid, $passwd ) = @_;

    my $telnet_obj = new Net::Telnet ( );

    $telnet_obj->open( $telnet_host );
    $telnet_obj->login( $userid, $passwd );
```

The subroutine takes three parameters:

$telnet_host – the IP name or IP address of the remote computer to establish a TELNET session with;

$userid – the user-id to log in as;

$passwd – the password to use.

An object of type Net::Telnet is then constructed as a result of calling the module's new method, and a reference to the created object is stored in the $telnet_obj scalar variable. A TELNET session is then established with the remote computer by calling two methods associated with the object: open establishes a reliable TCP connection to the TELNET port[19] on the remote computer, and login authenticates using the supplied user-id and password.

With the TELNET connection established and authenticated, the subroutine continues. Here is the second half:

```
    my @who_list = $telnet_obj->cmd( "/usr/bin/who" );

    $telnet_obj->close;

    $#who_list = $#who_list - 1;

    return @who_list;
}
```

An array called @who_list is assigned the result of an invocation of the cmd method associated with the $telnet_obj object. The single parameter to the cmd method is a Linux command-line, which issues the who command as located in the /usr/bin directory. The cmd method captures all of the output generated by the invoked program including the Linux *command prompt*, the significance of which will become clearer in just a moment.

The Net::Telnet object is then closed, as the program is finished with the TELNET session. The length of the *captured* array is then shortened by one. This ensures that the Linux command prompt returned by the cmd method is discarded and not included as part of the output from the who command, which is stored as an array of lines in the @who_list variable. The subroutine ends by returning the array of lines to its caller.

---

[19]Typically, port 23.

The rest of the code for `multiwho` is very straightforward. Here it is:

```
my @list;

@list = do_who( 'linux303', 'barryp', 'passwordhere' );
@list = (@list, do_who( '149.153.103.15',
                        'barryp', 'passwordhere' ));
@list = (@list, do_who( 'glasnost', 'barryp', 'passwordhere' ));

print "@list\n";
```

An array called `@list` is declared, then assigned to by three calls to the `do_who` subroutine. Note how the list is added to with the second and third invocations of `do_who`: the list becomes equal to itself plus the result of the next call to `do_who`. When the three calls to `do_who` complete, the `multiwho` program finishes by displaying the contents of the `@list` array to standard output.

Here are the results produced by `multiwho` when executed:

```
root       tty1      Apr 19 16:31
cno2031    pts/0     May 31 16:30 (pc310-10.itcarlow.ie)
cno2020    pts/1     May 31 16:14 (pc3-16.itcarlow.ie)
cno2020    pts/2     May 31 16:27 (pc3-16.itcarlow.ie)
cno2026    pts/3     May 31 16:18 (149.153.131.117)
cno2018    pts/4     May 31 16:30 (pc3-20.itcarlow.ie)
cno2019    pts/5     May 31 16:26 (pc3-21.itcarlow.ie)
COM2059    pts/8     May 31 15:20 (pc3-14.itcarlow.ie)
cno2006    pts/7     May 31 13:30 (pc3-13.itcarlow.ie)
barryp     pts/6     May 31 16:32 (PBMac.itcarlow.ie)
com3027    pts/0     May  9 09:52 (pc2-2.itcarlow.ie)
barryp     pts/1     May 31 16:23 (PBMac.itcarlow.ie)
meudecc    pts/0     May 31 16:30 (staff102.itcarlow.ie)
hickeypm   pts/1     May 31 16:14 (staff23.itcarlow.ie)
kinsella   pts/2     May 31 16:27 (akmac.itcarlow.ie)
whyte      pts/3     May 31 16:18 (149.153.100.117)
barryp     pts/4     May 31 16:31 (PBMac.itcarlow.ie)
```

Note that user `barryp` appears three times. This corresponds with the fact that three TELNET sessions were established by the `multiwho` program with each of the remote computers, and that the user-id used by `multiwho` on each of the computers was `barryp`. As the `who` program details the time at which each user logged in, we can confirm that on each of the three remote computers, user `barryp` is the most recent addition. Note that the clocks on the three computers are not synchronized: `barryp` is reported to have logged in at 16:32, 16:23 and 16:31 by each of the remote computers, even though `multiwho` is establishing TELNET sessions with the computers sequentially and within a very short period of time (seconds). Of more interest is the fact that the user `root` is logged into `linux303` at the console (device `tty1`). The system administrator should be concerned that `root` has been active on the system in this way for close to six weeks! It would appear that someone logged in as `root` on April 19th, but forgot to logout.

4.13   Where To From Here?

This chapter concentrated on programming to Internet standard protocols. In addition to using the Perl Socket API, two large add-on module libraries to Perl, `libwww-perl` and `libnet`, were described. A number of simple, yet useful, client and server programs were written in Perl to demonstrate interactions with a number of standard Internet protocols.

Using `Net::SMTP` is not the only way of automatically generating email messages with Perl. Visit your local CPAN and browse the *Mail and Usenet News* category. There you will find a large and growing collection of email add-on modules for Perl.

Those readers interested in building a Web server from scratch should start with the code from Chapter 15 of Lincoln Stein's book (refer to the *Print Resources* section from the last chapter). If writing a Web browser is more your thing, take a look at the fully functioning Web browsing demo application (called `tkweb`) written in the Tk GUI extension module and `libwww-perl`. Download Tk from a nearby CPAN.

4.14   Print Resources

A great little book (if somewhat out of date) on programming the Web is *Web Client Programming with Perl* by Clinton Wong (O'Reilly, 1997). This book provides excellent coverage of programming HTTP using the Perl Socket API and `libwww-perl` technologies. Unfortunately, the book is out of print. Fortunately, O'Reilly has included the book in its 'Open Books Project', which means that the text is online at the `http://www.oreilly.com/openbook/` website. It is somewhat of a shame that neither the author nor O'Reilly plan a second edition.

Chapter 9 of Lincoln Stein's *Network Programming with Perl* is devoted to coverage of `libnet` and `libwww-perl`. The examples which combine `libnet`'s email modules with HTML browsing and NNTP newsfeeds are especially instructive.

Chapters 18 and 20 from the *Perl Cookbook* (see the *Print Resources* section at the end of Chapter 1) provide many examples of programming to Internet standard protocols and Web technologies, respectively. Like Stein's book, `libnet` and `libwww-perl` feature heavily.

4.15   Web Resources

The latest version of the HTTP standard document is the Internet Engineering Task Force's RFC 2616, and it is widely available on the Internet. Go to the home of Web standards, `http://www.w3.org`, for more information. The text of any RFC can be located by following the link from `http://www.ietf.org`.

The `http://www.apache.org` website has all the information anyone could possibly need on the *Apache Web Server*.

The add-on modules discussed in this chapter are all available on CPAN, and can be found at the `http://search.cpan.org` website.

Gisle Aas maintains a website at `http://www.linpro.no/lwp` containing information on the current state of the `libwww-perl` project. A list of links to software built on top of `libwww-perl` is included. Gisle's CPAN directory is `http://www.cpan.org/authors/id/GAAS/`.

Graham Barr's CPAN directory is `http://www.cpan.org/authors/id/GBARR/`. Graham has also written a number of articles for *The Perl Journal* which cover programming FTP, Mail and Usenet applications with the `libnet` technologies. These articles are available online at the `http://www.tpj.com` website. Follow the link for the 'Archives' section to access these (as well as many other) interesting articles.

Additional information on *InterMapper* can be found at the *Dartware*'s website: `http://www.dartware.com`. Originally developed at *Dartmouth College* to assist in the management of a large AppleTalk and IP network, ownership of this network management technology was 'spun-out' and transferred to *Dartware* in April 2000.

Jay Rogers's CPAN directory is `http://www.cpan.org/authors/id/JROGERS/`.

Exercises

1. What changes are required to wwwb to support the POST method? Choose a popular search engine that uses POST and update wwwb to send a search term to your chosen engine.

2. Rewrite LWPwwwb to use the facilities provided by the LWP::Simple module.

3. Create a new parser, based on the parsewwwb code, which retrieves any HTML Web page from a remote Web server, parsing the retrieved page for any embedded graphic links, creating a list of names. When the parsing is complete, contact the Web server again and request the list of graphic files from the server, storing the files in the current working directory. When using libwww-perl, can the program take advantage of a *persistent connection* to the Web server?

4. Use the perldoc -f command to learn about chroot, and then change the simplehttpd Web server to use chroot as a means of limiting the visibility of the server's file system to a remote Web browser. What is the downside of using chroot?

5. Search the Internet for a description of the Common Gateway Interface (CGI) standard, then add support for CGI scripts (written in any programming language, not just Perl) to the simplehttpd Web server.

6. Add the ability to handle the POST method to the simplehttpd Web server. You are to ensure both the GET and POST methods work with the CGI mechanism from the previous question.

7. Extend the simplehttpd Web server to support FTP client requests from FTP-enabled Web browsers. [Hint: search CPAN for any third-party add-on modules to incorporate into simplehttpd.] Once simplehttpd can support both HTTP and FTP requests from clients, use the FTP client technology found in either libwww-perl or libnet to extend wwwb to enable the issuing of FTP requests and the processing of FTP responses. Test this new version of wwwb against simplehttpd and the *Apache* Web server.

8. Identify the modifications required to the HTTP::Daemon module to enable it to conform to RFC 2616.

9. Research the facilities provided by the Net::POP3 module included in the libnet library. Develop a small utility in Perl that checks your Internet mailbox for new mail (without actually downloading the messages from the server).

10. The Net::NNTP module supports RFC 977. Identify an RFC which updates the NNTP protocol standard, then create a new version of Net::NNTP to support the newer RFC.

11. Rewrite nws to use the NNTP support provided by libwww-perl as opposed to libnet. Which API do you prefer? Why?

12. The multiwho program only communicates with remote computers running the TELNET daemon, which is an inherently insecure service[20]. Create a new version of

---

[20]Among other things, passwords are transmitted as 'clear text' and are visible to any unscrupulous individual running tools like *The Network Debugger* from Chapter 2.

the `multiwho` program which is capable of communication with a remote server running the secure shell environment (SSH). [Hint: are there any CPAN modules that might help?] It is also a good idea to add error-checking code to the `Net::Telnet` method calls in this program.

Management

The last two chapters were concerned with programming the network. This chapter is concerned with another important topic: network management.

Programming the Network with Perl has already included an entire chapter on some aspects of network management. Chapter 2, *Snooping*, described how to build a network debugger in Perl. The ability to capture and analyse traffic on a network is of critical importance to the network manager when all other techniques have failed, and such tools can provide the vital clue which often results in the successful resolution of a problem. Recall from Chapter 2 how the snooper identified a *broadcast storm* occurring as a result of a large collection of misconfigured workstations. As this chapter will show, there is a lot more to network management than using snoopers.

The management of computer networks is a complex and difficult activity. One need only consider the vast array of diverse equipment connected to modern networks to develop an appreciation of what is involved. Typically, there is a large collection of devices connected: personal computers, workstations, repeaters, hubs, switches, routers, printers, scanners, wireless base-stations, uninterruptable power supplies, and so on. It is very rarely the case that every single piece of equipment on a network is built and supplied by one equipment manufacturer[1], so relying on a single vendor's network management technology is rarely a viable solution, especially when the network is a heterogeneous mix. Centrally managing a diverse network is difficult. Centrally managing the Internet is all but impossible.

Dealing with the diversity and complexity of computer networks is accomplished *in general* by the widespread adoption and adherence to standards. This is especially important when it comes to network management. On TCP/IP networks, two protocols provide support for managing networks: the *Internet Control Message Protocol* (ICMP) and the *Simple Network Management Protocol* (SNMP).

---

[1]If you know of such a network, email the author.

After a brief description of ICMP and two ICMP-based applications, this chapter examines SNMP from the perspective of the Perl programmer building programs to assist in the process of network management.

5.1   Simple Management with ICMP

Every implementation of the Internet Protocol, including the current IPv4 standard, must include support for ICMP, the *Internet Control Message Protocol*, as defined in the Internet standards document RFC 792. This simple technology provides IP with a means of indicating when certain problems have occurred on an IP network. These problems include, but are not limited to, the following.

A discarded datagram – an IP datagram was discarded and was not delivered to its destination network device.

A routing inconsistency – a router has noticed a routing inconsistency, which may mean that IP datagrams are being incorrectly routed within the network (resulting in their eventual discarding).

Destination not found – an IP datagram could not be delivered because the destination network device could not be found. Alternatively, the network to which the destination network device is attached could not be found.

A busy network device – a network device, typically a router, is busy and cannot accept any more datagrams (at this time).

To keep things simple (and easily implementable), ICMP does not concern itself with the cause of any problem, only its occurrence.

In addition to identifying problems (or errors), ICMP also provides an *informational service*. These informational messages include the following.

Timer messages – provide a mechanism to determine the round-trip time lag between the local and a remote network device.

Echo messages – provide a mechanism to determine whether or not a specified network device is operating and potentially willing to accept IP datagrams.

RFC 792 documents the ICMP informational and error messages in detail.

5.2   Doing the Ping Thing

The ping program[2] uses the *Echo Request* and *Echo Response* messages from ICMP to help network managers determine the operational status of a network device. When a device is *pinged* with ICMP's *Echo Request* message, it is generally

---

[2]Which takes its name from the sound submarines make when determining the closeness of objects underwater.

required to respond with ICMP's *Echo Response* message. Note that the device is not obliged to respond to the request, and many Internet sites configure devices to block ping traffic (due to security concerns).

5.2.1   Some ping examples

The ping program is installed on most Linux systems. The following command-line can be used to check the operational status of the network device running the HTTP server at *Linux Journal* magazine. Note the -c4 argument which tells ping to send four *Echo Request* messages to the named network device:

```
ping -c4 www.linuxjournal.com
```

When executed on pbmac.itcarlow.ie, the following results were reported by ping:

```
PING www.linuxjournal.com (64.39.18.136)
        from 149.153.100.65 : 56(84) bytes of data.
64 bytes from 64.39.18.136: icmp_seq=0 ttl=235 time=137.581 msec
64 bytes from 64.39.18.136: icmp_seq=1 ttl=235 time=139.957 msec
64 bytes from 64.39.18.136: icmp_seq=2 ttl=235 time=139.975 msec
64 bytes from 64.39.18.136: icmp_seq=3 ttl=235 time=139.977 msec

--- www.linuxjournal.com ping statistics ---
4 packets transmitted, 4 packets received, 0% packet loss
round-trip min/avg/max/mdev = 137.581/139.372/139.977/1.099 ms
```

The output (ping statistics) shows the receipt of four ICMP datagrams, which are encapsulated within their own IP datagram. Each ICMP datagram is 64 bytes in length. The TTL value associated with each IP datagram is shown, as is an ICMP sequence number and round-trip timings in milliseconds.

The ping program can be used to quickly determine a list of devices attached to a particular network. This is accomplished by sending a *directed broadcast* to the network under examination. When this happens, any network devices that are configured to respond to the *Echo Request* message will do so. To determine the list of devices operating on the 149.153.100.0 network, an ICMP message is sent to this network's *directed broadcast* address, which is 149.153.100.255. Use this Linux command-line:

```
ping -c2 -b 149.153.100.255
```

The -b argument instructs ping to broadcast to the address given. On first glance, the -c2 argument seems strange. Why are two broadcast messages being sent to all the devices on the network? Surely only a single ICMP message need be broadcast?

The reason for the use of two broadcasts has more to do with how the ping program in implemented than with how ICMP is implemented. When the first broadcast message is sent, ping waits for *exactly one reply* before proceeding with any other business that it may have. If this 'any other business' is to terminate, the ping program receives a reply from the first network device to respond to the broadcast, displays the ping statistics and then exits. The other ICMP *Echo Response* messages generated by the 'slower' network devices are discarded due to the fact that there is no application waiting to receive them (as ping has now terminated). By instructing ping to send two broadcast messages, it will not terminate until two *Echo Response* messages (with unique sequence numbers) have been received. When the 'slower' network devices now respond to the first broadcast, the ping program has not terminated, receives the *Echo Response* messages and reports them as duplicates.

Here is the output generated by the above directed broadcast:

```
PING 149.153.100.255 (149.153.100.255)
        from 149.153.100.65 : 56(84) bytes of data.
64 bytes from 149.153.100.65: icmp_seq=0 ttl=255 time=367 usec
64 bytes from 149.153.100.67: icmp_seq=0 ttl=255 time=678 usec (DUP!)
64 bytes from 149.153.100.18: icmp_seq=0 ttl=128 time=723 usec (DUP!)
64 bytes from 149.153.100.106: icmp_seq=0 ttl=255 time=817 usec (DUP!)
64 bytes from 149.153.100.15: icmp_seq=0 ttl=128 time=914 usec (DUP!)
64 bytes from 149.153.100.4: icmp_seq=0 ttl=255 time=1.012 msec (DUP!)
64 bytes from 149.153.100.253: icmp_seq=0 ttl=255 time=1.156 msec (DUP!)
64 bytes from 149.153.100.243: icmp_seq=0 ttl=60 time=2.070 msec (DUP!)
64 bytes from 149.153.100.65: icmp_seq=1 ttl=255 time=89 usec

--- 149.153.100.255 ping statistics ---
2 packets transmitted, 2 packets received, +7 duplicates, 0% packet loss
round-trip min/avg/max/mdev = 0.089/0.869/2.070/0.524 ms
```

Note that the fastest device, 149.153.100.65, is reported as responding twice (with unique sequence numbers). All the other network devices are reported as duplicates (with common sequence numbers). The list of devices operating[3] on the network has now been determined. Note that all of the network devices listed have an IP address starting with the 149.153.100 prefix.

The above broadcast was issued on pbmac.itcarlow.ie, which has an IP address of 149.153.100.65. So, it is not too surprising to see this network device respond first (after all, the broadcast goes to the local device too). On pbmac, the ping program waits for one second between creations of each request message. To ask ping to wait for longer, use the -iX command-line argument, where X is a positive integer representing the number of seconds to wait. This may have the effect of allowing ping to receive more duplicates from 'slow' network devices that do not respond within the number of seconds it takes ping to send and receive the two *Echo Request* messages (that is, within two seconds).

Another useful ping example pertains to the discovery of any routers on a network. RFC 1256 describes enhancements to ICMP that can assist in determining the IP address of any routers operating on a network. By sending an *Echo Request*

---

[3]Where 'operating' is defined as 'responding to ICMP *Echo Request* messages'.

message to the *Router Solicitation* address, a program can process any responses to determine the IP addresses of any routers. An IP address is reserved for this exact purpose and it is 224.0.0.2. The following command-line was used from pbmac.itcarlow.ie to generate a list of routers visible from pbmac's network segment:

```
ping -c2 224.0.0.2
```

Here is the output generated by this command:

```
PING 224.0.0.2 (224.0.0.2) from 149.153.100.65 : 56(84) bytes of data.
64 bytes from 149.153.100.18: icmp_seq=0 ttl=128 time=1.620 msec
64 bytes from 149.153.100.253: icmp_seq=0 ttl=255 time=1.620 msec (DUP!)
64 bytes from 149.153.2.30: icmp_seq=0 ttl=254 time=1.620 msec (DUP!)
64 bytes from 149.153.2.31: icmp_seq=0 ttl=254 time=21.620 msec (DUP!)
64 bytes from 149.153.2.32: icmp_seq=0 ttl=254 time=21.620 msec (DUP!)
64 bytes from 149.153.100.18: icmp_seq=1 ttl=128 time=9.963 msec

--- 224.0.0.2 ping statistics ---
2 packets transmitted, 2 packets received, +4 duplicates, 0% packet loss
round-trip min/avg/max/mdev = 1.620/9.677/21.620/8.945 ms
```

Again, within two seconds, five devices responded to the *Router Solicitation* message and declared themselves to be routers. Unlike the earlier broadcast, this *Echo Request* has been responded to by devices on the 149.153.2.0 network in addition to those on the 149.153.100.0 network.

5.3   Doing the Net::Ping Thing

Support for programming ping with Perl is provided by the Net::Ping module, as written by Russell Mosemann (and now included as a standard part of Perl). This is a simple module that provides an object-oriented interface to the ICMP *Echo Request* and *Echo Response* messages.

Three methods are associated with a Net::Ping object as follows.

new – creates a Net::Ping object. Three optional parameters can be specified: *protocol* (either icmp, udp or tcp, with udp as the default); *timeout* (the number of seconds to wait for an *Echo Response* to arrive, with a default value of 5 seconds); and *bytes* (the number of bytes to send to the remote system, with defaults of 0 for tcp and icmp and 1 for udp).

ping – sends an *Echo Request* and waits for an *Echo Response*. Two parameters can be specified. The first, which is required, identifies the remote network device to send the request to. The second, which is optional, specifies a number of seconds to wait for a response to arrive. When specified, this overrides the *timeout* value associated with the Net::Ping object.

close – destroys the Net::Ping object created by the call to new.

Of interest is the fact that Net::Ping can use one of three protocols when performing the *Echo Request*. Here is a small program, called multiping, that demonstrates the standard usage of the Net::Ping module:

```perl
#! /usr/bin/perl -w

use strict;
use Net::Ping;

my $host = shift || 'localhost';

my @protos = qw( icmp tcp udp );

foreach my $proto ( @protos )
{
    if ( ( $proto eq 'icmp' ) and ( $> ) )
    {
        print "multiping: 'icmp' only available to root.\n";
        next;
    }

    my $pinger = Net::Ping->new( $proto );

    if ( $pinger->ping( $host ) )
    {
        print "$host is alive to '$proto' pinging.\n";
    }
    else
    {
        print "$host did not respond to '$proto' pinging.\n";
    }

    $pinger->close;
}
```

After the usual start and the use of the Net::Ping module, the $host scalar is set to either localhost or the value passed from the Linux command-line. The list of Net::Ping supported protocols is assigned to the @protos array. The code then iterates over the @protos array.

Within the foreach loop, a check is performed on the protocol to see if it is equal to icmp. If it is, a further check is made to see if the program is being executed under root privilege by examining the value of the built-in $> variable. If the value of this variable is true, then the program is not running as root, and the iteration ends (as Net::Ping cannot use ICMP if it is not running as root).

When the protocol can be used, a Net::Ping object is created based on the protocol value and assigned to the $pinger scalar. The ping method associated with $pinger is then invoked. An appropriate message is displayed if the call to ping succeeds, that is, an *Echo Response* was received as a result of an *Echo Request*

being sent. Otherwise, another message declares that the `ping` was not successful. The iteration ends by destroying the `$pinger` object, invoking its associated
`close` method.

In addition to the restriction that ICMP can only be used by `Net::Ping` when
running as root (with superuser privilege), most Internet sites block TCP and
UDP *Echo Request* messages for security reasons. Increasingly, sites also block
`ping` traffic. This has the unfortunate effect of reducing the usefulness of the
`Net::Ping` module. For instance, when using Linux with standard user privilege,
`multiping` can be invoked to 'contact' the *Linux Journal* website as follows:

```
./multiping www.linuxjournal.com
```

which generates the following results:

```
multiping: 'icmp' only available to root.
www.linuxjournal.com did not respond to 'tcp' pinging.
www.linuxjournal.com did not respond to 'udp' pinging.
```

As can be seen from the above, the use of `Net::Ping` has turned out to be of
little benefit here. It is unclear whether the *Linux Journal* site is operational or
not. Executing `multiping` when logged in as root, produces these results:

```
www.linuxjournal.com is alive to 'icmp' pinging.
www.linuxjournal.com did not respond to 'tcp' pinging.
www.linuxjournal.com did not respond to 'udp' pinging.
```

This is somewhat more useful, but the requirement to be logged in as root limits
`multiping`'s usability. Refer to the exercises at the end of this chapter for some
suggested improvements to `Net::Ping`.

5.4   Tracing Routes

Another important use of ICMP occurs during the execution of the `traceroute`
program. In addition to using the *Echo Request* and *Echo Response* messages,
`traceroute` uses two additional ICMP messages to accomplish its goal, which is
to list (or *trace*) the routers between the network device `traceroute` is executing
on and some other network device. Before discussing the two ICMP messages, let
us take a look at an example of `traceroute` in action. This next command-line
requests the list of routers between `pbmac.itcarlow.ie` and the network device
hosting the *Linux Journal* website:

```
traceroute www.linuxjournal.com
```

This command produces these results:

```
traceroute to www.linuxjournal.com (64.39.18.136), 30 hops max, 38 byte packets
 1  149.153.100.253 (149.153.100.253)  0.617 ms  0.515 ms  0.493 ms
 2  gw.itcarlow.ie (149.153.1.2)  0.979 ms  0.951 ms  0.944 ms
 3  Carlow-7206.itnet.ie (193.1.206.34)  5.349 ms  5.151 ms  5.172 ms
```

```
 4  schiphol-atm3-0-3-itnet.hea.net (193.1.195.217)  6.779 ms  6.600 ms  6.664 ms
 5  miranda-f2-2.dublin.core.hea.net (193.1.195.169)  6.672 ms  6.603 ms  6.720 ms
 6  Uther-g1-0-0.dublin.core.hea.net (193.1.195.242)  6.896 ms  6.891 ms  6.785 ms
 7  158.43.111.41 (158.43.111.41)  34.965 ms  26.386 ms  26.734 ms
 8  ge3-0.cr1.dub2.gbb.uk.uu.net (158.43.152.33)  27.534 ms  27.686 ms  27.064 ms
 9  so3-1-0.tr2.lnd2.alter.net (158.43.253.5)  27.083 ms  27.488 ms  27.984 ms
10  SO-6-0-0.IR1.DCA4.Alter.Net (146.188.8.169)  100.694 ms  100.536 ms  100.212 ms
11  SO-1-0-0.IR1.DCA6.Alter.Net (146.188.13.37)  100.465 ms  100.994 ms  99.924 ms
12  118.at-4-1-0.TR1.DCA6.ALTER.NET (152.63.10.122)  100.342 ms  100.060 ms  99.837 ms
13  287.at-7-2-0.XR1.DCA8.ALTER.NET (152.63.33.249)  102.591 ms  102.765 ms  102.926 ms
14  POS6-0.BR1.DCA8.ALTER.NET (146.188.162.209)  102.968 ms  102.673 ms  102.603 ms
15  wdc-brdr-03.inet.qwest.net (205.171.4.69)  104.287 ms  103.475 ms  101.703 ms
16  wdc-core-03.inet.qwest.net (205.171.24.69)  102.285 ms  101.830 ms  101.909 ms
17  iah-core-01.inet.qwest.net (205.171.5.187)  136.107 ms  137.366 ms  136.327 ms
18  iah-edge-02.inet.qwest.net (205.171.31.14)  136.105 ms  136.530 ms  140.655 ms
19  63-145-96-242.cust.qwest.net (63.145.96.242)  141.461 ms  141.659 ms  141.474 ms
20  vl131.aggr2.sat.rackspace.com (64.39.2.50)  148.885 ms  146.822 ms  146.682 ms
21  64.39.18.136 (64.39.18.136)  141.371 ms  141.704 ms  141.706 ms
```

A total of 20 routers exist between the two network devices. This version of `traceroute` lists the IP name and IP address of each device, together with some timing information. Three time values are shown, and they provide for the calculation of a round-trip delay average.

5.4.1   How `traceroute` works

The `traceroute` program starts by sending some data (usually UDP data) to an *unused* protocol port-number on the remote network device. Prior to sending any data, `traceroute` sets the *Time-To-Live* value in the IP datagram header to 1. When the IP datagram is sent on its way, the first router[4] to receive it decrements the *Time-To-Live* value, realizes that it is now zero and discards the IP datagram (which is what the IP standard dictates should happen when the *Time-To-Live* value included with an IP datagram reaches zero). Immediately prior to the discardation, the router sends an ICMP message back to the network device that initially created the IP datagram. The message, the *Time Exceeded* message, informs the receiver that an IP datagram was discarded due to the *Time-To-Live* value reaching zero. To send the ICMP message, the router encapsulates the ICMP *Time Exceeded* message within an IP datagram prior to delivery. When this datagram arrives at the originating network device, it is passed to the application it is destined for, which, in this case, is the `traceroute` program. Noting the arrival of a *Time Exceeded* message, `traceroute` examines the IP datagram's header and extracts the contents of the *Source IP Address* field. This IP address identifies the router that sent the *Time Exceeded* message.

Next, `traceroute` sends the original datagram again, this time setting the *Time-To-Live* value to 2. The datagram gets past the first router (which decrements the *Time-To-Live* field giving it the value 1) but, at the second router, the *Time-To-Live* value again reaches zero and another ICMP *Time Exceeded* message is generated, which allows `traceroute` to determine the IP address of the second router. This

---

[4]Often referred to as the first *hop*.

process iterates (identifying all the routers between the source and destination network devices) until the datagram arrives at its ultimate destination. As this device is unlikely to be a router, the *Time-To-Live* field will never again reach zero. So how does `traceroute` know when to stop?

The answer has to do with the fact that `traceroute` started out sending data to an *unused* protocol port-number on the remote network device (a fact that the routers ignore, as they operate at the network layer and have no requirement to understand what higher layer protocols are doing). When the datagram arrives at the destination device, it has nowhere to go. The device discards the datagram and sends an ICMP *Destination Unreachable: Port Unreachable* message to the source network device. When `traceroute` receives this ICMP message (which can only have been sent from the remote network device) it knows that the process of listing the routes through the network is complete.

A `Net::Traceroute` module, written by Daniel Hagerty at MIT, is available for download from CPAN. Although useful, `Net::Traceroute` implements its functionality by invoking the operating system's `traceroute` command and parsing any returned results.

5.5 Not So Simple Management with SNMP

The process of using ICMP to learn about a network is simple, and the data gleaned from the results produced by programs such as `ping` and `traceroute` can be very useful. But, what if more data are required? How does the network manager determine how long a network device has been operating? Can a router be asked to specify the contents of its internal routing table? Can a network device indicate when certain things have happened? Perhaps the network manager would like to know when a network device is processing an inordinate amount of IP datagrams containing errors? ICMP cannot help here, as its purpose is solely to report on errors and data pertaining to individual IP datagrams. Some other technology is required and, on the Internet and TCP/IP networks, this technology is SNMP, the *Simple Network Management Protocol*.

5.5.1 A little SNMP history

The process of producing a standardized framework for network management is one of the Internet's greatest technical (and political) sagas. Initially perceived as an interim solution to a problem that would be solved by an all-seeing, all-knowing, all-powerful technical standards committee, the 'stop-gap technology' developed in the short term proved so successful that the 'ultimate solution' struggled in the marketplace. The short-term solution was, of course, the first version of the *Simple Network Management Protocol (SNMP)* and the ultimate solution was the *Common Management Information Protocol (CMIP)*, as proposed by the International Standards Organization's *Open Systems Interconnect (OSI)* model.

As there was a pressing need for some sort of standard network management technology, and as no one was willing to wait for the release of the first version of CMIP, the first version of SNMP (SNMPv1) was quickly deployed. Due to its widespread adoption, SNMPv1 became the de facto standard for network management. Later, a very protracted process produced SNMPv2, which added much needed functionality to the protocol. This included a more efficient *bulk transfer* mechanism as well as additional SNMP operations[5]. With the release of SNMPv2 and its widespread adoption, all hopes of 'migrating' SNMPv1 users to the now-ready CMIP standard were lost. CMIP as an all-encompassing network management technology had lost the battle, although in some market segments (most notably, telecommunications) it is experiencing something of a revival. However, on computer networks and the Internet, SNMP rules.

SNMPv3 (the most recent standard) added security features to the technology, which were missing or incomplete in the previous versions of the technology primarily – it seems – because no one on the standards working group could agree on how security should be handled. The various SNMP authors[6] fought about security for ages, all got rather huffy, then decided not to include security mechanisms in SNMPv2 at all!

5.6   The SNMP Management Framework

SNMP is only one component of the four-part *SNMP Management Framework*. The four components are as follows.

Managed device – a network device capable of being managed (referred to as a *Managed Agent* within the standards documents), and which can respond to requests for management information from another network device.

Management station – a network device capable of sending requests for management information to a *Managed Device* and interpreting any responses. The *Management Station* is often referred to as a *Network Management System (NMS)*.

Managed data – a collection of management data items associated with a particular *Managed Device*, referred to as a *Management Information Base (MIB)* within the standards documents.

Communication protocol – a standard mechanism for sending requests and responses to and from the *Management Station* and any number of *Managed Devices*. This is the role of SNMP.

On closer inspection, *Managed Device* conforms to the description of a *Server* from Chapter 3, and that is what it is: a server capable of responding to requests

---

[5]To be discussed shortly.
[6]Warring factions, if truth be told.

from any number of clients. The *Management Station* conforms to the description of *Client* from Chapter 3. Requests are made to any number of remote servers for service, and an interpretation is performed on the results. In their wisdom, the creators of the framework decided to retain the client/server model, but change the word 'server' to 'agent' and the word 'client' to 'station'. If this all seems rather confusing, do not worry: most think it is.

5.7 Managed Data

The data that allow a device to be managed are stored on a *Managed Device*. How these data are stored is not specified in the standards documents. For instance, the data may be held in a database, a flat-file or in memory. The standards allow the implementer of the *Managed Device* to choose whichever storage mechanism suits. What is specified in the documents is the constitution of the *Managed Data*, that is, what the data items are and what they mean. These metadata[7] are defined in a *Management Information Base (MIB)*.

An MIB is a standardized description of the data items maintained by the *Managed Device*. A large collection of MIBs exist, and it is possible for a single *Managed Device* to maintain data items drawn from more than one MIB. For instance, one MIB describes a collection of data relating to maintaining a network device running TCP/IP, and another describes data relating to Ethernet interface cards. It is not uncommon for a *Managed Device* to maintain the data items described within the TCP/IP MIB and the Ethernet MIB, and to make the values of any data item (regardless of MIB) available to a *Management Station*.

5.7.1 The TCP/IP MIB

When a device that is running SNMP is connected to a TCP/IP network, the *Managed Data* must conform to *at least* the TCP/IP MIB. A number of versions of this MIB exist, with the most recent known as MIB-II (reflecting a reorganization due to the release of SNMPv2). MIB-II is defined in RFC 1213.

Within MIB-II, the *Managed Data* is organized by category (or group), and there are 11 categories in all, as follows.

system – data about the network device, including its administrator-assigned name and the length of time it has been operational.

interfaces – data about the number and type of network interfaces attached to the network device.

at – data about the device's address translation table (which is now deprecated, but is included in MIB-II to maintain backward compatibility).

---

[7]Metadata: data about data.

ip – data about the current state of the IP software running on the network device. This includes details of the internal routing table.

icmp – data about any ICMP messages processed by the network device.

tcp – data about the current state of the TCP software running on the network device.

udp – data about the current state of the UDP software running on the network device.

egp – data about the current state of the EGP (Exterior Gateway Protocol) software running on the network device.

cmot – a category reserved for future use by CMIP, but not presently used.

transmission – data about the underlying transmission media employed by the network device.

snmp – data about the current state of the SNMP software running on the device.

Within each category, specific data items are defined. As an example, let us look at the data items associated with UDP. Within the standards document, each data item (within each category) has a unique name. Here is the unique name and a brief description of the UDP data items.

udpInDatagrams – a count of the total number of UDP datagrams delivered to waiting UDP applications on the network device.

udpNoPorts – a count of the total number of UDP datagrams received but which could not be delivered due to the fact that an application was not waiting for data at the specified protocol port-number.

udpInErrors – a count of the total number of UDP datagrams that could not be delivered (excluding any *udpNoPorts*).

udpOutDatagrams – a count of the total number of UDP datagrams sent to the network by the network device.

udpTable – data items describing the network device's *UDP Listener Table*, which may have a number of entries (see *udpEntry*, below).

udpEntry – data relating to a current listening UDP client, which consists of two additional data items for each *udpEntry*: the IP address of the local network device (referred to as **udpLocalAddress**) and the protocol port-number associated with the listening UDP application (referred to as **udpLocalPort**).

In addition to employing unique names (known as *descriptor*s within the standards), it was decided to assign each MIB data item a unique numeric identifier (known as an *object identifier* within the standards, or *OID* for short). Rather than define a new unique numbering system, the authors of SNMP applied for and were granted exclusive use of a subtree of the ISO's *OSI Management Information Tree*. The subtree is referred to mnemonically as `iso.org.dod.internet` (which is human friendly) or numerically as 1.3.6.1 (which is computer friendly). Below the internet branch, an mgmt subtree contains MIB-II (mnemonically referred to as mib-2). Below this branch are declared the 11 MIB-II categories.

It is therefore possible to refer to each of the categories uniquely and unambiguously using either the mnemonic or numeric identifier, as follows.

system
> iso.org.dod.internet.mgmt.mib-2.system
> 1.3.6.1.2.1.1

interfaces
> iso.org.dod.internet.mgmt.mib-2.interfaces
> 1.3.6.1.2.1.2

at
> iso.org.dod.internet.mgmt.mib-2.at
> 1.3.6.1.2.1.3

ip
> iso.org.dod.internet.mgmt.mib-2.ip
> 1.3.6.1.2.1.4

icmp
> iso.org.dod.internet.mgmt.mib-2.icmp
> 1.3.6.1.2.1.5

tcp
> iso.org.dod.internet.mgmt.mib-2.tcp
> 1.3.6.1.2.1.6

udp
> iso.org.dod.internet.mgmt.mib-2.udp
> 1.3.6.1.2.1.7

egp
> iso.org.dod.internet.mgmt.mib-2.egp
> 1.3.6.1.2.1.8

cmot
> iso.org.dod.internet.mgmt.mib-2.cmot
> 1.3.6.1.2.1.9

transmission
> iso.org.dod.internet.mgmt.mib-2.transmission
> 1.3.6.1.2.1.10

snmp
> iso.org.dod.internet.mgmt.mib-2.snmp
> 1.3.6.1.2.1.11

This scheme is carried further into each of the categories. Continuing with UDP as an example, here are the unique descriptors and object identifiers for the UDP group.

udpInDatagrams

    iso.org.dod.internet.mgmt.mib-2.udp.udpInDatagrams
    1.3.6.1.2.1.7.1

udpNoPorts

    iso.org.dod.internet.mgmt.mib-2.udp.udpNoPorts
    1.3.6.1.2.1.7.2

udpInErrors

    iso.org.dod.internet.mgmt.mib-2.udp.udpInErrors
    1.3.6.1.2.1.7.3

udpOutDatagrams

    iso.org.dod.internet.mgmt.mib-2.udp.udpOutDatagrams
    1.3.6.1.2.1.7.4

udpTable

    iso.org.dod.internet.mgmt.mib-2.udp.udpTable
    1.3.6.1.2.1.7.5

udpEntry

    iso.org.dod.internet.mgmt.mib-2.udp.udpTable.udpEntry
    1.3.6.1.2.1.7.5.1

udpLocalAddress

    iso.org.dod.internet.mgmt.mib-2.udp.udpTable.udpEntry.udpLocalAddress
    1.3.6.1.2.1.7.5.1.1

udpLocalPort

    iso.org.dod.internet.mgmt.mib-2.udp.udpTable.udpEntry.udpLocalPort
    1.3.6.1.2.1.7.5.1.2

If this all looks over elaborate, bear in mind that the purpose of the scheme is to ensure that MIB data items can be referred to uniquely and unambiguously.

Referring to the actual data item when performing an SNMP request adds a kink to this naming scheme. If the data item requested is not part of a table, a 0 needs to be appended to the descriptor or object identifier. So, to request the current value of **udpInErrors** it is necessary to refer to it as udpInErrors.0 within a request. This, in effect, requests the first *instance* of the **udpInErrors** data item, with the first (and, in this case, only) value being found at instance location zero. As is the case with most other computing technologies, the MIB-II definitions start counting at zero, not one. When working with data items from tables, a slightly different instance-specifying mechanism is used. This mechanism will be discussed by way of example later in this chapter.

5.8   The SNMP Protocol

When the framework is considered in its entirety, one can easily become overwhelmed by the details. And this is *before* any discussion of SNMP's operations has taken place. What then makes SNMP *simple*?

The answer has to do in part with the fact that SNMP views data within any MIB as containing a collection of scalar data items[8]. The refusal of the SNMP standards authors to allow for more complex data structures is one of the main differences between SNMP and CMIP (as the latter allows for very complex data structures). As scalars are easy to implement, implementations of the framework are kept simple. Additionally, SNMP supports a very small set of operations which are, again, designed to be easy to implement. By keeping the framework easy to implement, the authors of SNMP hoped to make its adoption an automatic decision, which is precisely what it is. SNMP is, by far, the most widely deployed network management technology in use today.

5.8.1   SNMP's operational model

SNMP supports two broad types of operation: *get* and *set*. In essence, this means that a *Management Station* can *get* an instance value from a *Managed Device*, or *set* the value of an instance on a *Managed Device*, assuming permission to do so has been granted. Every other operation is defined to be a side effect of either *get* or *set*.

This keeps things simple. Rather than have an operation for every conceivable thing a *Management Station* might want to do, all operations are defined in terms of getting a value from, or setting a value on, the *Managed Device*. As an example, this means that rather than having to define a 'shutdown' operation on each *Managed Device*, all that is required is a 'time to next shutdown' instance value in the MIB, which can then be *set* to an appropriate value to signal when the shutdown should occur. The shutdown occurs as a side effect of setting an instance value.

5.8.2   A brief tour of SNMPv1, SNMPv2 and SNMPv3

Within this operational model, SNMPv1 defines five *protocol messages*, three generated on the *Management Station* and two generated on the *Managed Device*. The *Management Station* messages are as follows.

get-request - in its simplest form, this message requests the value of an OID from a *Managed Device*. This is typically the value of the first instance of the OID. Additionally, a list of OIDs can be requested by a single `get-request` message. If a single OID is requested, or a list of OIDs is requested, each OID/value pairing is referred to as a *variable binding*.

---

[8]The fact that Perl has a fundamental data type *scalar* is purely coincidental, albeit pleasantly so.

get-next-request – when requesting a collection of data items (which may be stored within a table), the value of the first instance of the OID is requested with `get-request`. Subsequent values (that is, all other instances) can be requested by iteration and the use of `get-next-request`.

set-request – sends a request to a *Managed Device* to set the value associated with a specified OID.

The *Managed Device* messages are as follows.

get-response – is sent in response to a `get-request`, `get-next-request` and `set-request` message. For *get* operations, the response will contain the value requested (or an error code if things went wrong). For *set* operations, the response will indicate success or failure.

trap – is an unsolicited message from the *Managed Device* to the *Management Station*. This is generated due to the occurrence of some activity that the *Management Station* expressed an interest in. For instance, a *Management Station* may want to know when the amount of discarded IP datagrams reaches a certain threshold. Rather than poll the *Managed Device* by iterating with a `get-request` message, a `trap` could be *set* to tell the *Managed Device* to monitor the threshold and generate the `trap` message appropriately. Of course, to receive the `trap`, the *Management Station* needs to be listening.

The advent of SNMPv2[9] introduced two additional protocol messages and replaced another as follows.

get-bulk-request – provides a mechanism for requesting a large amount of instance values within a single request. This mechanism is much improved over the `get-request`/`get-next-request` mechanism from SNMPv1.

inform-request – allows one *Management Station* to communicate with another *Management Station* by way of requests and responses.

snmpV2-trap – replaces the `trap` message from SNMPv1, and improves the trapping mechanism by making the format of the Protocol Data Unit (PDU) conform with those employed by the other messages.

Unfortunately, the development and release of SNMPv2 introduced a number of problems, not least of which was that the new technology standards were no longer compatible with SNMPv1. This has been addressed somewhat with the release of SNMPv3 which attempts to coexist with both SNMPv1 and SNMPv2, as well as provide for the easier integration of future functionality. As a technology, SNMPv3 is best known for *finally* providing the SNMP framework with a *real* security mechanism.

---

[9]Often referred to as *SNMPv2C*.

5.8.3   SNMP communities

Each of the SNMP versions share the notion of *community*. It can be useful to think of SNMP communities as domains. *Managed Devices* within organizations belong to a specific, named community. When requests are made to a *Managed Device* from a *Management Station*, the *community string* must be specified. In this way, SNMP supports a simple, community-based access policy. Typically, devices that are globally visible belong to a community called `public`. If access is to be restricted, the network administrator can assign whichever community string is deemed appropriate.

For instance, on the network used during the writing of *Programming the Network with Perl*, a small number of devices use `public` as their community string. The `private` string is also used. Devices managed by the campus's *Computing Services Department* have a different, closely guarded community string. The campus is connected to the Internet via *ITnet*, one of the large, third-level academic networks in Ireland. Devices on *ITnet* have another community string. It is sometimes necessary for a *Management Station* to try a number of community strings in an attempt to communicate with a collection of *Managed Devices*.

5.9   The Net::SNMP Module

As with most areas of computer networking, Perl programmers have been busy developing add-on modules to make the life of protocol programmers easier. Happily, there is no shortage of modules to ease the programming of SNMP-based applications. In the sections which follow, Net::SNMP, by David M. Town, is used to develop a collection of *Management Station* utility programs.

Net::SNMP is available on CPAN, and is installed and tested with the usual set of commands, as follows:

```
gunzip Net-SNMP-3.60.tar.gz
tar xvf Net-SNMP-3.60.tar
cd Net-SNMP-3.6
perl Makefile.PL
make
make test
su
make install
<ctrl-D>
man Net::SNMP
perl -e 'use Net::SNMP'
```

One of the great things about Net::SNMP is that it removes the need to understand all of the nitty-gritty details of programming SNMP. SNMP is the most involved and detailed Internet protocol. The devil is *most definitely* in the details. And this is before discussing *Abstract Syntax Notation One (ASN.1)* and the *Basic Encoding Rules (BERs)*, two technologies that SNMP relies on internally, and which are (rather conveniently) ignored in *Programming the Network with Perl*. All this complexity can be off-putting to many. But do not worry. When `Net::SNMP` is used, programming SNMP is, well, *simple*.

`Net::SNMP` supports SNMPv1 and SNMPv2C. The API is object oriented in nature: an object of type `Net::SNMP` is created, then methods associated with the object are called as required. Two distinct object-oriented interfaces are provided: *blocking* and *non-blocking*. When the *blocking* interface is used, an invocation of a method halts (or 'blocks') further program execution until the method returns. When the *non-blocking* interface is used, an invocation of a method returns immediately, allowing program execution to continue. The code in the method is queued, and a *callback* subroutine is associated with it. Later, when a program requests that the methods in the queue be processed, the *callback* subroutines are executed in response to the queued methods being invoked. Typically, the arguments provided to a method differ as to whether it is called using the *blocking* or *non-blocking* interface.

The programs developed during the remainder of this chapter use the *blocking* interface. This keeps things as simple and understandable as possible. That said, the *non-blocking* interface is very useful, and readers are encouraged to explore the mechanism, starting with the example code included as part of the `Net::SNMP` documentation[10].

5.9.1   The `Net::SNMP` methods

The methods associated with a `Net::SNMP` object are as follows.

session – creates a new `Net::SNMP` object.

close – destroys a previously created `Net::SNMP` object.

snmp_event_loop – processes any queued methods (when the *non-blocking* interface is used).

get_request – sends the SNMP `get-request` message to a *Managed Device*, and waits for a response.

get_next_request – sends the SNMP `get-next-request` message to a *Managed Device*, and waits for a response.

set_request – sends the SNMP `set_request` message to a *Managed Device*, and waits for a response.

trap – sends the SNMPv1 `trap` message to a *Managed Device*.

---

[10]Another great thing about `Net::SNMP` is that David M. Town provides *excellent* documentation, both in POD and manpage format.

get_bulk_request – sends the SNMPv2 get_bulk_request message to a *Managed Device* and waits for a response.

inform_request – sends the SNMPv2 inform_request to a *Management Station*.

snmpV2_trap – sends the SNMPv2 snmpV2-trap message to a *Managed Device*.

get_table – uses a collection of get_next_request messages (SNMPv1) or a get_bulk_request message (SNMPv2) to request the retrieval of a table of data from a *Managed Device*.

version – provides a mechanism to get or set the SNMP version associated with the Net::SNMP object.

error – returns the current error message associated with the Net::SNMP object.

hostname – returns the IP name or address of the *Managed Device* associated with the Net::SNMP object.

error_status – returns the current numeric error status associated with the Net::SNMP object.

error_index – returns the current numeric error index associated with the Net::SNMP object.

var_bind_list – returns a hash reference to the variable binding associated with the Net::SNMP object, and created as a result of the last successfully received SNMP response.

timeout – gets or sets the number of seconds to wait for a response to a request. The default is 5 seconds.

retries – gets or sets the number of times Net::SNMP tries to send a message to a *Managed Device*. The default is one time.

mtu – gets or sets the Maximum Transmission Unit associated with the Net::SNMP object. The default is 1500 octets[11].

translate – gets or sets the Net::SNMP objects translation modes.

debug – switches on or off the Net::SNMP internal debugging messages. By default, debugging messages are off. It can be quite instructive to switch them on (occasionally).

In addition to the methods associated with a Net::SNMP object, the module provides three (non-OO) subroutines:

oid_context_match – provides a mechanism to check if one OID is equal to, or a subtree of, another;

oid_lex_sort – sorts a list of OIDs into lexicographical order;

ticks_to_time – takes a raw 'timeticks' value and converts it to a human-readable time string.

---

[11]An *octet* is an 8 bit byte.

When communicating with a *Managed Device*, `session` is called to *prepare* for the SNMP interaction. Note that SNMP uses UDP as its transport protocol, so do not assume that a connection is established by the call to `session`. A *facility* is prepared and the `Net::SNMP` object is created, providing a means to call any of the above methods. When the SNMP interaction is over, the `close` method is called to destroy the facility.

It may seem strange that SNMP uses the unreliable, connectionless UDP to carry its data. Surely network management data are important, requiring the use of a reliable transport protocol to get the data through? Yes, network management data are important, but networks do not exist to carry network management traffic, do they? The SNMP architects decided that the impact of carrying network management data on a network should be kept to a minimum, so UDP was chosen as the transport technology. Additionally, it was felt that a *Management Station* would, typically, be pressed into service when a network was experiencing problems. If the problems were severe, the network may be unable to establish any reliable connections using TCP. However, low-overhead UDP data *may* get through, allowing some sort of diagnosis to be determined from the received network management responses.

5.10 Working With Net::SNMP

For now, let us stick with UDP as the protocol of interest to the network manager. A program (called `udpstats`) contacts a *Managed Device* and requests the current values for the MIB-II udp group. As was shown in the discussion of the udp group earlier, four instance values and a table of UDP listeners are maintained.

Assuming the existence of the `udpstats` program, here is the Linux command-line to use to request the MIB-II udp group from one of the routers identified earlier in this chapter:

```
./udpstats 149.153.100.253 xxxxxx
```

In this example, xxxxxx is the SNMP community string required by this router (which operates on the network running at *The Institute of Technology, Carlow*)[12].

This invocation of `udpstats` produces the following results:

```
Requesting 'udp' group data for: 149.153.100.253, xxxxxx, SNMPv2

UDP instance values:

1.3.6.1.2.1.7.1.0 => 18821809
1.3.6.1.2.1.7.2.0 => 5303516
1.3.6.1.2.1.7.3.0 => 1
1.3.6.1.2.1.7.4.0 => 10495825
```

---

[12]The actual community string is not shown in an attempt to protect your author from the wrath of the on-campus *Computing Services Department*.

```
UDP table values:

1.3.6.1.2.1.7.5.1.1.149.153.1.253.496 => 149.153.1.253
1.3.6.1.2.1.7.5.1.1.149.153.1.253.520 => 149.153.1.253
1.3.6.1.2.1.7.5.1.1.149.153.1.253.1985 => 149.153.1.253
1.3.6.1.2.1.7.5.1.1.149.153.2.253.49 => 149.153.2.253
1.3.6.1.2.1.7.5.1.1.149.153.2.253.51505 => 149.153.2.253
1.3.6.1.2.1.7.5.1.1.149.153.2.253.56134 => 149.153.2.253
1.3.6.1.2.1.7.5.1.1.149.153.100.253.67 => 149.153.100.253
1.3.6.1.2.1.7.5.1.1.149.153.100.253.161 => 149.153.100.253
1.3.6.1.2.1.7.5.1.2.149.153.1.253.496 => 496
1.3.6.1.2.1.7.5.1.2.149.153.1.253.520 => 520
1.3.6.1.2.1.7.5.1.2.149.153.1.253.1985 => 1985
1.3.6.1.2.1.7.5.1.2.149.153.2.253.49 => 49
1.3.6.1.2.1.7.5.1.2.149.153.2.253.51505 => 51505
1.3.6.1.2.1.7.5.1.2.149.153.2.253.56134 => 56134
1.3.6.1.2.1.7.5.1.2.149.153.100.253.67 => 67
1.3.6.1.2.1.7.5.1.2.149.153.100.253.161 => 161
```

Which, admittedly, looks a little complicated. However, it is relatively easy to decipher. The first thing to bear in mind is that the Net::SNMP module works with numeric OIDs (1.3.6.1.2.1.7.1.0), as opposed to human-friendly mnemonics (udpInDatagrams). So, all of the values to the left of the => symbol are numeric OIDs. This means that the 'UDP instance values' lines of output correspond to the current counts for udpInDatagrams, udpNoPorts, udpInErrors and udpOutDatagrams. The numbers reported (except for udpInErrors) are very large. It is reasonable to assume that the device in question has been operating for quite some time. As will be seen later in this chapter, it is possible to ask the device how long it has been running in its current state.

The 'UDP table values' come next. The OIDs look strange, as they appear to contain embedded IP addresses, specifically 149.153.1.253, 149.153.2.253 and 149.153.100.253. The trailing positive integers add to the confusion.

Recall from earlier that the instance specifying mechanism used with tables differs from that used by single instance OIDs. Rather than appending a trailing '.0' to the OID to retrieve the value, with tables some other value is appended. Typically, this is some data that uniquely identify the row in the multi-columnar table. For the MIB-II udp group, the combination of an IP address and a protocol port-number is used, and this combination is appended to the *base* numeric OID. With UDP, the base numeric OIDs are 1.3.6.1.2.1.7.5.1.1 for udpLocalAddress and 1.3.6.1.2.1.7.5.1.2 for udpLocalPort. It is now possible to work out that this device currently has eight UDP listeners active, as follows:

149.153.1.253 using port 496;

149.153.1.253 using port 520;

149.153.1.253 using port 1985;

149.153.2.253 using port 49;

149.153.2.253 using port 51505;

149.153.2.253 using port 56134;

149.153.100.253 using port 67;

149.153.100.253 using port 161.

Eight listeners seems like a lot for an on-campus router. However, a review of the IANA protocol port-number assignments (first used in Chapter 2, *Snooping*), uncovers the purpose of most of these UDP listeners, as follows:

496 is used by the *Protocol Independent Multicasting* technology;

520 is used by the on-site local routing process, which is a variation on the established *Routing Information Protocol (RIP)*;

1985 is used by the *Hot Standby Router Protocol*;

49 is used by the *TACACS Login Host Protocol*;

67 is used by the *Bootstrap Protocol Server*;

161 is used by *SNMP*.

Any self-respecting network manager should be able to say why these UDP listeners exist on this router. As for the other two listeners, at ports 51505 and 56134, they fall within the range of the dynamically assigned or private protocol port-numbers. What they are listening for is a mystery. However, that self-same network manager should find their existence very interesting (if not *alarming*).

It is also somewhat strange that the *Managed Device* queried appears to have more than one IP address, namely 149.153.1.253, 149.153.2.253 and (as expected) 149.153.100.253. When one considers that routers exist to connect two or more separate networks together, this strangeness is explainable. As routers have two or more connections, and as each *connection* on an IP network must have its own unique IP address, it follows that routers have more than one assigned IP address. It is therefore reasonable to assume that this router (149.153.100.253) has three connections to three individual networks, each with their own unique IP address.

5.10.1 Working with mnemonic object identifiers

The Net::SNMP module also uses numeric OIDs when specifying the MIB data to access when getting or setting data. This is great for the computer, but quickly becomes tedious for the programmer. To provide for increased convenience, a Perl module called OIDs.pm allows OIDs to be specified using their mnemonic, programmer-friendly descriptor. The entire source code for this module can be found in Appendix E.

The OIDs.pm module is a large collection of Perl constant definitions. By default, nothing is exported to a program using the module. Any single OID descriptor can be imported by name, as can collections of descriptors by group. Here are some examples:

```
use OIDs qw( sysUpTime ipForwarding udpInDatagrams );

use OIDs qw( :interfaces );

use OIDs qw( :tcp :udp ifNumber );
```

The first example imports three individual OID descriptors, one from the MIB-II system group, another from the ip group, and the last from the udp group.

The second example imports the entire collection of OIDs included in the MIB-II interfaces group.

The last example imports the ifNumber OID from the MIB-II interfaces group, together with the entire collection of OIDs included in the tcp and udp groups. Note that the order is important here, as the individually imported items must come after the group tags.

5.10.2   The udpstats source code

And now, after all that, here is the entire source code to the udpstats program, followed by a detailed description of its function:

```
#! /usr/bin/perl -w

use strict;
use Socket;
use Net::SNMP qw( oid_lex_sort );
use OIDs qw( :udp );

sub udp_get_table {
    my ( $sess, $requestOID ) = @_;

    my $responsePDU = $sess->get_table( $requestOID );

    if ( !defined( $responsePDU ) )
    {
        print "udpstats: OID: ", $requestOID, " : ",
                $sess->error, "\n";
    }

    foreach my $resp ( oid_lex_sort ( keys %{ $responsePDU } ) )
    {
        print "$resp => ", $responsePDU->{ $resp }, "\n";
    }
    print "\n";
}
```

```perl
my $snmp_host       = shift || 'localhost';
my $snmp_community  = shift || 'public';
my $snmp_version    = shift || '2';
my $snmp_port       = shift || 161;

$snmp_host = inet_ntoa( scalar gethostbyname( $snmp_host ) );

print "Requesting 'udp' group data for: $snmp_host, ";
print "$snmp_community, SNMPv$snmp_version\n\n";

my ( $snmp_session, $snmp_error ) = Net::SNMP->session(
                         -hostname   => $snmp_host,
                         -community  => $snmp_community,
                         -version    => $snmp_version,
                         -port       => $snmp_port,
                         -debug      => 0 );

if ( !defined( $snmp_session ) )
{
    die "udpstats: an error occurred: ", $snmp_error, "\n";
}

my @udpOIDs = ( udpInDatagrams, udpNoPorts,
                udpInErrors, udpOutDatagrams );

my $responsePDU = $snmp_session->get_request( @udpOIDs );

if ( !defined( $responsePDU ) )
{
    warn "udpstats: ", $snmp_session->error, "\n";
}

print "UDP instance values:\n\n";

foreach my $resp ( oid_lex_sort ( keys %{ $responsePDU } ) )
{
    print "$resp => ", $responsePDU->{ $resp }, "\n";
}

print "\nUDP table values:\n\n";

udp_get_table( $snmp_session, udpTable );

$snmp_session->close;
```

The program starts with the usual first line, followed by the importation of
four modules. Strictness is switched on and the Socket module is included.
The Net::SNMP module is included and the code explicitly asks to include the
oid_lex_sort subroutine, which is not imported by default. The OIDs module is
included and the entire MIB-II udp group comes with it:

```
#! /usr/bin/perl -w

use strict;
use Socket;
use Net::SNMP qw( oid_lex_sort );
use OIDs qw( :udp );
```

A subroutine called `udp_get_table` is then defined. This subroutine will be examined after the rest of the `udpstats` program has been described.

Four lexically scoped scalars are then defined, taking their values from command-line arguments (if they are available) or from default values specified in the code. Note that the default SNMP version is SNMPv2 and the protocol port-number is 161:

```
my $snmp_host      = shift || 'localhost';
my $snmp_community = shift || 'public';
my $snmp_version   = shift || '2';
my $snmp_port      = shift || 161;
```

The SNMP *Managed Device* is identified by the `$snmp_host` scalar variable. This value is passed through `gethostbyname` and `inet_ntoa` to convert it to dotted-decimal. A brief message is then displayed on screen which describes what the program is about to try and do:

```
$snmp_host = inet_ntoa( scalar gethostbyname( $snmp_host ) );

print "Requesting 'udp' group data for: $snmp_host, ";
print "$snmp_community, SNMPv$snmp_version\n\n";
```

The `session` constructor from Net::SNMP is then invoked. Upon success, this method creates the Net::SNMP object and assigns it to the `$snmp_session` scalar. Upon failure, `$snmp_session` is set to `undef` and an appropriate error message is assigned to the `$snmp_error` scalar. Note how this call to `session` takes five named parameters: the values of the four lexically scoped scalars, together with a value for the –debug parameter. Set this to 1 to switch on the Net::SNMP debugging messages but be warned, the output can be very verbose:

```
my ( $snmp_session, $snmp_error ) = Net::SNMP->session(
                         -hostname    => $snmp_host,
                         -community   => $snmp_community,
                         -version     => $snmp_version,
                         -port        => $snmp_port,
                         -debug       => 0 );

if ( !defined( $snmp_session ) )
{
    die "udpstats: an error occurred: ", $snmp_error, "\n";
}
```

A check is performed on the value of $snmp_session to see whether or not the call to session was successful. If it was not, the udpstats program dies with an appropriate error message. Otherwise, the program proceeds.

A list of mnemonic OIDs is assigned to the @udpOIDs array. This array is then passed to the get_request method associated with the newly created Net::SNMP object. As this code is running in 'blocking mode' by default, udpstats waits for a response to arrive for this request. If no response arrives within 5 seconds (the default) or if an error occurred, the $responsePDU scalar is set to undef. If a response does arrive, a reference to a hash is assigned to $responsePDU. This hash is keyed by OID, allowing easy access to the values contained in the variable binding list included with the response PDU. Again, this code checks the value returned from the method call. If the value is undefined, a warning message is displayed:

```
my @udpOIDs = ( udpInDatagrams, udpNoPorts,
                    udpInErrors, udpOutDatagrams );

my $responsePDU = $snmp_session->get_request( @udpOIDs );

if ( !defined( $responsePDU ) )
{
    warn "udpstats: ", $snmp_session->error, "\n";
}
```

The now-familiar hash traversal mechanism is used to print the contents of the hash referred to by $responsePDU. The oid_lex_sort subroutine is used to sort the OIDs in lexicographical order:

```
print "UDP instance values:\n\n";

foreach my $resp ( oid_lex_sort ( keys %{ $responsePDU } ) )
{
    print "$resp => ", $responsePDU->{ $resp }, "\n";
}
```

A single call to the udp_get_table subroutine is then made, then the Net::SNMP object is destroyed by a call to close. The udpstats program then terminates:

```
print "\nUDP table values:\n\n";

udp_get_table( $snmp_session, udpTable );

$snmp_session->close;
```

Let us look at the source code to the udp_get_table subroutine, which expects to receive two parameters: a valid Net::SNMP object and a numeric OID. These values are placed into the $sess and $requestOID scalar variables, respectively:

```
sub udp_get_table {
    my ( $sess, $requestOID ) = @_;
```

The `get_table` method associated with the Net::SNMP object is then invoked and, as with the call to the `get_request` method, a hash reference is returned upon success, whereas `undef` is returned if an error or a timeout occurred. The code checks for this and prints an error message, if required:

```perl
my $responsePDU = $sess->get_table( $requestOID );

if ( !defined( $responsePDU ) )
{
    print "udpstats: OID: ", $requestOID, " : ",
                $sess->error, "\n";
}
```

If all is well (that is, the hash reference does exist and is populated with the contents of the response's variable bindings), standard hash traversal code prints out the contents, which are keyed by OID:

```perl
foreach my $resp ( oid_lex_sort ( keys %{ $responsePDU } ) )
{
    print "$resp => ", $responsePDU->{ $resp }, "\n";
}
print "\n";
}
```

Which, when invoked, displays the entire table of UDP listeners.

In order to fully analyse the data returned from `udpstats` and consider the data in context, a requirement exists to determine the length of time the device has been operational. A small program called `howlongup` does just that.

5.10.3   The `howlongup` program

The MIB-II `system` group contains the data item needed to determine how long a device has been operating[13], and it is called `sysUpTime`. Here is the source code to the `howlongup` program, which, in addition to retrieving the value of `sysUpTime`, also requests the value of the system description (`sysDescr`) and name (`sysName`):

```perl
#! /usr/bin/perl -w

use strict;
use Socket;
use Net::SNMP;
use OIDs qw( sysDescr sysName sysUpTime );

my $snmp_host      = shift || 'localhost';
my $snmp_community = shift || 'public';
my $snmp_version   = shift || '2';
my $snmp_port      = shift || 161;
```

---

[13]Actually, it contains a value that indicates how long the SNMP agent has been running on the *Managed Device*.

```
$snmp_host = inet_ntoa( scalar gethostbyname( $snmp_host ) );

print "Requesting system data items for: $snmp_host, ";
print "$snmp_community, SNMPv$snmp_version\n\n";

my ( $snmp_session, $snmp_error ) = Net::SNMP->session(
                          -hostname    => $snmp_host,
                          -community   => $snmp_community,
                          -version     => $snmp_version,
                          -port        => $snmp_port,
                          -debug       => 0 );

if ( !defined( $snmp_session ) )
{
    die "howlongup: an error occurred: ", $snmp_error, "\n";
}

my @sysOIDs = ( sysDescr, sysUpTime, sysName );

my $responsePDU = $snmp_session->get_request( @sysOIDs );

if ( !defined( $responsePDU ) )
{
    warn "howlongup: ", $snmp_session->error, "\n";
}

print "Descr. => ", $responsePDU->{ OIDs::sysDescr }, "\n";
print "Name   => ", $responsePDU->{ OIDs::sysName }, "\n";
print "UpTime => ", $responsePDU->{ OIDs::sysUpTime }, "\n\n";

$snmp_session->close;
```

Having worked through the source code to udpstats, understanding this program is easy. A single get_request method call requests the value of the three MIB-II system group data items. The results of the request are (on success) entered into the hash referenced by $responsePDU and then displayed on screen using three print statements.

The howlongup program can be executed from the Linux command-line as follows:

```
./howlongup 149.153.100.253 xxxxxx
```

This produces the following results:

```
Requesting system data items for: 149.153.100.253, xxxxxx, SNMPv2

Descr. => Cisco Internetwork Operating System Software
          IOS (tm) MSFC Software (C6MSFC-JSV-M), Version 12.1(6)E,
          EARLY DEPLOYMENT RELEASE SOFTWARE (fc3)
          TAC Support: http://www.cisco.com/cgi-bin/
                            ibld/view.pl?i=support
          Copyright (c) 1986-2001 by cisco Systems, In
Name   => CAT6000_MSFC
UpTime => 82 days, 18:34:42.41
```

The system description clearly shows that this device is one of the many available from *cisco Systems*. The system name is locally assigned by the network manager, although the value of sysName for this device looks like it is set to some factory-set default. The system 'uptime' value gives some clue as to the large numbers reported by the udpstats program. Eighty-two days is a long time for any device to operate continually, but does this explain over five million udpNoPorts? That is an awful lot of traffic, averaging approximately 64 000 datagrams per day! It is time for the network manager to snoop the traffic arriving at the 149.153.100.253 router (perhaps over a 48 hour period) in an attempt to determine why so many UDP datagrams are arriving, yet have no destination application waiting to receive them.

It is a simple exercise to create udpstats2, which combines sysUpTime with data from the MIB-II udp group, producing output as follows:

```
Requesting 'udp' group data for: 149.153.100.253, xxxxxx, SNMPv2

UpTime => 82 days, 18:35:04.64

UDP instance values:

1.3.6.1.2.1.7.1.0 => 19079331
1.3.6.1.2.1.7.2.0 => 5356687
1.3.6.1.2.1.7.3.0 => 1
1.3.6.1.2.1.7.4.0 => 10707080

UDP table values:

1.3.6.1.2.1.7.5.1.1.149.153.1.253.496 => 149.153.1.253
1.3.6.1.2.1.7.5.1.1.149.153.1.253.520 => 149.153.1.253
1.3.6.1.2.1.7.5.1.1.149.153.1.253.1985 => 149.153.1.253
1.3.6.1.2.1.7.5.1.1.149.153.2.253.49 => 149.153.2.253
1.3.6.1.2.1.7.5.1.1.149.153.2.253.51505 => 149.153.2.253
1.3.6.1.2.1.7.5.1.1.149.153.2.253.56134 => 149.153.2.253
1.3.6.1.2.1.7.5.1.1.149.153.100.253.67 => 149.153.100.253
1.3.6.1.2.1.7.5.1.1.149.153.100.253.161 => 149.153.100.253
1.3.6.1.2.1.7.5.1.2.149.153.1.253.496 => 496
1.3.6.1.2.1.7.5.1.2.149.153.1.253.520 => 520
1.3.6.1.2.1.7.5.1.2.149.153.1.253.1985 => 1985
1.3.6.1.2.1.7.5.1.2.149.153.2.253.49 => 49
1.3.6.1.2.1.7.5.1.2.149.153.2.253.51505 => 51505
1.3.6.1.2.1.7.5.1.2.149.153.2.253.56134 => 56134
1.3.6.1.2.1.7.5.1.2.149.153.100.253.67 => 67
1.3.6.1.2.1.7.5.1.2.149.153.100.253.161 => 161
```

5.11   What's Up?

The udpstats2 program demonstrates an important technique, which is that it is often necessary to draw on data items from more than one MIB-II group to deduce meaning from network management raw data. However, it is possible to monitor a single data item and still perform a useful function.

Consider a network manager who wishes to keep track of a collection of network devices. In addition to determining the 'uptime' for each device, the network manager also wants to know which device (if any) has restarted recently.

One strategy is to set a `trap` on each and every device to signal a *Management Station* whenever a restart occurs. However, this assumes a *Management Station* is operating continuously.

Another strategy is to use the value of `sysUpTime` from the MIB-II `system` group, and note when the value returned from a *Managed Device* is less than some previously retrieved value.

This is what the `whatsup` program does. Prior to issuing any SNMP requests, the `whatsup` program pre-processes a small text file called `whatsup.txt`. This file contains the IP name or address of the device to keep track of, the community string to use when querying the device, and the most recent value of the `sysUpTime` in *timeticks*[14]. Within `whatsup.txt`, each of these values are delimited by the : character.

Here is the contents of `whatsup.txt` as it exists on `pbmac.itcarlow.ie`:

```
149.153.100.10:public:0
gw.itcarlow.ie:wwwwww:0
149.153.100.253:xxxxxx:0
glasnost.itcarlow.ie:public:0
193.1.206.34:zzzzzz:0
```

As before, the actual community strings have been changed to protect the networks used during the production of *Programming the Network with Perl*.

When the `whatsup` program is executed, each *Managed Device* in the file is contacted, and the value of the `sysUpTime` OID is requested. The retrieved value is compared with the value in the `whatsup.txt` file. If the retrieved value is a larger timeticks value than that stored in the file, the *Managed Device* is assumed to still be operating. Otherwise, the *Managed Device* is assumed to have been restarted. At the end of each execution, the `whatsup` program updates the `whatsup.txt` file with the most recently available data. As long as the `whatsup` program is executed with some reasonable frequency (perhaps once a day[15]), this strategy should produce usable results.

Let us work through the source code to the `whatsup` program. The first five lines are as expected. Of note is the fact that the `ticks_to_time` subroutine is imported from `Net::SNMP` and the `sysUpTime` OID is imported from the `OIDs.pm` module:

---

[14]The number of hundredths of a second since the SNMP agent on the *Managed Device* started executing.

[15]On Linux and UNIX-like systems, the `cron` program can automate program execution.

```
#! /usr/bin/perl -w

use strict;
use Socket;
use Net::SNMP qw( ticks_to_time );
use OIDs qw( sysUpTime );
```

Two lexically scoped variables are then defined. The $whatsupfile scalar is set to the supplied command-line value, or to whatsup.txt by default. A hash called %managed_agents is also defined, and is initially empty:

```
my $whatsupfile = shift || 'whatsup.txt';
my %managed_agents = ();
```

The file referred to by $whatsupfile is then opened for reading, and the content of the file is brought into the program one line at a time. For each line, the %managed_agents hash is updated. Referring to the three colon-delimited fields from the whatsup.txt file above, the IP name or address of the *Managed Device* is used as the hash key. The hash value is a reference to an anonymous, two-element array, and the array takes its values from the community string and timeticks value as read in from the file. When the entire file has been processed and the hash populated, the file is closed:

```
open WHATSUPFILE_IN, $whatsupfile
    or die "whatsup: could not open file: $whatsupfile.\n";

while ( <WHATSUPFILE_IN> )
{
    my ( $host, $comm, $ticks ) = split /:/;
    chomp( $ticks );
    $managed_agents{ $host } = [ $comm, $ticks ];
}

close WHATSUPFILE_IN;
```

The code then iterates. Each *Managed Device* stored in the %managed_agents hash is processed sequentially. The first order of business is to create a Net::SNMP object to enable SNMP communication with the *Managed Device*:

```
print "\nThe whatsup results:\n\n";

foreach my $h ( keys %managed_agents )
{
    my $snmp_host      = inet_ntoa( scalar gethostbyname( $h ) );
    my $snmp_community = $managed_agents{ $h }->[0];

    my ( $snmp_session, $snmp_error ) = Net::SNMP->session(
                        -hostname    => $snmp_host,
                        -community   => $snmp_community,
                        -translate   => [ -timeticks => 0x0 ] );
```

```
if ( !defined( $snmp_session ) )
{
    warn "whatsup: an error occurred: ", $snmp_error, "\n";
    next;
}
```

Note the inclusion of the -translate parameter to the session method. By setting the -timeticks mode to false (0x0), the object has been instructed not
to convert the raw timeticks values received from the *Managed Device* into a
human-readable form. This allows for simple numeric comparisons later in the
code.

Note too the use of next if the object cannot be created. A get_request for
the sysUpTime OID is then sent to the *Managed Device* and, if the request is
successful, a scalar called $sysTm is assigned the 'uptime' value:

```
my $responsePDU = $snmp_session->get_request( sysUpTime );

if ( !defined( $responsePDU ) )
{
    warn "whatsup: ", $snmp_session->error, "\n";
}

my $sysTm = $responsePDU->{ OIDs::sysUpTime };
```

If the current value of the sysUpTime OID is greater than the value stored in the
whatsup.txt file, a message is displayed indicating that the *Managed Device* is
still operating. The timeticks value (as stored in the $sysTm scalar) is converted
into a human-readable form prior to display, by passing it to the ticks_to_time
subroutine:

```
if ( $sysTm > $managed_agents{ $h }->[1] )
{
    print "\'$h\' is still up, with uptime reported as ",
        ticks_to_time( $sysTm ), "\n\n";
}
```

If the current value of the sysUpTime OID is not greater than the value stored in
the whatsup.txt file, a message is displayed indicating that the *Managed Device*
may have restarted. The previously reported value of sysUpTime is displayed
together with the current one:

```
else
{
    print "WARNING: \'$h\' may have restarted:\n";
    print "\tit has a reported uptime of ",
        ticks_to_time( $sysTm ), "\n";
    print "\tbut previously reported uptime of ",
        ticks_to_time( $managed_agents{ $h }->[1] ),
            "\n\n";
}
```

The value of `sysUpTime` contained in the `%managed_agents` hash is then updated with the most recently retrieved value (contained in `$sysTm`). The `Net::SNMP` object is then destroyed by calling its associated `close` method, and the iteration ends:

```
$managed_agents{ $h }->[1] = $sysTm;

$snmp_session->close;
}
```

With the entire collection of *Managed Devices* processed, the contents of the `whatsup.txt` file is updated. The file is opened for writing (destroying any existing contents), then the `%managed_agents` hash is iterated over once again to output its contents to the file. The `whatsup` program then terminates:

```
open WHATSUPFILE_OUT, ">$whatsupfile"
    or die "whatsup: could not open file: $whatsupfile to write.\n";

foreach my $h ( keys %managed_agents )
{
    my $c = $managed_agents{ $h }->[0];
    my $t = $managed_agents{ $h }->[1];

    print WHATSUPFILE_OUT "$h:$c:$t\n";
}

close WHATSUPFILE_OUT;
```

Invoking the program could not be easier. Assuming the existence of a file called `whatsup.txt` in the same directory as the `whatsup` program, use this command-line:

```
./whatsup
```

On `pbmac.itcarlow.ie`, the following results were produced:

```
The whatsup results:
'149.153.100.10' is still up, with uptime reported as 83 days, 19:48:25.84
'gw.itcarlow.ie' is still up, with uptime reported as 35 days, 18:24:41.76
'149.153.100.253' is still up, with uptime reported as 83 days, 19:48:25.86
'glasnost.itcarlow.ie' is still up, with uptime reported as 23 days, 01:31:33.36
'193.1.206.34' is still up, with uptime reported as 56 days, 18:14:13.88
```

All of the managed devices are up and running. Note that data on `glasnost.itcarlow.ie` are included. This device is not a router (it is a Web server). However, this does not stop it running an SNMP agent and responding to SNMP requests. The `whatsup.txt` file now looks like this:

```
149.153.100.10:public:724250584
gw.itcarlow.ie:wwwwww:309028176
149.153.100.253:xxxxxx:724250586
glasnost.itcarlow.ie:public:199269336
193.1.206.34:zzzzzz:490405388
```

The timeticks field has been updated for each *Managed Device*. A short time later, `glasnost.itcarlow.ie` is restarted. When the `whatsup` program is executed again, the results reflect this:

```
The whatsup results:

'149.153.100.10' is still up, with uptime reported as 83 days, 19:52:09.95

'gw.itcarlow.ie' is still up, with uptime reported as 35 days, 18:28:25.87

WARNING: 'glasnost.itcarlow.ie' may have restarted:
             it has a reported uptime of 1 minute, 29.07
             but previously reported uptime of 23 days, 01:31:33.36

'149.153.100.253' is still up, with uptime reported as 83 days, 19:52:09.97

'193.1.206.34' is still up, with uptime reported as 56 days, 18:17:57.98
```

And the `whatsup.txt` file is updated again, thus:

```
149.153.100.10:public:724272995
gw.itcarlow.ie:wwwwww:309050587
glasnost.itcarlow.ie:public:8907
149.153.100.253:xxxxxx:724272997
193.1.206.34:zzzzzz:490427798
```

Note that the ordering in the file has changed. This has to do with the fact that the details of each *Managed Device* are stored in a hash. Consequently, the ordering of the hash does not necessarily remain constant between invocations of the `whatsup` program. If order is important, change the first line of the last `foreach` iteration to:

```
foreach my $h ( sort ( keys %managed_agents ) )
```

5.11.1 Being more careful

All of the `Net::SNMP` programs developed to date have assumed the presence of a functioning SNMP agent on the *Managed Device*. This is too optimistic an assumption to make. When the `session` constructor is invoked, a new `Net::SNMP` object comes into existence. However, no attempt is made to contact the *Managed Device* and interact. So, when `session` returns normally (that is, it does not return `undef`), this *only* means that the object has been successfully created, not that the *Managed Device* is up and running and waiting to service SNMP requests.

To improve upon this, a small subroutine (called `snmp_connect`) creates the `Net::SNMP` object and then attempts to retrieve one data item from the MIB-II `system` group. If the request is successful, the subroutine returns the `Net::SNMP` object, otherwise `undef` is returned. Here is the `snmp_connect` source code:

```
use OIDs.pm qw( sysDescr );
        .
        .
        .
sub snmp_connect {
return undef unless $#_ == 3;

my $try = Net::SNMP->session(
            -hostname      => shift,
            -community     => shift,
            -version       => shift,
            -port          => shift
        );

my $responsePDU = $try->get_request( sysDescr );

return ( !defined( $responsePDU ) ? undef : $try );
}
```

Note that this subroutine expects to receive four parameters: the IP address or name of the *Managed Device*; the community string; the SNMP version; and the SNMP protocol port-number. If anything other than four parameters are received, the code exits early and returns `undef`. After creating the `Net::SNMP` object, the subroutine attempts to retrieve the value of the `sysDescr` OID. Note the inclusion of this OID in the import-list for the `OIDs.pm` module at the top of the program. The last line of code in the subroutine checks the response from the *Managed Device* and returns either `undef` or the `Net::SNMP` object, based upon whether or not the response was defined.

As the use of this subroutine provides an added layer of robustness to programs that use it, it will be used throughout the remainder of this chapter. Rather than invoking the `session` method directly, the `snmp_connect` subroutine is invoked instead.

Assuming the existence of scalars for the four required parameters, the standard idiom is:

```
my $snmp_session = snmp_connect( $snmp_host, $snmp_community,
                                 $snmp_version, $snmp_port );

if ( !defined( $snmp_session ) )
{
    die "Whoops: an error occurred: cannot establish session.\n";
}
```

5.12   Setting MIB-II Data

The Net::SNMP module supports the setting of data on a *Managed Device*. That is, assuming the following two conditions hold.

The MIB-II data item is read/write – only a small percentage of all MIB-II data items are classified as 'read-write' within the standards document. It is impossible to set a data item that is designated 'read-only' and any attempt to do so will not succeed.

The *managed device* allows setting – the SNMP agent software executing on a *Managed Device* must be configured by a Systems Administrator to support the setting of data items. Even if the standards document indicates that an MIB-II data item is 'read-write', any attempt to set the data item on a *Managed Device* that has been explicitly configured to disallow the set_request operation will fail.

Most SNMP agent implementations provide a mechanism to configure the community string to associate with 'read-only' and 'read-write' operations.

To configure the desired values, a file called /usr/local/share/snmp/snmpd.conf on pblinux.itcarlow.ie can be edited. Here is the contents of this file:

```
####################################################
# snmpd.conf
####################################################

syslocation "Paul Barry's Laptop"
sysservices 12
syscontact  paul.barry@itcarlow.ie


rwcommunity  private
rocommunity  public
```

Lines that start with # are comments and can be ignored. The rest of the lines are SNMP agent software *configuration directives*.

The first three directives set the value of three data items from the MIB-II system group, and are relatively self-explanatory[16]. When it comes to configuring access, the two remaining directives are of more interest.

The rwcommunity directive configures the community string to use for 'read-write' access, which is the string private. 'Read-only' access is configured with the rocommunity directive, which uses the string public. Note that the use of 'private' and 'public' as community strings is regarded by many to be merely default values that should never be used within a production environment (as they are too common and too easy to guess). They are fine to use during testing and for illustrative purposes, but real community strings should be chosen with the same care as would any systems administration password.

---

[16]The reader is referred to RFC 1213 for more details.

The Net::SNMP module supports setting MIB-II data items through the use of the set_request method. This method takes three parameters as follows.

Object identifier – a numeric object identifier.

Object type – the ASN.1 object type of the value to be set.

Object value – the actual value to set.

Of the three, the middle parameter requires further explanation. It is only reasonable to expect that each MIB-II data item has a *type* associated with it. For example, the data item might be a positive integer or a zero-terminated string. Within the SNMP Framework, the allowed data types are rigidly defined in a document known as *The Structure of Management Information (SMI)*. The Net::SNMP module defines a set of constants corresponding to the allowed data types. This is a list of the most commonly used (note that the names of the types are taken from the Net::SNMP module's constant definitions):

INTEGER and INTEGER32 – machine independent integer types;

OCTET_STRING – binary and textual data in 8 bit byte format;

OBJECT_IDENTIFIER – type for defining the position of the OID in the MIB;

IPADDRESS – an IP address in dotted-decimal notation;

COUNTER, COUNTER32 and COUNTER64 – non-negative integers which *wrap around* when they reach their maximum value;

GAUGE and GAUGE32 – non-negative integers that do not *wrap around*, but instead 'cap' at their maximum value (until such time as their value decreases);

TIMETICKS – non-negative integer in hundredths of a second since some start time.

The following code snippet demonstrates the standard usage of the set_request method:

```
my $newLocation = "Paul Barry's Desktop";

my $respPDU = $snmp_session->set_request( sysLocation,
                                          OCTET_STRING,
                                          $newLocation );

if ( !defined( $responsePDU ) )
{
    warn "set_request did not work: ", $snmp_session->error, "\n";
}
```

The sysLocation data item from the MIB-II system group is set to 'Paul Barry's Desktop' by this code, assuming, of course, that the SNMP agent software on the *Managed Device* has been configured to allow such operations. If the set_request fails, an appropriate error message is displayed.

5.13   IP Router Mapping

Earlier in this chapter, the traceroute program was used to determine the list of routers between two network devices on the Internet. Another, related requirement often exists, and it is to determine all of the routes through an internet. The ultimate outcome of this requirement is to draw a map of the maze of routers that are currently operating.

The MIB-II ip group contains 23 data items relating to the current state of the IP software running on a *Managed Device*. Item number 21, ipRouteTable, contains a collection of ipRouteEntry data items, each relating to a route to a particular destination. Each ipRouteEntry contains a further 13 data items. Of these, the following are of most interest to the network manager attempting to map the routers on a network:

ipRouteDest - the IP address of a destination network;

ipRouteNextHop - the IP address of the next hop for a route;

ipRouteType - the type of the route.

The ipRouteType data item can have one of four values:

4 - the route is to a device on a non-local network;

3 - the route is to a device on a local network;

2 - the route is (temporarily) invalid;

1 - the route is not of type 2, 3 or 4.

The contents of a table from any *Managed Device* can be retrieved by an invocation of the Net::SNMP module's get_table method (as was demonstrated in the udpstats program). So, the contents of a routing table can be requested by passing the ipRouteTable OID to get_table. Once the routing table is retrieved, its contents can be processed to extract the ipRouteDest, ipRouteNextHop and ipRouteType values.

This is the function of the subroutine which follows (which is part of the iproutedata program).

Taking two parameters, a Net::SNMP object and an OID, the subroutine begins by requesting the table associated with the OID from the *Managed Device* associated with the Net::SNMP object:

```
sub iptables_get_table {
    my ( $sess, $requestOID ) = @_;
```

```
      my $responsePDU = $sess->get_table( $requestOID );

      if ( !defined( $responsePDU ) )
      {
          print "iproutedata: OID: ", $requestOID, " : ",
                        $sess->error, "\n";
      }
```

If the retrieval is successful, the $responsePDU scalar references a hash populated with the name/value pairings of the data from the table (which are themselves generated from the variable bindings). The referenced hash is then iterated over:

```
      foreach my $resp ( oid_lex_sort ( keys %{ $responsePDU } ) )
      {
```

As the routing table can be quite large, only the entries associated with the ipRouteDest, ipRouteNextHop and ipRouteType data items are displayed. So, for each hash entry, three checks are performed against each of the OID *patterns*. The pattern to look for is assigned to the $oid_pat scalar, then it is checked against the current hash key (which is in the $resp scalar). If a match is made, the value associated with the hash key is displayed.

The first check is performed against the ipRouteDest OID:

```
          my $oid_pat = OIDs::ipRouteDest;
          if ( $resp =~ /^$oid_pat\./ )
          {
              print "Dest:    $resp => ",
                        $responsePDU->{ $resp }, "\n";
          }
```

The second check is performed against the ipRouteNextHop OID:

```
          $oid_pat = OIDs::ipRouteNextHop;
          if ( $resp =~ /^$oid_pat\./ )
          {
              print "NextHop: $resp => ",
                        $responsePDU->{ $resp }, "\n";
          }
```

The third and final check is performed against the ipRouteType OID:

```
          $oid_pat = OIDs::ipRouteType;
          if ( $resp =~ /^$oid_pat\./ )
          {
              print "Type:    $resp => ",
                        $responsePDU->{ $resp }, "\n";
          }
      }
      print "\n";
  }
```

Assuming the existence of a `Net::SNMP` object called `$snmp_session`, the subroutine would be invoked as follows:

```
iptables_get_table( $snmp_session, ipRouteTable );
```

The `iproutedata` program can be executed against the 149.153.100.10 router with the following Linux command-line:

```
./iproutedata 149.153.100.10 public
```

The following output is displayed:

```
Requesting 'ip' tables for: 149.153.100.10, public, SNMPv2

Dest:    1.3.6.1.2.1.4.21.1.1.0.0.0.0 => 0.0.0.0
Dest:    1.3.6.1.2.1.4.21.1.1.127.0.0.0 => 127.0.0.0
Dest:    1.3.6.1.2.1.4.21.1.1.149.153.1.0 => 149.153.1.0
Dest:    1.3.6.1.2.1.4.21.1.1.149.153.2.0 => 149.153.2.0
Dest:    1.3.6.1.2.1.4.21.1.1.149.153.3.0 => 149.153.3.0
Dest:    1.3.6.1.2.1.4.21.1.1.149.153.6.0 => 149.153.6.0
Dest:    1.3.6.1.2.1.4.21.1.1.149.153.9.0 => 149.153.9.0
Dest:    1.3.6.1.2.1.4.21.1.1.149.153.16.0 => 149.153.16.0
Dest:    1.3.6.1.2.1.4.21.1.1.149.153.50.0 => 149.153.50.0
Dest:    1.3.6.1.2.1.4.21.1.1.149.153.97.0 => 149.153.97.0
Dest:    1.3.6.1.2.1.4.21.1.1.149.153.98.0 => 149.153.98.0
Dest:    1.3.6.1.2.1.4.21.1.1.149.153.100.0 => 149.153.100.0
Dest:    1.3.6.1.2.1.4.21.1.1.149.153.103.0 => 149.153.103.0
Dest:    1.3.6.1.2.1.4.21.1.1.149.153.128.0 => 149.153.128.0
Dest:    1.3.6.1.2.1.4.21.1.1.149.153.198.0 => 149.153.198.0
Dest:    1.3.6.1.2.1.4.21.1.1.149.153.200.0 => 149.153.200.0
Dest:    1.3.6.1.2.1.4.21.1.1.149.153.201.0 => 149.153.201.0
Dest:    1.3.6.1.2.1.4.21.1.1.149.153.201.2 => 149.153.201.2
Dest:    1.3.6.1.2.1.4.21.1.1.149.153.204.0 => 149.153.204.0
Dest:    1.3.6.1.2.1.4.21.1.1.149.153.205.0 => 149.153.205.0
Dest:    1.3.6.1.2.1.4.21.1.1.149.153.205.2 => 149.153.205.2
Dest:    1.3.6.1.2.1.4.21.1.1.149.153.212.0 => 149.153.212.0
Dest:    1.3.6.1.2.1.4.21.1.1.149.153.216.0 => 149.153.216.0
Dest:    1.3.6.1.2.1.4.21.1.1.149.153.253.0 => 149.153.253.0
NextHop: 1.3.6.1.2.1.4.21.1.7.0.0.0.0 => 149.153.1.2
NextHop: 1.3.6.1.2.1.4.21.1.7.127.0.0.0 => 127.0.0.12
NextHop: 1.3.6.1.2.1.4.21.1.7.149.153.1.0 => 149.153.1.253
NextHop: 1.3.6.1.2.1.4.21.1.7.149.153.2.0 => 149.153.2.253
NextHop: 1.3.6.1.2.1.4.21.1.7.149.153.3.0 => 149.153.3.253
NextHop: 1.3.6.1.2.1.4.21.1.7.149.153.6.0 => 149.153.6.253
NextHop: 1.3.6.1.2.1.4.21.1.7.149.153.9.0 => 149.153.9.253
NextHop: 1.3.6.1.2.1.4.21.1.7.149.153.16.0 => 149.153.31.253
NextHop: 1.3.6.1.2.1.4.21.1.7.149.153.50.0 => 149.153.50.253
NextHop: 1.3.6.1.2.1.4.21.1.7.149.153.97.0 => 149.153.100.253
NextHop: 1.3.6.1.2.1.4.21.1.7.149.153.98.0 => 149.153.100.12
NextHop: 1.3.6.1.2.1.4.21.1.7.149.153.100.0 => 149.153.100.253
```

```
NextHop:  1.3.6.1.2.1.4.21.1.7.149.153.103.0 => 149.153.103.253
NextHop:  1.3.6.1.2.1.4.21.1.7.149.153.128.0 => 149.153.100.253
NextHop:  1.3.6.1.2.1.4.21.1.7.149.153.198.0 => 149.153.2.100
NextHop:  1.3.6.1.2.1.4.21.1.7.149.153.200.0 => 149.153.2.100
NextHop:  1.3.6.1.2.1.4.21.1.7.149.153.201.0 => 149.153.2.100
NextHop:  1.3.6.1.2.1.4.21.1.7.149.153.201.2 => 149.153.2.100
NextHop:  1.3.6.1.2.1.4.21.1.7.149.153.204.0 => 149.153.2.100
NextHop:  1.3.6.1.2.1.4.21.1.7.149.153.205.0 => 149.153.2.100
NextHop:  1.3.6.1.2.1.4.21.1.7.149.153.205.2 => 149.153.2.100
NextHop:  1.3.6.1.2.1.4.21.1.7.149.153.212.0 => 149.153.2.22
NextHop:  1.3.6.1.2.1.4.21.1.7.149.153.216.0 => 149.153.216.253
NextHop:  1.3.6.1.2.1.4.21.1.7.149.153.253.0 => 149.153.253.253
Type:     1.3.6.1.2.1.4.21.1.8.0.0.0.0 => 4
Type:     1.3.6.1.2.1.4.21.1.8.127.0.0.0 => 3
Type:     1.3.6.1.2.1.4.21.1.8.149.153.1.0 => 3
Type:     1.3.6.1.2.1.4.21.1.8.149.153.2.0 => 3
Type:     1.3.6.1.2.1.4.21.1.8.149.153.3.0 => 3
Type:     1.3.6.1.2.1.4.21.1.8.149.153.6.0 => 3
Type:     1.3.6.1.2.1.4.21.1.8.149.153.9.0 => 3
Type:     1.3.6.1.2.1.4.21.1.8.149.153.16.0 => 3
Type:     1.3.6.1.2.1.4.21.1.8.149.153.50.0 => 3
Type:     1.3.6.1.2.1.4.21.1.8.149.153.97.0 => 3
Type:     1.3.6.1.2.1.4.21.1.8.149.153.98.0 => 4
Type:     1.3.6.1.2.1.4.21.1.8.149.153.100.0 => 3
Type:     1.3.6.1.2.1.4.21.1.8.149.153.103.0 => 3
Type:     1.3.6.1.2.1.4.21.1.8.149.153.128.0 => 3
Type:     1.3.6.1.2.1.4.21.1.8.149.153.198.0 => 4
Type:     1.3.6.1.2.1.4.21.1.8.149.153.200.0 => 4
Type:     1.3.6.1.2.1.4.21.1.8.149.153.201.0 => 4
Type:     1.3.6.1.2.1.4.21.1.8.149.153.201.2 => 4
Type:     1.3.6.1.2.1.4.21.1.8.149.153.204.0 => 4
Type:     1.3.6.1.2.1.4.21.1.8.149.153.205.0 => 4
Type:     1.3.6.1.2.1.4.21.1.8.149.153.205.2 => 4
Type:     1.3.6.1.2.1.4.21.1.8.149.153.212.0 => 4
Type:     1.3.6.1.2.1.4.21.1.8.149.153.216.0 => 3
Type:     1.3.6.1.2.1.4.21.1.8.149.153.253.0 => 3
```

This is all well and good, but what does it mean? Taken individually, the long list of destinations (ipRouteDest), next hops (ipRouteNextHop) and types (ipRouteType) have little meaning. When mapping routers on an IP-based network, it is not enough to display the list of destination values, as they are the IP addresses of destination networks, *not* routers. The list of next hop values (after the duplicates have been removed) does indeed identify a list of routers. However, the resulting list does not identify a collection of individual routers, only a collection of individual *connections to networks*. Recall that an IP address identifies a *connection*, not a network device.

The significance of this statement becomes clear when the function of a router is considered. That is, a router connects two or more physical networks together.

Consequently, routers have connections to at least two networks, which results in routers having more than one IP address (as was discussed when describing the output from the `udpstats` program earlier in this chapter). The existence of these multiple connections within a single routing device manifests itself as an individual entry in the next hop list. So, using the next hop list as the list of routers to map causes problems as some of the IP addresses on the list refer to connections on the router itself.

Determining which of the IP addresses refer to the router itself and which refer to some other router is accomplished by examining the list of types associated with each destination. If the type value is 4, the connection type is *indirect* and the destination refers to a non-local network. The next hop value associated with the destination refers to another router somewhere on the network. Note that the `ipRouteType` OID value reported above (to the left of the `=>` symbol) is a concatenation of the OID for `ipRouteType` and the IP address of a destination.

The `ipdetermine` program implements the functionality described above for a single router. Given the IP name or address of a router, `ipdetermine` retrieves the routing table from the *Managed Device* then, following the above technique, produces a list of routers that the *Managed Device* has connections to. The source code to `ipdetermine` is shown in its entirety prior to describing it in detail:

```perl
#! /usr/bin/perl -w

use strict;
use Socket;
use Net::SNMP;
use OIDs qw( sysDescr
             ipRouteTable ipRouteDest
             ipRouteType ipRouteNextHop );

sub snmp_connect {
    return undef unless $#_ == 3;

    my $try = Net::SNMP->session(
                -hostname    => shift,
                -community   => shift,
                -version     => shift,
                -port        => shift
            );

    my $responsePDU = $try->get_request( sysDescr );

    return ( !defined( $responsePDU ) ? undef : $try );
}

my $snmp_host      = shift || 'localhost';
my $snmp_community = shift || 'public';
my $snmp_version   = '2';
```

```perl
my $snmp_port      = 161;

$snmp_host = inet_ntoa( scalar gethostbyname( $snmp_host ) );

print "Determining 'ip' next hop data for: $snmp_host, ";
print "$snmp_community, SNMPv$snmp_version\n\n";

my $snmp_session = snmp_connect( $snmp_host, $snmp_community,
                                 $snmp_version, $snmp_port );

if ( !defined( $snmp_session ) )
{
    die "ipdetermine: an error occurred: cannot " .
                "establish session.\n";
}

my $responsePDU = $snmp_session->get_table( ipRouteTable );

if ( !defined( $responsePDU ) )
{
    print "ipdetermine: OID: ", ipRouteTable, " : ";
    print $snmp_session->error, "\n";
}

my @dests = ();

foreach my $resp ( keys %{ $responsePDU } )
{
    my $oid_pat = ipRouteDest;
    if ( $resp =~ /^$oid_pat\./ )
    {
        @dests = ( @dests, $responsePDU->{ $resp } );
    }
}

my %unique_next_hops = ();

foreach my $dest ( @dests )
{
    my $oid_type = ipRouteType . ".$dest";

    if ( $responsePDU->{ $oid_type } eq '4' )
    {
        my $oid_nexthop = ipRouteNextHop . ".$dest";
        $unique_next_hops{ $responsePDU->{ $oid_nexthop } }++;
    }
}

foreach my $unique ( keys %unique_next_hops )
```

```
    {
        print "Next hop: $unique\n";
    }

    $snmp_session->close;
```

The program begins as expected. After using the required collection of modules, the `snmp_connect` subroutine is defined. The program then initializes four lexically scoped scalars (`$snmp_host`, `$snmp_community`, `$snmp_version` and `$snmp_port`). The values for the first two scalars are initialized with values from the command-line if provided, otherwise defaults are used. The value of `$snmp_host` is converted to its dotted-decimal equivalent, then `snmp_connect` is invoked to create a `Net::SNMP` object. The result returned by `$snmp_connect` is assigned to the `$snmp_session` scalar, and a check is performed on the scalar to ensure SNMP is operating on the *Managed Device* referred to by `$snmp_host`.

The program then requests the contents of the routing table from the *Managed Device* with a call to the `Net::SNMP` object's `get_table` method. If something goes wrong, the `ipdetermine` program promptly dies:

```
    my $responsePDU = $snmp_session->get_table( ipRouteTable );

    if ( !defined( $responsePDU ) )
    {
        die "ipdetermine: OID: ", ipRouteTable, " : ",
            $snmp_session->error, "\n";
    }
```

The response received from the *Managed Device* is then processed in order to determine the list of destinations contained in the routing table's variable bindings. An array called `@dests` is defined to be initially empty, prior to a `foreach` statement processing the response. Using the technique employed by `iproutedata`, the code looks for a match to the `ipRouteDest` OID value and, if one is found, adds the value of the destination to the `@dests` array:

```
    my @dests = ();

    foreach my $resp ( keys %{ $responsePDU } )
    {
        my $oid_pat = ipRouteDest;
        if ( $resp =~ /^$oid_pat\./ )
        {
            @dests = ( @dests, $responsePDU->{ $resp } );
        }
    }
```

A hash called `%unique_next_hops` is defined to be initially empty. Another `foreach` statement then processes the `@dests` array. By concatenating each destination with the `ipRouteType` OID value, a check is made to see if the type of connection is 4. If it is, another concatenation combines the current destination ($dest) with the OID value for ipRouteNextHop, and assigns the value to the $oid_nexthop scalar. This scalar is then used to refer to the next hop value associated with the destination, and the resultant IP address is added into the %unique_next_hops hash. Note how the now familiar idiom of using a hash to store a unique list of items is once again employed to good effect in this code:

```
my %unique_next_hops = ();

foreach my $dest ( @dests )
{
    my $oid_type = ipRouteType . ".$dest";

    if ( $responsePDU->{ $oid_type } eq '4' )
    {
        my $oid_nexthop = ipRouteNextHop . ".$dest";
        $unique_next_hops{ $responsePDU->{ $oid_nexthop } }++;
    }
}
```

With the entire list of destinations processed, all that remains is to print the results contained in the %unique_next_hops hash. One final foreach statement does just that. The Net::SNMP object is destroyed and the ipdetermine program terminates:

```
foreach my $unique ( keys %unique_next_hops )
{
    print "Next hop: $unique\n";
}

$snmp_session->close;
```

The ipdetermine program is invoked from the Linux command-line as follows:

```
./ipdetermine 149.153.100.10 public
```

The following output is generated:

```
Determining 'ip' next hop data for: 149.153.100.10, public, SNMPv2

Next hop: 149.153.100.12
Next hop: 149.153.1.2
Next hop: 149.153.2.22
Next hop: 149.153.2.100
```

This is much less verbose and much more manageable than the output generated by the iproutedata program. This output also has more *meaning*. The 149.153.100.10 router has identified the routers that it has connections to (and the map of routers on the network can begin to be drawn).

The next step would be to contact these four routers, and determine their list of routers, expand the map, and iterate over the list of routers determined from each of the four (being careful, of course, not to return to a router already processed by an earlier iteration). Implementing this strategy is left as an exercise for the reader (refer to the *Exercises* at the end of this chapter).

5.14   Where To From Here?

This chapter concentrated on network management, with the majority of the discussion given over to SNMP. The `Net::SNMP` add-on module provides a Perl API to SNMP, and formed the basis of a collection of *Management Station* utilities.

An alternative Perl API to SNMP is provided by the `net-snmp` project (previously known as `ucd-snmp` and before that as `cmu-snmp`). An open-source, SourceForge project, this technology provides an API to SNMP for C and Perl programmers, and can be downloaded from the `net-snmp` website located at `http://www.net-snmp.org`. The Perl API is written and maintained by Giovanni S. Marzot. In addition to the programming APIs, this technology provides a fully functioning SNMP agent that can be built, installed and queried on most systems (including those using Linux). The Perl API is not unlike that provided by `Net::SNMP`, in that there is support for performing `get-request`, `get-next-request`, and so on. However, the API is somewhat more involved than that provided by `Net::SNMP` and can take some getting used to. In the technology's favour, `net-snmp` provides support for all three versions of SNMP. The `Net::SNMP` module supports only SNMPv1 and SNMPv2[17].

Another CPAN module, `SNMP::Util` by Wayne Marquette, provides a set of SNMP utilities that work in conjunction with Marzot's Perl API to `net-snmp`. Jochen Wiedmann has created `SNMP::Monitor`, which provides for the creation of automated SNMP monitoring mechanisms. Available on CPAN, the `SNMP::Monitor` module also builds on `net-snmp`.

5.15   Print Resources

Chapter 5 of Eric A. Hall's *Internet Core Protocols: The Definitive Guide* (see the *Print Resources* section from Chapter 2) contains an excellent description of ICMP, together with a discussion of its relationship to the `ping` and `traceroute` programs.

A thorough treatment of the field of network management is *Network Management: Principles and Practice* by Mani Subramanian (Addison Wesley, 2000). Referred to extensively during the writing of this chapter, this book shows that there is more to an understanding of network management than SNMP. *ASN.1* and

---

[17]However, this situation may have changed by the time this book is published.

BER are described, and an appendix presents the *CMIP* technology as promoted by the ISO.

The classic SNMP introduction is *The Simple Book: An Introduction to Network Management* by Marshall T. Rose (Prentice Hall, 1996). Rose is one of the principal architects of the SNMP framework and supporting technologies.

To learn most of what there is to know about routing, refer to *Routing in the Internet*, 2nd edn, by Christian Huitema (Prentice Hall, 2000). There simply is no more comprehensive routing resource.

5.16 Web Resources

Find the RFCs referenced in this chapter at the `http://www.ietf.org` website.

The *Internet Control Message Protocol* is documented in the following RFCs.

RFC 792 – the official standard for ICMP.

RFC 1256 – a description of the ICMP Router Discovery Messages.

There is a vast array of RFC documents relating to network management. What follows is an abbreviated list.

RFC 1155 – the Structure and Identification of Management Information for TCP/IP-based Internets (commonly referred to as *SMIv1*) details the types that can be used with MIB data items.

RFC 1157 – the official standard for SNMPv1.

RFC 1213 – a description of the MIB-II data items.

RFC 1902, 1903 and 1904 – Multiple updates to RFC 1155, referred to collectively as *SMIv2* and tailored to SNMPv2.

RFC 1905 and 1906 – the official standard for SNMPv2.

RFC 1907 – the update to RFC 1213 which tailors MIB-II to SNMPv2.

Daniel Hagerty's `Net::Traceroute` add-on module can be downloaded from the following CPAN directory: `http://www.cpan.org/authors/id/H/HA/HAG/`.

David M. Town's `Net::SNMP` add-on module can be downloaded from this CPAN directory: `http://www.cpan.org/authors/id/D/DT/DTOWN/`.

The ISO maintains an online presence at `http://www.iso.ch`.

Exercises

1. The standard Net::Ping module is useful. However, support for *directed broadcast* is not provided. Investigate what would be required to enhance the Net::Ping source code to support such a broadcast, thus allowing the module to be used in the creation of a network discovery application.

2. Another limitation with Net::Ping is the restriction that the ICMP protocol is only available to a user operating under superuser privilege. Why do you think this is? What would be the impact of removing this restriction from the Net::Ping module?

3. Would Net::Ping be more useful if a protocol port-number (other than the *Echo* port) were used when pinging with TCP and UDP?

4. Referring to the Net::Ping source code as appropriate, implement a version of the traceroute program in Perl. What value will you use for your *unused port*?

5. Review the data items included in the MIB-II icmp group. Would the retrieval of any of the ICMP data items help in determining the source of the large number of udpNoPorts reported by the udpstats2 program?

6. Create a program called tcpstats, based on the udpstats2 program, which requests and displays the MIB-II tcp group data.

7. Develop an IP Router Mapping program which is based on and expands upon the ipdetermine source code. How will you ensure that the program does not iterate forever? Is there a benefit to be gained from using a recursive algorithm?

8. Download the net-snmp technology from the http://www.net-snmp.org website. Install this technology on your Linux computer and configure the supplied SNMP agent software to process traps. Develop a *Management Station* utility using the Net::SNMP module to set a trap and then react to trap messages arriving from the net-snmp SNMP agent software.

6

Mobile Agents

And now for something completely different.

The last three chapters concerned themselves with a discussion of programming the network with what can be termed *traditional techniques*. Specifically, the use of the *client/server model* is so common that one could be forgiven for assuming it is the only usable network application development model. Today, the vast majority of Internet-based applications conform to the client/server model. And for good reason: it works well, is well understood and is easy to work with. However, there are other models, some of which were briefly discussed at the start of Chapter 3, *Sockets*. Of them all, one of the most interesting is the *mobile-agent model*, and its study forms the basis of this, the final chapter of *Programming the Network with Perl*.

6.1 What is a Mobile Agent?

The cute answer is: *it depends on who is asked.* Due to the relative immaturity of this field, the study of mobile-agent technologies has produced a number of often conflicting definitions. Rather than discuss the various definitions and risk confusing the reader, a simple 'working definition' is presented here (with the keywords emphasized).

> A mobile agent is a *network-aware* software application that can, under certain circumstances, *suspend* its execution on one network device, *transport* to another network device and *resume* execution there.

The *mobile* designation is due to the software application's ability to relocate from one network device to another. The *agent* designation is due to the software application doing something on behalf of a user, that is, it acts as an *agent* for the user.

This model is very different to the client/server model. Instead of a standard, formatted message being sent from one software application to another over a network, the entire software application is sent. In the course of its execution, a mobile agent may *relocate* to *multiple* network devices, that is, it can *roam*.

6.1.1   Mobile agent = code + state ·

A mobile agent has two main components: *code* and *state*.

Obviously, in order for a software application to relocate from one network device to another, its code has to travel. It will depend on the mobile-agent environment whether or not the code is in source code form, compiled form or in some intermediate form (such as *bytecode*).

The software application's *state* also has to travel. This refers to the resources the software application is currently using. Do any variables exist, and what are their values? Are any disk-files open? Does the software application hold any other resources? Again, depending on the mobile-agent environment, none, some or all of the software application's resources may travel. The entire set of resources are referred to as the software application's *state*.

6.1.2   What is a mobile-agent environment?

A mobile-agent environment (MAE) is a set of technologies that provides a working space for mobile agents. The MAE has to exist on each network device that the mobile agent can execute on (and relocate to), and this includes the device that starts the mobile agent. Throughout this chapter, the device that starts the mobile agent is referred to as the *initiating network device.*

The technologies used to provide an MAE vary widely. Some are network servers that operate on any compatible network device, while others are entire operating systems built from scratch to support mobile agents.

Within the literature, MAEs are referred to by a number of names, with *site*, *location* and *place* the most popular monikers.

6.2   Mobile-Agent Examples

In light of an understanding of what a mobile agent is, let us revisit two applications from earlier in this book and consider their re-implementation as mobile agents.

6.2.1   Revisiting `multiwho`

Chapter 4, *Protocols*, includes the `multiwho` program, which uses the TELNET protocol to automate the production of the list of logged-in users on a collection of network devices. The TELNET protocol is classically client/server, whereby the server on a remote network device provides a terminal emulation service to a local client program. The `multiwho` program, built to exploit TELNET, contacts a list of network devices (each of which runs a TELNET server) and interacts with them in order to determine the list of logged-in users. It is the responsibility of the `multiwho` program to monitor the entire execution process, as well as process the results of each interaction and produce the concatenated list of logged-in users (the *master list*).

The `multiwho` program exhibits two identifiable characteristics as follows.

It is client-centric – the client-side of the interaction does all the real work. In comparison, the server-side of the interaction provides a fixed set of services which cannot be easily changed or expanded. If additional processing of the results generated by the service request is required, then this processing *must* occur on the client (as is the case with `multiwho`).

It is bandwidth-intensive – the network traffic generated by `multiwho` in relation to the results produced is disproportionate. A small amount of output results from a large amount of network traffic. This is worsened by the fact that TELNET is a very 'chatty' protocol.

A mobile-agent implementation of `multiwho` would begin by relocating to the first network device on the list. Once there[1], `multiwho` would determine the list of logged-in users and concatenate them with the master list (which would have started out empty). The `multiwho` mobile agent then relocates to the next network device on the list and iterates. This procedure repeats until each network device on the list is visited and the master list of logged-in users is complete. The `multiwho` mobile agent then returns to the initiating network device and displays the entire list of logged-in users.

The mobile-agent-based `multiwho` is no longer client-centric, nor is it bandwidth-intensive. Network traffic is generated when a relocation from one network device to another occurs. Thankfully, the 'chatty' TELNET protocol is nowhere to be seen.

6.2.2 Revisiting `ipdetermine`

Chapter 5, *Management*, includes the `ipdetermine` program, which uses SNMP to determine a list of routers contactable from a specified routing device. The technique employed requests the contents of the routing table from a *Managed Device*, then processes the table to extract the required information. Typically, the routing table has tens (and sometimes hundreds) of entries, which are transferred

---

[1]Note that the mobile agent is *no longer executing* on the initiating network device.

from the SNMP server (the *Managed Device*) to the SNMP client (the *Management Station*) for processing.

Like TELNET, the SNMP technologies are client/server. The `ipdetermine` program is both client-centric and bandwidth-intensive. Returning to the example invocation of `ipdetermine` from the end of the last chapter, when executed against the `149.153.100.10` router, it produced a list of just four contactable routers from the entire routing table (which had considerably more entries, 312 in all).

Now, imagine a mobile-agent-capable router exists. An `ipdetermine` mobile agent transfers itself to the router, processes the routing table to determine the list of contactable routers, then returns to the initiating network device with the list. The entire contents of the routing table are no longer transferred across the network, and the reliance on SNMP is greatly reduced.

An improved implementation of the `ipdetermine` mobile agent would involve `ipdetermine` *cloning* itself prior to its transfer to the router. The original `ipdetermine` mobile agent would then wait (on the initiating network device) to receive the results produced by its clone and sent to it from the router. The clone *never* returns to the initiating host, only the results of its execution on the router are transmitted. In this way, the network traffic generated by the clone is kept to a minimum.

6.3   Mobile-Agent Advantages/Disadvantages

Before discussing the advantages of the mobile-agent model over others (notable the client/server model), it is important to point out that it is possible to use *any* development model to solve a problem. The client/server and mobile-agent versions of both `multiwho` and `ipdetermine` solve the problems they set out to. The methods used are very different, but the results *are the same*. The trick is to identify when it is appropriate and advantageous to use one model over the other.

It might seem obvious, but the fact that mobile agents have the ability to relocate is a huge advantage. For example, if a mobile agent cannot find what it needs on one network device, it relocates to another and continues looking. As such, the *mobility advantage* removes some of the limitations of traditional techniques. The mobile agent can, therefore, make the most of its *autonomy*.

Related to the mobility advantage is the ability of a mobile agent to *adapt* to the job at hand, providing a potentially powerful problem-solving technology. Granted, this typically involves combining mobile-agent techniques with those of the Artificial Intelligence community[2]. The *adaptability advantage* provides a level of customization which is superior to other models. When mobile agents

---

[2]A topic very much beyond the scope of *Programming the Network with Perl*.

collaborate at locations, this advantage can enable unique and elegant solutions to problems.

Efficiency is another advantage, especially as it relates to network bandwidth utilization. As the complexity of the mobile agent increases, the bandwidth requirements do not necessarily.

As an example of the *efficiency advantage*, consider a website indexing program. When developed using traditional client/server techniques, one possible strategy employed by the client would be to request every document accessible on the website. Each document is retrieved from the HTTP server (with its own individual *HTTP Request*) and then stored on the client's local storage. Only then can indexing occur. Even when HTTP/1.1 (with its persistent connections) is employed, the network traffic produced by this strategy is large, and gets larger as more documents are added to the website. The resulting index might be small, but, as this is produced on the client, its size has no bearing on the network bandwidth used.

When a mobile-agent strategy is employed, the mobile agent relocates from the initiating network device to the website and performs the indexing *in situ*. When the index is created, it is transferred back to the initiating network device. The index is small and the bandwidth that it consumes pales in comparison with that generated by the client/server approach. Granted, the processing burden (that is, the creation of the index) has been shifted from the initiating network device to the website. But, bear in mind that the website no longer has to process all those *HTTP Request* messages, as it is assumed the mobile agent has access to the website's documents in a manner which is independent of the HTTP access mechanisms.

The web-indexing example also serves to highlight the major disadvantage of using mobile agents: *security concerns*. For the mobile-agent model to work well, all of the participating network devices must *trust* each other to a high degree, or to a level of trust that is deemed acceptable by some local administrative policy. For instance, it would be foolish to widely advertise the existence of an MAE on any network device, as not all users of the network are trustworthy. The problem worsens when one considers that an MAE provides a facility to execute arbitrary blocks of code as received from another remote network device. A malicious mobile agent could wreak havoc on the network device hosting the MAE if given free rein to execute *any code* on the MAE. Another concern is the existence of malicious MAEs which await the arrival of non-malicious mobile agents. When they arrive, these mobile agents find themselves operating in a hostile environment.

Any further discussion of the solutions to the *security disadvantage* are beyond the scope of *Programming the Network with Perl*, as the intent here is to introduce the mobile-agent model and demonstrate examples of its use. Security in mobile agents is generating considerable ongoing research among academics and commercial interests. Refer to the *Web Resources* section at the end of this chapter for further details.

6.4 Perl Agents

The application of Perl to the development of mobile-agent technologies has, unfortunately, not produced a great wealth of activity (as compared with the other networking technologies discussed in the rest of *Programming the Network with Perl*). Despite this fact, the area does have its pioneers. One such pioneer is Steve Purkis, who, as an undergraduate at *Carleton University* in Canada, developed the Agent.pm module. An unfinished, proof-of-concept technology, Agent.pm can nevertheless be used to develop working mobile agents in Perl.

6.4.1 Preparing Perl for mobile agents

To use Agent.pm, the Class::Tom module (written by James Duncan) needs to be installed. Class::Tom, which can be used to transfer an object from one network device to another, expects to find Crypt::MD5, Data::Dumper, UNIVERSAL and MIME::Base64 installed. For readers working through this book, these modules should already be installed, as they either come as standard with Perl 5.6 or were needed in an earlier chapter. If this is not the case (that is, one or more of them is not installed), visit the nearest CPAN, then download and install whichever modules are missing.

Note that there are multiple versions of Class::Tom on CPAN. To work with Agent.pm, version 2.04 should be installed, not the more recent version of the module (which is version 3.02).

After downloading version 2.04 of Class::Tom, use these commands to install the module into Perl and test that the installation was successful:

```
gunzip Class-Tom-2.04.tar.gz
tar xvf Class-Tom-2.04.tar
cd Class-Tom-2.04
perl Makefile.PL
make
make test
su
make install
<ctrl-D>
man Class::Tom
perl -e 'use Class::Tom'
```

In addition to Class::Tom and any prerequisites it may have, Agent.pm requires the IO::Socket module, which is standard with the Perl 5.6 distribution.

To install and test the most recent version of Agent.pm, download the module from CPAN and use these commands:

```
gunzip Agent-3.20.tar.gz
tar xvf Agent-3.20.tar
cd Agent-3.20
```

```
perl Makefile.PL
make
make test
su
make install
<ctrl-D>
man Agent
perl -e 'use Agent'
```

6.5 The Agent.pm Module

The 3.20 release of Agent.pm includes four object-oriented classes that can be used to build mobile agents and mobile-agent environments.

The four classes are

Agent – used to instantiate and run a mobile agent;

Agent::Message – used to send code from one MAE to another;

Agent::Transport – used to receive code from an MAE;

Agent::Transport::TCP – provides a transport mechanism for mobile-agent developers to use. At the time of writing, Agent.pm supports only TCP, which means that when relocation occurs, it occurs reliably.

To build a functioning mobile agent, the programmer needs to create the following three programs using the Agent.pm technologies.

A launching MAE – this program provides a mechanism to start (or launch) a mobile agent on the initiating network device. Although it is useful to think of this program as an MAE, it primarily exists to kick-start the execution of a mobile agent, not to receive a mobile agent from another MAE. Note, too, that this program does not send a mobile agent to another MAE. The decision as to whether or not to relocate is taken by the mobile agent, not the MAE. However, the *Launching MAE* does provide a *relocation service* to the mobile agent.

A receiving MAE – using the facilities provided by Agent::Transport, this program receives a mobile agent from an MAE and executes it. Like the *Launching MAE*, the *Receiving MAE* provides a relocation service to a mobile agent.

A loadable mobile agent – inheriting its functionality from the Agent class, this program can use the facilities of Agent::Message to relocate from one MAE to another. This program cannot start its execution cycle without the assistance of a *Launching MAE*[3]. Once relocated, this program cannot execute nor relocate without the assistance of a *Receiving MAE*.

Later in this chapter, examples of each of these programs are developed.

---

[3]So it is probably inappropriate to call it a 'program'.

6.6   Ooooh, Objects!

As if all this talk of 'classes' and 'inheriting' was not a big enough clue, it should now be clear that `Agent.pm` is a purely object-oriented (OO) add-on module to Perl. Throughout *Programming the Network with Perl*, object-oriented technologies created by other Perl programmers have been used to great effect. To use `Agent.pm`, a greater understanding of Perl's OO mechanisms is required.

Developing classes in Perl is straightforward and follows a simple recipe.

Declare a package – the `package` subroutine declares a namespace, and in OO Perl, each class has a unique namespace (usually stored within its own module file).

Add functionality with methods – behaviour is added to an OO Perl class by writing methods that reside within the namespace. As was the case in earlier chapters, *method* is the OO name for *subroutine*.

To create an object, bless it – the inbuilt `bless` subroutine takes a reference to something and turns it into an object of some named class. In Perl, the 'something' can be anything at all (although hashes are very popular with OO Perl programmers). Blessing typically occurs when the object (of a certain class) is being instantiated by its *constructor*. Constructor is another fancy OO name for a special object instantiation subroutine, which is – again, typically – called new in Perl[4]. When the word 'instantiate' is used, think 'create'.

In addition to satisfying this OO Perl recipe, classes based on the `Agent.pm` technologies must contain two specific methods:

new – a constructor that instantiates a mobile-agent object which is inherited from the `Agent` class;

agent_main – a method that belongs to the mobile agent's class, but is invoked by the MAE.

It is also recommended that the mobile agent be contained in a disk-file named with a '.pa' extension.

Looking at some code should help to make sense of all this OO speak, and in the sections which follow, a number of code samples illustrate Perl's OO technology.

6.7   The Default Mobile Agent

Here is the source code to a simple *mobile agent* called `onedefault.pa`:

```
#! /usr/bin/perl -w

use strict;
use 5.6.0;
```

---

[4]Although it does not *have* to be called new. Recall from the last chapter that objects of type `Net::SNMP` were constructed with a call to the `session` method.

```perl
package Agent::OneDefault;

our @ISA = qw( Agent );

sub new {
    my ( $class, %args ) = @_;

    my $self = {};

    foreach ( keys( %args ) )
    {
        $self->{ "$_" } = $args{ "$_" };
    }

    bless $self, $class;
}

sub agent_main {
    my ( $self, @args ) = @_;

    my $to = delete( $self->{ 'Host' } );

    unless ( $to )
    {
        print "Hello from the onedefault.pa mobile agent.\n";

        return 1;
    }

    my $msg = new Agent::Message(
            'Body'      => [ "OneDefault.\n", $self->store() ],
            'Transport' => 'TCP',
            'Address'   => $to );

    if ( !$msg->send )
    {
        print "onedefault: could not send agent!\n";
    }
}

1;
```

This may look like a functioning Perl program, but is, in fact, a mobile agent (contained in a Perl module). If the Perl interpreter executes this code as is, nothing happens. To make this code do something useful, a *Launching MAE* is required. But more on that later.

The mobile agent's source code starts with the strange first line, two familiar use statements, and these two statements:

```perl
package Agent::OneDefault;

our @ISA = qw( Agent );
```

The first line sets the namespace to Agent::OneDefault, which can be thought of as the mobile agent's class name. It is a convention to prefix the class name of mobile agents based on Agent.pm with the 'Agent::' string, but this could just as easily be any string. The second line tells Perl that this class inherits functionality from the Agent class by setting the @ISA array to the name of the class from which to inherit.

Next comes the code for the new method:

```perl
sub new {
    my ( $class, %args ) = @_;

    my $self = {};

    foreach ( keys( %args ) )
    {
        $self->{ "$_" } = $args{ "$_" };
    }

    bless $self, $class;
}
```

When used to instantiate an object, the Perl interpreter always ensures that new receives the name of the class to construct as its first parameter, followed by any other parameters. The first line of the new method assigns the class name to the $class scalar, and then uses any parameters to initialize a hash called %args. A scalar called $self is then set to reference an empty (anonymous) hash. This reference to a hash is used to refer to the state of the object, and is called $self by convention[5]. A foreach statement then processes any parameters passed to new and copies them into the hash referenced by $self. Note the use of the -> symbol to refer to the referenced hash entries. Once the hash referred to by $self is populated, a call to the inbuilt bless subroutine turns $self (which is, after all, just a reference) into an object of type $class. As the invocation of bless occurs as the last statement of the new method, an implicit return statement returns the result of bless to the method's caller.

When the Agent class relocates a mobile agent from one MAE to another, it does so by transferring the object. The object is made up of the data items stored in the $self referenced hash (*state*), together with the methods that act upon the data items (*code*).

A single method, the agent_main subroutine, resides in the class Agent::OneDefault. As Perl arranges to include a reference to the object as the first parameter to each called method, the code begins by placing the reference into a scalar called $self and any other parameters into an array called @args:

---

[5] Again, it could have been called anything. Perl is not fussy, but standard naming conventions are generally a good idea.

```
sub agent_main {
    my ( $self, @args ) = @_;
```

The hash referenced by $self is then accessed to determine the value associated with the Host key, which is then assigned to the $to scalar. As a result of the assignment, the inbuilt delete subroutine removes the Host key/value pairing from the hash. Note that the value associated with the Host key is not set in the onedefault.pa source code. The value was passed to the new constructor when it was invoked, and the invocation and assignment occur elsewhere. A check is performed on the value of $to, and a message is displayed on screen if its value is undefined. Assuming the initial existence of a value associated with the Host key, the $to scalar is defined and, consequently, the message will not display the first time this method is executed:

```
my $to = delete( $self->{ 'Host' } );

unless ( $to )
{
    print "Hello from the onedefault.pa mobile agent.\n";

    return 1;
}
```

The agent_main subroutine then instantiates an Agent::Message object by calling its new constructor:

```
my $msg = new Agent::Message(
            'Body'      => [ "OneDefault.\n", $self->store() ],
            'Transport' => 'TCP',
            'Address'   => $to );
```

The Agent::Message class supports the sending of code from one MAE to another. The parameters to new identify the code to send (Body), the protocol to use (Transport) and the location of the MAE (Address). The code is the second element in an anonymous array associated with the Body parameter. A call is made to the store method associated with the mobile agent's object. The store method belongs to the Agent class (from which Agent::OneDefault inherits its functionality), and it returns the object (code and state) in a *stringified form*. To do this, Agent.pm uses the facilities provided by Class::Tom.

Once the Agent::Message object has been instantiated and stored in the $msg scalar, the mobile agent asks the MAE to relocate. A call to the send method associated with the Agent::Message object is performed, together with a simple check to see that all went well. If an error occurs, a message is displayed on screen and the relocation does not occur. Either way, the agent_main method terminates, and the module code ends with a true value (the 1; line), which is a requirement that Perl places on modules:

```
        if ( !$msg->send )
        {
            print "onedefault: could not send agent!\n";
        }
    }
    1;
```

The first time this method is executed (by a *Launching MAE*) the value of $to will be set to the value of the Host hash entry referenced by $self. The unless code is not executed, as $to has a value. The mobile agent then relocates to a *Receiving MAE*. Once relocated, the code executes for a second time. This time the value of $to is undefined due to the fact that the first execution of the code used the inbuilt delete subroutine to remove the Host entry from the referenced hash. With an undefined $to, the unless code now executes, the mobile agent displays the message 'Hello from the onedefault.pa mobile agent.' on screen, then invokes return with a value of 1. No further relocation occurs, and the mobile agent terminates. This, therefore, is a default mobile agent that does something (displays a message) on a single *Receiving MAE*, then terminates. Hence its name: onedefault.pa.

6.8   A Launching Mobile-Agent Environment

In the last section it was stated that the onedefault.pa mobile agent, if executed as is, does nothing. To make it do something, a *Launching MAE* is required. The onelaunchma program serves as the first example of such a program:

```
#! /usr/bin/perl -w

use strict;
use Socket;
use Agent;

my $ma_name = shift || 'onedefault.pa';
my $ma_host = shift || 'localhost';
my $ma_port = shift || 40000;

$ma_host = inet_ntoa( scalar gethostbyname( $ma_host ) );

my $ma_hostport = $ma_host . ':' . $ma_port;

my %args = ( 'Name' => $ma_name,
             'Host' => $ma_hostport );

my $perlagent = new Agent ( %args );

my $agentresults = eval { $perlagent->run; };
```

```
if ( $@ )
{
    print "onelaunchma: something went wrong: $@\n";
}
if ( $agentresults )
{
    print "onelaunchma: results: ", $agentresults, "\n";
}
```

Compared with the complexity of the mobile agent's source code, there is not much to onelaunchma. After the usual first line and a collection of use statements, three scalars are set to either default values, or to values entered at the Linux command-line:

```
my $ma_name = shift || 'onedefault.pa';
my $ma_host = shift || 'localhost';
my $ma_port = shift || 40000;
```

The $ma_name scalar identifies the mobile-agent disk-file to use, and it defaults to the onedefault.pa mobile agent. The $ma_host and $ma_port scalars identify the IP name (or IP address) and protocol port-number of the network device hosting the *Receiving MAE*, respectively.

When one relocates a mobile agent from one MAE to another using Agent.pm, MAEs are identified by a combination of their dotted-decimal IP address and protocol port-number. The two values are concatenated together and separated by a colon. The next two lines of code convert the IP name (or IP address) into its dotted-decimal equivalent, and then assign the address and protocol port-number (in the required format) to a scalar called $ma_hostport:

```
$ma_host = inet_ntoa( scalar gethostbyname( $ma_host ) );

my $ma_hostport = $ma_host . ':' . $ma_port;
```

The value of $ma_hostport is immediately used in the initialization of a hash called %args:

```
my %args = ( 'Name' => $ma_name,
             'Host' => $ma_hostport );
```

Note that the value of $ma_hostport is assigned to the hash entry called Host. One other hash entry is assigned: the Name entry is assigned the value of the $ma_name scalar (i.e. the name of the disk-file which contains the mobile agent's source code).

With the %args hash populated, the next line of code instantiates an object of type Agent and passes the %args hash as the new constructor's sole parameter. The object is assigned to the $perlagent scalar:

```
my $perlagent = new Agent ( %args );
```

With the object in existence, its `run` method is invoked. This has the effect of calling the `agent_main` method contained within the mobile agent's source code:

```
my $agentresults = eval { $perlagent->run; };
```

The invocation of `run` occurs within an `eval` block. This lets the mobile agent terminate abnormally (perhaps by calling `die`) without impacting the execution of `onelaunchma`. If the `run` method returns results, they are assigned to the `$agentresults` scalar. If the `eval` block terminates abnormally, the built-in `$@` variable is assigned the reason. The `onelaunchma` program concludes with two `if` statements that check these scalars and display messages on screen, if appropriate:

```
if ( $@ )
{
    print "onelaunchma: something went wrong: $@\n";
}
if ( $agentresults )
{
    print "onelaunchma: results: ", $agentresults, "\n";
}
```

6.9   A One-Shot Location

With the mobile agent written (`onedefault.pa`) and the *Launching MAE* in place (`onelaunchma`), all that remains is an MAE to which the mobile agent can relocate. The `oneshotloc` program is a *Receiving MAE*, and here it is:

```
#! /usr/bin/perl -w

use strict;
use Socket;
use Sys::Hostname;

use Agent;
use Agent::Transport;

my $mae_name = inet_ntoa( scalar gethostbyname( hostname ) );
my $mae_port = shift || 40000;
my $mae_address = $mae_name . ':' . $mae_port;

my $mae = new Agent::Transport( 'Medium'  => 'TCP',
                                'Address' => $mae_address );

my ( $from, @recv_code ) = $mae->recv( 'Timeout' => 120 )
    or die "oneshotloc: timed out waiting: no code.\n";

my $stored_agent = join( '', @recv_code );
```

```
my $ma = new Agent( 'Stored' => $stored_agent )
    or die "oneshotloc: could not create agent.\n";

my $res = eval { $ma->run; };

if ( $@ )
{
    warn "oneshotloc: could not run agent: $@\n";
}
```

In addition to the modules included at the start of onelaunchma, this program also includes the standard Sys::Hostname module, in addition to the Agent::Transport class. Code similar to that used to produce the $ma_hostport scalar (in onelaunchma) is used to assign the IP address/protocol port-number combination to a scalar called $mae_address. Note that this program takes a single command-line argument, the value for the protocol port-number to use (which defaults to 40000). Rather than require the user of the program to enter the IP name of the network device hosting this *Receiving MAE*, the hostname subroutine (as provided by the Sys::Hostname module) is used to determine the correct value to use:

```
my $mae_name = inet_ntoa( scalar gethostbyname( hostname ) );
my $mae_port = shift || 40000;
my $mae_address = $mae_name . ':' . $mae_port;
```

The value of $mae_address is used in the instantiation of an object of type Agent::Transport:

```
my $mae = new Agent::Transport( 'Medium' => 'TCP',
                                'Address' => $mae_address );
```

With the $mae scalar referring to the just created object, the oneshotloc program now has the ability to receive a mobile agent from another MAE, as this is what the Agent::Transport class provides. A receipt is requested by invoking the recv method:

```
my ( $from, @recv_code ) = $mae->recv( 'Timeout' => 120 )
    or die "oneshotloc: timed out waiting (2 minutes).\n";
```

The recv method now waits (i.e. *blocks*) for 120 seconds for a mobile agent to arrive. In actual fact, the recv method is waiting for some mobile agent somewhere to invoke its send method. Referring back to the onedefault.pa source code, note how the two parameters to send match up with the two values returned from a successful invocation of recv.

The mobile agent's *code* now resides in the @recv_code array[6]. To get to a point where the code can be executed by the Agent class, the contents of the array are converted to a scalar, as follows:

```
my $stored_agent = join( '', @recv_code );
```

---

[6]Stored in an internal format used by the Class::Tom module

The mobile agent now exists in the `$stored_agent` scalar, and is then passed to the new constructor and assigned to the `Stored` hash entry. This ensures the correct code is invoked when the mobile agent is executed by the *Receiving MAE*:

```
my $ma = new Agent( 'Stored' => $stored_agent )
    or die "oneshotloc: could not create agent.\n";
```

As in the *Launching MAE*, an invocation of the run method associated with the `Agent` object occurs, again within an `eval` block, prior to the program terminating:

```
my $res = eval { $ma->run; };

if ( $@ )
{
    warn "oneshotloc: could not run agent: $@\n";
}
```

To run the `oneshotloc` program and use protocol port-number 35000, use the following command-line:

```
./oneshotloc 35000
```

And nothing happens. The *Receiving MAE* is waiting for some other MAE somewhere to send a mobile agent to it.

Assuming `oneshotloc` is executing on `pbmac.itcarlow.ie`, the following command-line is used to send the `onedefault.pa` mobile agent to it:

```
./onelaunchma onedefault.pa pbmac.itcarlow.ie 35000
```

If all goes well, the 'Hello from the onedefault.pa mobile agent.' message appears on `pbmac`'s screen, then `oneshotloc` terminates. Which helps explain its name, as it is a one-shot *Receiving MAE*. A single mobile agent is received, executed and that is all. In the section which follows, these programs will be updated to support the receipt and delivery of multiple mobile agents.

6.10 Relocating To Multiple Locations

The `oneshotloc` *Receiving MAE* terminates after the receipt of a single mobile agent. The addition of a simple loop to the source code adapts `oneshotloc` to support the receipt of more than one mobile agent. In effect, the program is now a network server that waits forever at some specified IP address/protocol port-number to service clients (received from other MAEs, be they of the *Receiving* or *Launching* kind).

6.10.1 Processing multiple mobile agents

The `multishotloc` program includes the modified `oneshotloc` source code. This code, up to and including the instantiation of the `$mae` object of type `Agent::Transport`, is exactly as it was in `oneshotloc`. Here is the rest of the source code from `multishotloc`:

```
while (1)
{
    my ( $from, @recv_code ) = $mae->recv( 'Timeout' => 120 );

    unless ( @recv_code )
    {
        warn "multishotloc: timed out waiting: no code.\n";
        next;
    }

    my $stored_agent = join( '', @recv_code );

    my $ma = new Agent( 'Stored' => $stored_agent );

    my $res = eval { $ma->run; };

    if ( $@ )
    {
        warn "multishotloc: could not run agent: $@\n";
    }
}
```

The body of the `while` loop is similar to that used by `oneshotloc`. If the invocation of the `recv` method times out, this program does not call `die` as `oneshotloc` did. Instead, a warning message is displayed, and the code calls `next` to jump to the start of the next iteration. Other than that, only the additional looping code is new, and it could not be easier. The `multishotloc` program loops forever (or until killed by a signal from the underlying operating system).

6.10.2 Identifying multiple locations

Changing the `onelaunchma` program to identify a list of mobile agents is also straightforward. Rather than having a single IP address/protocol port-number combination to relocate to, the `multilaunchma` program supports any number of locations. Requiring the user to enter the list of locations at the command-line (as is the case with the single location used by `onelaunchma`) is unwieldy at best. So `multilaunchma` provides for the list of locations to exist in a disk-file.

The name of this disk-file is `multilaunchma.rc`. Here is the content of the file as it exists on `pbmac.itcarlow.ie`:

```
glasnost.itcarlow.ie:35000
149.153.103.5:40000
149.153.103.15:40000
pbmac.itcarlow.ie:35000
```

On each line, the file identifies the IP name (or address) of the MAE, together with the protocol port-number that the MAE is using. Note how this file has, as the last location on the list, a *Receiving MAE* executing at protocol port-number 35000 on the self same `pbmac.itcarlow.ie`. This allows the roaming mobile agent to return to `pbmac` when it has finished doing what it set out to do. The list can be any length, and users are free to mix IP names with IP addresses when identifying the network device. Any protocol port-number can be specified, unless a well-known protocol port-number is specified, which requires the *Receiving MAE* to execute with superuser privilege[7].

Rather than a single `Host` entry in the `%args` hash, the `multilaunchma` program places an anonymous array into the hash, keyed on `Hosts`. In order to populate the array referred to by `Hosts`, the contents of the `multilaunchma.rc` disk-file are read into the program and processed. Here is the first half of the `multilaunchma` program which includes the code which processes the disk-file:

```perl
#! /usr/bin/perl -w

use strict;
use Socket;

use Agent;

my $mae_name  = shift || 'multidefault.pa';

my %args = ( 'Name' => $mae_name );

open RCFILE, 'multilaunchma.rc'
    or die "multilaunchma: could not open RC file.\n";

while ( <RCFILE> )
{
    my ( $mae_host, $mae_port ) = split /:/;

    chomp( $mae_port );

    $mae_host = inet_ntoa( scalar gethostbyname( $mae_host ) );

    push( @{$args{ 'Hosts' }}, ( $mae_host . ':' . $mae_port ) );
}

close RCFILE;
```

---

[7]Which is a really, really, *really* bad idea! When executing as root, a mobile agent can perform any operation on the network device hosting the *Receiving MAE*. Oh dear.

The `multilaunchma.rc` disk-file is opened and processed one line at a time. With each iteration, the IP name (or IP address) and protocol port-number are extracted. The dotted-decimal IP address is determined, then the location in the required `Agent.pm` format is appended onto the anonymous array referred to by `Hosts` within the `%args` hash. The disk-file is then closed.

The rest of the code to the `multilaunchma` mobile agent is as it was in the `onelaunchma` program. An object of type `Agent` is instantiated with the values contained in `%args`, then the mobile agent is executed by invoking its `run` method:

```perl
my $perlagent = new Agent ( %args );

my $agentresults = eval { $perlagent->run; };

if ( $@ )
{
    print "multilaunchma: something went wrong: $@\n";
}
if ( $agentresults )
{
    print "multilaunchma: results: ", $agentresults, "\n";
}
```

Note that the mobile agent carries with it (as part of its *state*) the current value of the `%args` hash, which contains the list of *Receiving MAE* network devices to visit. In addition, `multilaunchma` specifies the default name of the mobile agent to execute as `multidefault.pa`.

6.10.3   A multi-location mobile agent

The code to the `multidefault.pa` mobile agent needs to be aware of and process the multiple locations. The source code to `multidefault.pa` starts by declaring its own namespace, inheriting from the `Agent` class and defining the new constructor:

```perl
#! /usr/bin/perl -w

use strict;
use 5.6.0;

package Agent::MultiDefault;

our @ISA = qw( Agent );

sub new {
    my ( $class, %args ) = @_;
    my $self = {};
```

```
foreach ( keys( %args ) )
{
    $self->{ "$_" } = $args{ "$_" };
}

bless $self, $class;
}
```

Other than the different value for the namespace, this code is identical to the code from onedefault.pa. In fact, it will rarely be the case that the new constructor differs to that shown above for any developed mobile agent.

The other required method is agent_main. Its code starts as expected, assigning the reference to the object to $self, and any supplied arguments to the @args array:

```
sub agent_main {
    my ( $self, @args ) = @_;
```

As $self refers to the object (which is a blessed reference to a hash), the $to scalar is assigned the first value of the anonymous array referred to by the Hosts entry, which is the first IP address/protocol port-number combination from the multilaunchma.rc disk-file. Note how the inbuilt shift subroutine removes the element from the array. This use of shift ensures the mobile agent eventually exhausts the list of locations:

```
my $to = shift @{ $self->{ 'Hosts' }};
```

If the $to scalar is defined, the mobile agent executes a method called do_it, which is associated with the mobile agent's object:

```
if ( $to )
{
    $self->do_it;
}
```

If the $to scalar is undefined, the mobile agent executes a method called at_end which, again, is associated with the mobile agent's object. The $to scalar is undefined as soon as the anonymous array of locations is exhausted. Consequently, the at_end method executes when the mobile agent reaches the final *Receiving MAE*:

```
unless ( $to )
{
    return $self->at_end;
}
```

The agent_main method concludes with code similar to that seen in the source code to onedefault.pa. An object of type Agent::Message is instantiated and sent to a *Receiving MAE*:

```
    my $msg = new Agent::Message(
            'Body'      => [ "MultiDefault.\n", $self->store() ],
            'Transport' => 'TCP',
            'Address'   => $to );

    if ( !$msg->send )
    {
        print "multidefault: could not send agent!\n";
    }
}
```

The code to the `multidefault.pa` mobile agent concludes with the definition of the `do_it` and `at_end` methods. As this is the default multi-location mobile agent, these methods simply display a message on the screen of the *Receiving MAE*. As both methods belong to the `Agent::MultiDefault` class, they are always invoked with a reference to the object as their first parameter. As a result, the `$self` scalar is assigned the value of this first parameter (a reference to a blessed hash) and the `@args` array is assigned any other parameters passed to the method:

```
sub do_it {
    my ( $self, @args ) = @_;

    print "This is do_it.\n";
}

sub at_end {
    my ( $self, @args ) = @_;

    print "This is at_end.\n";
}

1;
```

To execute the multi-location mobile agent, edit the `multilaunchma.rc` disk-file as required, then invoke the `multilaunchma` *Launching MAE* to send the mobile agent on its way, as follows:

```
./multilaunchma
```

Assuming *Receiving MAE* programs are executing on the network devices referred to in the `multilaunchma.rc` disk-file, the mobile agent relocates to each MAE and displays 'This is do_it.' on the MAE's screen, except for the final MAE, where the message 'This is at_end.' appears. The mobile agent has successfully roamed to a list of MAEs and executed specific methods at each.

Or has it? The 'This is do_it.' message also appears on the screen of the *Launching MAE*, which (being an MAE just like any other) executes the `agent_main` method, removes a location from the anonymous array, finds the `$to` scalar to be defined and invokes the `do_it` method. If the programmer wishes the code in do_it to execute on the *Launching MAE* as well as all the *Receiving MAEs* (bar the last), this behaviour is fine. However, what if this is not the case? What if the do_it method needs to be invoked after the first relocation, not before it?

The problem is that the $to scalar is assigned a location from the anonymous array too early. Consequently, as $to is defined, the do_it method is invoked by the *Launching MAE*.

One solution to this problem employs a variation on a strategy developed by Steve Purkis. Rather than assign a location from the list to the $to scalar before the call to do_it, it is assigned after. A trick which exploits the behaviour of arrays, hashes and references is used to ensure that the definedness of $to can be checked before a value has been assigned to it.

A slightly modified multi-location mobile agent (multidefault2.pa) implements this strategy. Changes are only required to the agent_main method. Here is the source code:

```perl
sub agent_main {
    my ( $self, @args ) = @_;

    my $to = \$self->{ 'ToValue' };

    $self->do_it if ( $$to && ($#{$self->{ 'Hosts' }} > -1) );

    $self->{ 'ToValue' } = shift @{ $self->{ 'Hosts' }};

    return $self->at_end unless ( $$to );

    my $msg = new Agent::Message(
            'Body'      => [ "MultiDefault.\n", $self->store() ],
            'Transport' => 'TCP',
            'Address'   => $$to );

    if ( !$msg->send )
    {
        print "multidefault2: could not send agent!\n";
    }
}
```

The method begins by processing any parameters. The $to scalar is then assigned a reference to the value of the ToValue hash entry (which is part of the $self object):

```perl
sub agent_main {
    my ( $self, @args ) = @_;

    my $to = \$self->{ 'ToValue' };
```

When agent_main is executed for the first time (by the *Launching MAE*), the ToValue hash entry does not exist in the hash referred to by $self. Referring to ToValue in this way dynamically adds the hash entry to $self and sets its initial value to undef[8]. A reference to ToValue is then assigned to the $to scalar. So, unlike the code from multidefault.pa, $to contains a reference to some value, not an actual value.

It is then possible to check the value referred to by $to to see if it is undefined, as in the next line:

```
$self->do_it if ( $$to && ($#{$self->{ 'Hosts' }} > -1) );
```

This line also checks to ensure that the anonymous array has at least one element by testing against the array index value (the array's $# value). If the *Launching MAE* determines that the value referred to by $to is undef or the anonymous array is empty, it skips the invocation of the do_it method.

A location is then assigned to the ToValue hash entry, as follows:

```
$self->{ 'ToValue' } = shift @{ $self->{ 'Hosts' }};
```

A location is removed from the anonymous array referred to by Hosts and assigned to ToValue. The critical side effect of this assignment is that the value that $to references is also assigned the location. Remember, the $to scalar refers to the ToValue hash entry. If one value changes, so does the other.

The rest of the agent_main code is similar to that from the mobile agent multidefault.pa, except that the value referred to by $to is used:

```
return $self->at_end unless ( $$to );

my $msg = new Agent::Message(
          'Body'      => [ "MultiDefault.\n", $self->store() ],
          'Transport' => 'TCP',
          'Address'   => $$to );

if ( !$msg->send )
{
    print "multidefault2: could not send agent!\n";
}
}
```

The multi-location mobile agent now behaves as required. The do_it method is invoked by each MAE, except for the *Launching MAE* and the final *Receiving MAE*. The final *Receiving MAE* invokes the at_end method instead.

By combining this improved version of the multi-location mobile agent with the multilaunchma and multishotloc programs, there now exists a platform upon which useful mobile agents can be developed. Other than changing the contents of the multilaunchma.rc disk-file, the multilaunchma and multishotloc programs should never change. Starting with the multidefault2.pa source code, follow this recipe to develop a custom mobile agent.

---

[8]Which is, after all, standard hash behaviour.

Make a copy – copy the `multidefault2.pa` source code to a new disk-file (ensuring, for the sake of consistency, that the name of the disk-file ends in the '.pa' extension).

Change `do_it` – change the code that is executed by each *Receiving MAE* to perform the desired operation.

Change `at_end` – change the code that is executed by the final *Receiving MAE* to perform any post-relocation processing (such as displaying results).

Add hash entries – add hash entries to the mobile agent's object whenever additional state information needs to be manipulated and relocated. When objects based on the `Agent` class travel, the `Agent.pm` technologies ensure that all data associated with the object relocate from one MAE to another.

And that is all there is to it. The three 'multi' programs provide the mobile-agent machinery. The `do_it` and `at_end` methods provide standard points within the mobile-agent source code to allow for customization of the default behaviour.

With the mobile-agent machinery in place, it is time to develop a mobile-agent version of the client/server `multiwho` and `ipdetermine` programs.

6.11   The Mobile-Agent `multiwho`

Producing the mobile-agent version of `multiwho` is easy, as all that is required is the definition of the `do_it` and `at_end` methods. Here is the code to the `do_it` method from the `multiwhoma.pa` program:

```
sub do_it {
    my ( $self, @args ) = @_;

    @{$self->{ 'WhoList' }} = ( @{$self->{ 'WhoList' }}, 'who' );
}
```

Another anonymous array is stored within the object's hash and is referred to by the `WhoList` key. Each time the `do_it` method is invoked, the anonymous array's contents are reassigned to a copy of its current contents together with the results of the underlying operating system executing the who command. Perl's *back-tick* operator is used to execute who and return any results to the mobile agent. Once again, the dynamic addition of entries to an existing hash is exploited by this code.

Eventually, the mobile agent arrives at the final *Receiving MAE*, and the `at_end` method is invoked. This method simply displays the contents of the anonymous array referred to by `WhoList`:

```
sub at_end {
    my ( $self, @args ) = @_;

    print @{$self->{ 'WhoList' }}, "\n";
}
```

And that is it. The mobile-agent version of the client/server multiwho program is ready. After adjusting the contents of the multilaunchma.rc disk-file, and assuming MAEs are executing at each of the locations referred to in the disk-file, execute multiwhoma.pa as follows:

```
./multilaunchma multiwhoma.pa
```

This mobile agent relocates to each of the locations identified in the disk-file and interacts with the *Receiving MAE* operating there. Unlike the multidefault.pa mobile agent, multiwhoma.pa executes silently at each of the locations until it arrives at the final *Receiving MAE*, where the concatenated results of each of the who commands are displayed on screen. Here is a copy of the results generated when multiwhoma.pa relocated to the same set of servers contacted by the multiwho program from Chapter 4:

```
root       tty1       Apr 19 16:31
cno2031    pts/0      May 31 16:30 (pc310-10.itcarlow.ie)
cno2020    pts/1      May 31 16:14 (pc3-16.itcarlow.ie)
cno2020    pts/2      May 31 16:27 (pc3-16.itcarlow.ie)
cno2026    pts/3      May 31 16:18 (149.153.131.117)
cno2018    pts/4      May 31 16:30 (pc3-20.itcarlow.ie)
cno2019    pts/5      May 31 16:26 (pc3-21.itcarlow.ie)
COM2059    pts/8      May 31 15:20 (pc3-14.itcarlow.ie)
cno2006    pts/7      May 31 13:30 (pc3-13.itcarlow.ie)
com3027    pts/0      May  9 09:52 (pc2-2.itcarlow.ie)
meudecc    pts/0      May 31 16:30 (staff102.itcarlow.ie)
hickeypm   pts/1      May 31 16:14 (staff23.itcarlow.ie)
kinsella   pts/2      May 31 16:27 (akmac.itcarlow.ie)
whyte      pts/3      May 31 16:18 (149.153.100.117)
```

The multiwhoma.pa mobile agent was dispatched just after the client/server multiwho was executed. Comparing these results with those from Chapter 4 (on p. 216) confirms that the mobile agent has produced the same results, with one notable exception: the details of user-id barryp are missing from the results produced by multiwhoma.pa. This has to do with the fact that the client/server multiwho is required to establish a connection with each TELNET server and log into the network device using an identified user-id. This logged-in user then appears as an active user on the output generated by the who command. As no such logged-in user is associated with each of the *Receiving MAE* programs, no additional user-ids are reported by who[9].

6.12   The Mobile-Agent ipdetermine

The mobile-agent version of the ipdetermine program from Chapter 5, *Management*, is somewhat more involved than multiwhoma.pa. The source code

---

[9]For argument's sake, it is assumed that any MAEs are configured to operate as non-superuser, background processes at each location.

needs to incorporate the SNMP code from the client/server ipdetermine, as well as the code from multidefault2.pa. This version of the program is called ipdeterminema.pa.

After the usual first few lines of code, an appropriate namespace is declared, then the code includes a collection of use statements. These come after the package statement as the facilities they provide are needed by the mobile agent itself, so they need to be declared *inside* the namespace:

```
package Agent::IpDetermineMA;

use Net::SNMP;
use OIDs qw( sysDescr
             ipRouteTable ipRouteDest
             ipRouteType ipRouteNextHop );
```

The new and agent_main methods are exactly the same as they are in the multidefault2.pa program. Only the do_it and at_end methods need to be changed. Here is the source code to do_it:

```
sub do_it {
    my ( $self, @args ) = @_;

    my $snmp_session = Net::SNMP->session(
                        -hostname    => 'localhost',
                        -community   => 'public',
                        -version     => '2',
                        -port        => 161
                     );

    if ( !defined( $snmp_session ) )
    {
        print "ipdeterminema: error: cannot establish session.\n";

        return;
    }

    my $responsePDU = $snmp_session->get_table( ipRouteTable );

    if ( !defined( $responsePDU ) )
    {
        print "ipdeterminema: OID: ", ipRouteTable, " : ",
            $snmp_session->error, "\n";

        return;
    }

    $snmp_session->close;

    my @dests = ();
```

```perl
foreach my $resp ( keys %{ $responsePDU } )
{
    my $oid_pat = ipRouteDest;
    if ( $resp =~ /^$oid_pat\./ )
    {
        @dests = ( @dests, $responsePDU->{ $resp } );
    }
}

my %unique_next_hops = ();

foreach my $dest ( @dests )
{
    my $oid_type = ipRouteType . ".$dest";

    if ( $responsePDU->{ $oid_type } eq '4' )
    {
        my $oid_nexthop = ipRouteNextHop . ".$dest";
        $unique_next_hops{ $responsePDU->{ $oid_nexthop } }++;
    }
}

foreach my $unique ( keys %unique_next_hops )
{
    push @{$self->{ 'Routers' }}, $unique;
}
}
```

This code does two things.

Firstly, drawing on the code from the client/server ipdetermine, the collection of unique routing network devices contactable from the router executing the mobile agent is determined, and placed into the %unique_next_hops hash. Note that this SNMP code communicates with the *Managed Device* identified as localhost. That is, the mobile agent sends its requests to the SNMP software executing on *the same network device* executing the mobile agent. Although SNMP is still employed, the high-bandwidth network transfer has been avoided[10].

Secondly, the hash is processed (at the bottom of the do_it method), and the list of routers is assigned to the anonymous array referenced by the Routers hash entry of the $self object. Note the use of the inbuilt push subroutine which assigns the list of routers (one at a time) to the array.

After the do_it method executes, the mobile agent relocates to the final *Receiving MAE* and the at_end method executes. This method simply processes the anonymous array associated with the Routers hash entry and prints the list of contactable routers to the screen:

---

[10]As is always the case when localhost is used.

```
sub at_end {
    my ( $self, @args ) = @_;

    print "Determined 'ip' next hop data:\n\n";

    foreach my $router ( @{$self->{ 'Routers' }} )
    {
        print "$router\n";
    }
}
```

Finding a commercial router that can be configured to run an MAE is difficult. To demonstrate the mobile agent in action, the network device glasnost. itcarlow.ie will act as a surrogate router. Although configured primarily as a Web server, glasnost.itcarlow.ie runs both IP and SNMP. Despite not operating on a router, the SNMP software executing on glasnost.itcarlow.ie can be asked to provide its routing table[11].

When the client/server ipdetermine is executed with the following command-line:

```
./ipdetermine glasnost.itcarlow.ie public
```

it produces the following results:

```
Requesting 'ip' next hop data for: 149.153.100.67, public, SNMPv2

Next hop: 149.153.100.10
```

With the multishotloc MAE executing at protocol port-number 40000 on glasnost.itcarlow.ie and at protocol port-number 44444 on the initiating network device (which is pbmac.itcarlow.ie), the mobile agent ipdeterminema.pa can be sent on its way (from pbmac.itcarlow.ie) with this command-line:

```
./multilaunchma ipdeterminema.pa
```

Assuming, of course, that the multilaunchma.rc disk-file contains these two lines:

```
glasnost.itcarlow.ie:40000
pbmac.itcarlow.ie:44444
```

When the mobile agent returns to pbmac.itcarlow.ie it displays the following results on screen:

```
Determined 'ip' next hop data:

149.153.100.10
```

---

[11]Which, admittedly, is quite small.

These results, thankfully, exactly match those produced by the client/server ipdetermine. An exercise at the end of the current chapter uses *The Network Debugger* to establish that the network traffic generated by the mobile agent ipdeterminema.pa is less than that produced by the client/server ipdetermine.

6.13 The Cloning Mobile-Agent ipdetermine

The bandwidth utilized by the ipdeterminema.pa mobile agent can be further reduced by arranging for just the results produced by the mobile agent to travel back to the initiating network device, as opposed to the entire mobile agent.

To accomplish this, ipdeterminema.pa needs to include some standard Socket API sending and receiving code, in addition to the SNMP processing code. The strategy employed borrows code from the UDP client and server examples from Chapter 3, *Sockets*. UDP is chosen as the transport service for the same reasons it is used by SNMP: it is lightweight, incurs little overhead and is easy to implement. The mobile-agent machinery available (multilaunchma and multishotloc) are designed to allow a mobile agent to roam to a collection of MAEs, performing processing at each *intermediate* MAE before processing any results at the final *Receiving MAE*. This design worked well with the ipdeterminema.pa program. However, with the cloned version of the program, the mobile agent travels to only one MAE (on the routing device), interacts with the SNMP software executing there, then sends back the results to the initiating network device. With only one MAE identified in the multilaunchma.rc disk-file, the current design would never execute the do_it method (as the design arranges never to execute the method on the final *Receiving MAE*). Consequently, any code that needs to execute on the routing device needs to reside in the at_end method, *not* in do_it.

A new version of the mobile agent called ipdetermineclonema.pa implements the strategy outlined above, and here is the entire source code:

```
#! /usr/bin/perl -w

use strict;
use 5.6.0;

package Agent::IpDetermineCloneMA;

use Socket;
use Net::SNMP;
use OIDs qw( sysDescr
             ipRouteTable ipRouteDest
             ipRouteType ipRouteNextHop );

use constant SENDTO_UDP_PORT    => 40001;
use constant REMOTE_HOST        => 'localhost';
use constant RESULTS_RECV_PORT  => 40001;
use constant MAX_RECV_LEN       => 65536;
```

```perl
our @ISA = qw( Agent );

sub new {
    my ( $class, %args ) = @_;
    my $self = {};

    foreach ( keys( %args ) )
    {
        $self->{ "$_" } = $args{ "$_" };
    }

    bless $self, $class;
}

sub agent_main {
    my ( $self, @args ) = @_;

    my $to = \$self->{ 'ToValue' };

    $self->do_it if ( $$to && ($#{$self->{ 'Hosts' }} > -1) );

    $self->{ 'ToValue' } = shift @{ $self->{ 'Hosts' }};

    return $self->at_end unless $$to;

    my $msg = new Agent::Message(
                        'Body'      => [ "IpDetermineCloneMA.\n",
                                         $self->store() ],
                        'Transport' => 'TCP',
                        'Address'   => $$to );

    if ( !$msg->send )
    {
        print "ipclonema: could not send agent!\n";
    }
    else
    {
        my $local_port = RESULTS_RECV_PORT;
        my $trans_serv = getprotobyname( 'udp' );
        my $local_addr = sockaddr_in( $local_port, INADDR_ANY );

        socket( MARECV_UDP_SOCK, PF_INET, SOCK_DGRAM, $trans_serv )
            or die "ipclonema: socket creation failed: $!\n";
        bind( MARECV_UDP_SOCK, $local_addr )
            or die "ipclonema: bind to address failed: $!\n";

        my $data;

        my $from_who = recv( MARECV_UDP_SOCK, $data,
                                         MAX_RECV_LEN, 0 );

        close MARECV_UDP_SOCK;

        if ( $from_who )
        {
            print "Determined 'ip' next hop data:\n\n";
            print "$data\n";
```

```perl
        }
        else
        {
            warn "ipclonema: Problem with recv: $!\n";
        }
    }

    return undef;
}

sub do_it {
    my ( $self, @args ) = @_;
}

sub at_end {
    my ( $self, @args ) = @_;

    my $snmp_session = Net::SNMP->session(
                        -hostname    => 'localhost',
                        -community   => 'public',
                        -version     => '2',
                        -port        => 161
                    );

    if ( !defined( $snmp_session ) )
    {
        print "ipclonema: error: cannot establish session.\n";

        return;
    }

    my $responsePDU = $snmp_session->get_table( OIDs::ipRouteTable );

    if ( !defined( $responsePDU ) )
    {
        print "ipclonema: OID: ", OIDs::ipRouteTable, " : ",
            $snmp_session->error, "\n";

        return;
    }

    $snmp_session->close;

    my @dests = ();

    foreach my $resp ( keys %{ $responsePDU } )
    {
        my $oid_pat = OIDs::ipRouteDest;
        if ( $resp =~ /^$oid_pat\./ )
        {
            @dests = ( @dests, $responsePDU->{ $resp } );
        }
    }

    my %unique_next_hops = ();

    foreach my $dest ( @dests )
```

```
    {
        my $oid_type = OIDs::ipRouteType . ".$dest";

        if ( $responsePDU->{ $oid_type } eq '4' )
        {
            my $oid_nexthop = OIDs::ipRouteNextHop . ".$dest";
            $unique_next_hops{ $responsePDU->{ $oid_nexthop } }++;
        }
    }

    foreach my $unique ( keys %unique_next_hops )
    {
        push @{$self->{ 'Routers' }}, $unique;
    }

    my $remote      = REMOTE_HOST;
    my $remote_port = SENDTO_UDP_PORT;
    my $trans_serv  = getprotobyname( 'udp' );
    my $remote_host = gethostbyname( $remote )
        or die "ipclonema: name lookup failed: $remote\n";
    my $destination = sockaddr_in( $remote_port, $remote_host );

    sleep( 1 );

    socket( MASEND_UDP_SOCK, PF_INET, SOCK_DGRAM, $trans_serv )
        or die "ipclonema: socket creation failed: $!\n";

    my $data = join( '', @{$self->{ 'Routers' }} );

    send( MASEND_UDP_SOCK, $data, 0, $destination )
        or warn "ipclonema: send to socket failed.\n";
    close MASEND_UDP_SOCK
        or die "ipclonema: close socket failed: $!\n";
}

1;
```

The program begins very much like the code to `ipdeterminema.pa`. Note the additional use of the standard Socket module within the namespace. Three constant definitions appear near the top of the source code, and are used by the UDP sending and receiving parts of the program:

```
use constant SENDTO_UDP_PORT   => 40001;
use constant RESULTS_RECV_PORT => 40001;
use constant MAX_RECV_LEN      => 65536;
```

The new method is unchanged. The `agent_main` method does differ from the other mobile agents based on `multidefault2.pa`. The first half of the method (up to and including the invocation of $msg->send) is as expected. The addition of an `else` part to the `if` statement provides a mechanism to perform additional processing after the mobile agent has successfully been sent on its way. Here, the `ipdetermineclonema.pa` mobile agent becomes a UDP server and waits at the protocol port-number identified by RESULTS_RECV_PORT, declared earlier to be 40001. When data arrive at the socket associated with the protocol port-number, it is displayed on screen in a similar fashion to the previous versions of ipdetermine[12]:

```perl
if ( !$msg->send )
{
    print "ipclonema: could not send agent!\n";
}
else
{
    my $local_port = RESULTS_RECV_PORT;
    my $trans_serv = getprotobyname( 'udp' );
    my $local_addr = sockaddr_in( $local_port, INADDR_ANY );

    socket( MARECV_UDP_SOCK, PF_INET, SOCK_DGRAM, $trans_serv )
        or die "ipclonema: socket creation failed: $!\n";
    bind( MARECV_UDP_SOCK, $local_addr )
        or die "ipclonema: bind to address failed: $!\n";

    my $data;

    my $from_who = recv( MARECV_UDP_SOCK, $data,
                                MAX_RECV_LEN, 0 );

    close MARECV_UDP_SOCK;

    if ( $from_who )
    {
        print "Determined 'ip' next hop data:\n\n";
        print "$data\n";
    }
    else
    {
        warn "ipclonema: Problem with recv: $!\n";
    }
}

return undef;
}
```

The do_it method is relegated to doing nothing in this mobile agent as, with only a single *Receiving MAE* relocated to, do_it is never invoked. Consequently, this method is empty:

```perl
sub do_it {
    my ( $self, @args ) = @_;
}
```

---

[12]Refer to Chapter 3, *Sockets*, for an explanation of the Socket API code used here.

The remaining changes (i.e. additions of code) occur within the at_end method. The SNMP processing code from the ipdeterminema.pa program is copied verbatim into this mobile agent's at_end method. Rather than display any results on screen, the at_end method now sends them to the waiting UDP server that was established by the agent_main method on the initiating network device. Again, this code is borrowed from the UDP client examples from Chapter 3, *Sockets*:

```
my $remote = $self->{ 'Home' };
my $remote_port = SENDTO_UDP_PORT;
my $trans_serv  = getprotobyname( 'udp' );
my $remote_host = gethostbyname( $remote )
    or die "ipclonema: name lookup failed: $remote\n";
my $destination = sockaddr_in( $remote_port, $remote_host );

sleep( 1 );

socket( MASEND_UDP_SOCK, PF_INET, SOCK_DGRAM, $trans_serv )
    or die "ipclonema: socket creation failed: $!\n";

my $data = join( "\n", @{$self->{ 'Routers' }} );

send( MASEND_UDP_SOCK, $data, 0, $destination )
    or warn "ipclonema: send to socket failed.\n";
close MASEND_UDP_SOCK
    or die "ipclonema: close socket failed: $!\n";
}
```

Three lines are worth noting. The first sets the remote UDP server's network address to the value associated with the object's Home hash entry. This will necessitate a small change to the multilaunchma program, which will be discussed shortly:

```
my $remote = $self->{ 'Home' };
```

Prior to creating the socket and sending the determined list of routers to the waiting UDP server, the at_end method pauses for one second:

```
sleep( 1 );
```

This may seem like a strange thing to do. Unfortunately, under certain circumstances (most notably when testing with localhost), a situation can arise where the code to establish the UDP server (as executed by agent_main) has not executed in the time it takes the mobile agent to relocate, perform some processing and send any data back to the waiting UDP server. If the send occurs with no server in existence, the UDP data simply disappear. The UDP server code then executes, and the server waits, and waits, and waits.

The addition of a small, artificial delay guards against this happening. The final line of code worth highlighting takes the results from the SNMP processing and assigns the array of determined routing devices to a scalar called $data. The scalar is then sent via the created client socket to the waiting UDP server on the initiating network device:

```
my $data = join( "\n", @{$self->{ 'Routers' }} );
```

To support the use of the $self->{ 'Home ' } value, a small change is needed to the multilaunchma program. Replace the single-line assignment to the %args hash (near the top of the program) with these lines, creating multilaunchma2:

```
my $initiating = inet_ntoa( scalar gethostbyname( hostname ) );

my %args = ( 'Name' => $mae_name,
             'Home' => $initiating );
```

These lines ensure that the value of Home is set to the IP address of the initiating network device whenever the mobile agent is launched. This then allows the UDP client code within ipdetermineclonema.pa to identify the correct network device to which to send results.

The multilaunchma.rc disk-file now has a single entry, as follows:

```
glasnost.itcarlow.ie:40000
```

With the multishotloc MAE executing on glasnost.itcarlow.ie at protocol port-number 40000, the cloning mobile agent can now be sent on its way with the following command:

```
./multilaunchma2 ipdetermineclonema.pa
```

After a short pause, the following results are displayed on the initiating network device's screen:

```
Determined 'ip' next hop data:

149.153.100.10
```

Once again, these results match those of the previous implementations of this program. Of interest is the fact that the ipdetermineclonema.pa combines the strengths of the *mobile-agent model* (mobility, low bandwidth) with those of the *client/server model* (simplicity, short messages). When it comes to choosing a model to work with, it is not an either-or decision. It is perfectly acceptable to mix'n'match.

Of course, despite the fact that this most recent version of ipdetermine uses the least amount of network bandwidth, one needs to ask whether or not the increased complexity in the code was worth the effort? There is no simple answer to this question, as specific application requirements always dictate the design decisions made. In some cases, this level of complexity is tolerable, in others, it is not. Choose wisely.

6.14 Other Perl Agent Examples

The release distribution of Agent.pm includes a collection of instructive example programs. What follows is a brief description of each.

dcalc.pl – a distributed mobile-agent calculator, capable for relocating to a list of MAEs.

Eval.pa – a mobile-agent code evaluator, which relocates to an MAE, executes specified code with eval, then returns any results to a specified network location.

ex.pl – a *Launching MAE* designed to execute the mobile agents distributed with Agent.pm. It can also be used to launch any other mobile agent developed using the Agent.pm technologies.

FreeSpace.pa – a mobile agent capable of relocating to a list of MAEs in order to determine the amount of free hard-disk storage available on each MAE. Unlike the multidefault2.pa mobile agent, FreeSpace.pa executes its equivalent of the do_it method on the final *Receiving MAE*, as well as all others.

HelloWorld.pa – a simple mobile agent that relocates to a specified MAE and displays a 'Hello World!' message on the MAE's screen.

keepalive.pl – a small program that uses the inbuilt fork subroutine to demonstrate sustained (or persistent) connections using the Agent.pm technologies and the TCP transport service.

Loop.pa – this mobile agent can be started as a *sender* or a *receiver*. When operating as either, it communicates with another Loop.pa mobile agent, sending a small message repeatedly (back and forth).

MyAgent.pl – written by James Duncan, this small program combines the code for a mobile agent with that of a *Launching MAE*. When executed, it relocates to a specified *Receiving MAE* and displays the string '**** A Test from James ****' on screen.

Static.pa – the distribution's MAE, which can be executed by the ex.pl program. Described by Steve Purkis as an 'agent server', this program provides functionality similar to the multishotloc program, yet uses a very different implementation strategy. It does more, but is more complex as a result.

Template.pa – an empty mobile agent that can form the basis of any custom mobile agent. An empty shell, the Template.pa code is, nevertheless, not unlike the onedefault.pa and multidefault2.pa programs.

6.15   Where To From Here?

Another interesting Perl mobile code technology is Penguin by *Felix Gallo*. Penguin provides functionality not unlike that provided by Agent.pm, but in a very different manner. A related module is Penguin-Easy, by James Duncan, which provides a simpler API to the Penguin facilities. Note that the development of these modules, which are both available on CPAN, has not seen any activity for a number of years.

There is a lot of ongoing research within the mobile-agent community. Refer to the *Web Resources* section at the end of this chapter for more details.

As stated at the start of this chapter, Agent.pm is an unfinished, proof-of-concept technology. Readers are encouraged to extend and expand upon the capabilities of Agent.pm, and share their code with the Perl programming community.

6.16   Print Resources

A good introduction to mobile-agent technology is the book *Mobile Agents* by William T. Cockayne and Michael Zyda (Manning, 1998). This includes a description of four (non-Perl) mobile-agent implementations: Telescript, Agent TCL (now called D'Agents), ARA and IBM's Aglets.

Understanding Code Mobility by Alfonso Fuggetta, Gian Pietro Picco and Giovanni Vigna (IEEE Transactions on Software Engineering, 1998) is an excellent article describing a collection of mobile code technologies, design paradigms and proposed application areas. The inclusion of a network management case-study is highly relevant in light of this book's last chapter.

6.17   Web Resources

Steve Purkis's CPAN directory is http://www.cpan.org/authors/id/SPURKIS. An old and somewhat out-of-date Agent.pm website can be found at http://tiamat.epn.nu/~spurkis/Agent.

The CPAN directory devoted to the work of James Duncan can be found at: http://www.cpan.org/authors/id/JDUNCAN.

An excellent and very well maintained website devoted to listing online mobile-agent resources can be found at http://www.cetus-links.org/oo_mobile_agents.html. Refer to the *Bibliography* section of this page for a link to a large collection of mobile-agent security references.

Exercises

1. . The multishotloc program has the potential to miss the receipt of a mobile agent if it is currently servicing another (that is, the $mae->recv call cannot execute because $ma->run is executing). Adapt the multishotloc program to support the creation of a forked child process to execute each received mobile agent.

2. Explore the support Agent.pm has for exploiting Perl's threading technology. Revisit the program developed from the last exercise and adapt it to use threads as opposed to the forking mechanism. What advantages does the threading implementation have over the forking one, if any?

3. Use *The Network Debugger* from Chapter 2 to capture the network traffic generated by the client/server version of the multiwho program. Note the amount of traffic generated by the computer running multiwho. Next, configure the *Network Debugger* to capture the network traffic generated by the multiwhoma.pa mobile agent on the network device executing the *Launching MAE*. Compare the results with those of the client/server version.

4. Repeat the last exercise for the client/server and mobile-agent version of the ipdetermine program.

5. The multidefault2.pa mobile agent halts when it cannot relocate to an MAE (perhaps due to the MAE's inability to accept connections). For example, when roaming to a list of five MAEs, if the third MAE is unavailable, the multidefault2.pa will terminate at the second MAE (never returning to the final MAE to process any results from the mobile agent's computations). Develop a more robust implementation of this mobile agent which is capable of withstanding any number of unavailable MAEs. When this new version of multidefault2.pa arrives at the final MAE, in addition to processing the at_end results, it should report the list of MAEs visited.

6. Research the Safe module which comes as standard with the Perl distribution. Once you understand the facilities provided by this module, investigate its use within the Agent.pm classes. Can the use of Safe improve upon the security vulnerabilities of the oneshotloc and multishotloc MAEs? Change these programs to switch on the use of Safe. What effect does this have?

Appendix A
Essential Linux Commands

To learn more about a particular command, view the *manual page* associated with it – simply type man followed by the name of the command you want to learn about. To exit from a manual page, press the q key (where 'q' stands for 'quit'). Most commands have options associated with them – do not try to guess the options. Read the manual page!

Working with Files and Directories

cat	type a file to the screen
cd	change directory (or return to %HOME directory)
chmod	change the mode of a file (e.g. to make it executable)
chown	change the owner of a file or directory
cp	copy a file/directory to a new location
find	search for a file on the system (see 'locate')
ftp	transfer files from one system to another
grep	search for a text string in a group of files
gzip/gunzip	compress/uncompress a file or group of files
head	display the first few lines of a file on the screen
ispell	spell-check a file using the system dictionary
less	type a file to the screen one screenfull at a time
locate	locate a specific file on the system (see 'find')
ln	create a symbolic link (alias/shortcut) to a file
ls	list the contents of a directory to the screen
mkdir	create a new directory
mv	move or rename a currently existing file/directory

pwd	display the name of current working directory
rm	delete one or more files
rmdir	delete a directory
sort	sort a file (using various techniques)
tac	type a file to the screen in reverse order (see 'cat')
tail	display the last few lines of a file on the screen
wc	display the character, word, or line count of a file
zcat	type the contents of a compressed file to the screen
zmore	like 'zcat', only display the file one screenful at a time

Printing Commands

lpq	check the status of your entries on the print queue
lpr	add an entry to the print queue
lprm	remove an entry from the print queue

Networking Commands

netstat	show the network status for this system
ping	is there anybody out there? Check a host for existence
traceroute	show me how to get from here to there

Working with Processes

kill	stop a process (program) from running
ps	report on the active processes
top	who is doing what, and how much CPU are they using?
w	display a summary of system usage on the screen

Working with Disks

df	how much free disk space is there?
du	how is the disk space being used?

Miscellaneous Commands

cal	display a calendar on the screen
clear	clear the screen
date	display the current date and time on the screen
echo	display a message on the screen

man	read a manual page (type 'man man' to learn more)
passwd	change your password
perl	run Perl (a great programming language ...)
su	create a shell under the ID of some other user
telnet	log into a remote computer
uname	display the machine and operating system name
users	list the current login sessions on the system
vi	run vi (a great text editor ...)
whereis	locate a binary (executable), source, or manual page file
which	list the path to a particular binary file (executable)
who	who is currently logged in
whoami	'cause I've forgotten ...
Ctrl-D	signal end-of-file to running process (key combination)

Essential Systems Administrator Commands

Note that you will need to be logged in as *root* to use these commands effectively. Remember, as *root* you have complete power over Linux (so be careful).

cron	execute commands at scheduled times
dmesg	display the system control messages
e2fsck	check the health of a disk
fdisk	fiddle with disk partitions (be very, very careful)
fdisk	you are being careful with fdisk, aren't you?
ifconfig	configure your network interface card
kill	see kill above (much more fun as root)
lilo	install the Linux Loader (read the 'man' page)
lpc	control a print queue
mke2fs	create a file system (i.e. format a disk)
mount	add a disk into the active file system (read the 'man' page)
reboot	reboot now!
rpm	the RedHat Package Manager
shutdown	perform a nice safe, graceful, shutdown of the system
tar	work with 'tarred' files (read the 'man' page)
umount	remove a disk from the active file system

Appendix B
vi *Quick*
Reference

This quick reference will get you started. To learn more, from the Linux command-line, type: man vi.

Invoking the vi Text Editor

vi - start the vi editor with an empty edit buffer.

vi *file* - edit a file called *file*.

vi +n *file* - edit a file called *file* and go to line *n*.

vi +/*pattern* *file* - edit a file called *file* and go to the first line that matches the string *pattern*.

vi's modes

vi can be in one of three modes:

edit mode - keys typed are added to the edit buffer;

non-edit mode - keys typed adjust or move around the edit buffer;

ex mode - commands are executed within vi, and the commands affect the edit buffer.

To enter *edit mode*, press the Esc key then type i.
To enter *non-edit mode*, simply press Esc.
To enter *ex mode*, press Esc then type :.

Non-edit mode keystrokes

^	go to start of current line (first non-blank character)
0	go to start of current line
$	go to end of current line
w	go to next word
b	go to previous word (back)
o	insert blank line below current one, enter *edit mode*
O	insert blank line above current one, enter *edit mode*
i	enter *edit mode* by inserting text at current location
a	enter *edit mode* by appending text after current location
A	enter *edit mode* by appending to the end of the current line
J	join the current line with the line immediately below it
Ctrl-G	show current line number
*n*G	go to line *n* within the edit buffer
G	go to bottom of edit buffer

Deleting text (in non-edit mode)

dd	delete current line
dw	delete next word
d^	delete to start of line
d$	delete to end of line
x	delete a single character

Changing text (in non-edit mode)

cc	change the current line, and enter *edit mode*
cw	change the current word, and enter *edit mode*
r	replace a single character
R	replace characters until Esc is pressed

Cutting and Pasting (in non-edit mode)

yy	copy current line (the line is now *yanked*)
*n*yy	copy *n* current lines (multi-yank)
ye	copy to the end of next word (little-yank)
p	paste yanked text after or below cursor
P	paste yanked text before or above cursor

Some ex mode commands

:w	write the edit buffer (i.e. save the file)
:w *file*	write a copy of the edit buffer as *file*
:wq	write the edit buffer then quit
:q!	quit without writing any changes (called 'force quit')
:w! *file*	overwrite *file* with current edit buffer
:sh	temporarily exit vi to access a Linux shell
:help	access the vi online help
:help *cmd*	access the online help for subject *cmd*
:set	used to set and unset vi settings
:set all	display the entire list of vi's current settings

Searching

/*pattern*	search forward in edit buffer for a match to *pattern*
/	repeat last forward search
?*pattern*	search backward in edit buffer for a match to *pattern*
?	repeat last backward search
n	repeat previous search (regardless of direction)

Appendix C

Network Employed

The network employed during the development of *Programming the Network with Perl* resides at *The Institute of Technology, Carlow* in Ireland. Although the entire network consists of hundreds of interconnected network devices on a number of LAN segments, only a handful were used to test the example programs in this book. These devices are identified on the network diagram over the page, together with the LAN segments they are attached to.

Those network devices sporting an 'R' identify routers running proprietary 'network' operating systems. All of the other network devices are running some version of the Linux Operating System, except for `elmo` (Mac OS) and `mossy` (Windows). A square denotes a client (or workstation) network device, whereas a rectangle denotes a server-class network device.

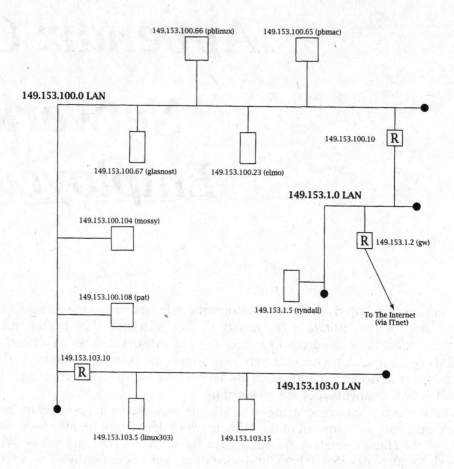

Appendix D
Sample
NetDebug
Results

In this appendix, the results generated by a number of *NetDebug* invocations are presented. A brief commentary accompanies each example. Although some of the captured traffic is quite voluminous, it is illustrative of the amount of data typically transferred for all but the simplest of network interactions. Note that for each capture, any datagrams larger than 1500 bytes are split over a number of Ethernet frames, as the underlying network is one built from this popular LAN technology.

NetDebugging Web Traffic

The following invocation of *NetDebug* captures *HTTP* traffic, which uses the well-known TCP protocol port-number 80:

    ./netdb -s 149.153.100.67 -p 80

The glasnost.itcarlow.ie (149.153.100.67) Web server services a number of requests from mossy.itcarlow.ie (which is identified as 149.153.100.104). The vast majority of the traffic captured is textual (as the Web uses the text-based HTML extensively). The transfer of a number of binary graphic files is also captured, and these are identified by the 'GIF89a' character sequence. To conserve space, only a small portion of each graphic file's capture is shown.

The user on `mossy.itcarlow.ie` uses a Web browser to request (using the GET method) the `index.html` homepage from `glasnost.itcarlow.ie`. Once the entire page (HTML and any embedded graphics) is received, the user then clicks on the link to Paul Barry's homepage. Once this page is transferred, the user clicks on a link (at the bottom of Paul Barry's homepage) which redirects the browser to the *Programming the Network with Perl* website. Here is the traffic captured by *NetDebug*:

```
Fri Aug  3 15:11:32 2001 - netdebug BEGIN run.

- - - - - - - - - - - - - - - - - - - - - - - - - - - - - - - - - -
149.153.100.104 -> 149.153.100.67 (id: 13062, ttl: 128)

TCP Source: 1115 -> TCP Destination: 80
TCP Header Length: 7, TCP Checksum: 43539
TCP Data:

^E´^A^A^D^B
- - - - - - - - - - - - - - - - - - - - - - - - - - - - - - - - - -
149.153.100.67 -> 149.153.100.104 (id: 36536, ttl: 64)

TCP Source: 80 -> TCP Destination: 1115
TCP Header Length: 7, TCP Checksum: 54195
TCP Data:

^E´^A^A^D^B
- - - - - - - - - - - - - - - - - - - - - - - - - - - - - - - - - -
149.153.100.104 -> 149.153.100.67 (id: 13318, ttl: 128)

TCP Source: 1115 -> TCP Destination: 80
TCP Header Length: 5, TCP Checksum: 22020
TCP Data:

^@^@^@^@^@^@
- - - - - - - - - - - - - - - - - - - - - - - - - - - - - - - - - -
149.153.100.104 -> 149.153.100.67 (id: 13574, ttl: 128)

TCP Source: 1115 -> TCP Destination: 80
TCP Header Length: 5, TCP Checksum: 48444
TCP Data:

GET / HTTP/1.0
Connection: Keep-Alive
User-Agent: Mozilla/4.75 [en] (Win98; U)
Host: glasnost.itcarlow.ie
Accept: image/gif, image/x-xbitmap, image/jpeg, image/pjpeg, image/png, */*
Accept-Encoding: gzip
Accept-Language: en
Accept-Charset: iso-8859-1,*,utf-8

- - - - - - - - - - - - - - - - - - - - - - - - - - - - - - - - - -
149.153.100.67 -> 149.153.100.104 (id: 36537, ttl: 64)
TCP Source: 80 -> TCP Destination: 1115
TCP Header Length: 5, TCP Checksum: 65386
TCP Data:

UUUUUU
- - - - - - - - - - - - - - - - - - - - - - - - - - - - - - - - - -
149.153.100.67 -> 149.153.100.104 (id: 36538, ttl: 64)

TCP Source: 80 -> TCP Destination: 1115
TCP Header Length: 5, TCP Checksum: 6689
TCP Data:
```

```
HTTP/1.1 200 OK
Date: Fri, 03 Aug 2001 15:12:28 GMT
Server: Apache/1.3.14 (Unix) (Red-Hat/Linux) mod_perl/1.23
Last-Modified: Tue, 05 Jun 2001 10:24:17 GMT
ETag: "17942-687-3b1cb351"
Accept-Ranges: bytes
Content-Length: 1671
Keep-Alive: timeout=15, max=100
Connection: Keep-Alive
Content-Type: text/html

<!DOCTYPE HTML PUBLIC "-//W3C//DTD HTML 3.2 Final//EN">
<HTML>
 <HEAD> <TITLE>Welcome to glasnost.itcarlow.ie</TITLE> </HEAD>
 <BODY>
<CENTER>
  <H1>Welcome to Glasnost!</H1>
This is the staff Web server at the <a href="http://www.itcarlow.ie/">
Institute of Technology, Carlow</a> in Ireland.<P> <HR>
Note: this service is in 'beta' and, as such, is limited to a small
number of (Computing) staff.<BR>
The plan is to make the service available to all staff at the start of
the next academic session (2001/2002).  <HR><P>
The following staff members maintain Web pages on (or accessible from)
this server:<P>
<a href="~barryp/index.html">Paul Barry</a>, Computing<BR>
<a href="~casse/index.html">Eamon Cass</a>, Computing<BR>
<a href="~hickeypm/index.html">Philip Hickey</a>, Computing<BR>
<a href="http://akmac.itcarlow.ie/local/">Austin Kinsella</a>, Computing<BR>
<a href="~lowep/index.html">Peter Lowe</a>, Computing<BR>
<a href="~meudecc/index.html">Dr. Christophe Meudec</a>, Computing<BR>
<a href="~moloneyg/index.html">Gerry Moloney</a>, Computing<BR>
<!--
<a href="~palmerr/ind
- - - - - - - - - - - - - - - - - - - - - - - - - - - - - - - - - -
149.153.100.67 -> 149.153.100.104 (id: 36539, ttl: 64)

TCP Source: 80 -> TCP Destination: 1115
TCP Header Length: 5, TCP Checksum: 60617
TCP Data:

Palmer</a>, Computing<BR>
-->
<!--
<a href="~powerb/index.html">Bernadette Power</a>, Computing<BR>
-->
<a href="~powerk/index.html">Ken Power</a>, Computing<BR>
<a href="~whyte/index.html">Nigel Whyte</a>, Computing<BR> <P>
Usage Guidelines for staff can be found <a href="guide.html">here</a>.
<P><HR>
Report any problems to the <A HREF="mailto:paul.barry@itcarlow.ie">
server administrator</A>.<BR>
If you take issue with any of the content, please direct your comments
to the author of the material.
</CENTER> </BODY> <HTML>

- - - - - - - - - - - - - - - - - - - - - - - - - - - - - - - - - -
149.153.100.104 -> 149.153.100.67 (id: 13830, ttl: 128)

TCP Source: 1115 -> TCP Destination: 80
TCP Header Length: 5, TCP Checksum: 19763
TCP Data:

^@^@^@^@^@^@
- - - - - - - - - - - - - - - - - - - - - - - - - - - - - - - - - -
149.153.100.104 -> 149.153.100.67 (id: 14086, ttl: 128)
```

```
TCP Source: 1115 -> TCP Destination: 80
TCP Header Length: 5, TCP Checksum: 62950
TCP Data:

GET /~barryp/index.html HTTP/1.0
Referer: http://glasnost.itcarlow.ie/
Connection: Keep-Alive
User-Agent: Mozilla/4.75 [en] (Win98; U)
Host: glasnost.itcarlow.ie
Accept: image/gif, image/x-xbitmap, image/jpeg, image/pjpeg, image/png, */*
Accept-Encoding: gzip
Accept-Language: en
Accept-Charset: iso-8859-1,*,utf-8


- - - - - - - - - - - - - - - - - - - - - - - - - - - - - - - -
149.153.100.67 -> 149.153.100.104 (id: 36540, ttl: 64)

TCP Source: 80 -> TCP Destination: 1115
TCP Header Length: 5, TCP Checksum: 61612
TCP Data:

UUUUUU
- - - - - - - - - - - - - - - - - - - - - - - - - - - - - - - -
149.153.100.67 -> 149.153.100.104 (id: 36541, ttl: 64)

TCP Source: 80 -> TCP Destination: 1115
TCP Header Length: 5, TCP Checksum: 28822
TCP Data:

HTTP/1.1 200 OK
Date: Fri, 03 Aug 2001 15:12:33 GMT
Server: Apache/1.3.14 (Unix)  (Red-Hat/Linux) mod_perl/1.23
Last-Modified: Tue, 17 Jul 2001 18:16:47 GMT
ETag: "13b52-a0e-3b54810f"
Accept-Ranges: bytes
Content-Length: 2574
Keep-Alive: timeout=15, max=99
Connection: Keep-Alive
Content-Type: text/html

<!doctype html public "-//W3C//DTD HTML 3.2 Final//EN">
<html>
<head> <title>Welcome to Paul Barry's Web-Site</title> </head>

<body>
<center>
<img src="star_bar.gif"> <p>
<h2>Welcome to Paul Barry's Web-Site</h2> <p>
If you are one of my students, and you are looking for the <b>Course
Support Materials</b> Web site, then click <a href="elmo/index.html">
here</a>.<p>
<img src="star_bar.gif"> <p>
<h2>Courses</h2>
I am teaching two courses this academic year (2000/2001): <UL>
<LI>BSc Software Engineering (4th Year Class): <b>Networking and
Operating Systems</b><p>
<LI>BSc Computer Networking (2nd Year Class): <b>Networking and
Internetworking</b> </UL>
<img src="star_bar.gif"> <p>
<h2>Articles and Book Reviews</h2>
<p><a href="http://www.linuxjournal.com"><img src="lj.gif"></a><p>
Recently written for <a href="http://www.linuxjournal.com">Linux
Journal</a> magazine: <UL>
<LI>August 2001: Article: <A HREF="http://www.linuxjournal.com/
lj-issues/issue88/index.html"><i>The Trials and Tribulations of
Installing LinuxPPC 2000 Q4</i></A>.<br>Note: this article is
```

```
available in print form only.<p>
<LI>March 2001: Book Review
- - - - - - - - - - - - - - - - - - - - - - - - - - - - - - -
149.153.100.67 -> 149.153.100.104 (id: 36542, ttl: 64)

TCP Source: 80 -> TCP Destination: 1115
TCP Header Length: 5, TCP Checksum: 64553
TCP Data:

p://www.linuxjournal.com/articles/linux_review/0032.html"><i>Perl:
The Programmer's Companion</i></A><p>
<LI>February 2001: Book Review: <A HREF="http://www.linuxjournal.com
/articles/linux_review/0031.html"><i>Debugging Perl: Troubleshooting
for Programmers</i></A><p>
<LI>February 2001: Article: <A HREF="http://www.linuxjournal.com/
articles/linux_review/0027.html"><i>Which Programming Language?</i>
</A><p>
<LI>December 2000: Article: <A HREF="http://www.linuxjournal.com/
articles/misc/0035.html"><i>Mac OS X: First Impressions</i></A><p>
<LI>December 2000: Book Review: <A HREF="http://www.linuxjournal.com
/lj-issues/issue80/index.html"><i>Programming Perl, 3rd Edition</i>
</A>.<br>Note: this review is available in print form only.  </UL>
Copies of a selection of <a href="http://www.linuxjournal.com">
Linux Journal</a> back-issues can be found in the Institute's <a
href="http://www.itcarlow.ie/facilities/fac_libr_it004.html">Learning
Resource Centre</a>.<p> <p>
<img src="star_bar.gif">
<P>E-mail me by clicking on this email address: <A HREF="mailto:
paul.barry@itcarlow.ie">paul.barry@itcarlow.ie</A></P> <p>
Information on "Programming the Network with Perl" is available
<a href="http://glasnost.itcarlow.ie/~pnb/index.html">here</a>.
Note that I'm at an advanced stage of writing this book (as of July
2001).<p> <img src="star_bar.gif"> <p>
Return to the <a href="/index.html">main page</a>.
</center> </body> </html>

- - - - - - - - - - - - - - - - - - - - - - - - - - - - - - -
149.153.100.104 -> 149.153.100.67 (id: 14342, ttl: 128)

TCP Source: 1115 -> TCP Destination: 80
TCP Header Length: 5, TCP Checksum: 16547
TCP Data:

^@^@^@^@^@^@
- - - - - - - - - - - - - - - - - - - - - - - - - - - - - - -
149.153.100.104 -> 149.153.100.67 (id: 14598, ttl: 128)

TCP Source: 1116 -> TCP Destination: 80
TCP Header Length: 7, TCP Checksum: 38438
TCP Data:

^E'^A^A^D^B
- - - - - - - - - - - - - - - - - - - - - - - - - - - - - - -
149.153.100.67 -> 149.153.100.104 (id: 36543, ttl: 64)

TCP Source: 80 -> TCP Destination: 1116
TCP Header Length: 7, TCP Checksum: 48548
TCP Data:

^E'^A^A^D^B
- - - - - - - - - - - - - - - - - - - - - - - - - - - - - - -
149.153.100.104 -> 149.153.100.67 (id: 14854, ttl: 128)

TCP Source: 1116 -> TCP Destination: 80
TCP Header Length: 5, TCP Checksum: 16373
TCP Data:
```

```
^@^@^@^@^@^@
- - - - - - - - - - - - - - - - - - - - - - - - - - - - - - - - - -
149.153.100.104 -> 149.153.100.67 (id: 15110, ttl: 128)

TCP Source: 1117 -> TCP Destination: 80
TCP Header Length: 7, TCP Checksum: 38434
TCP Data:

^E´^A^A^D^B
- - - - - - - - - - - - - - - - - - - - - - - - - - - - - - - - - -
149.153.100.67 -> 149.153.100.104 (id: 36544, ttl: 64)

TCP Source: 80 -> TCP Destination: 1117
TCP Header Length: 7, TCP Checksum: 59307
TCP Data:

^E´^A^A^D^B
- - - - - - - - - - - - - - - - - - - - - - - - - - - - - - - - - -
149.153.100.104 -> 149.153.100.67 (id: 15366, ttl: 128)

TCP Source: 1117 -> TCP Destination: 80
TCP Header Length: 5, TCP Checksum: 27132
TCP Data:

^@^@^@^@^@^@
- - - - - - - - - - - - - - - - - - - - - - - - - - - - - - - - - -
149.153.100.104 -> 149.153.100.67 (id: 15622, ttl: 128)

TCP Source: 1116 -> TCP Destination: 80
TCP Header Length: 5, TCP Checksum: 17686
TCP Data:

GET /~barryp/star_bar.gif HTTP/1.0
Referer: http://glasnost.itcarlow.ie/~barryp/index.html
Connection: Keep-Alive
User-Agent: Mozilla/4.75 [en] (Win98; U)
Host: glasnost.itcarlow.ie
Accept: image/gif, image/x-xbitmap, image/jpeg, image/pjpeg, image/png
Accept-Encoding: gzip
Accept-Language: en
Accept-Charset: iso-8859-1,*,utf-8


- - - - - - - - - - - - - - - - - - - - - - - - - - - - - - - - - -
149.153.100.67 -> 149.153.100.104 (id: 36545, ttl: 64)

TCP Source: 80 -> TCP Destination: 1116
TCP Header Length: 5, TCP Checksum: 59667
TCP Data:

UUUUUU
- - - - - - - - - - - - - - - - - - - - - - - - - - - - - - - - - -
149.153.100.104 -> 149.153.100.67 (id: 15878, ttl: 128)

TCP Source: 1117 -> TCP Destination: 80
TCP Header Length: 5, TCP Checksum: 49228
TCP Data:

GET /~barryp/lj.gif HTTP/1.0
Referer: http://glasnost.itcarlow.ie/~barryp/index.html
Connection: Keep-Alive
User-Agent: Mozilla/4.75 [en] (Win98; U)
Host: glasnost.itcarlow.ie
Accept: image/gif, image/x-xbitmap, image/jpeg, image/pjpeg, image/png
Accept-Encoding: gzip
Accept-Language: en
Accept-Charset: iso-8859-1,*,utf-8
```

```
- - - - - - - - - - - - - - - - - - - - - - - - - - - - - - - - -
149.153.100.67 -> 149.153.100.104 (id: 36546, ttl: 64)

TCP Source: 80 -> TCP Destination: 1117
TCP Header Length: 5, TCP Checksum: 4897
TCP Data:

UUUUUU
- - - - - - - - - - - - - - - - - - - - - - - - - - - - - - - - -
149.153.100.67 -> 149.153.100.104 (id: 36547, ttl: 64)

TCP Source: 80 -> TCP Destination: 1116
TCP Header Length: 5, TCP Checksum: 25171
TCP Data:

HTTP/1.1 200 OK
Date: Fri, 03 Aug 2001 15:12:33 GMT
Server: Apache/1.3.14 (Unix)  (Red-Hat/Linux) mod_perl/1.23
Last-Modified: Tue, 22 May 2001 11:33:18 GMT
ETag: "13b58-530-3b0a4e7e"
Accept-Ranges: bytes
Content-Length: 1328
Keep-Alive: timeout=15, max=100
Connection: Keep-Alive
Content-Type: image/gif

GIF89aûˆAˆRˆ@÷ˆ@ ...
- - - - - - - - - - - - - - - - - - - - - - - - - - - - - - - - -
149.153.100.67 -> 149.153.100.104 (id: 36548, ttl: 64)

TCP Source: 80 -> TCP Destination: 1116
TCP Header Length: 5, TCP Checksum: 10340
TCP Data:

... Q@ˆ@;
- - - - - - - - - - - - - - - - - - - - - - - - - - - - - - - - -
149.153.100.67 -> 149.153.100.104 (id: 36549, ttl: 64)

TCP Source: 80 -> TCP Destination: 1117
TCP Header Length: 5, TCP Checksum: 305
TCP Data:

HTTP/1.1 200 OK
Date: Fri, 03 Aug 2001 15:12:33 GMT
Server: Apache/1.3.14 (Unix)  (Red-Hat/Linux) mod_perl/1.23
Last-Modified: Tue, 22 May 2001 11:33:18 GMT
ETag: "13b53-20a1-3b0a4e7e"
Accept-Ranges: bytes
Content-Length: 8353
Keep-Alive: timeout=15, max=100
Connection: Keep-Alive
Content-Type: image/gif

GIF89aˆ@ˆA<ˆ@÷ˆ@ˆ@ï ...
- - - - - - - - - - - - - - - - - - - - - - - - - - - - - - - - -
149.153.100.104 -> 149.153.100.67 (id: 16134, ttl: 128)

TCP Source: 1116 -> TCP Destination: 80
TCP Header Length: 5, TCP Checksum: 14387
TCP Data:

ˆ@ˆ@ˆ@ˆ@ˆ@ˆ@
- - - - - - - - - - - - - - - - - - - - - - - - - - - - - - - - -
149.153.100.67 -> 149.153.100.104 (id: 16582, ttl: 64)

TCP Source: 80 -> TCP Destination: 1117
TCP Header Length: 5, TCP Checksum: 38910
TCP Data:
```

```
... ãêo=>oxÄˆHˆ@ˆ[ðØßˆEˆP«Éˆ@¦@ˆFC±Â2o#oWsoÁÀEGuˆZþoˆ@Õ\oˆ[oØ
- - - - - - - - - - - - - - - - - - - - - - - - - - - - - - - - - - - -
149.153.100.67 -> 149.153.100.104 (id: 36551, ttl: 64)

TCP Source: 80 -> TCP Destination: 1117
TCP Header Length: 5, TCP Checksum: 305
TCP Data:

HTTP/1.1 200 OK
Date: Fri, 03 Aug 2001 15:12:33 GMT
Server: Apache/1.3.14 (Unix)  (Red-Hat/Linux) mod_perl/1.23
Last-Modified: Tue, 22 May 2001 11:33:18 GMT
ETag: "13b53-20a1-3b0a4e7e"
Accept-Ranges: bytes
Content-Length: 8353
Keep-Alive: timeout=15, max=100
Connection: Keep-Alive
Content-Type: image/gif

GIF89aˆ@ˆA<ˆ@÷ˆ@ˆ@ ...
- - - - - - - - - - - - - - - - - - - - - - - - - - - - - - - -
149.153.100.104 -> 149.153.100.67 (id: 16390, ttl: 128)

TCP Source: 1117 -> TCP Destination: 80
TCP Header Length: 5, TCP Checksum: 25337
TCP Data:

ˆ@ˆ@ˆ@ˆ@ˆ@
- - - - - - - - - - - - - - - - - - - - - - - - - - - - - - - -
149.153.100.67 -> 149.153.100.104 (id: 36552, ttl: 64)

TCP Source: 80 -> TCP Destination: 1117
TCP Header Length: 5, TCP Checksum: 38910
TCP Data:

... >êx=ˆHoˆ[ÄØˆ@ˆEð«ßˆ@ˆP@ÉC¦ÂˆFo±o2s#ÁWEouÁþGˆ@ˆZ\oˆ[Õø ...
- - - - - - - - - - - - - - - - - - - - - - - - - - - - - - - - -
149.153.100.104 -> 149.153.100.67 (id: 16646, ttl: 128)

TCP Source: 1117 -> TCP Destination: 80
TCP Header Length: 5, TCP Checksum: 23877
TCP Data:

ˆ@ˆ@ˆ@ˆ@ˆ@
- - - - - - - - - - - - - - - - - - - - - - - - - - - - - - - -
149.153.100.67 -> 149.153.100.104 (id: 36553, ttl: 64)

TCP Source: 80 -> TCP Destination: 1117
TCP Header Length: 5, TCP Checksum: 22433
TCP Data:

... o¦dYo)0ˆAo%W¦ˆV|@ÊˆD®ooJy|ˆEAy0ˆTˆF| ...
- - - - - - - - - - - - - - - - - - - - - - - - - - - - - - - -
149.153.100.67 -> 149.153.100.104 (id: 36554, ttl: 64)

TCP Source: 80 -> TCP Destination: 1117
TCP Header Length: 5, TCP Checksum: 45879
TCP Data:

... ˆ_àˆOopˆBboÅ ...
- - - - - - - - - - - - - - - - - - - - - - - - - - - - - - - -
149.153.100.67 -> 149.153.100.104 (id: 36555, ttl: 64)

TCP Source: 80 -> TCP Destination: 1117
TCP Header Length: 5, TCP Checksum: 14645
TCP Data:
```

```
... TˆEˆURØÀoˆE¨nw˚E ...
- - - - - - - - - - - - - - - - - - - - - - - - - - - - - - - - - - - -
149.153.100.104 -> 149.153.100.67 (id: 16902, ttl: 128)

TCP Source: 1117 -> TCP Destination: 80
TCP Header Length: 5, TCP Checksum: 20957
TCP Data:

ˆ@ˆ@ˆ@ˆ@ˆ@ˆ@
- - - - - - - - - - - - - - - - - - - - - - - - - - - - - - - - - - - -
149.153.100.67 -> 149.153.100.104 (id: 36556, ttl: 64)

TCP Source: 80 -> TCP Destination: 1117
TCP Header Length: 5, TCP Checksum: 30368
TCP Data:

... Ix9Ô-¨u¬gÝhR§úÒμþu˚oÝçˆAˆAˆ@; ...
- - - - - - - - - - - - - - - - - - - - - - - - - - - - - - - - - - - -
149.153.100.104 -> 149.153.100.67 (id: 17158, ttl: 128)

TCP Source: 1117 -> TCP Destination: 80
TCP Header Length: 5, TCP Checksum: 18126
TCP Data:

ˆ@ˆ@ˆ@ˆ@ˆ@ˆ@
- - - - - - - - - - - - - - - - - - - - - - - - - - - - - - - - - - - -
149.153.100.104 -> 149.153.100.67 (id: 17414, ttl: 128)

TCP Source: 1115 -> TCP Destination: 80
TCP Header Length: 5, TCP Checksum: 60757
TCP Data:

GET /˜pnb/index.html HTTP/1.0
Referer: http://glasnost.itcarlow.ie/˜barryp/index.html
Connection: Keep-Alive
User-Agent: Mozilla/4.75 [en] (Win98; U)
Host: glasnost.itcarlow.ie
Accept: image/gif, image/x-xbitmap, image/jpeg, image/pjpeg, image/png, */*
Accept-Encoding: gzip
Accept-Language: en
Accept-Charset: iso-8859-1,*,utf-8


- - - - - - - - - - - - - - - - - - - - - - - - - - - - - - - - - - - -
149.153.100.67 -> 149.153.100.104 (id: 36557, ttl: 64)

TCP Source: 80 -> TCP Destination: 1115
TCP Header Length: 5, TCP Checksum: 58381
TCP Data:

UUUUUU
- - - - - - - - - - - - - - - - - - - - - - - - - - - - - - - - - - - -
149.153.100.67 -> 149.153.100.104 (id: 36558, ttl: 64)

TCP Source: 80 -> TCP Destination: 1115
TCP Header Length: 5, TCP Checksum: 29732
TCP Data:

HTTP/1.1 200 OK
Date: Fri, 03 Aug 2001 15:12:41 GMT
Server: Apache/1.3.14 (Unix)  (Red-Hat/Linux) mod_perl/1.23
Last-Modified: Wed, 18 Jul 2001 10:36:56 GMT
ETag: "bf30-1d28-3b5566c8"
Accept-Ranges: bytes
Content-Length: 7464
Keep-Alive: timeout=15, max=98
Connection: Keep-Alive
Content-Type: text/html
```

```
<HTML>
<HEAD>
   <TITLE>Welcome to the &quot;Programming the Network with Perl&quot;
Web site</TITLE> </HEAD>
<BODY>
<CENTER><IMG SRC="pnb.gif" WIDTH=500 HEIGHT=50 X-CLARIS-USEIMAGEWIDTH
X-CLARIS-USEIMAGEHEIGHT ALIGN=bottom></CENTER>

<H2><CENTER>Hello and Welcome!</CENTER></H2>
<CENTER>This site supports the activities of reviewers and readers of
<P><I>Programming the Network with Perl<BR>
</I>by <BR> Paul Barry.</P>
<P>To be published by <A HREF="http://www.wiley.co.uk/compbooks">John
Wiley &amp; Sons</A></P>
<P> </P>
<P><B>This book is currently at an advanced stage of development (as
of July 2001)</B></P>
<P> </P></CENTER>
<H2><CENTER>Contents</CENTER></H2>
<CENTER><A HREF="#Diagrams">Diagrams</A><BR>
<A HREF="#SourceCode">Source Code</A><BR>
<A HREF="#Links">Links</A><BR>
<A HREF="#MailingList">Mailing List</A><BR
- - - - - - - - - - - - - - - - - - - - - - - - - - - - - - - - - - -
149.153.100.67 -> 149.153.100.104 (id: 36559, ttl: 64)

TCP Source: 80 -> TCP Destination: 1115
TCP Header Length: 5, TCP Checksum: 54498
TCP Data:

ontactDetails">Contact Details</A>

<P> </P></CENTER>
<H2><CENTER><A NAME=Diagrams></A>Diagrams</CENTER></H2>

<CENTER>My apologies, in advance, for the poor quality of these
diagrams.
<P>Chapter 2, Snooping, has a number of diagrams (missing from the
review text).</P>
<P>Here they are (in hand-drawn form - sorry):</P></CENTER> <UL>
   <LI><CENTER><A HREF="BA02F01.JPG">Figure 1</A>: How EtherSnooper
   Works.</CENTER></LI>
   <LI><CENTER><A HREF="BA02F02.jpg">Figure 2</A>: UDP/IP
   Fragmentation.</CENTER></LI>
   <LI><CENTER><A HREF="BA02F03.jpg">Figure 3</A>: TCP/IP
   Fragmentation.</CENTER></LI> </UL>

<CENTER>The final appendix (Network Employed) is also missing the
diagram. <BR>
Here is a <A HREF="BA10F01.jpg">hand-drawn copy</A> (again - sorry
for the poor quality).

<P> </P></CENTER>
<H2><CENTER><A NAME=SourceCode></A>Source Code</CENTER></H2>
<CENTER>Each "tarball" archive contains the code for a chapter from
the book.<BR>
Read the file called MANIFEST to see what's included in each archive.

<P> There is no source code for <B>Chapter 1: Meet Perl<BR>
</B>This is deliberate, as it will do you good to type in the sample
code and get it working on your computer.</P>

<P><A HREF="chapter2.tar.gz">Chapter 2: Snooping</A><BR>
(pay particular attention to the "<B>fix-Ethernet.pm</B>" file in
this archive)</P> <P><A HREF="chapter3.tar.gz">Chapter
- - - - - - - - - - - - - - - - - - - - - - - - - - - - - - - - - - -
149.153.100.67 -> 149.153.100.104 (id: 36560, ttl: 64)
```

```
TCP Source: 80 -> TCP Destination: 1115
TCP Header Length: 5, TCP Checksum: 49315
TCP Data:

></P> <P><A HREF="chapter4.tar.gz">Chapter 4: Protocols</A></P>
<P><A HREF="chapter5.tar.gz">Chapter 5: Management</A></P>
<P>Chapter 6: Mobile Agents - source code will be available soon.</P>
<P> </P></CENTER> <H2><CENTER><A NAME=Links></A>Links</CENTER></H2>

<H4><CENTER> Chapter 1: Meet Perl</CENTER></H4>

<CENTER>The home of the Perl community, the <A HREF="http://www.perl.
com">Perl Web site</A> <BR>
The Perl <A HREF="http://use.perl.org">gossip-site</A><BR>
The Perl <A HREF="http://www.perl.org">advocacy-site</A> (This is
also the home of <I>The Perl Mongers</I>) <BR>
The official location of the <A HREF="http://www.cpan.org">CPAN</A>
(Search the archive <A HREF="http://search.cpan.org">here</A>)<BR>
The Perl 5.6 <A HREF="http://www.perldoc.com">online
documentation</A> as a searchable Web site

<P> </P></CENTER> <H4><CENTER>Chapter 2: Snooping</CENTER></H4>

<CENTER><I>libpcap</I> can be downloaded from the <A HREF="http://
www.tcpdump.org">tcpdump</A> Web site<BR>
<A HREF="http://www.cpan.org/modules/by-module/Net/TIMPOTTER/">Tim
Potter</A>'s CPAN directory (NetPacket, etc.)<BR>
Shomiti Systems' <A HREF="http://www.shomiti.com">Surveyor Lite</A>
is available for the Windows platform<BR>
Macintosh users can download a demo of <I>EtherPeek</I> from
<A HREF="http://www.aggroup.com">WildPackets</A> (formerly: <I>The AG
Group</I>)<BR> Search for analysers for the
- - - - - - - - - - - - - - - - - - - - - - - - - - - - - - - - - -
149.153.100.104 -> 149.153.100.67 (id: 17670, ttl: 128)

TCP Source: 1115 -> TCP Destination: 80
TCP Header Length: 5, TCP Checksum: 13286
TCP Data:

^@^@^@^@^@^@^@
- - - - - - - - - - - - - - - - - - - - - - - - - - - - - - - - - -
149.153.100.67 -> 149.153.100.104 (id: 36561, ttl: 64)

TCP Source: 80 -> TCP Destination: 1115
TCP Header Length: 5, TCP Checksum: 28546
TCP Data:

 at the <A HREF="http://www.freshmeat.net">FreshMeat</A>
Web site<BR>
The list of Ethernet Frame Types can be accessed <A HREF="http://
www.iana.org/assignments/ethernet-numbers">here</A><BR>
The Transport Protocol Number Assignments can be accessed <A HREF="
http://www.iana.org/assignments/port-numbers">here</A>

<P> </P></CENTER> <H4><CENTER>Chapter 3: Sockets</CENTER></H4>

<CENTER>The <A HREF="http://www.perl.com">Perl Web site</A> maintains
a short list of networking links<BR>
A excellent <A HREF="http://www.sockets.com">resource</A> for Windows
programmers

<P> </P></CENTER> <H4><CENTER>Chapter 4: Protocols</CENTER></H4>

<CENTER>The HTTP standard document is available from the home of
<A HREF="http://www.w3.org">web standards</A><BR>
The text to any RFC can be found on the <A HREF="http://www.ietf.org">
IETF</A> Web site<BR>
```

```
All about the <A HREF="http://www.apache.org">Apache Web Server</A><BR>
The <A HREF="http://www.linpro.no/lwp">Gisle Aas</A> Web site (for
the <I>libwww-perl</I> project)<BR>
Gisle's <A HREF="http://www.cpan.org/authors/id/GAAS/">CPAN 
directory</A><BR>
Graham Barr's <A HREF="http://www.cpan.org/authors/id/GBARR/}">CPAN
directory</A> (libnet)<BR>
Find out about <A HREF="http://www.dartware.com">InterMapper</A> for
the Macintosh<BR>
Jay Rogers' <A HREF="http://www.cpan.org/authors/id/JROGERS/">CPAN
directory</A> (Net::Telnet) <P> </P></CENT
- - - - - - - - - - - - - - - - - - - - - - - - - - - - - - - - - -


    ...


- - - - - - - - - - - - - - - - - - - - - - - - - - - - - - - - - -
413 datagrams/segments processed.

Fri Aug  3 15:12:33 2001 - netdebug END run.
```

NetDebugging NetNews Traffic

The following invocation of *NetDebug* captures *NNTP* traffic generated by the
`mossy.itcarlow.ie` (`149.153.100.104`) network device, and destined for a
remote *NNTP* server located at `193.10.250.164`:

```
./netdb -s 149.153.100.104 -p 119
```

The *NNTP* client operating on `149.153.100.104` requests two articles, numbered
1639 and 1642.

These articles are currently contained in the newsgroup `comp.lang.perl.`
`announce`. Like the vast majority of Internet standard protocols, *NNTP* is primarily textual, and the captured results reflect this. Only a small number of
the datagrams involved in the communication contain binary data (such as
`^@^@^@^@^@^@`):

```
Fri Aug  3 15:08:25 2001 - netdebug BEGIN run.
- - - - - - - - - - - - - - - - - - - - - - - - - - - - - - - - - -
149.153.100.104 -> 193.10.250.164 (id: 8710, ttl: 128)

TCP Source: 1112 -> TCP Destination: 119
TCP Header Length: 5, TCP Checksum: 4373
TCP Data:

ARTICLE 1639


- - - - - - - - - - - - - - - - - - - - - - - - - - - - - - - - - -
193.10.250.164 -> 149.153.100.104 (id: 34287, ttl: 46)

TCP Source: 119 -> TCP Destination: 1112
TCP Header Length: 5, TCP Checksum: 16704
TCP Data:

^@^@^@^@^@^@
- - - - - - - - - - - - - - - - - - - - - - - - - - - - - - - - - -
193.10.250.164 -> 149.153.100.104 (id: 34288, ttl: 46)

TCP Source: 119 -> TCP Destination: 1112
TCP Header Length: 5, TCP Checksum: 5052
TCP Data:
```

```
220 1639 <t1k18a6164iab6@corp.supernews.com> article
From: ebohlman@omsdev.com (Eric Bohlman)
Newsgroups: comp.lang.perl.announce,comp.lang.perl.modules
Subject: ANNOUNCE: XML::Records 0.10
Approved: merlyn@stonehenge.com (comp.lang.perl.announce)
Date: 21 Jul 2001 21:55:08 GMT
Organization: OMS Development
Message-ID: <t1k18a6164iab6@corp.supernews.com>
X-Disclaimer: The "Approved" header verifies header information
for article transmission and does not imply approval of content.
X-Complaints-To: newsabuse@supernews.com
Lines: 11
Path: news.ind.mh.se!grendel.df.1th.se!snopp!newsfeed.sunet.se!
news01.sunet.se!uninett.no!asap-asp.net!Norway.EU.net!uio.no!
news.tele.dk!171.64.14.106!newsfeed.stanford.edu!sn-xit-01!sn-post-02!
sn-post-01!supernews.com!not-for-mail
Xref: news.ind.mh.se comp.lang.perl.announce:1639
comp.lang.perl.modules:42175

Version 0.10 of XML::Records is now available on CPAN.  It allows
you to pull "records" out of XML documents and turn them into
Perl data st
- - - - - - - - - - - - - - - - - - - - - - - - - - - - - - - - - -
149.153.100.104 -> 193.10.250.164 (id: 8966, ttl: 128)

TCP Source: 1112 -> TCP Destination: 119
TCP Header Length: 5, TCP Checksum: 39656
TCP Data:

^@^@^@^@^@^@
- - - - - - - - - - - - - - - - - - - - - - - - - - - - - - - - - -
193.10.250.164 -> 149.153.100.104 (id: 34289, ttl: 46)

TCP Source: 119 -> TCP Destination: 1112
TCP Header Length: 5, TCP Checksum: 6767
TCP Data:

ructures (similar to Grant McLean's XML::Simple, but without having to
read the entire document into memory), create simple tree structures (same
as XML::Parser::EasyTree) from them, or generate PerlSAX events from them,
allowing you to build DOM, XPath or similar structures from selected parts
of a document.  Since it's now a subclass of XML::TokeParser, it allows
you to read token-by-token as well as record-by-record.

- - - - - - - - - - - - - - - - - - - - - - - - - - - - - - - - - -
149.153.100.104 -> 193.10.250.164 (id: 9222, ttl: 128)

TCP Source: 1112 -> TCP Destination: 119
TCP Header Length: 5, TCP Checksum: 39656
TCP Data:

^@^@^@^@^@^@
- - - - - - - - - - - - - - - - - - - - - - - - - - - - - - - - - -
149.153.100.104 -> 193.10.250.164 (id: 9478, ttl: 128)

TCP Source: 1112 -> TCP Destination: 119
TCP Header Length: 5, TCP Checksum: 2648
TCP Data:

ARTICLE 1642

- - - - - - - - - - - - - - - - - - - - - - - - - - - - - - - - - -
193.10.250.164 -> 149.153.100.104 (id: 34290, ttl: 46)

TCP Source: 119 -> TCP Destination: 1112
TCP Header Length: 5, TCP Checksum: 15226
TCP Data:
```

```
^@^@^@^@^@^@
- - - - - - - - - - - - - - - - - - - - - - - - - - - - - - - - - - - - - -
193.10.250.164 -> 149.153.100.104 (id: 34291, ttl: 46)

TCP Source: 119 -> TCP Destination: 1112
TCP Header Length: 5, TCP Checksum: 15482
TCP Data:

220 1642 <tmboo378u0ab4c@corp.supernews.com> article
From: jmcnamara@cpan.org (John McNamara)
Newsgroups: comp.lang.perl.announce,comp.lang.perl.modules
Subject: ANNOUNCE: Spreadsheet::WriteExcel 0.33
Approved: merlyn@stonehenge.com (comp.lang.perl.announce)
Date: Mon, 30 Jul 2001 22:31:14 GMT
Organization: Eircom.Net http://www.eircom.net
Message-ID: <tmboo378u0ab4c@corp.supernews.com>
X-Disclaimer: The "Approved" header verifies header information for
article transmission and does not imply approval of content.
X-Complaints-To: newsabuse@supernews.com
Lines: 140
Path: news.ind.mh.se!newsrelay.mitt.mh.se!newsfeed.sunet.se!
news01.sunet.se!uninett.no!howland.erols.net!news.maxwell.syr.edu!
newsfeed.stanford.edu!sn-xit-01!sn-post-01!supernews.com!
corp.supernews.com!not-for-mail
Xref: news.ind.mh.se comp.lang.perl.announce:1642
comp.lang.perl.modules:42426
```

==
ANNOUNCE

    Spreadsheet::WriteExcel version 0.33 has been uploaded t
```
- - - - - - - - - - - - - - - - - - - - - - - - - - - - - - - - - - - - - -
193.10.250.164 -> 149.153.100.104 (id: 34292, ttl: 46)

TCP Source: 119 -> TCP Destination: 1112
TCP Header Length: 5, TCP Checksum: 60014
TCP Data:

o CPAN.
```

==
NAME

    Spreadsheet::WriteExcel - Write formatted text and numbers to a
    cross-platform Excel binary file.

==
CHANGES

    Added (hopefully) easier mechanism to add format properties.

    Added more page setup options: repeat rows and columns, hide
    gridlines, print area, fit to pages and page breaks.

    Added more examples.

==
DESCRIPTION

    The Spreadsheet::WriteExcel module can be used create a cross-
    platform Excel binary file. Multiple worksheets can be added to a
    workbook and formatting can be applied to cells. Text, numbers,
    formulas and hyperlinks can be written to the cells.

    The Excel file produced by this module is compatible with Excel 5,
    95, 97 and 2000.

The module will work on the majority of Windows, UNIX and Macintosh platforms. Generated files are also compatible with the Linux/UNIX spreadsheet applications OpenOffice, Gnumeric and XESS. The generated files are not compatible with MS Access.

This module cannot be used to read an Excel file. See Spreadsheet::ParseExcel or look at the main documentation for some suggestions. This module cannot be uses to write to an existing Excel file.

```
==
- - - - - - - - - - - - - - - - - - - - - - - - - - - - - - - - - - -
149.153.100.104 -> 193.10.250.164 (id: 9734, ttl: 128)

TCP Source: 1112 -> TCP Destination: 119
TCP Header Length: 5, TCP Checksum: 36718
TCP Data:

^@^@^@^@^@^@
- - - - - - - - - - - - - - - - - - - - - - - - - - - - - - - - - - -
193.10.250.164 -> 149.153.100.104 (id: 34293, ttl: 46)

TCP Source: 119 -> TCP Destination: 1112
TCP Header Length: 5, TCP Checksum: 7329
TCP Data:

==========================================================
```

SYNOPSIS

To write a string, a formatted string, a number and a formula to the first worksheet in an Excel workbook called perl.xls:

```perl
use Spreadsheet::WriteExcel;

# Create a new Excel workbook
my $workbook = Spreadsheet::WriteExcel->new("perl.xls");

# Add a worksheet
$worksheet = $workbook->addworksheet();

#  Add and define a format
$format = $workbook->addformat();       # Add a format
$format->set_bold();
$format->set_color('red');
$format->set_align('center');

# Write a formatted and unformatted string
$col = $row = 0;
$worksheet->write($row, $col, "Hi Excel!", $format);
$worksheet->write(1,     $col, "Hi Excel!");

# Write a number and a formula using A1 notation
$worksheet->write('A3', 1.2345);
$worksheet->write('A4', '=SIN(PI()/4)');
```

```
======================================================================
```

REQUIREMENTS

This module requires Perl 5.005 (or later) and Parse::RecDescent: http://search.cpan.org/search?dist=Parse-RecDescent

```
======================================================================
```

INSTALLATION

Method 1
Download the zipped tar file from one of the following:
    http://search.cpan.org/search?dist=Spreadsheet-WriteExcel
    http://th
- -
193.10.250.164 -> 149.153.100.104 (id: 34296, ttl: 46)

TCP Source: 119 -> TCP Destination: 1112
TCP Header Length: 5, TCP Checksum: 18128
TCP Data:

eg.ca/mod_perl/cpan-search?idinfo=154

ftp://ftp.funet.fi/pub/languages/perl/CPAN/authors/id/J/JM/JMCNAMARA/

    Unzip the module as follows or use winzip:
        tar -zxvf Spreadsheet-WriteExcel-0.xx.tar.gz

    The module can be installed using the standard Perl procedure:

        perl Makefile.PL
        make
        make test
        make install   # You may need to be root
        make clean   # or make realclean

    Windows users without a working "make" can get nmake from:
        ftp://ftp.microsoft.com/Softlib/MSLFILES/nmake15.exe

    Method 2
    If you have CPAN.pm configured you can install the module as
    follows:
        perl -MCPAN -e "install 'Spreadsheet::WriteExcel'"

    Method 3
    ActivePerl users can use PPM as follows:

    C:\> ppm
    PPM> set repository tmp
    http://homepage.eircom.net/~jmcnamara/perl
    PPM> install Spreadsheet-WriteExcel
    PPM> quit
    C:\>

    If this fails try the following:

    PPM>install

http://homepage.eircom.net/~jmcnamara/perl/Spreadsheet-WriteExcel.ppd

    If you wish to perform a local PPM install you can get the files
    from:

http://homepage.eircom.net/~jmcnamara/perl/Spreadsheet-WriteExcel.ppd

http://homepage.eircom.net/~jmcnamara/perl/Spreadsheet-WriteExcel-0.xx-PPM.tar.gz

===
AUTHOR

- -
149.153.100.104 -> 193.10.250.164 (id: 9990, ttl: 128)

TCP Source: 1112 -> TCP Destination: 119
TCP Header Length: 5, TCP Checksum: 33798
TCP Data:

```
^@^@^@^@^@^@
- - - - - - - - - - - - - - - - - - - - - - - - - - - - - - -
193.10.250.164 -> 149.153.100.104 (id: 34303, ttl: 46)

TCP Source: 119 -> TCP Destination: 1112
TCP Header Length: 5, TCP Checksum: 22766
TCP Data:

a (jmcnamara@cpan.org)

--

.

- - - - - - - - - - - - - - - - - - - - - - - - - - - - - - -
149.153.100.104 -> 193.10.250.164 (id: 10246, ttl: 128)

TCP Source: 1112 -> TCP Destination: 119
TCP Header Length: 5, TCP Checksum: 33798
TCP Data:

^@^@^@^@^@^@
- - - - - - - - - - - - - - - - - - - - - - - - - - - - - - -
18 datagrams/segments processed.

Fri Aug  3 15:09:25 2001 - netdebug END run.
```

NetDebugging TELNET Traffic

The following invocation of *NetDebug*:

```
./netdb -s 149.153.100.65 -p 23
```

captures traffic aimed at protocol port-number 23 (used by *TELNET*) on the 149.153.100.65 network device (which is pbmac.itcarlow.ie). A user called barryp connects to the *TELNET* server from the network device 149.153. 100.104 (mossy), supplying a login-id and password when prompted. The ls command is issued, then the user disconnects from the *TELNET* server.

This interaction produced the following results:

```
Mon Sep  3 14:22:46 2001 - netdebug BEGIN run.
- - - - - - - - - - - - - - - - - - - - - - - - - - - - - - -
149.153.100.104 -> 149.153.100.65 (id: 41479, ttl: 128)

TCP Source: 1070 -> TCP Destination: 23
TCP Header Length: 7, TCP Checksum: 14431
TCP Data:

- - - - - - - - - - - - - - - - - - - - - - - - - - - - - - -
149.153.100.65 -> 149.153.100.104 (id: 136, ttl: 64)

TCP Source: 23 -> TCP Destination: 1070
TCP Header Length: 7, TCP Checksum: 47017
TCP Data:

- - - - - - - - - - - - - - - - - - - - - - - - - - - - - - -
149.153.100.104 -> 149.153.100.65 (id: 41735, ttl: 128)
```

```
TCP Source: 1070 -> TCP Destination: 23
TCP Header Length: 5, TCP Checksum: 14842
TCP Data:

^@^@^@^@^@^@
- - - - - - - - - - - - - - - - - - - - - - - - - - - - - - -
149.153.100.65 -> 149.153.100.104 (id: 137, ttl: 64)

TCP Source: 23 -> TCP Destination: 1070
TCP Header Length: 5, TCP Checksum: 42850
TCP Data:

ÿý^Xÿý ÿý#ÿý'
- - - - - - - - - - - - - - - - - - - - - - - - - - - - - - -
149.153.100.104 -> 149.153.100.65 (id: 41991, ttl: 128)

TCP Source: 1070 -> TCP Destination: 23
TCP Header Length: 5, TCP Checksum: 8691
TCP Data:

ÿû^X^@^@^@
- - - - - - - - - - - - - - - - - - - - - - - - - - - - - - -
149.153.100.65 -> 149.153.100.104 (id: 138, ttl: 64)

TCP Source: 23 -> TCP Destination: 1070
TCP Header Length: 5, TCP Checksum: 57005
TCP Data:

UUUUUU
- - - - - - - - - - - - - - - - - - - - - - - - - - - - - - -
149.153.100.104 -> 149.153.100.65 (id: 42247, ttl: 128)

TCP Source: 1070 -> TCP Destination: 23
TCP Header Length: 5, TCP Checksum: 62920
TCP Data:

ÿü ÿü#ÿü'
- - - - - - - - - - - - - - - - - - - - - - - - - - - - - - -
149.153.100.65 -> 149.153.100.104 (id: 139, ttl: 64)

TCP Source: 23 -> TCP Destination: 1070
TCP Header Length: 5, TCP Checksum: 50854
TCP Data:

ÿú^X^Aÿð
- - - - - - - - - - - - - - - - - - - - - - - - - - - - - - -
149.153.100.104 -> 149.153.100.65 (id: 42503, ttl: 128)

TCP Source: 1070 -> TCP Destination: 23
TCP Header Length: 5, TCP Checksum: 36184
TCP Data:

ÿú^X^@ANSIÿð
- - - - - - - - - - - - - - - - - - - - - - - - - - - - - - -
149.153.100.65 -> 149.153.100.104 (id: 140, ttl: 64)

TCP Source: 23 -> TCP Destination: 1070
TCP Header Length: 5, TCP Checksum: 41340
TCP Data:

ÿû^Cÿý^Aÿý^_ÿû^Eÿý!
- - - - - - - - - - - - - - - - - - - - - - - - - - - - - - -
149.153.100.104 -> 149.153.100.65 (id: 42759, ttl: 128)

TCP Source: 1070 -> TCP Destination: 23
TCP Header Length: 5, TCP Checksum: 14043
TCP Data:
```

ÿý^C^@^@^@
- -
149.153.100.65 -> 149.153.100.104 (id: 141, ttl: 64)

TCP Source: 23 -> TCP Destination: 1070
TCP Header Length: 5, TCP Checksum: 56962
TCP Data:

UUUUUU
- -
149.153.100.104 -> 149.153.100.65 (id: 43015, ttl: 128)

TCP Source: 1070 -> TCP Destination: 23
TCP Header Length: 5, TCP Checksum: 14738
TCP Data:

ÿû^Aÿü^_ÿþ^Eÿü!
- -
149.153.100.65 -> 149.153.100.104 (id: 142, ttl: 64)

TCP Source: 23 -> TCP Destination: 1070
TCP Header Length: 5, TCP Checksum: 56962
TCP Data:

UUUUUU
- -
149.153.100.65 -> 149.153.100.104 (id: 143, ttl: 64)

TCP Source: 23 -> TCP Destination: 1070
TCP Header Length: 5, TCP Checksum: 39768
TCP Data:

ÿþ^Aÿû^A
Linux/PPC 2000 Q4
Packages current to December 25 2000
Kernel 2.2.18-4hpmac on a ppc

- -
149.153.100.104 -> 149.153.100.65 (id: 43271, ttl: 128)

TCP Source: 1070 -> TCP Destination: 23
TCP Header Length: 5, TCP Checksum: 14541
TCP Data:

ÿü^A^@^@^@
- -
149.153.100.65 -> 149.153.100.104 (id: 144, ttl: 64)

TCP Source: 23 -> TCP Destination: 1070
TCP Header Length: 5, TCP Checksum: 31729
TCP Data:

login:
- -
149.153.100.104 -> 149.153.100.65 (id: 43527, ttl: 128)

TCP Source: 1070 -> TCP Destination: 23
TCP Header Length: 5, TCP Checksum: 14537
TCP Data:

ÿý^A^@^@^@
- -
149.153.100.65 -> 149.153.100.104 (id: 145, ttl: 64)

TCP Source: 23 -> TCP Destination: 1070
TCP Header Length: 5, TCP Checksum: 56838
TCP Data:

```
UUUUUU
- - - - - - - - - - - - - - - - - - - - - - - - - - - - - - - - - - -
149.153.100.104 -> 149.153.100.65 (id: 43783, ttl: 128)

TCP Source: 1070 -> TCP Destination: 23
TCP Header Length: 5, TCP Checksum: 55237
TCP Data:

b^@^@^@^@^@
- - - - - - - - - - - - - - - - - - - - - - - - - - - - - - - - - - -
149.153.100.65 -> 149.153.100.104 (id: 146, ttl: 64)

TCP Source: 23 -> TCP Destination: 1070
TCP Header Length: 5, TCP Checksum: 31740
TCP Data:

bUUUUU
- - - - - - - - - - - - - - - - - - - - - - - - - - - - - - - - - - -
149.153.100.104 -> 149.153.100.65 (id: 44039, ttl: 128)

TCP Source: 1070 -> TCP Destination: 23
TCP Header Length: 5, TCP Checksum: 55492
TCP Data:

a^@^@^@^@^@
- - - - - - - - - - - - - - - - - - - - - - - - - - - - - - - - - - -
149.153.100.65 -> 149.153.100.104 (id: 147, ttl: 64)

TCP Source: 23 -> TCP Destination: 1070
TCP Header Length: 5, TCP Checksum: 31994
TCP Data:

aUUUUU
- - - - - - - - - - - - - - - - - - - - - - - - - - - - - - - - - - -
149.153.100.104 -> 149.153.100.65 (id: 44295, ttl: 128)

TCP Source: 1070 -> TCP Destination: 23
TCP Header Length: 5, TCP Checksum: 14797
TCP Data:

^@^@^@^@^@^@
- - - - - - - - - - - - - - - - - - - - - - - - - - - - - - - - - - -
149.153.100.104 -> 149.153.100.65 (id: 44551, ttl: 128)

TCP Source: 1070 -> TCP Destination: 23
TCP Header Length: 5, TCP Checksum: 51139
TCP Data:

r^@^@^@^@^@
- - - - - - - - - - - - - - - - - - - - - - - - - - - - - - - - - - -
149.153.100.65 -> 149.153.100.104 (id: 148, ttl: 64)

TCP Source: 23 -> TCP Destination: 1070
TCP Header Length: 5, TCP Checksum: 27640
TCP Data:

rUUUUU
- - - - - - - - - - - - - - - - - - - - - - - - - - - - - - - - - - -
149.153.100.104 -> 149.153.100.65 (id: 44807, ttl: 128)

TCP Source: 1070 -> TCP Destination: 23
TCP Header Length: 5, TCP Checksum: 51138
TCP Data:

r^@^@^@^@^@
- - - - - - - - - - - - - - - - - - - - - - - - - - - - - - - - - - -
149.153.100.65 -> 149.153.100.104 (id: 149, ttl: 64)
```

```
TCP Source: 23 -> TCP Destination: 1070
TCP Header Length: 5, TCP Checksum: 27638
TCP Data:

rUUUUU
- - - - - - - - - - - - - - - - - - - - - - - - - - - - - -
149.153.100.104 -> 149.153.100.65 (id: 45063, ttl: 128)

TCP Source: 1070 -> TCP Destination: 23
TCP Header Length: 5, TCP Checksum: 14795
TCP Data:

^@^@^@^@^@^@
- - - - - - - - - - - - - - - - - - - - - - - - - - - - - -
149.153.100.104 -> 149.153.100.65 (id: 45319, ttl: 128)

TCP Source: 1070 -> TCP Destination: 23
TCP Header Length: 5, TCP Checksum: 49345
TCP Data:

y^@^@^@^@^@
- - - - - - - - - - - - - - - - - - - - - - - - - - - - - -
149.153.100.65 -> 149.153.100.104 (id: 150, ttl: 64)

TCP Source: 23 -> TCP Destination: 1070
TCP Header Length: 5, TCP Checksum: 25844
TCP Data:

yUUUUU
- - - - - - - - - - - - - - - - - - - - - - - - - - - - - -
149.153.100.104 -> 149.153.100.65 (id: 45575, ttl: 128)

TCP Source: 1070 -> TCP Destination: 23
TCP Header Length: 5, TCP Checksum: 51648
TCP Data:

p^@^@^@^@^@
- - - - - - - - - - - - - - - - - - - - - - - - - - - - - -
149.153.100.65 -> 149.153.100.104 (id: 151, ttl: 64)

TCP Source: 23 -> TCP Destination: 1070
TCP Header Length: 5, TCP Checksum: 28146
TCP Data:

pUUUUU
- - - - - - - - - - - - - - - - - - - - - - - - - - - - - -
149.153.100.104 -> 149.153.100.65 (id: 45831, ttl: 128)

TCP Source: 1070 -> TCP Destination: 23
TCP Header Length: 5, TCP Checksum: 14793
TCP Data:

^@^@^@^@^@^@
- - - - - - - - - - - - - - - - - - - - - - - - - - - - - -
149.153.100.104 -> 149.153.100.65 (id: 46087, ttl: 128)

TCP Source: 1070 -> TCP Destination: 23
TCP Header Length: 5, TCP Checksum: 11445
TCP Data:

ÚÚÚÚ
- - - - - - - - - - - - - - - - - - - - - - - - - - - - - -
149.153.100.65 -> 149.153.100.104 (id: 152, ttl: 64)

TCP Source: 23 -> TCP Destination: 1070
TCP Header Length: 5, TCP Checksum: 53476
TCP Data:
```

```
UUUU
- - - - - - - - - - - - - - - - - - - - - - - - - - - - - - - - -
149.153.100.104 -> 149.153.100.65 (id: 46343, ttl: 128)

TCP Source: 1070 -> TCP Destination: 23
TCP Header Length: 5, TCP Checksum: 14791
TCP Data:

^@^@^@^@^@^@
- - - - - - - - - - - - - - - - - - - - - - - - - - - - - - - - -
149.153.100.65 -> 149.153.100.104 (id: 153, ttl: 64)

TCP Source: 23 -> TCP Destination: 1070
TCP Header Length: 5, TCP Checksum: 63003
TCP Data:

Password:
- - - - - - - - - - - - - - - - - - - - - - - - - - - - - - - - -
149.153.100.104 -> 149.153.100.65 (id: 46599, ttl: 128)

TCP Source: 1070 -> TCP Destination: 23
TCP Header Length: 5, TCP Checksum: 14791
TCP Data:

^@^@^@^@^@^@
- - - - - - - - - - - - - - - - - - - - - - - - - - - - - - - - -
149.153.100.104 -> 149.153.100.65 (id: 46855, ttl: 128)

TCP Source: 1070 -> TCP Destination: 23
TCP Header Length: 5, TCP Checksum: 51645
TCP Data:

p^@^@^@^@^@
- - - - - - - - - - - - - - - - - - - - - - - - - - - - - - - - -
149.153.100.65 -> 149.153.100.104 (id: 154, ttl: 64)

TCP Source: 23 -> TCP Destination: 1070
TCP Header Length: 5, TCP Checksum: 56811
TCP Data:

UUUUUU
- - - - - - - - - - - - - - - - - - - - - - - - - - - - - - - - -
149.153.100.104 -> 149.153.100.65 (id: 47111, ttl: 128)

TCP Source: 1070 -> TCP Destination: 23
TCP Header Length: 5, TCP Checksum: 55484
TCP Data:

a^@^@^@^@^@
- - - - - - - - - - - - - - - - - - - - - - - - - - - - - - - - -
149.153.100.65 -> 149.153.100.104 (id: 155, ttl: 64)

TCP Source: 23 -> TCP Destination: 1070
TCP Header Length: 5, TCP Checksum: 56810
TCP Data:

UUUUUU
- - - - - - - - - - - - - - - - - - - - - - - - - - - - - - - - -
149.153.100.104 -> 149.153.100.65 (id: 47367, ttl: 128)

TCP Source: 1070 -> TCP Destination: 23
TCP Header Length: 5, TCP Checksum: 50875
TCP Data:

s^@^@^@^@^@
- - - - - - - - - - - - - - - - - - - - - - - - - - - - - - - - -
149.153.100.65 -> 149.153.100.104 (id: 156, ttl: 64)
```

```
TCP Source: 23 -> TCP Destination: 1070
TCP Header Length: 5, TCP Checksum: 56809
TCP Data:

UUUUUU
- - - - - - - - - - - - - - - - - - - - - - - - - - - - - - - - - -
149.153.100.104 -> 149.153.100.65 (id: 47623, ttl: 128)

TCP Source: 1070 -> TCP Destination: 23
TCP Header Length: 5, TCP Checksum: 50874
TCP Data:

s^@^@^@^@^@
- - - - - - - - - - - - - - - - - - - - - - - - - - - - - - - - - -
149.153.100.65 -> 149.153.100.104 (id: 157, ttl: 64)

TCP Source: 23 -> TCP Destination: 1070
TCP Header Length: 5, TCP Checksum: 56808
TCP Data:

UUUUUU
- - - - - - - - - - - - - - - - - - - - - - - - - - - - - - - - - -
149.153.100.104 -> 149.153.100.65 (id: 47879, ttl: 128)

TCP Source: 1070 -> TCP Destination: 23
TCP Header Length: 5, TCP Checksum: 49849
TCP Data:

w^@^@^@^@^@
- - - - - - - - - - - - - - - - - - - - - - - - - - - - - - - - - -
149.153.100.65 -> 149.153.100.104 (id: 158, ttl: 64)

TCP Source: 23 -> TCP Destination: 1070
TCP Header Length: 5, TCP Checksum: 56807
TCP Data:

UUUUUU
- - - - - - - - - - - - - - - - - - - - - - - - - - - - - - - - - -
149.153.100.104 -> 149.153.100.65 (id: 48135, ttl: 128)

TCP Source: 1070 -> TCP Destination: 23
TCP Header Length: 5, TCP Checksum: 51896
TCP Data:

o^@^@^@^@^@
- - - - - - - - - - - - - - - - - - - - - - - - - - - - - - - - - -
149.153.100.65 -> 149.153.100.104 (id: 159, ttl: 64)

TCP Source: 23 -> TCP Destination: 1070
TCP Header Length: 5, TCP Checksum: 56806
TCP Data:

UUUUUU
- - - - - - - - - - - - - - - - - - \- - - - - - - - - - - - - - - -
149.153.100.104 -> 149.153.100.65 (id: 48391, ttl: 128)

TCP Source: 1070 -> TCP Destination: 23
TCP Header Length: 5, TCP Checksum: 51127
TCP Data:

r^@^@^@^@^@
- - - - - - - - - - - - - - - - - - - - - - - - - - - - - - - - - -
149.153.100.65 -> 149.153.100.104 (id: 160, ttl: 64)

TCP Source: 23 -> TCP Destination: 1070
TCP Header Length: 5, TCP Checksum: 56805
TCP Data:
```

```
UUUUUU
- - - - - - - - - - - - - - - - - - - - - - - - - - - - - - - - - -
149.153.100.104 -> 149.153.100.65 (id: 48647, ttl: 128)

TCP Source: 1070 -> TCP Destination: 23
TCP Header Length: 5, TCP Checksum: 54710
TCP Data:

d^@^@^@^@^@
- - - - - - - - - - - - - - - - - - - - - - - - - - - - - - - - - -
149.153.100.65 -> 149.153.100.104 (id: 161, ttl: 64)

TCP Source: 23 -> TCP Destination: 1070
TCP Header Length: 5, TCP Checksum: 56804
TCP Data:

UUUUUU
- - - - - - - - - - - - - - - - - - - - - - - - - - - - - - - - - -
149.153.100.104 -> 149.153.100.65 (id: 48903, ttl: 128)

TCP Source: 1070 -> TCP Destination: 23
TCP Header Length: 5, TCP Checksum: 53685
TCP Data:

h^@^@^@^@^@
- - - - - - - - - - - - - - - - - - - - - - - - - - - - - - - - - -
149.153.100.65 -> 149.153.100.104 (id: 162, ttl: 64)

TCP Source: 23 -> TCP Destination: 1070
TCP Header Length: 5, TCP Checksum: 56803
TCP Data:

UUUUUU
- - - - - - - - - - - - - - - - - - - - - - - - - - - - - - - - - -
149.153.100.104 -> 149.153.100.65 (id: 49159, ttl: 128)

TCP Source: 1070 -> TCP Destination: 23
TCP Header Length: 5, TCP Checksum: 54452
TCP Data:

e^@^@^@^@^@
- - - - - - - - - - - - - - - - - - - - - - - - - - - - - - - - - -
149.153.100.65 -> 149.153.100.104 (id: 163, ttl: 64)

TCP Source: 23 -> TCP Destination: 1070
TCP Header Length: 5, TCP Checksum: 56802
TCP Data:

UUUUUU
- - - - - - - - - - - - - - - - - - - - - - - - - - - - - - - - - -
149.153.100.104 -> 149.153.100.65 (id: 49415, ttl: 128)

TCP Source: 1070 -> TCP Destination: 23
TCP Header Length: 5, TCP Checksum: 51123
TCP Data:

r^@^@^@^@^@
- - - - - - - - - - - - - - - - - - - - - - - - - - - - - - - - - -
149.153.100.65 -> 149.153.100.104 (id: 164, ttl: 64)

TCP Source: 23 -> TCP Destination: 1070
TCP Header Length: 5, TCP Checksum: 56801
TCP Data:

UUUUUU
- - - - - - - - - - - - - - - - - - - - - - - - - - - - - - - - - -
149.153.100.104 -> 149.153.100.65 (id: 49671, ttl: 128)
```

```
TCP Source: 1070 -> TCP Destination: 23
TCP Header Length: 5, TCP Checksum: 54450
TCP Data:

e^@^@^@^@^@^@
- - - - - - - - - - - - - - - - - - - - - - - - - - - - - - - - - - -
149.153.100.65 -> 149.153.100.104 (id: 165, ttl: 64)

TCP Source: 23 -> TCP Destination: 1070
TCP Header Length: 5, TCP Checksum: 56800
TCP Data:

UUUUUU
- - - - - - - - - - - - - - - - - - - - - - - - - - - - - - - - - - -
149.153.100.104 -> 149.153.100.65 (id: 49927, ttl: 128)

TCP Source: 1070 -> TCP Destination: 23
TCP Header Length: 5, TCP Checksum: 11431
TCP Data:

^X^X^X^X
- - - - - - - - - - - - - - - - - - - - - - - - - - - - - - - - - - -
149.153.100.65 -> 149.153.100.104 (id: 166, ttl: 64)

TCP Source: 23 -> TCP Destination: 1070
TCP Header Length: 5, TCP Checksum: 53450
TCP Data:

UUUU
- - - - - - - - - - - - - - - - - - - - - - - - - - - - - - - - - - -
149.153.100.104 -> 149.153.100.65 (id: 50183, ttl: 128)

TCP Source: 1070 -> TCP Destination: 23
TCP Header Length: 5, TCP Checksum: 14777
TCP Data:

^@^@^@^@^@^@^@
- - - - - - - - - - - - - - - - - - - - - - - - - - - - - - - - - - -
149.153.100.65 -> 149.153.100.104 (id: 167, ttl: 64)

TCP Source: 23 -> TCP Destination: 1070
TCP Header Length: 5, TCP Checksum: 431
TCP Data:

Last login: Mon Sep  3 14:23:11 from 149.153.100.104
- - - - - - - - - - - - - - - - - - - - - - - - - - - - - - - - - - -
149.153.100.104 -> 149.153.100.65 (id: 50439, ttl: 128)

TCP Source: 1070 -> TCP Destination: 23
TCP Header Length: 5, TCP Checksum: 14777
TCP Data:

^@^@^@^@^@^@^@
- - - - - - - - - - - - - - - - - - - - - - - - - - - - - - - - - - -
149.153.100.65 -> 149.153.100.104 (id: 168, ttl: 64)

TCP Source: 23 -> TCP Destination: 1070
TCP Header Length: 5, TCP Checksum: 12716
TCP Data:

[barryp@pbmac barryp]$
- - - - - - - - - - - - - - - - - - - - - - - - - - - - - - - - - - -
149.153.100.104 -> 149.153.100.65 (id: 50695, ttl: 128)
```

```
TCP Source: 1070 -> TCP Destination: 23
TCP Header Length: 5, TCP Checksum: 14777
TCP Data:

^@^@^@^@^@^@
- - - - - - - - - - - - - - - - - - - - - - - - - - - - - - - -
149.153.100.104 -> 149.153.100.65 (id: 50951, ttl: 128)

TCP Source: 1070 -> TCP Destination: 23
TCP Header Length: 5, TCP Checksum: 52655
TCP Data:

l^@^@^@^@^@
- - - - - - - - - - - - - - - - - - - - - - - - - - - - - - - -
149.153.100.65 -> 149.153.100.104 (id: 169, ttl: 64)

TCP Source: 23 -> TCP Destination: 1070
TCP Header Length: 5, TCP Checksum: 29061
TCP Data:

lUUUUU
- - - - - - - - - - - - - - - - - - - - - - - - - - - - - - -
149.153.100.104 -> 149.153.100.65 (id: 51207, ttl: 128)

TCP Source: 1070 -> TCP Destination: 23
TCP Header Length: 5, TCP Checksum: 50862
TCP Data:

s^@^@^@^@^@
- - - - - - - - - - - - - - - - - - - - - - - - - - - - - - - -
149.153.100.65 -> 149.153.100.104 (id: 170, ttl: 64)

TCP Source: 23 -> TCP Destination: 1070
TCP Header Length: 5, TCP Checksum: 27267
TCP Data:

sUUUUU
- - - - - - - - - - - - - - - - - - - - - - - - - - - - - - - - - -
149.153.100.104 -> 149.153.100.65 (id: 51463, ttl: 128)

TCP Source: 1070 -> TCP Destination: 23
TCP Header Length: 5, TCP Checksum: 14775
TCP Data:

^@^@^@^@^@^@
- - - - - - - - - - - - - - - - - - - - - - - - - - - - - - - -
149.153.100.104 -> 149.153.100.65 (id: 51719, ttl: 128)

TCP Source: 1070 -> TCP Destination: 23
TCP Header Length: 5, TCP Checksum: 11427
TCP Data:


7777
- - - - - - - - - - - - - - - - - - - - - - - - - - - - - - - - -
149.153.100.65 -> 149.153.100.104 (id: 171, ttl: 64)

TCP Source: 23 -> TCP Destination: 1070
TCP Header Length: 5, TCP Checksum: 53365
TCP Data:


UUUU
- - - - - - - - - - - - - - - - - - - - - - - - - - - - - - - -
149.153.100.104 -> 149.153.100.65 (id: 51975, ttl: 128)

TCP Source: 1070 -> TCP Destination: 23
TCP Header Length: 5, TCP Checksum: 14773
TCP Data:
```

^@^@^@^@^@^@
- -
149.153.100.65 -> 149.153.100.104 (id: 172, ttl: 64)

TCP Source: 23 -> TCP Destination: 1070
TCP Header Length: 5, TCP Checksum: 24666
TCP Data:

^[[0m^[[01;34mDesktop^[[0m
^[[m[barryp@pbmac barryp]$
- -
149.153.100.104 -> 149.153.100.65 (id: 52231, ttl: 128)

TCP Source: 1070 -> TCP Destination: 23
TCP Header Length: 5, TCP Checksum: 14773
TCP Data:

^@^@^@^@^@^@
- -
149.153.100.104 -> 149.153.100.65 (id: 52487, ttl: 128)

TCP Source: 1070 -> TCP Destination: 23
TCP Header Length: 5, TCP Checksum: 49835
TCP Data:

w^@^@^@^@^@
- -
149.153.100.65 -> 149.153.100.104 (id: 173, ttl: 64)

TCP Source: 23 -> TCP Destination: 1070
TCP Header Length: 5, TCP Checksum: 26186
TCP Data:

wUUUUU
- -
149.153.100.104 -> 149.153.100.65 (id: 52743, ttl: 128)

TCP Source: 1070 -> TCP Destination: 23
TCP Header Length: 5, TCP Checksum: 14772
TCP Data:

^@^@^@^@^@^@
- -
149.153.100.104 -> 149.153.100.65 (id: 52999, ttl: 128)

TCP Source: 1070 -> TCP Destination: 23
TCP Header Length: 5, TCP Checksum: 53674
TCP Data:

h^@^@^@^@^@
- -
149.153.100.65 -> 149.153.100.104 (id: 174, ttl: 64)

TCP Source: 23 -> TCP Destination: 1070
TCP Header Length: 5, TCP Checksum: 30024
TCP Data:

hUUUUU
- -
149.153.100.104 -> 149.153.100.65 (id: 53255, ttl: 128)

TCP Source: 1070 -> TCP Destination: 23
TCP Header Length: 5, TCP Checksum: 51881
TCP Data:

o^@^@^@^@^@
- -
149.153.100.65 -> 149.153.100.104 (id: 175, ttl: 64)

```
TCP Source: 23 -> TCP Destination: 1070
TCP Header Length: 5, TCP Checksum: 28230
TCP Data:

oUUUUU
- - - - - - - - - - - - - - - - - - - - - - - - - - - - - - - - - - -
149.153.100.104 -> 149.153.100.65 (id: 53511, ttl: 128)

TCP Source: 1070 -> TCP Destination: 23
TCP Header Length: 5, TCP Checksum: 14770
TCP Data:

^@^@^@^@^@^@
- - - - - - - - - - - - - - - - - - - - - - - - - - - - - - - - - - -
149.153.100.104 -> 149.153.100.65 (id: 53767, ttl: 128)

TCP Source: 1070 -> TCP Destination: 23
TCP Header Length: 5, TCP Checksum: 55464
TCP Data:

a^@^@^@^@^@
- - - - - - - - - - - - - - - - - - - - - - - - - - - - - - - - - - -
149.153.100.65 -> 149.153.100.104 (id: 176, ttl: 64)

TCP Source: 23 -> TCP Destination: 1070
TCP Header Length: 5, TCP Checksum: 31812
TCP Data:

aUUUUU
- - - - - - - - - - - - - - - - - - - - - - - - - - - - - - - - - - -
149.153.100.104 -> 149.153.100.65 (id: 54023, ttl: 128)

TCP Source: 1070 -> TCP Destination: 23
TCP Header Length: 5, TCP Checksum: 52391
TCP Data:

m^@^@^@^@^@
- - - - - - - - - - - - - - - - - - - - - - - - - - - - - - - - - - -
149.153.100.65 -> 149.153.100.104 (id: 177, ttl: 64)

TCP Source: 23 -> TCP Destination: 1070
TCP Header Length: 5, TCP Checksum: 28738
TCP Data:

mUUUUU
- - - - - - - - - - - - - - - - - - - - - - - - - - - - - - - - - - -
149.153.100.104 -> 149.153.100.65 (id: 54279, ttl: 128)

TCP Source: 1070 -> TCP Destination: 23
TCP Header Length: 5, TCP Checksum: 14768
TCP Data:

^@^@^@^@^@^@
- - - - - - - - - - - - - - - - - - - - - - - - - - - - - - - - - - -
149.153.100.104 -> 149.153.100.65 (id: 54535, ttl: 128)

TCP Source: 1070 -> TCP Destination: 23
TCP Header Length: 5, TCP Checksum: 53414
TCP Data:

i^@^@^@^@^@
- - - - - - - - - - - - - - - - - - - - - - - - - - - - - - - - - - -
149.153.100.65 -> 149.153.100.104 (id: 178, ttl: 64)

TCP Source: 23 -> TCP Destination: 1070
TCP Header Length: 5, TCP Checksum: 29760
TCP Data:
```

```
¡UUUUU
- - - - - - - - - - - - - - - - - - - - - - - - - - - - - -
149.153.100.104 -> 149.153.100.65 (id: 54791, ttl: 128)

TCP Source: 1070 -> TCP Destination: 23
TCP Header Length: 5, TCP Checksum: 14767
TCP Data:

^@^@^@^@^@^@
- - - - - - - - - - - - - - - - - - - - - - - - - - - - - -
149.153.100.104 -> 149.153.100.65 (id: 55047, ttl: 128)

TCP Source: 1070 -> TCP Destination: 23
TCP Header Length: 5, TCP Checksum: 11419
TCP Data:


7777
- - - - - - - - - - - - - - - - - - - - - - - - - - - - - -
149.153.100.65 -> 149.153.100.104 (id: 179, ttl: 64)

TCP Source: 23 -> TCP Destination: 1070
TCP Header Length: 5, TCP Checksum: 53298
TCP Data:


UUUU
- - - - - - - - - - - - - - - - - - - - - - - - - - - - - -
149.153.100.104 -> 149.153.100.65 (id: 55303, ttl: 128)

TCP Source: 1070 -> TCP Destination: 23
TCP Header Length: 5, TCP Checksum: 14765
TCP Data:

^@^@^@^@^@^@
- - - - - - - - - - - - - - - - - - - - - - - - - - - - - -
149.153.100.65 -> 149.153.100.104 (id: 180, ttl: 64)

TCP Source: 23 -> TCP Destination: 1070
TCP Header Length: 5, TCP Checksum: 54771
TCP Data:

barryp
[barryp@pbmac barryp]$
- - - - - - - - - - - - - - - - - - - - - - - - - - - - - -
149.153.100.104 -> 149.153.100.65 (id: 55559, ttl: 128)

TCP Source: 1070 -> TCP Destination: 23
TCP Header Length: 5, TCP Checksum: 14765
TCP Data:

^@^@^@^@^@^@
- - - - - - - - - - - - - - - - - - - - - - - - - - - - - -
149.153.100.104 -> 149.153.100.65 (id: 55815, ttl: 128)

TCP Source: 1070 -> TCP Destination: 23
TCP Header Length: 5, TCP Checksum: 13732
TCP Data:

^D^@^@^@^@^@
- - - - - - - - - - - - - - - - - - - - - - - - - - - - - -
149.153.100.65 -> 149.153.100.104 (id: 181, ttl: 64)

TCP Source: 23 -> TCP Destination: 1070
TCP Header Length: 5, TCP Checksum: 34487
TCP Data:

logout
```

```
- - - - - - - - - - - - - - - - - - - - - - - - - - - - - - - - - -
149.153.100.65 -> 149.153.100.104 (id: 182, ttl: 64)

TCP Source: 23 -> TCP Destination: 1070
TCP Header Length: 5, TCP Checksum: 7757
TCP Data:

^[[H^[[J
- - - - - - - - - - - - - - - - - - - - - - - - - - - - - - - - - -
149.153.100.104 -> 149.153.100.65 (id: 56071, ttl: 128)

TCP Source: 1070 -> TCP Destination: 23
TCP Header Length: 5, TCP Checksum: 14763
TCP Data:

^@^@^@^@^@^@
- - - - - - - - - - - - - - - - - - - - - - - - - - - - - - - - - -
149.153.100.104 -> 149.153.100.65 (id: 56327, ttl: 128)

TCP Source: 1070 -> TCP Destination: 23
TCP Header Length: 5, TCP Checksum: 14762
TCP Data:

^@^@^@^@^@^@
- - - - - - - - - - - - - - - - - - - - - - - - - - - - - - - - - -
149.153.100.65 -> 149.153.100.104 (id: 183, ttl: 64)

TCP Source: 23 -> TCP Destination: 1070
TCP Header Length: 5, TCP Checksum: 56597
TCP Data:

UUUUUU
- - - - - - - - - - - - - - - - - - - - - - - - - - - - - - - - - -
107 datagrams/segments processed.

Mon Sep  3 14:23:46 2001 - netdebug END run.
```

The *TELNET* protocol is very *chatty*, and the captured results confirm this: a large number of small datagrams are travelling to/from the *TELNET* server. As *TELNET* transfers data as clear text, it is possible to determine where in the stream of datagrams the server prompts the user for a login-id and password, as the `Password:` prompts are clearly visible. After each prompt, a collection of datagrams carry the login-id (which is `barryp` in this case) and password (which is `passwordhere`), again in clear-text. Note that the *TELNET* server echoes each character typed by the user, resulting in the following datagram sequences: `bbaarryypp` and `ppaasswwoorrddhheerree`. Each character typed is sent and echoed in its own *TELNET* datagram, which only adds to the *chatty* nature of this protocol.

NetDebugging Secure Shell Traffic

The following invocation of *NetDebug* captures network traffic to and from the `pbmac.itcarlow.ie` (`149.153.100.65`) network device. The well-known protocol port-number of the *Secure Shell Protocol* is 22, and any captured traffic is filtered on this value:

```
./netdb -s 149.153.100.65 -p 22
```

Unlike the traffic captured during the TELNET example, this captured traffic reveals little, as the communication session between the two network devices is encrypted and, consequently, secure. The general advice is clear: *do not use TELNET when privacy is important*[1]. As the bulk of the traffic captured is unintelligible, what follows is a small extract of the *NetDebug* results:

```
Fri Aug  3 16:20:32 2001 - netdebug BEGIN run.

- - - - - - - - - - - - - - - - - - - - - - - - - - - - - - - - - -
149.153.100.66 -> 149.153.100.65 (id: 3515, ttl: 64)

TCP Source: 1030 -> TCP Destination: 22
TCP Header Length: 10, TCP Checksum: 23666
TCP Data:

^B^H
^@^G#ó^@^@^@^@^A^C^C^@
- - - - - - - - - - - - - - - - - - - - - - - - - - - - - - - - - -
149.153.100.65 -> 149.153.100.66 (id: 48, ttl: 64)

TCP Source: 22 -> TCP Destination: 1030
TCP Header Length: 10, TCP Checksum: 64392
TCP Data:

^B^H
^@^@Q8^@^G#ó^A^C^C^@
- - - - - - - - - - - - - - - - - - - - - - - - - - - - - - - - - -
149.153.100.66 -> 149.153.100.65 (id: 3516, ttl: 64)

TCP Source: 1030 -> TCP Destination: 22
TCP Header Length: 8, TCP Checksum: 35650
TCP Data:


^@^G#ó^@^@Q8
- - - - - - - - - - - - - - - - - - - - - - - - - - - - - - - - - -
149.153.100.65 -> 149.153.100.66 (id: 49, ttl: 64)

TCP Source: 22 -> TCP Destination: 1030
TCP Header Length: 8, TCP Checksum: 35458
TCP Data:


^@^@Q8^@^G#óSSH-1.99-OpenSSH_2.2.0p1

- - - - - - - - - - - - - - - - - - - - - - - - - - - - - - - - - -
149.153.100.66 -> 149.153.100.65 (id: 3517, ttl: 64)

TCP Source: 1030 -> TCP Destination: 22
TCP Header Length: 8, TCP Checksum: 35625
TCP Data:


^@^G#ó^@^@Q8
- - - - - - - - - - - - - - - - - - - - - - - - - - - - - - - - - -
149.153.100.66 -> 149.153.100.65 (id: 3518, ttl: 64)

TCP Source: 1030 -> TCP Destination: 22
TCP Header Length: 8, TCP Checksum: 28869
TCP Data:


^@^G#ó^@^@Q8SSH-2.0-OpenSSH_2.5.2p2
```

---

[1]Many network administrators take this further and advise *never* to use *TELNET*.

```
- - - - - - - - - - - - - - - - - - - - - - - - - - - - - - - - - - - - -
149.153.100.65 -> 149.153.100.66 (id: 50, ttl: 64)

TCP Source: 22 -> TCP Destination: 1030
TCP Header Length: 8, TCP Checksum: 9585
TCP Data:


^@^@Q8^@^G#ó
- - - - - - - - - - - - - - - - - - - - - - - - - - - - - - - - - - - - -
149.153.100.66 -> 149.153.100.65 (id: 3519, ttl: 64)

TCP Source: 1030 -> TCP Destination: 22
TCP Header Length: 8, TCP Checksum: 16624
TCP Data:


^@^G#ó^@^@Q8^@^@^Bt^K^TÀ'oo^Z(¢x¼+Y»^Vo^_¸^@^@^@=diffie-hellman-
group-exchange-sha1,diffie-hellman-group1-sha1^@^@^@Ossh-rsa,ss
h-dss^@^@^@oaes128-cbc,3des-cbc,blowfish-cbc,cast128-cbc,arcfour
,aes192-cbc,aes256-cbc,rijndael128-cbc,rijndael192-cbc,rijndael2
56-cbc,rijndael-cbc@lysator.liu.se^@^@^@oaes128-cbc,3des-cbc,blo
wfish-cbc,cast128-cbc,arcfour,aes192-cbc,aes256-cbc,rijndael128-
cbc,rijndael192-cbc,rijndael256-cbc,rijndael-cbc@lysator.liu.se^
@^@^Uhmac-md5,hmac-sha1,hmac-ripemd160,hmac-ripemd160@openssh.c
om,hmac-sha1-96,hmac-md5-96^@^@^@Uhmac-md5,hmac-sha1,hmac-ripemd
160,hmac-ripemd160@openssh.com,hmac-sha1-96,hmac-md5-96^@^@^Dn
one^@^@^@^Dnone^@^@^@^@^@^@^@^@^@^@^@^@^@
- - - - - - - - - - - - - - - - - - - - - - - - - - - - - - - - - - - - -
149.153.100.65 -> 149.153.100.66 (id: 51, ttl: 64)

TCP Source: 22 -> TCP Destination: 1030
TCP Header Length: 8, TCP Checksum: 56660
TCP Data:


^@^@Q8^@^G#ó^@^@^A$^F^T^E½SY¡í^C^Ñqo^H‰uxo^@^@^@Zdiffie-hellman-
group1-sha1^@^@^@^Gssh-dss^@^@^@)3des-cbc,blowfish-cbc,arcfour,ca
st128-cbc^@^@^@)3des-cbc,blowfish-cbc,arcfour,cast128-cbc^@^@^@-h
mac-sha1,hmac-md5,hmac-ripemd160@openssh.com^@^@^@-hmac-sha1,hmac
-md5,hmac-ripemd160@openssh.com^@^@^@Izlib,none^@^@^@^Izlib,none
^@^@^@^@^@^@^@^@^@^@^@^@^@^@^@^@^@^@^@
- - - - - - - - - - - - - - - - - - - - - - - - - - - - - - - - - - - - -
149.153.100.65 -> 149.153.100.66 (id: 52, ttl: 64)

TCP Source: 22 -> TCP Destination: 1030
TCP Header Length: 8, TCP Checksum: 8656
TCP Data:


^@^@Q9^@^G#ó
- - - - - - - - - - - - - - - - - - - - - - - - - - - - - - - - - - - - -
149.153.100.66 -> 149.153.100.65 (id: 3520, ttl: 64)

TCP Source: 1030 -> TCP Destination: 22
TCP Header Length: 8, TCP Checksum: 34077
TCP Data:


^@^G#÷^@^@Q8
- - - - - - - - - - - - - - - - - - - - - - - - - - - - - - - - - - - - -
149.153.100.66 -> 149.153.100.65 (id: 3521, ttl: 64)

TCP Source: 1030 -> TCP Destination: 22
TCP Header Length: 8, TCP Checksum: 9769
TCP Data:
```

```
^@^G#÷^@^@Q8^@^@^@o^F^^^@^@^@oBoÐ‚V^^^Uo‚ÈTooÃËO‚ØÈ^A³Nh/wÕ+^D4J]^Y
e¾oäçïf¾Äï^O²^Tïö36[Î^C^KÍÁVktÇ,SoW~&ooÊ=^V^V=^G[^O^¾ÉDvo½^\"Îôo[b½
.4e^Ê^Gèáçoÿ5Îæ$nÿ·§¿IoÅÆ¤u"-^P£½Ü^G^OÎ^XÜ2^@^@^@^@^@^@
- - - - - - - - - - - - - - - - - - - - - - - - - - - - - - -
149.153.100.65 -> 149.153.100.66 (id: 53, ttl: 64)

TCP Source: 22 -> TCP Destination: 1030
TCP Header Length: 8, TCP Checksum: 8503
TCP Data:


^@^@Q>^@^G#÷
- - - - - - - - - - - - - - - - - - - - - - - - - - - - - - -

        .
        .
        .

- - - - - - - - - - - - - - - - - - - - - - - - - - - - - - -
149.153.100.65 -> 149.153.100.66 (id: 100, ttl: 64)

TCP Source: 22 -> TCP Destination: 1030
TCP Header Length: 8, TCP Checksum: 63926
TCP Data:


^@^@X'^@^G+^[
- - - - - - - - - - - - - - - - - - - - - - - - - - - - - - -
149.153.100.66 -> 149.153.100.65 (id: 0, ttl: 255)

TCP Source: 1030 -> TCP Destination: 22
TCP Header Length: 8, TCP Checksum: 17527
TCP Data:


^@^G+^[^@^@X'
- - - - - - - - - - - - - - - - - - - - - - - - - - - - - - -
123 datagrams/segments processed.

Fri Aug  3 16:21:32 2001 - netdebug END run.
```

NetDebugging Network Management Traffic

The following invocation of *NetDebug* captures *SNMP* traffic generated by the pbmac.itcarlow.ie (149.153.100.65) network device, resulting from the execution of the ipdetermine program from Chapter 5, *Management*, against the 149.153.100.10 router. As *SNMP* uses UDP and the well-known protocol port-number 161, this needs to be specified on the command-line, as follows:

```
./netdb -s 149.153.100.65 -p 161 -u
```

The results produced are all but unintelligible due to the fact that *SNMP* uses the *Basic Encoding Rules* to encode its data prior to transfer. However, the entire capture is included here to support the examples in Chapter 5, *Management*, and Chapter 6, *Mobile Agents*. Specifically, the *volume* of data captured is most interesting (enlightening):

```
Fri Aug  3 15:56:31 2001 - netdebug BEGIN run.

- - - - - - - - - - - - - - - - - - - - - - - - - - - - - - - - - -
149.153.100.65 -> 149.153.100.10 (id: 44735, ttl: 64)

UDP Source: 1042 -> UDP Destination: 161
UDP Length: 48, UDP Checksum: 53718
UDP Data:

0&^B^A^A^D^Fpublic|^Y^B^AN^B^A^@^B^A^@0^NO^L^F^H+^F^A^B^A^A^A^@^E^@
- - - - - - - - - - - - - - - - - - - - - - - - - - - - - - - - - -
149.153.100.10 -> 149.153.100.65 (id: 61004, ttl: 255)

UDP Source: 161 -> UDP Destination: 1042
UDP Length: 312, UDP Checksum: 48913
UDP Data:

Oo^A,^B^A^A^D^Fpublic¢o^A^]^B^AN^B^A^@^B^A^@Oo^A^POo^A^L^F^H+^F^A
^B^A^A^A^@^DoÿCisco Internetwork Operating System Software
IOS (tm) MSFC Software (C6MSFC-JSV-M), Version 12.1(6)E, EARLY
DEPLOYMENT RELEASE SOFTWARE (fc3)
TAC Support: http://www.cisco.com/cgi-bin/ibld/view.pl?i=support
Copyright (c) 1986-2001 by cisco Systems, In
- - - - - - - - - - - - - - - - - - - - - - - - - - - - - - - - - -
149.153.100.65 -> 149.153.100.10 (id: 44736, ttl: 64)

UDP Source: 1042 -> UDP Destination: 161
UDP Length: 47, UDP Checksum: 50116
UDP Data:

0%^B^A^A^D^Fpublic¥^X^B^AO^B^A^@^B^A
00^K^F^G+^F^A^B^A^D^U^E^@
- - - - - - - - - - - - - - - - - - - - - - - - - - - - - - - - - -
149.153.100.10 -> 149.153.100.65 (id: 61005, ttl: 255)

UDP Source: 161 -> UDP Destination: 1042
UDP Length: 285, UDP Checksum: 9234
UDP Data:

Oo^A^Q^B^A^A^D^Fpublic¢o^A^B^B^AO^B^A^@^B^A^@0oö0^U^F+^F^A^B^A^D^U
^A^A^@^@^@^@@^D^@^@^@0^U^F+^F^A^B^A^D^U^A^A^¿^@^@^@@^D^¿^@^@^@0^
W^F^O+^F^A^B^A^D^U^A^Ao^Uo^Y^A^@@^Doo^A^@0^W^F^O+^F^A^B^A^D^U^A^Ao
^Uo^Y^B^@@^Doo^B^@0^W^F^O+^F^A^B^A^D^U^A^Ao^Uo^Y^C^@@^Doo^C^@0^W^F
^O+^F^A^B^A^D^U^A^Ao^Uo^Y^F^@@^Doo^F^@0^W^F^O+^F^A^B^A^D^U^A^Ao^Uo
^Y^I^@@^Doo^I^@0^W^F^O+^F^A^B^A^D^U^A^Ao^Uo^Y^P^@@^Doo^P^@0^W^F^O+
^F^A^B^A^D^U^A^Ao^Uo^Y2^@@^Doo2^@0^W^F^O+^F^A^B^A^D^U^A^Ao^Uo^Ya^@
@^Dooa^@
- - - - - - - - - - - - - - - - - - - - - - - - - - - - - - - - - -
149.153.100.65 -> 149.153.100.10 (id: 44737, ttl: 64)

UDP Source: 1042 -> UDP Destination: 161
UDP Length: 55, UDP Checksum: 35631
UDP Data:

0-^B^A^A^D^Fpublic¥ ^B^AP^B^A^@^B^A
0^U0^S^F^O+^F^A^B^A^D^U^A^Ao^Uo^Ya^@^E^@
- - - - - - - - - - - - - - - - - - - - - - - - - - - - - - - - - -
149.153.100.10 -> 149.153.100.65 (id: 61006, ttl: 255)

UDP Source: 161 -> UDP Destination: 1042
UDP Length: 297, UDP Checksum: 62904
UDP Data:

Oo^A^]^B^A^A^D^Fpublic¢o^A^N^B^AP^B^A^@^B^A^@Oo^A^A0^W^F^O+^F^A^B^
A^D^U^A^Ao^Uo^Yb^@@^Doob^@0^W^F^O+^F^A^B^A^D^U^A^Ao^Uo^Yd^@@^Dood^
@0^W^F^O+^F^A^B^A^D^U^A^Ao^Uo^Yg^@@^Doog^@0^X^F^P+^F^A^B^A^D^U^A^A
o^Uo^Yo^@^@@^Dooo^@0^X^F^P+^F^A^B^A^D^U^A^Ao^Uo^YoF^@@^DooÆ^@0^X^F
```

```
^P+^F^A^B^A^D^U^A^Ao^Uo^YoH^@@^DooÈ^@0^X^F^P+^F^A^B^A^D^U^A^Ao^Uo^
YoI^@@^DooÉ^@0^X^F^P+^F^A^B^A^D^U^A^Ao^Uo^YoI^B@^DooÉ^B0^X^F^P+^F^
A^B^A^D^U^A^Ao^Uo^YoL^@@^DooÌ^@0^X^F^P+^F^A^B^A^D^U^A^Ao^Uo^YoM^@@
^DooÍ^@
- - - - - - - - - - - - - - - - - - - - - - - - - - - - - - - - - -
149.153.100.65 -> 149.153.100.10 (id: 44738, ttl: 64)

UDP Source: 1042 -> UDP Destination: 161
UDP Length: 56, UDP Checksum: 14349
UDP Data:

0.^B^A^A^D^Fpublic¥!^B^AQ^B^A^@^B^A
0^V0^T^F^P+^F^A^B^A^D^U^A^Ao^Uo^YoM^@^E^@
- - - - - - - - - - - - - - - - - - - - - - - - - - - - - - - - - -
149.153.100.10 -> 149.153.100.65 (id: 61007, ttl: 255)

UDP Source: 161 -> UDP Destination: 1042
UDP Length: 270, UDP Checksum: 42465
UDP Data:

Oo^A^B^B^A^A^D^Fpublic¢oô^B^AQ^B^A^@^B^A^@Ooè0^X^F^P+^F^A^B^A^D^U^i
A^Ao^Uo^YoM^B@^DooÍ^B0^X^F^P+^F^A^B^A^D^U^A^Ao^Uo^YoT^@@^DooÔ^@0^X^
F^P+^F^A^B^A^D^U^A^Ao^Uo^YoX^@@^DooØ^@0^X^F^P+^F^A^B^A^D^U^A^Ao^Uo^
Yo)^@@^Dooý^@0^R^F+^F^A^B^A^D^U^A^B^@^@^@^@^B^A^@0^R^F+^F^A^B^A^D^U
^A^B^¿^@^@^@^B^A^A0^T^F^O+^F^A^B^A^D^U^A^Bo^Uo^Y^A^@^B^A^X0^T^F^O+^
F^A^B^A^D^U^A^Bo^Uo^Y^B^@^B^A^C0^T^F^O+^F^A^B^A^D^U^A^Bo^Uo^Y^C^@^B
^A^E0^T^F^O+^F^A^B^A^D^U^A^Bo^Uo^Y^F^@^B^A^H
- - - - - - - - - - - - - - - - - - - - - - - - - - - - - - - - - -
149.153.100.65 -> 149.153.100.10 (id: 44739, ttl: 64)

UDP Source: 1042 -> UDP Destination: 161
UDP Length: 55, UDP Checksum: 35464
UDP Data:

0-^B^A^A^D^Fpublic¥ ^B^AR^B^A^@^B^A
0^U0^S^F^O+^F^A^B^A^D^U^A^Bo^Uo^Y^F^@^E^@
- - - - - - - - - - - - - - - - - - - - - - - - - - - - - - - - - -
149.153.100.10 -> 149.153.100.65 (id: 61008, ttl: 255)

UDP Source: 161 -> UDP Destination: 1042
UDP Length: 260, UDP Checksum: 2434
UDP Data:

Ooù^B^A^A^D^Fpublic¢oë^B^AR^B^A^@^B^A^@Ooß0^T^F^O+^F^A^B^A^D^U^A^Boi
^Uo^Y^I^@^B^A^P0^T^F^O+^F^A^B^A^D^U^A^Bo^Uo^Y^P^@^B^A^R0^T^F^O+^F^A^
B^A^D^U^A^Bo^Uo^Y2^@^B^A^S0^T^F^O+^F^A^B^A^D^U^A^Bo^Uo^Ya^@^B^A^D0^T
^F^O+^F^A^B^A^D^U^A^Bo^Uo^Yb^@^B^A^@0^T^F^O+^F^A^B^A^D^U^A^Bo^Uo^Yd^
@^B^A^D0^T^F^O+^F^A^B^A^D^U^A^Bo^Uo^Yg^@^B^A^G0^U^F^P+^F^A^B^A^D^U^A
^Bo^Uo^Yo^@^@^B^A^D0^U^F^P+^F^A^B^A^D^U^A^Bo^Uo^YoF^@^B^A^C0^U^F^P+^
F^A^B^A^D^U^A^Bo^Uo^YoH^@^B^A^C
- - - - - - - - - - - - - - - - - - - - - - - - - - - - - - - - - -
149.153.100.65 -> 149.153.100.10 (id: 44740, ttl: 64)

UDP Source: 1042 -> UDP Destination: 161
UDP Length: 56, UDP Checksum: 15371
UDP Data:

0.^B^A^A^D^Fpublic¥!^B^AS^B^A^@^B^A
0^V0^T^F^P+^F^A^B^A^D^U^A^Bo^Uo^YoH^@^E^@
- - - - - - - - - - - - - - - - - - - - - - - - - - - - - - - - - -
149.153.100.10 -> 149.153.100.65 (id: 61009, ttl: 255)

UDP Source: 161 -> UDP Destination: 1042
UDP Length: 261, UDP Checksum: 1703
UDP Data:
```

```
OoúˆBˆAˆAˆDˆFpublic¢oiˆBˆASˆBˆAˆ@ˆBˆAˆ@Ooà0ˆUˆFˆP+ˆFˆAˆBˆAˆDˆUˆABo
ˆUoˆYoIˆ@ˆBˆAˆCO0ˆUˆFˆP+ˆFˆAˆBˆAˆDˆUˆABoˆUoˆYoIˆBˆBˆAˆCO0ˆUˆFˆP+ˆFˆA
ˆBˆAˆDˆUˆABoˆUoˆYoLˆ@ˆBˆAˆCO0ˆUˆFˆP+ˆFˆAˆBˆAˆDˆUˆABoˆUoˆYoMˆ@ˆBˆAˆ
CO0ˆUˆFˆP+ˆFˆAˆBˆAˆDˆUˆABoˆUoˆYoMˆBˆBˆAˆCO0ˆUˆFˆP+ˆFˆAˆBˆAˆDˆUˆABo
UoˆYoTˆ@ˆBˆAˆCO0ˆUˆFˆP+ˆFˆAˆBˆAˆDˆUˆABoˆUoˆYoXˆ@ˆBˆAˆVO0ˆUˆFˆP+ˆFˆA
BˆAˆDˆUˆABoˆUoˆYo)ˆ@ˆBˆAˆWO0ˆRˆF+ˆFˆAˆBˆAˆDˆUˆAˆCˆ@ˆ@ˆ@ˆBˆAˆ@O0ˆRˆ
F+ˆFˆAˆBˆAˆDˆUˆAˆCˆ¿ˆ@ˆ@ˆ@ˆBˆAˆ@
- - - - - - - - - - - - - - - - - - - - - - - - - - - - - - - - -
149.153.100.65 -> 149.153.100.10 (id: 44741, ttl: 64)

UDP Source: 1042 -> UDP Destination: 161
UDP Length: 53, UDP Checksum: 47643
UDP Data:

0.ˆBˆAˆAˆDˆFpublic¥!ˆBˆASˆBˆAˆ@ˆBˆA
0ˆVO0ˆTˆFˆP+ˆFˆAˆBˆAˆDˆUˆABoˆUoˆYoHˆ@ˆEˆ@
- - - - - - - - - - - - - - - - - - - - - - - - - - - - - - - - -
149.153.100.10 -> 149.153.100.65 (id: 61010, ttl: 255)

UDP Source: 161 -> UDP Destination: 1042
UDP Length: 257, UDP Checksum: 30171
UDP Data:

OoöˆBˆAˆAˆDˆFpublic¢oèˆBˆATˆBˆAˆ@ˆBˆAˆ@OoÜ0ˆTˆFˆO+ˆFˆAˆBˆAˆDˆUˆACo
ˆUoˆYˆAˆ@ˆBˆAˆ@0ˆTˆFˆO+ˆFˆAˆBˆAˆDˆUˆACoˆUoˆYˆBˆ@ˆBˆAˆ@0ˆTˆFˆO+ˆFˆA
ˆBˆAˆDˆUˆACoˆUoˆYˆCˆ@ˆBˆAˆ@0ˆTˆFˆO+ˆFˆAˆBˆAˆDˆUˆACoˆUoˆYˆFˆ@ˆBˆAˆ
@0ˆTˆFˆO+ˆFˆAˆBˆAˆDˆUˆACoˆUoˆYˆIˆ@ˆBˆAˆ@0ˆTˆFˆO+ˆFˆAˆBˆAˆDˆUˆACoˆ
UoˆYˆPˆ@ˆBˆAˆ@0ˆTˆFˆO+ˆFˆAˆBˆAˆDˆUˆACoˆUoˆY2ˆ@ˆBˆAˆ@0ˆTˆFˆO+ˆFˆAˆB
ˆAˆDˆUˆACoˆUoˆYaˆ@ˆBˆAˆ@0ˆTˆFˆO+ˆFˆAˆBˆAˆDˆUˆACoˆUoˆYbˆ@ˆBˆAˆ@0ˆT
ˆFˆO+ˆFˆAˆBˆAˆDˆUˆACoˆUoˆYdˆ@ˆBˆAˆ@
- - - - - - - - - - - - - - - - - - - - - - - - - - - - - - - - -
149.153.100.65 -> 149.153.100.10 (id: 44742, ttl: 64)

UDP Source: 1042 -> UDP Destination: 161
UDP Length: 55, UDP Checksum: 35111
UDP Data:

0-ˆBˆAˆAˆDˆFpublic¥ ˆBˆAUˆBˆAˆ@ˆBˆA
0ˆUO0ˆSˆFˆO+ˆFˆAˆBˆAˆDˆUˆACoˆUoˆYdˆ@ˆEˆ@
- - - - - - - - - - - - - - - - - - - - - - - - - - - - - - - - -
149.153.100.10 -> 149.153.100.65 (id: 61011, ttl: 255)

UDP Source: 161 -> UDP Destination: 1042
UDP Length: 266, UDP Checksum: 55129
UDP Data:

OoÿˆBˆAˆAˆDˆFpublic¢oñˆBˆAUˆBˆAˆ@ˆBˆAˆ@Ooà0ˆTˆFˆO+ˆFˆAˆBˆAˆDˆUˆACo
ˆUoˆYgˆ@ˆBˆAˆ@0ˆUˆFˆP+ˆFˆAˆBˆAˆDˆUˆACoˆUoˆYoˆ@ˆ@ˆBˆAˆ@0ˆUˆFˆP+ˆFˆA
ˆBˆAˆDˆUˆACoˆUoˆYoFˆ@ˆBˆAˆA0ˆUˆFˆP+ˆFˆAˆBˆAˆDˆUˆACoˆUoˆYoHˆ@ˆBˆAˆ
B0ˆUˆFˆP+ˆFˆAˆBˆAˆDˆUˆACoˆUoˆYoIˆ@ˆBˆAˆA0ˆUˆFˆP+ˆFˆAˆBˆAˆDˆUˆACoˆ
UoˆYoIˆBˆBˆAˆA0ˆUˆFˆP+ˆFˆAˆBˆAˆDˆUˆACoˆUoˆYoLˆ@ˆBˆAˆB0ˆUˆFˆP+ˆFˆAˆ
BˆAˆDˆUˆACoˆUoˆYoMˆ@ˆBˆAˆA0ˆUˆFˆP+ˆFˆAˆBˆAˆDˆUˆACoˆUoˆYoMˆBˆBˆAˆA
0ˆUˆFˆP+ˆFˆAˆBˆAˆDˆUˆACoˆUoˆYoTˆ@ˆBˆAˆA
- - - - - - - - - - - - - - - - - - - - - - - - - - - - - - - - -
149.153.100.65 -> 149.153.100.10 (id: 44743, ttl: 64)

UDP Source: 1042 -> UDP Destination: 161
UDP Length: 56, UDP Checksum: 12040
UDP Data:

0.ˆBˆAˆAˆDˆFpublic¥!ˆBˆAVˆBˆAˆ@ˆBˆA
0ˆVO0ˆTˆFˆP+ˆFˆAˆBˆAˆDˆUˆACoˆUoˆYoTˆ@ˆEˆ@
- - - - - - - - - - - - - - - - - - - - - - - - - - - - - - - - -
149.153.100.10 -> 149.153.100.65 (id: 61012, ttl: 255)

UDP Source: 161 -> UDP Destination: 1042
UDP Length: 255, UDP Checksum: 62150
UDP Data:
```

```
Ooÿ^B^A^A^D^Fpublic¢oñ^B^AU^B^A^@^B^A^@Ooå0^T^F^O+^F^A^B^A^D^U^A^Co
^Uo^YoX^@^B^A^@0^U^F^P+^F^A^B^A^D^U^A^Co^Uo^Yo)^@^B^A^@0^R^F+^F^A^B
^A^D^U^A^D^@^@^@^@^B^Aÿ0^R^F+^F^A^B^A^D^U^A^D^¿^@^@^@^B^Aÿ0^T^F^O+^
F^A^B^A^D^U^A^Do^Uo^Y^A^@^B^Aÿ0^T^F^O+^F^A^B^A^D^U^A^Do^Uo^Y^B^@^B^
Aÿ0^T^F^O+^F^A^B^A^D^U^A^Do^Uo^Y^C^@^B^Aÿ0^T^F^O+^F^A^B^A^D^U^A^Do^
Uo^Y^F^@^B^Aÿ0^T^F^O+^F^A^B^A^D^U^A^Do^Uo^Y^I^@^B^Aÿ0^T^F^O+^F^A^B^
A^D^U^A^Do^Uo^Y^P^@^B^Aÿ
- - - - - - - - - - - - - - - - - - - - - - - - - - - - - - - - - -
149.153.100.65 -> 149.153.100.10 (id: 44744, ttl: 64)

UDP Source: 1042 -> UDP Destination: 161
UDP Length: 55, UDP Checksum: 34937
UDP Data:

0-^B^A^A^D^Fpublic¥ ^B^AW^B^A^@^B^A
0^U0^S^F^O+^F^A^B^A^D^U^A^Do^Uo^Y^P^@^E^@
- - - - - - - - - - - - - - - - - - - - - - - - - - - - - - - - - -
149.153.100.10 -> 149.153.100.65 (id: 61013, ttl: 255)

UDP Source: 161 -> UDP Destination: 1042
UDP Length: 262, UDP Checksum: 7957
UDP Data:

Ooû^B^A^A^D^Fpublic¢oí^B^AW^B^A^@^B^A^@Ooá0^T^F^O+^F^A^B^A^D^U^A^Do
^Uo^Y2^@^B^Aÿ0^T^F^O+^F^A^B^A^D^U^A^Do^Uo^Ya^@^B^Aÿ0^T^F^O+^F^A^B^A
^D^U^A^Do^Uo^Yb^@^B^Aÿ0^T^F^O+^F^A^B^A^D^U^A^Do^Uo^Yd^@^B^Aÿ0^T^F^O
+^F^A^B^A^D^U^A^Do^Uo^Yg^@^B^Aÿ0^U^F^P+^F^A^B^A^D^U^A^Do^Uo^Yo^@^@^
B^Aÿ0^U^F^P+^F^A^B^A^D^U^A^Do^Uo^YoF^@^B^Aÿ0^U^F^P+^F^A^B^A^D^U^A^D
o^Uo^YoH^@^B^Aÿ0^U^F^P+^F^A^B^A^D^U^A^Do^Uo^YoI^@^B^Aÿ0^U^F^P+^F^A^
B^A^D^U^A^Do^Uo^YoI^B^B^Aÿ
- - - - - - - - - - - - - - - - - - - - - - - - - - - - - - - - - -
149.153.100.65 -> 149.153.100.10 (id: 44745, ttl: 64)

UDP Source: 1042 -> UDP Destination: 161
UDP Length: 56, UDP Checksum: 14596
UDP Data:

0.^B^A^A^D^Fpublic¥!^B^AX^B^A^@^B^A
0^V0^T^F^P+^F^A^B^A^D^U^A^Do^Uo^YoI^B^E^@
- - - - - - - - - - - - - - - - - - - - - - - - - - - - - - - - - -
149.153.100.10 -> 149.153.100.65 (id: 61014, ttl: 255)

UDP Source: 161 -> UDP Destination: 1042
UDP Length: 259, UDP Checksum: 27146
UDP Data:

Ooø^B^A^A^D^Fpublic¢oê^B^AX^B^A^@^B^A^@OoÞ0^U^F^P+^F^A^B^A^D^U^A^Do
^Uo^YoL^@^B^Aÿ0^U^F^P+^F^A^B^A^D^U^A^Do^Uo^YoM^@^B^Aÿ0^U^F^P+^F^A^B
^A^D^U^A^Do^Uo^YoM^B^B^Aÿ0^U^F^P+^F^A^B^A^D^U^A^Do^Uo^YoT^@^B^Aÿ0^U
^F^P+^F^A^B^A^D^U^A^Do^Uo^YoX^@^B^Aÿ0^U^F^P+^F^A^B^A^D^U^A^Do^Uo^Yo
)^@^B^Aÿ0^R^F+^F^A^B^A^D^U^A^E^@^@^@^@^B^Aÿ0^R^F+^F^A^B^A^D^U^A^E^¿
^@^@^@^B^Aÿ0^T^F^O+^F^A^B^A^D^U^A^Eo^Uo^Y^A^@^B^Aÿ0^T^F^O+^F^A^B^A^
D^U^A^Eo^Uo^Y^B^@^B^Aÿ
- - - - - - - - - - - - - - - - - - - - - - - - - - - - - - - - - -
149.153.100.65 -> 149.153.100.10 (id: 44746, ttl: 64)

UDP Source: 1042 -> UDP Destination: 161
UDP Length: 55, UDP Checksum: 34693
UDP Data:

0-^B^A^A^D^Fpublic¥ ^B^AY^B^A^@^B^A
0^U0^S^F^O+^F^A^B^A^D^U^A^Eo^Uo^Y^B^@^E^@
- - - - - - - - - - - - - - - - - - - - - - - - - - - - - - - - - -
149.153.100.10 -> 149.153.100.65 (id: 61015, ttl: 255)

UDP Source: 161 -> UDP Destination: 1042
UDP Length: 258, UDP Checksum: 38070
UDP Data:
```

```
Oo÷^B^A^A^D^Fpublic¢oé^B^AY^B^A^@^B^A^@OoÝ0^T^F^O+^F^A^B^A^D^U^A^Eo
^Uo^Y^C^@^B^Aÿ0^T^F^O+^F^A^B^A^D^U^A^Eo^Uo^Y^F^@^B^Aÿ0^T^F^O+^F^A^B
^A^D^U^A^Eo^Uo^Y^I^@^B^Aÿ0^T^F^O+^F^A^B^A^D^U^A^Eo^Uo^Y^P^@^B^Aÿ0^T
^F^O+^F^A^B^A^D^U^A^Eo^Uo^Y2^@^B^Aÿ0^T^F^O+^F^A^B^A^D^U^A^Eo^Uo^Ya^
@^B^Aÿ0^T^F^O+^F^A^B^A^D^U^A^Eo^Uo^Yb^@^B^Aÿ0^T^F^O+^F^A^B^A^D^U^A^
Eo^Uo^Yd^@^B^Aÿ0^T^F^O+^F^A^B^A^D^U^A^Eo^Uo^Yg^@^B^Aÿ0^U^F^P+^F^A^B
^A^D^U^A^Eo^Uo^Yo^@^@^B^Aÿ
- - - - - - - - - - - - - - - - - - - - - - - - - - - - - - - - - - - - -
149.153.100.65 -> 149.153.100.10 (id: 44747, ttl: 64)

UDP Source: 1042 -> UDP Destination: 161
UDP Length: 56, UDP Checksum: 33028
UDP Data:

0.^B^A^A^D^Fpublic¥!^B^AZ^B^A^@^B^A
0^V0^T^F^P+^F^A^B^A^D^U^A^Eo^Uo^Yo^@^@^E^@
- - - - - - - - - - - - - - - - - - - - - - - - - - - - - - - - - - - - -
149.153.100.10 -> 149.153.100.65 (id: 61016, ttl: 255)

UDP Source: 161 -> UDP Destination: 1042
UDP Length: 268, UDP Checksum: 41860
UDP Data:

Oo^A^@^B^A^A^D^Fpublic¢oò^B^AZ^B^A^@^B^A^@Ooæ0^U^F^P+^F^A^B^A^D^U^A
^Eo^Uo^YoF^@^B^Aÿ0^U^F^P+^F^A^B^A^D^U^A^Eo^Uo^YoH^@^B^Aÿ0^U^F^P+^F^
A^B^A^D^U^A^Eo^Uo^YoI^@^B^Aÿ0^U^F^P+^F^A^B^A^D^U^A^Eo^Uo^YoI^B^B^Aÿ
0^U^F^P+^F^A^B^A^D^U^A^Eo^Uo^YoL^@^B^Aÿ0^U^F^P+^F^A^B^A^D^U^A^Eo^Uo
^YoM^@^B^Aÿ0^U^F^P+^F^A^B^A^D^U^A^Eo^Uo^YoM^B^B^Aÿ0^U^F^P+^F^A^B^A^
D^U^A^Eo^Uo^YoT^@^B^Aÿ0^U^F^P+^F^A^B^A^D^U^A^Eo^Uo^YoX^@^B^Aÿ0^U^F^
P+^F^A^B^A^D^U^A^Eo^Uo^Yo)^@^B^Aÿ
- - - - - - - - - - - - - - - - - - - - - - - - - - - - - - - - - - - - -
149.153.100.65 -> 149.153.100.10 (id: 44748, ttl: 64)

UDP Source: 1042 -> UDP Destination: 161
UDP Length: 56, UDP Checksum: 1027
UDP Data:

0.^B^A^A^D^Fpublic¥!^B^A[^B^A^@^B^A
0^V0^T^F^P+^F^A^B^A^D^U^A^Eo^Uo^Yo)^@^E^@
- - - - - - - - - - - - - - - - - - - - - - - - - - - - - - - - - - - - -
149.153.100.10 -> 149.153.100.65 (id: 61017, ttl: 255)

UDP Source: 161 -> UDP Destination: 1042
UDP Length: 253, UDP Checksum: 57106
UDP Data:

Ooò^B^A^A^D^Fpublic¢oä^B^A[^B^A^@^B^A^@OoØ0^R^F+^F^A^B^A^D^U^A^F^@^@
^@^@^B^Aÿ0^R^F+^F^A^B^A^D^U^A^F^¿^@^@^@^B^Aÿ0^T^F^O+^F^A^B^A^D^U^A^F
o^Uo^Y^A^@^B^Aÿ0^T^F^O+^F^A^B^A^D^U^A^Fo^Uo^Y^B^@^B^Aÿ0^T^F^O+^F^A^B
^A^D^U^A^Fo^Uo^Y^C^@^B^Aÿ0^T^F^O+^F^A^B^A^D^U^A^Fo^Uo^Y^F^@^B^Aÿ0^T^
F^O+^F^A^B^A^D^U^A^Fo^Uo^Y^I^@^B^Aÿ0^T^F^O+^F^A^B^A^D^U^A^Fo^Uo^Y^P^
@^B^Aÿ0^T^F^O+^F^A^B^A^D^U^A^Fo^Uo^Y2^@^B^Aÿ0^T^F^O+^F^A^B^A^D^U^A^F
o^Uo^Ya^@^B^Aÿ
- - - - - - - - - - - - - - - - - - - - - - - - - - - - - - - - - - - - -
149.153.100.65 -> 149.153.100.10 (id: 44749, ttl: 64)

UDP Source: 1042 -> UDP Destination: 161
UDP Length: 55, UDP Checksum: 34339
UDP Data:

0-^B^A^A^D^Fpublic¥ ^B^A\^B^A^@^B^A
0^U0^S^F^O+^F^A^B^A^D^U^A^Fo^Uo^Ya^@^E^@
- - - - - - - - - - - - - - - - - - - - - - - - - - - - - - - - - - - - -
149.153.100.10 -> 149.153.100.65 (id: 61018, ttl: 255)

UDP Source: 161 -> UDP Destination: 1042
UDP Length: 264, UDP Checksum: 23719
UDP Data:
```

```
Ooý^B^A^A^D^Fpublic¢oï^B^A\^B^A^@^B^A^@Ooã0^T^F^O+^F^A^B^A^D^U^A^Fo
^Uo^Yb^@^B^Aÿ0^T^F^O+^F^A^B^A^D^U^A^Fo^Uo^Yd^@^B^Aÿ0^T^F^O+^F^A^B^A
^D^U^A^Fo^Uo^Yg^@^B^Aÿ0^U^F^P+^F^A^B^A^D^U^A^Fo^Uo^Yo^@^@^B^Aÿ0^U^F
^P+^F^A^B^A^D^U^A^Fo^Uo^YoF^@^B^Aÿ0^U^F^P+^F^A^B^A^D^U^A^Fo^Uo^YoH^
@^B^Aÿ0^U^F^P+^F^A^B^A^D^U^A^Fo^Uo^YoI^@^B^Aÿ0^U^F^P+^F^A^B^A^D^U^A
^Fo^Uo^YoI^B^B^Aÿ0^U^F^P+^F^A^B^A^D^U^A^Fo^Uo^YoL^@^B^Aÿ0^U^F^P+^F^
A^B^A^D^U^A^Fo^Uo^YoM^@^B^Aÿ
- - - - - - - - - - - - - - - - - - - - - - - - - - - - - - - - - -
149.153.100.65 -> 149.153.100.10 (id: 44750, ttl: 64)

UDP Source: 1042 -> UDP Destination: 161
UDP Length: 56, UDP Checksum: 13057
UDP Data:

0.^B^A^A^D^Fpublic¥!^B^A]^B^A^@^B^A
0^V0^T^F^P+^F^A^B^A^D^U^A^Fo^Uo^YoM^@^E^@
- - - - - - - - - - - - - - - - - - - - - - - - - - - - - - - - - -
149.153.100.10 -> 149.153.100.65 (id: 61019, ttl: 255)

UDP Source: 161 -> UDP Destination: 1042
UDP Length: 276, UDP Checksum: 25888
UDP Data:

Oo^A^H^B^A^A^D^Fpublic¢oú^B^A]^B^A^@^B^A^@Ooî0^U^F^P+^F^A^B^A^D^U^A
^Fo^Uo^YoM^B^B^Aÿ0^U^F^P+^F^A^B^A^D^U^A^Fo^Uo^YoT^@^B^Aÿ0^U^F^P+^F^
A^B^A^D^U^A^Fo^Uo^YoX^@^B^Aÿ0^U^F^P+^F^A^B^A^D^U^A^Fo^Uo^Yo)^@^B^Aÿ
0^U^F+^F^A^B^A^D^U^A^G^@^@^@^@@^Doo^A^B0^U^F+^F^A^B^A^D^U^A^G^¿^@^@
^@@^D^¿^@^@^L0^W^F^O+^F^A^B^A^D^U^A^Go^Uo^Y^A^@@^Doo^Aÿ0^W^F^O+^F^A
^B^A^D^U^A^Go^Uo^Y^B^@@^Doo^Bý0^W^F^O+^F^A^B^A^D^U^A^Go^Uo^Y^C^@@^D
oo^Cý0^W^F^O+^F^A^B^A^D^U^A^Go^Uo^Y^F^@@^Doo^Fý
- - - - - - - - - - - - - - - - - - - - - - - - - - - - - - - - - -
149.153.100.65 -> 149.153.100.10 (id: 44751, ttl: 64)

UDP Source: 1042 -> UDP Destination: 161
UDP Length: 55, UDP Checksum: 34172
UDP Data:

0.^B^A^A^D^Fpublic¥!^B^A]^B^A^@^B^A
0^U0^S^F^O+^F^A^B^A^D^U^A^Go^Uo^Y^F^@^E^@
- - - - - - - - - - - - - - - - - - - - - - - - - - - - - - - - - -
149.153.100.10 -> 149.153.100.65 (id: 61020, ttl: 255)

UDP Source: 161 -> UDP Destination: 1042
UDP Length: 292, UDP Checksum: 11313
UDP Data:

^A^Go^Uo^Y^I^@@^Doo^Iý0^W^F^O+^F^A^B^A^D^U^A^Go^Uo^Y^P^@@^Doo^_ý0^W^
F^O+^F^A^B^A^D^U^A^Go^Uo^Y2^@@^Doo2ý0^W^F^O+^F^A^B^A^D^U^A^Go^Uo^Ya^
@@^Doodý0^W^F^O+^F^A^B^A^D^U^A^Go^Uo^Yb^@@^Dood^L0^W^F^O+^F^A^B^A^D^
U^A^Go^Uo^Yd^@@^Doodý0^W^F^O+^F^A^B^A^D^U^A^Go^Uo^Yg^@@^Doogý0^X^F^P
+^F^A^B^A^D^U^A^Go^Uo^Yo^@^@@^Doodý0^X^F^P+^F^A^B^A^D^U^A^Go^Uo^YoF^
@@^Doo^Bd0^X^F^P+^F^A^B^A^D^U^A^Go^Uo^YoH^@@^Doo^Bd
- - - - - - - - - - - - - - - - - - - - - - - - - - - - - - - - - -
149.153.100.65 -> 149.153.100.10 (id: 44752, ttl: 64)

UDP Source: 1042 -> UDP Destination: 161
UDP Length: 56, UDP Checksum: 14079
UDP Data:

0.^B^A^A^D^Fpublic¥!^B^A_^B^A^@^B^A
0^V0^T^F^P+^F^A^B^A^D^U^A^Go^Uo^YoH^@^E^@
- - - - - - - - - - - - - - - - - - - - - - - - - - - - - - - - - -
149.153.100.10 -> 149.153.100.65 (id: 61021, ttl: 255)

UDP Source: 161 -> UDP Destination: 1042
UDP Length: 287, UDP Checksum: 11891
UDP Data:
```

```
OoˆAˆSˆBˆAˆAˆDˆFpublic¢oˆAˆDˆBˆA_ˆBˆAˆ@ˆBˆAˆ@Ooø0ˆXˆFˆP+ˆFˆAˆBˆAˆD
ˆUˆAˆGoˆUoˆYoIˆ@@ˆDooˆBd0ˆXˆFˆP+ˆFˆAˆBˆAˆDˆUˆAˆGoˆUoˆYoIˆB@ˆDooˆBd
0ˆXˆFˆP+ˆFˆAˆBˆAˆDˆUˆAˆGoˆUoˆYoLˆ@@ˆDooˆBd0ˆXˆFˆP+ˆFˆAˆBˆAˆDˆUˆAˆG
oˆUoˆYoMˆ@@ˆDooˆBd0ˆXˆFˆP+ˆFˆAˆBˆAˆDˆUˆAˆGoˆUoˆYoMˆB@ˆDooˆBd0ˆXˆFˆ
P+ˆFˆAˆBˆAˆDˆUˆAˆGoˆUoˆYoTˆ@@ˆDooˆBˆV0ˆXˆFˆP+ˆFˆAˆBˆAˆDˆUˆAˆGoˆUoˆ
YoXˆ@@ˆDooØý0ˆXˆFˆP+ˆFˆAˆBˆAˆDˆUˆAˆGoˆUoˆYo)ˆ@@ˆDooýý0ˆRˆF+ˆFˆAˆBˆ
AˆDˆUˆAˆHˆ@ˆ@ˆ@ˆ@ˆBˆAˆD0ˆRˆF+ˆFˆAˆBˆAˆDˆUˆAˆHˆ¿ˆ@ˆ@ˆ@ˆBˆAˆC
- - - - - - - - - - - - - - - - - - - - - - - - - - - - - - - - - -
149.153.100.65 -> 149.153.100.10 (id: 44753, ttl: 64)

UDP Source: 1042 -> UDP Destination: 161
UDP Length: 53, UDP Checksum: 46351
UDP Data:

O.ˆBˆAˆAˆDˆFpublic¥!ˆBˆA_ˆBˆAˆ@ˆBˆA
0ˆS0ˆQˆF+ˆFˆAˆBˆAˆDˆUˆAˆHˆ¿ˆ@ˆ@ˆ@ˆEˆ@
- - - - - - - - - - - - - - - - - - - - - - - - - - - - - - - - - -
149.153.100.10 -> 149.153.100.65 (id: 61022, ttl: 255)

UDP Source: 161 -> UDP Destination: 1042
UDP Length: 257, UDP Checksum: 22173
UDP Data:

OoöˆBˆAˆAˆDˆFpublic¢oèˆBˆA'ˆBˆAˆ@ˆBˆAˆ@OoÜ0ˆTˆFˆO+ˆFˆAˆBˆAˆDˆUˆAˆHo
ˆUoˆYˆAˆ@ˆBˆAˆC0ˆTˆFˆO+ˆFˆAˆBˆAˆDˆUˆAˆHoˆUoˆYˆBˆ@ˆBˆAˆC0ˆTˆFˆO+ˆFˆA
ˆBˆAˆDˆUˆAˆHoˆUoˆYˆCˆ@ˆBˆAˆC0ˆTˆFˆO+ˆFˆAˆBˆAˆDˆUˆAˆHoˆUoˆYˆFˆ@ˆBˆAˆ
C0ˆTˆFˆO+ˆFˆAˆBˆAˆDˆUˆAˆHoˆUoˆYˆIˆ@ˆBˆAˆC0ˆTˆFˆO+ˆFˆAˆBˆAˆDˆUˆAˆHoˆ
UoˆYˆPˆ@ˆBˆAˆC0ˆTˆFˆO+ˆFˆAˆBˆAˆDˆUˆAˆHoˆUoˆY2ˆ@ˆBˆAˆC0ˆTˆFˆO+ˆFˆAˆB
ˆAˆDˆUˆAˆHoˆUoˆYaˆ@ˆBˆAˆC0ˆTˆFˆO+ˆFˆAˆBˆAˆDˆUˆAˆHoˆUoˆYbˆ@ˆBˆAˆD0ˆT
ˆFˆO+ˆFˆAˆBˆAˆDˆUˆAˆHoˆUoˆYdˆ@ˆBˆAˆC
- - - - - - - - - - - - - - - - - - - - - - - - - - - - - - - - - -
149.153.100.65 -> 149.153.100.10 (id: 44754, ttl: 64)

UDP Source: 1042 -> UDP Destination: 161
UDP Length: 55, UDP Checksum: 33819
UDP Data:

O-ˆBˆAˆAˆDˆFpublic¥ ˆBˆAaˆBˆAˆ@ˆBˆA
0ˆU0ˆSˆFˆO+ˆFˆAˆBˆAˆDˆUˆAˆHoˆUoˆYdˆ@ˆEˆ@
- - - - - - - - - - - - - - - - - - - - - - - - - - - - - - - - - -
149.153.100.10 -> 149.153.100.65 (id: 61023, ttl: 255)

UDP Source: 161 -> UDP Destination: 1042
UDP Length: 266, UDP Checksum: 46369
UDP Data:

OooÿˆBˆAˆAˆDˆFpublic¢oñˆBˆAaˆBˆAˆ@ˆBˆAˆ@Ooå0ˆTˆFˆO+ˆFˆAˆBˆAˆDˆUˆAˆHo
ˆUoˆYgˆ@ˆBˆAˆC0ˆUˆFˆP+ˆFˆAˆBˆAˆDˆUˆAˆHoˆUoˆYoˆ@ˆ@ˆBˆAˆC0ˆUˆFˆP+ˆFˆA
ˆBˆAˆDˆUˆAˆHoˆUoˆYoFˆ@ˆBˆAˆD0ˆUˆFˆP+ˆFˆAˆBˆAˆDˆUˆAˆHoˆUoˆYoHˆ@ˆBˆAˆ
D0ˆUˆFˆP+ˆFˆAˆBˆAˆDˆUˆAˆHoˆUoˆYoIˆ@ˆBˆAˆD0ˆUˆFˆP+ˆFˆAˆBˆAˆDˆUˆAˆHoˆ
UoˆYoIˆBˆBˆAˆD0ˆUˆFˆP+ˆFˆAˆBˆAˆDˆUˆAˆHoˆUoˆYoLˆ@ˆBˆAˆD0ˆUˆFˆP+ˆFˆA
BˆAˆDˆUˆAˆHoˆUoˆYoMˆ@ˆBˆAˆD0ˆUˆFˆP+ˆFˆAˆBˆAˆDˆUˆAˆHoˆUoˆYoMˆBˆBˆAˆD
0ˆUˆFˆP+ˆFˆAˆBˆAˆDˆUˆAˆHoˆUoˆYoTˆ@ˆBˆAˆD
- - - - - - - - - - - - - - - - - - - - - - - - - - - - - - - - - -
149.153.100.65 -> 149.153.100.10 (id: 44755, ttl: 64)

UDP Source: 1042 -> UDP Destination: 161
UDP Length: 56, UDP Checksum: 10748
UDP Data:

O.ˆBˆAˆAˆDˆFpublic¥!ˆBˆAbˆBˆAˆ@ˆBˆA
0ˆV0ˆTˆFˆP+ˆFˆAˆBˆAˆDˆUˆAˆHoˆUoˆYoTˆ@ˆEˆ@
- - - - - - - - - - - - - - - - - - - - - - - - - - - - - - - - - -
149.153.100.10 -> 149.153.100.65 (id: 61024, ttl: 255)

UDP Source: 161 -> UDP Destination: 1042
UDP Length: 255, UDP Checksum: 53906
UDP Data:
```

```
Ooô^B^A^A^D^Fpublic¢oæ^B^Ab^B^A^@^B^A^@OoÚO^U^F^P+^F^A^B^A^D^U^A^Ho
^Uo^YoX^@^B^A^CO^U^F^P+^F^A^B^A^D^U^A^Ho^Uo^Yo)^@^B^A^CO^R^F+^F^A^B
^A^D^U^A^I^@^@^@^@^B^A^BO^R^F+^F^A^B^A^D^U^A^I^¿^@^@^@^B^A^BO^T^F^O
+^F^A^B^A^D^U^A^Io^Uo^Y^A^@^B^A^BO^T^F^O+^F^A^B^A^D^U^A^Io^Uo^Y^B^@
^B^A^BO^T^F^O+^F^A^B^A^D^U^A^Io^Uo^Y^C^@^B^A^BO^T^F^O+^F^A^B^A^D^U^
A^Io^Uo^Y^F^@^B^A^BO^T^F^O+^F^A^B^A^D^U^A^Io^Uo^Y^I^@^B^A^BO^T^F^O+
^F^A^B^A^D^U^A^Io^Uo^Y^P^@^B^A^B
- - - - - - - - - - - - - - - - - - - - - - - - - - - - - - - - - -
149.153.100.65 -> 149.153.100.10 (id: 44756, ttl: 64)

UDP Source: 1042 -> UDP Destination: 161
UDP Length: 55, UDP Checksum: 33645
UDP Data:

O-^B^A^A^D^Fpublic¥ ^B^Ac^B^A^@^B^A
O^UO^S^F^O+^F^A^B^A^D^U^A^Io^Uo^Y^P^@^E^@
- - - - - - - - - - - - - - - - - - - - - - - - - - - - - - - - - -
149.153.100.10 -> 149.153.100.65 (id: 61025, ttl: 255)

UDP Source: 161 -> UDP Destination: 1042
UDP Length: 262, UDP Checksum: 63186
UDP Data:

Ooû^B^A^A^D^Fpublic¢oî^B^Ac^B^A^@^B^A^@OoáO^T^F^O+^F^A^B^A^D^U^A^Io
^Uo^Y2^@^B^A^BO^T^F^O+^F^A^B^A^D^U^A^Io^Uo^Ya^@^B^A^BO^T^F^O+^F^A^B
^A^D^U^A^Io^Uo^Yb^@^B^A^BO^T^F^O+^F^A^B^A^D^U^A^Io^Uo^Yd^@^B^A^BO^T
^F^O+^F^A^B^A^D^U^A^Io^Uo^Yg^@^B^A^BO^U^F^P+^F^A^B^A^D^U^A^Io^Uo^Yo
^@^@^B^A^BO^U^F^P+^F^A^B^A^D^U^A^Io^Uo^YoF^@^B^A^HO^U^F^P+^F^A^B^A^
D^U^A^Io^Uo^YoH^@^B^A^HO^U^F^P+^F^A^B^A^D^U^A^Io^Uo^YoI^@^B^A^HO^U^
F^P+^F^A^B^A^D^U^A^Io^Uo^YoI^B^B^A^H
- - - - - - - - - - - - - - - - - - - - - - - - - - - - - - - - - -
149.153.100.65 -> 149.153.100.10 (id: 44757, ttl: 64)

UDP Source: 1042 -> UDP Destination: 161
UDP Length: 56, UDP Checksum: 13304
UDP Data:

O.^B^A^A^D^Fpublic¥!^B^Ad^B^A^@^B^A
O^VO^T^F^P+^F^A^B^A^D^U^A^Io^Uo^YoI^B^E^@
- - - - - - - - - - - - - - - - - - - - - - - - - - - - - - - - - -
149.153.100.10 -> 149.153.100.65 (id: 61026, ttl: 255)

UDP Source: 161 -> UDP Destination: 1042
UDP Length: 259, UDP Checksum: 16845
UDP Data:

Ooø^B^A^A^D^Fpublic¢oê^B^Ad^B^A^@^B^A^@OoÞO^U^F^P+^F^A^B^A^D^U^A^Io
^Uo^YoL^@^B^A^HO^U^F^P+^F^A^B^A^D^U^A^Io^Uo^YoM^@^B^A^HO^U^F^P+^F^A
^B^A^D^U^A^Io^Uo^YoM^B^B^A^HO^U^F^P+^F^A^B^A^D^U^A^Io^Uo^YoT^@^B^A^
HO^U^F^P+^F^A^B^A^D^U^A^Io^Uo^YoX^@^B^A^BO^U^F^P+^F^A^B^A^D^U^A^Io^
Uo^Yo)^@^B^A^BO^R^F+^F^A^B^A^D^U^A
^@^@^@^@^B^A^CO^R^F+^F^A^B^A^D^U^A
^¿^@^@^@^B^A^@O^T^F^O+^F^A^B^A^D^U^A
o^Uo^Y^A^@^B^A^@O^T^F^O+^F^A^B^A^D^U^A
o^Uo^Y^B^@^B^A^@
- - - - - - - - - - - - - - - - - - - - - - - - - - - - - - - - - -
149.153.100.65 -> 149.153.100.10 (id: 44758, ttl: 64)

UDP Source: 1042 -> UDP Destination: 161
UDP Length: 55, UDP Checksum: 33401
UDP Data:

O-^B^A^A^D^Fpublic¥ ^B^Ae^B^A^@^B^A
O^UO^S^F^O+^F^A^B^A^D^U^A
o^Uo^Y^B^@^E^@
- - - - - - - - - - - - - - - - - - - - - - - - - - - - - - - - - -
149.153.100.10 -> 149.153.100.65 (id: 61027, ttl: 255)
```

```
UDP Source: 161 -> UDP Destination: 1042
UDP Length: 258, UDP Checksum: 35200
UDP Data:

Oo÷ˆBˆAˆAˆDˆFpublic¢oéˆBˆAeˆBˆAˆ@ˆBˆAˆ@OoÝ0ˆTˆFˆO+ˆFˆAˆBˆAˆDˆUˆA
oˆUoˆYˆCˆ@ˆBˆAˆ@0ˆTˆFˆO+ˆFˆAˆBˆAˆDˆUˆA
oˆUoˆYˆFˆ@ˆBˆAˆ@0ˆTˆFˆO+ˆFˆAˆBˆAˆDˆUˆA
oˆUoˆYˆIˆ@ˆBˆAˆ@0ˆTˆFˆO+ˆFˆAˆBˆAˆDˆUˆA
oˆUoˆYˆPˆ@ˆBˆAˆ@0ˆTˆFˆO+ˆFˆAˆBˆAˆDˆUˆA
oˆUoˆY2ˆ@ˆBˆAˆ@0ˆTˆFˆO+ˆFˆAˆBˆAˆDˆUˆA
oˆUoˆYaˆ@ˆBˆAˆ@0ˆTˆFˆO+ˆFˆAˆBˆAˆDˆUˆA
oˆUoˆYbˆ@ˆBˆAˆC0ˆTˆFˆO+ˆFˆAˆBˆAˆDˆUˆA
oˆUoˆYdˆ@ˆBˆAˆ@0ˆTˆFˆO+ˆFˆAˆBˆAˆDˆUˆA
oˆUoˆYgˆ@ˆBˆAˆ@0ˆUˆFˆP+ˆFˆAˆBˆAˆDˆUˆA
oˆUoˆYoˆ@ˆBˆAˆ@
- - - - - - - - - - - - - - - - - - - - - - - - - - - - - -
149.153.100.65 -> 149.153.100.10 (id: 44759, ttl: 64)

UDP Source: 1042 -> UDP Destination: 161
UDP Length: 56, UDP Checksum: 31736
UDP Data:

0.ˆBˆAˆAˆDˆFpublic¥!ˆBˆAfˆBˆAˆ@ˆBˆA
0ˆV0ˆTˆFˆP+ˆFˆAˆBˆAˆDˆUˆA
oˆUoˆYoˆ@ˆ@ˆEˆ@
- - - - - - - - - - - - - - - - - - - - - - - - - - - - - -
149.153.100.10 -> 149.153.100.65 (id: 61028, ttl: 255)

UDP Source: 161 -> UDP Destination: 1042
UDP Length: 268, UDP Checksum: 28244
UDP Data:

OoˆAˆ@ˆBˆAˆAˆDˆFpublic¢oòˆBˆAfˆBˆAˆ@ˆBˆAˆ@Ooæ0ˆUˆFˆP+ˆFˆAˆBˆAˆDˆUˆA
oˆUoˆYoFˆ@ˆBˆAˆD0ˆUˆFˆP+ˆFˆAˆBˆAˆDˆUˆA
oˆUoˆYoHˆ@ˆBˆAˆD0ˆUˆFˆP+ˆFˆAˆBˆAˆDˆUˆA
oˆUoˆYoIˆ@ˆBˆAˆD0ˆUˆFˆP+ˆFˆAˆBˆAˆDˆUˆA
oˆUoˆYoIˆBˆBˆAˆD0ˆUˆFˆP+ˆFˆAˆBˆAˆDˆUˆA
oˆUoˆYoLˆ@ˆBˆAˆD0ˆUˆFˆP+ˆFˆAˆBˆAˆDˆUˆA
oˆUoˆYoMˆ@ˆBˆAˆD0ˆUˆFˆP+ˆFˆAˆBˆAˆDˆUˆA
oˆUoˆYoMˆBˆBˆAˆD0ˆUˆFˆP+ˆFˆAˆBˆAˆDˆUˆA
oˆUoˆYoTˆ@ˆBˆAˆK0ˆUˆFˆP+ˆFˆAˆBˆAˆDˆUˆA
oˆUoˆYoXˆ@ˆBˆAˆ@0ˆUˆFˆP+ˆFˆAˆBˆAˆDˆUˆA
oˆUoˆYo)ˆ@ˆBˆAˆ@
- - - - - - - - - - - - - - - - - - - - - - - - - - - - - -
149.153.100.65 -> 149.153.100.10 (id: 44760, ttl: 64)

UDP Source: 1042 -> UDP Destination: 161
UDP Length: 56, UDP Checksum: 65270
UDP Data:

0.ˆBˆAˆAˆDˆFpublic¥!ˆBˆAgˆBˆAˆ@ˆBˆA
0ˆV0ˆTˆFˆP+ˆFˆAˆBˆAˆDˆUˆA
oˆUoˆYo)ˆ@ˆEˆ@
- - - - - - - - - - - - - - - - - - - - - - - - - - - - - -
149.153.100.10 -> 149.153.100.65 (id: 61029, ttl: 255)

UDP Source: 161 -> UDP Destination: 1042
UDP Length: 285, UDP Checksum: 60812
UDP Data:

OoˆAˆQˆBˆAˆAˆDˆFpublic¢oˆAˆBˆBˆAgˆBˆAˆ@ˆBˆAˆ@Ooö0ˆUˆF+ˆFˆAˆBˆAˆDˆUˆ
AˆKˆ@ˆ@ˆ@ˆ@@ˆDˆ@ˆ@ˆ@ˆ@0ˆUˆF+ˆFˆAˆBˆAˆDˆUˆAˆKˆ¿ˆ@ˆ@ˆ@@ˆDÿˆ@ˆ@ˆ@0ˆWˆF
ˆO+ˆFˆAˆBˆAˆDˆUˆAˆKoˆUoˆYˆAˆ@@ˆDÿÿÿˆ@0ˆWˆFˆO+ˆFˆAˆBˆAˆDˆUˆAˆKoˆUoˆY
ˆBˆ@@ˆDÿÿÿˆ@0ˆWˆFˆO+ˆFˆAˆBˆAˆDˆUˆAˆKoˆUoˆYˆCˆ@@ˆDÿÿÿˆ@0ˆWˆFˆO+ˆFˆAˆ
BˆAˆDˆUˆAˆKoˆUoˆYˆFˆ@@ˆDÿÿÿˆ@0ˆWˆFˆO+ˆFˆAˆBˆAˆDˆUˆAˆKoˆUoˆYˆIˆ@@ˆDÿ
ÿÿˆ@0ˆWˆFˆO+ˆFˆAˆBˆAˆDˆUˆAˆKoˆUoˆYˆPˆ@@ˆDÿÿÿðˆ@0ˆWˆFˆO+ˆFˆAˆBˆAˆDˆUˆ
AˆKoˆUoˆY2ˆ@@ˆDÿÿÿˆ@0ˆWˆFˆO+ˆFˆAˆBˆAˆDˆUˆAˆKoˆUoˆYaˆ@@ˆDÿÿÿˆ@
- - - - - - - - - - - - - - - - - - - - - - - - - - - - - -
149.153.100.65 -> 149.153.100.10 (id: 44761, ttl: 64)
```

UDP Source: 1042 -> UDP Destination: 161
UDP Length: 55, UDP Checksum: 33047
UDP Data:

0-^B^A^A^D^Fpublic¥ ^B^Ah^B^A^@^B^A
0^U0^S^F^O+^F^A^B^A^D^U^A^Ko^Uo^Ya^@^E^@
- -
149.153.100.10 -> 149.153.100.65 (id: 61030, ttl: 255)

UDP Source: 161 -> UDP Destination: 1042
UDP Length: 297, UDP Checksum: 16981
UDP Data:

Oo^A^]^B^A^A^D^Fpublic¢o^A^N^B^Ah^B^A^@^B^A^@Oo^A^A0^W^F^O+^F^A^B^A
^D^U^A^Ko^Uo^Yb^@@^Dÿÿÿ^@0^W^F^O+^F^A^B^A^D^U^A^Ko^Uo^Yd^@@^Dÿÿÿ^@0
^W^F^O+^F^A^B^A^D^U^A^Ko^Uo^Yg^@@^Dÿÿÿ^@0^X^F^P+^F^A^B^A^D^U^A^Ko^U
o^Yo^@^@@^Dÿÿä^@0^X^F^P+^F^A^B^A^D^U^A^Ko^Uo^YoF^@@^Dÿÿÿ^@0^X^F^P+^
F^A^B^A^D^U^A^Ko^Uo^YoH^@@^Dÿÿÿ^@0^X^F^P+^F^A^B^A^D^U^A^Ko^Uo^YoI^@
@^Dÿÿÿ^@0^X^F^P+^F^A^B^A^D^U^A^Ko^Uo^YoI B@^Dÿÿÿÿ0^X^F^P+^F^A^B^A^D
^U^A^Ko^Uo^YoL^@@^Dÿÿÿ^@0^X^F^P+^F^A^B^A^D^U^A^Ko^Uo^YoM^@@^Dÿÿÿ^@·
- -
149.153.100.65 -> 149.153.100.10 (id: 44762, ttl: 64)

UDP Source: 1042 -> UDP Destination: 161
UDP Length: 56, UDP Checksum: 11765
UDP Data:

0.^B^A^A^D^Fpublic¥!^B^Ai^B^A^@^B^A
0^V0^T^F^P+^F^A^B^A^D^U^A^Ko^Uo^YoM^@^E^@
- -
149.153.100.10 -> 149.153.100.65 (id: 61031, ttl: 255)

UDP Source: 161 -> UDP Destination: 1042
UDP Length: 270, UDP Checksum: 62328
UDP Data:

Oo^A^B^B^A^A^D^Fpublic¢oô^B^Ai^B^A^@^B^A^@Ooè0^X^F^P+^F^A^B^A^D^U^A
^Ko^Uo^YoM^B@^Dÿÿÿÿ0^X^F^P+^F^A^B^A^D^U^A^Ko^Uo^YoT^@@^Dÿÿÿ^@0^X^F^
P+^F^A^B^A^D^U^A^Ko^Uo^YoX^@@^Dÿÿÿ^@0^X^F^P+^F^A^B^A^D^U^A^Ko^Uo^Yo
)^@@^Dÿÿÿ^@0^R^F+^F^A^B^A^D^U^A^L^@^@^@^@^B^Aÿ0^R^F+^F^A^B^A^D^U^A^
L^¿^@^@^@^B^Aÿ0^T^F^O+^F^A^B^A^D^U^A^Lo^Uo^Y^A^@^B^Aÿ0^T^F^O+^F^A^B
^A^D^U^A^Lo^Uo^Y^B^@^B^Aÿ0^T^F^O+^F^A^B^A^D^U^A^Lo^Uo^Y^C^@^B^Aÿ0^T
^F^O+^F^A^B^A^D^U^A^Lo^Uo^Y^F^@^B^Aÿ
- -
149.153.100.65 -> 149.153.100.10 (id: 44763, ttl: 64)

UDP Source: 1042 -> UDP Destination: 161
UDP Length: 55, UDP Checksum: 32880
UDP Data:

0-^B^A^A^D^Fpublic¥ ^B^Aj^B^A^@^B^A
0^U0^S^F^O+^F^A^B^A^D^U^A^Lo^Uo^Y^F^@^E^@
- -
149.153.100.10 -> 149.153.100.65 (id: 61032, ttl: 255)

UDP Source: 161 -> UDP Destination: 1042
UDP Length: 260, UDP Checksum: 19473
UDP Data:

Ooù^B^A^A^D^Fpublic¢oë^B^Aj^B^A^@^B^A^@Ooß0^T^F^O+^F^A^B^A^D^U^A^Lo
^Uo^Y^I^@^B^Aÿ0^T^F^O+^F^A^B^A^D^U^A^Lo^Uo^Y^P^@^B^Aÿ0^T^F^O+^F^A^B
^A^D^U^A^Lo^Uo^Y2^@^B^Aÿ0^T^F^O+^F^A^B^A^D^U^A^Lo^Uo^Ya^@^B^Aÿ0^T^F
^O+^F^A^B^A^D^U^A^Lo^Uo^Yb^@^B^Aÿ0^T^F^O+^F^A^B^A^D^U^A^Lo^Uo^Yd^@^
B^Aÿ0^T^F^O+^F^A^B^A^D^U^A^Lo^Uo^Yg^@^B^Aÿ0^U^F^P+^F^A^B^A^D^U^A^Lo
^Uo^Yo^@^@^B^Aÿ0^U^F^P+^F^A^B^A^D^U^A^Lo^Uo^YoF^@^B^Aÿ0^U^F^P+^F^A^
B^A^D^U^A^Lo^Uo^YoH^@^B^Aÿ
- -
149.153.100.65 -> 149.153.100.10 (id: 44764, ttl: 64)

```
UDP Source: 1042 -> UDP Destination: 161
UDP Length: 56, UDP Checksum: 12787
UDP Data:

0.ˆBˆAˆAˆDˆFpublic¥!ˆBˆAkˆBˆAˆ@ˆBˆA
0ˆV0ˆTˆFˆP+ˆFˆAˆBˆAˆDˆUˆAˆLoˆUoˆYoHˆ@ˆEˆ@
```
- -
```
149.153.100.10 -> 149.153.100.65 (id: 61033, ttl: 255)

UDP Source: 161 -> UDP Destination: 1042
UDP Length: 261, UDP Checksum: 63089
UDP Data:

OoúˆBˆAˆAˆDˆFpublic¢oìˆBˆAkˆBˆAˆ@ˆBˆAˆ@0oà0ˆUˆFˆP+ˆFˆAˆBˆAˆDˆUˆAˆLoi
ˆUoˆYoIˆ@ˆBˆAÿ0ˆUˆFˆP+ˆFˆAˆBˆAˆDˆUˆAˆLoˆUoˆYoIˆBˆBˆAÿ0ˆUˆFˆP+ˆFˆAˆBˆ
AˆDˆUˆAˆLoˆUoˆYoLˆ@ˆBˆAÿ0ˆUˆFˆP+ˆFˆAˆBˆAˆDˆUˆAˆLoˆUoˆYoMˆ@ˆBˆAÿ0ˆUˆF
ˆP+ˆFˆAˆBˆAˆDˆUˆAˆLoˆUoˆYoMˆBˆBˆAÿ0ˆUˆFˆP+ˆFˆAˆBˆAˆDˆUˆAˆLoˆUoˆYoTˆ@
ˆBˆAÿ0ˆUˆFˆP+ˆFˆAˆBˆAˆDˆUˆAˆLoˆUoˆYoXˆ@ˆBˆAÿ0ˆUˆFˆP+ˆFˆAˆBˆAˆDˆUˆAˆL
oˆUoˆYo)ˆ@ˆBˆAÿ0ˆUˆRˆF+ˆFˆAˆBˆAˆDˆUˆAˆ@ˆ@ˆ@ˆ@ˆFˆAˆ@0ˆRˆF+ˆFˆAˆBˆAˆDˆUˆ
Aˆ¿ˆ@ˆ@ˆ@ˆFˆAˆ@
```
- -
```
149.153.100.65 -> 149.153.100.10 (id: 44765, ttl: 64)

UDP Source: 1042 -> UDP Destination: 161
UDP Length: 53, UDP Checksum: 45059
UDP Data:

0.ˆBˆAˆAˆDˆFpublic¥!ˆBˆAkˆBˆAˆ@ˆBˆA
0ˆS0ˆQˆF+ˆFˆAˆBˆAˆDˆUˆAˆ¿ˆ@ˆ@ˆ@ˆEˆ@
```
- -
```
149.153.100.10 -> 149.153.100.65 (id: 61034, ttl: 255)

UDP Source: 161 -> UDP Destination: 1042
UDP Length: 257, UDP Checksum: 19807
UDP Data:

OoöˆBˆAˆAˆDˆFpublic¢oèˆBˆAlˆBˆAˆ@ˆBˆAˆ@0oÜ0ˆTˆFˆO+ˆFˆAˆBˆAˆDˆUˆAoˆU
oˆYˆAˆ@ˆFˆAˆ@0ˆTˆFˆO+ˆFˆAˆBˆAˆDˆUˆAoˆUoˆYˆBˆ@ˆFˆAˆ@0ˆTˆFˆO+ˆFˆAˆBˆA
ˆDˆUˆAoˆUoˆYˆCˆ@ˆFˆAˆ@0ˆTˆFˆO+ˆFˆAˆBˆAˆDˆUˆAoˆUoˆYˆFˆ@ˆFˆAˆ@0ˆTˆFˆO
+ˆFˆAˆBˆAˆDˆUˆAoˆUoˆYˆIˆ@ˆFˆAˆ@0ˆTˆFˆO+ˆFˆAˆBˆAˆDˆUˆAoˆUoˆYˆPˆ@ˆFˆA
ˆ@0ˆTˆFˆO+ˆFˆAˆBˆAˆDˆUˆAoˆUoˆY2ˆ@ˆFˆAˆ@0ˆTˆFˆO+ˆFˆAˆBˆAˆDˆUˆAoˆUoˆY
aˆ@ˆFˆAˆ@0ˆTˆFˆO+ˆFˆAˆBˆAˆDˆUˆAoˆUoˆYbˆ@ˆFˆAˆ@0ˆTˆFˆO+ˆFˆAˆBˆAˆDˆUˆ
AoˆUoˆYdˆ@ˆFˆAˆ@
```
- -
```
149.153.100.65 -> 149.153.100.10 (id: 44766, ttl: 64)

UDP Source: 1042 -> UDP Destination: 161
UDP Length: 55, UDP Checksum: 32527
UDP Data:

0-ˆBˆAˆAˆDˆFpublic¥ ˆBˆAmˆBˆAˆ@ˆBˆA
0ˆU0ˆSˆFˆO+ˆFˆAˆBˆAˆDˆUˆAoˆUoˆYdˆ@ˆEˆ@
```
- -
```
149.153.100.10 -> 149.153.100.65 (id: 61035, ttl: 255)

UDP Source: 161 -> UDP Destination: 1042
UDP Length: 266, UDP Checksum: 40950
UDP Data:

OoÿˆBˆAˆAˆDˆFpublic¢oñˆBˆAmˆBˆAˆ@ˆBˆAˆ@0oà0ˆTˆFˆO+ˆFˆAˆBˆAˆDˆUˆAoˆUo
ˆYgˆ@ˆFˆAˆ@0ˆUˆFˆP+ˆFˆAˆBˆAˆDˆUˆAoˆUoˆYoˆ@ˆ@ˆFˆAˆ@0ˆUˆFˆP+ˆFˆAˆBˆAˆD
ˆUˆAoˆUoˆYoFˆ@ˆFˆAˆ@0ˆUˆFˆP+ˆFˆAˆBˆAˆDˆUˆAoˆUoˆYoHˆ@ˆFˆAˆ@0ˆUˆFˆP+ˆF
ˆAˆBˆAˆDˆUˆAoˆUoˆYoIˆ@ˆFˆAˆ@0ˆUˆFˆP+ˆFˆAˆBˆAˆDˆUˆAoˆUoˆYoIˆBˆFˆAˆ@0ˆ
UˆFˆP+ˆFˆAˆBˆAˆDˆUˆAoˆUoˆYoLˆ@ˆFˆAˆ@0ˆUˆFˆP+ˆFˆAˆBˆAˆDˆUˆAoˆUoˆYoMˆ@
ˆFˆAˆ@0ˆUˆFˆP+ˆFˆAˆBˆAˆDˆUˆAoˆUoˆYoMˆBˆFˆAˆ@0ˆUˆFˆP+ˆFˆAˆBˆAˆDˆUˆAoˆ
UoˆYoTˆ@ˆFˆAˆ@
```
- -
```
149.153.100.65 -> 149.153.100.10 (id: 44767, ttl: 64)
```

```
UDP Source: 1042 -> UDP Destination: 161
UDP Length: 56, UDP Checksum: 9456
UDP Data:

0.^B^A^A^D^Fpublic¥!^B^An^B^A^@^B^A
0^V0^T^F^P+^F^A^B^A^D^U^Ao^Uo^YoT^@^E^@
- - - - - - - - - - - - - - - - - - - - - - - - -
149.153.100.10 -> 149.153.100.65 (id: 61036, ttl: 255)

UDP Source: 161 -> UDP Destination: 1042
UDP Length: 261, UDP Checksum: 7176
UDP Data:

Ooú^B^A^A^D^Fpublic¢oì^B^An^B^A^@^B^A^@0oà0^U^F^P+^F^A^B^A^D^U^Ao^Uo
^YoX^@^F^A^@0^U^F^P+^F^A^B^A^D^U^Ao^Uo^Yo)^@^F^A^@0^S^F^N+^F^A^B^A^D
^V^A^A^A^¿^@^@^K^B^A^A0^S^F^N+^F^A^B^A^D^V^A^A^A^¿^@^@^L^B^A^A0^S^F^
N+^F^A^B^A^D^V^A^A^A^¿^@^@^U^B^A^A0^U^F^P+^F^A^B^A^D^V^A^A^Co^Uo^Y^B
^B^A^C0^U^F^P+^F^A^B^A^D^V^A^A^Co^Uo^Y^B^K^B^A^C0^U^F^P+^F^A^B^A^D^V
^A^A^Co^Uo^Y^B^L^B^A^C0^U^F^P+^F^A^B^A^D^V^A^A^Co^Uo^Y^B^B^A^C0^U^F^
P+^F^A^B^A^D^V^A^A^Co^Uo^Y^B^V^B^A^C
- - - - - - - - - - - - - - - - - - - - - - - - -
149.153.100.65 -> 149.153.1.5 (id: 44769, ttl: 64)

- - - - - - - - - - - - - - - - - - - - - - - - -
149.153.1.5 -> 149.153.100.65 (id: 0, ttl: 63)

- - - - - - - - - - - - - - - - - - - - - - - - -
68 datagrams/segments processed.

Fri Aug  3 15:57:31 2001 - netdebug END run.
```

Appendix E
The OIDs.pm
Module

The code which follows is the contents of the OIDs.pm module created in support of the SNMP programs developed during Chapter 5, *Management*:

```perl
package OIDs;

# Module for a large (but not complete) collection of MIB-II OID
# constants as defined in RFC 1156. (MIB-I), RFC 1213, RFC 1354
# and RFC 1907.

use 5.6.0;

require Exporter;

our @ISA        = qw( Exporter );

# Nothing exported by default.
our @EXPORT     = qw();

# Individual OID's exported by request.
our @EXPORT_OK  =

    qw(

        sysDescr sysObjectID sysUpTime sysContact sysName
        sysLocation sysServices

        sysORLastChange sysORTable

        ifNumber ifTable ifEntry ifIndex ifDescr ifType
        ifMtu ifSpeed ifPhysAddress ifAdminStatus ifOperStatus
        ifLastChange ifInOctets ifInUcastPkts ifInNUcastPkts
        ifInDiscards ifInErrors ifInUnknownProtos ifOutOctets
        ifOutUcastPkts ifOutNUcastPkts ifOutDiscards ifOutErrors
        ifOutQLen ifSpecific
```

```
            atTable atEntry atIfIndex atPhysAddress atNetAddress

            ipForwarding ipDefaultTTL ipInReceives ipInHdrErrors
            ipInAddrErrors ipForwDatagrams ipInUnknownProtos
            ipInDiscards ipInDelivers ipOutRequests ipOutOutDiscards
            ipOutNoRoutes ipReasmTimeOut ipReasmReqds ipReasmOKs
            ipReasmFails ipFragOKs ipFragFails ipFragCreates
            ipAddrTable ipRouteTable ipNetToMediaTable
            ipRoutingDiscards ipForward

            ipForward ipForwardNumber ipForwardTable ipForwardEntry

            ipRouteEntry ipRouteDest ipRouteIfIndex ipRouteMetric1
            ipRouteMetric2 ipRouteMetric3 ipRouteMetric4 ipRouteNextHop
            ipRouteType ipRouteProto ipRouteAge ipRouteMask
            ipRouteMetric5 ipRouteInfo

            icmpInMsgs icmpInErrors icmpInDestUnreachs icmpInTimeExcds
            icmpInParmProbs icmpInSrcQuenches icmpInRedirects
            icmpInEchos icmpInEchoReps icmpInTimestamps
            icmpInTimestampsReps icmpInAddrMasks icmpInAddrMaskReps
            icmpOutMsgs icmpOutErrors icmpOutDestUnreachs
            icmpOutTimeExcds icmpOutParmProbs icmpOutSrcQuenches
            icmpOutRedirects icmpOutEchos icmpOutEchoReps
            icmpOutTimestamps icmpOutTimestampReps
            icmpOutAddrMasks icmpOutAddrMaskReps

            tcpRtoAlgorithm tcpRtoMin tcpRtoMax tcpMaxConn
            tcpActiveOpens tcpPassiveOpens tcpAttemptFails
            tcpEstabResets tcpCurrEstab tcpInSegs tcpOutSegs
            tcpRetransSegs tcpConnTable tcpInErrs tcpOutRsts

            udpInDatagrams udpNoPorts udpInErrors udpOutDatagrams
            udpTable udpEntry udpLocalAddress udpLocalPort
        );

# Groups of OID's exported by request.
our %EXPORT_TAGS =
    (
        system => [ qw( sysDescr sysObjectID sysUpTime sysContact
            sysName sysLocation sysServices ) ],

        system2 => [ qw( sysDescr sysObjectID sysUpTime sysContact
            sysName sysLocation sysServices sysORLastChange
            sysORTable ) ],

        interfaces => [ qw( ifNumber ifTable ifEntry ifIndex ifDescr
            ifType ifMtu ifSpeed ifPhysAddress ifAdminStatus
            ifOperStatus ifLastChange ifInOctets ifInUcastPkts
            ifInNUcastPkts ifInDiscards ifInErrors ifInUnknownProtos
            ifOutOctets ifOutUcastPkts ifOutNUcastPkts
            ifOutDiscards ifOutErrors ifOutQLen ifSpecific ) ],

        at => [ qw ( atTable atEntry atIfIndex atPhysAddress
            atNetAddress ) ],
```

```
            ip => [ qw ( ipForwarding ipDefaultTTL ipInReceives
                 ipInHdrErrors ipInAddrErrors ipForwDatagrams
                 ipInUnknownProtos ipInDiscards ipInDelivers
                 ipOutRequests ipOutOutDiscards ipOutNoRoutes
                 ipReasmTimeOut ipReasmReqds ipReasmOKs ipReasmFails
                 ipFragOKs ipFragFails ipFragCreates ipAddrTable
                 ipRouteTable ipNetToMediaTable ipRoutingDiscards ) ],

            ipFwd => [ qw ( ipForward ipForwardNumber ipForwardTable
                 ipForwardEntry ) ],

            iproutetable => [ qw ( ipRouteEntry ipRouteDest
                 ipRouteIfIndex ipRouteMetric1 ipRouteMetric2
                 ipRouteMetric3 ipRouteMetric4 ipRouteNextHop
                 ipRouteType ipRouteProto ipRouteAge ipRouteMask
                 ipRouteMetric5 ipRouteInfo )],

            icmp => [ qw ( icmpInMsgs icmpInErrors icmpInDestUnreachs
                 icmpInTimeExcds icmpInParmProbs icmpInSrcQuenches
                 icmpInRedirects icmpInEchos icmpInEchoReps
                 icmpInTimestamps icmpInTimestampsReps icmpInAddrMasks
                 icmpInAddrMaskReps icmpOutMsgs icmpOutErrors
                 icmpOutDestUnreachs icmpOutTimeExcds icmpOutParmProbs
                 icmpOutSrcQuenches icmpOutRedirects icmpOutEchos
                 icmpOutEchoReps icmpOutTimestamps icmpOutTimestampReps
                 icmpOutAddrMasks icmpOutAddrMaskReps ) ],

            tcp => [ qw ( tcpRtoAlgorithm tcpRtoMin tcpRtoMax tcpMaxConn
                 tcpActiveOpens tcpPassiveOpens tcpAttemptFails
                 tcpEstabResets tcpCurrEstab tcpInSegs tcpOutSegs
                 tcpRetransSegs tcpConnTable tcpInErrs tcpOutRsts ) ],

            udp => [ qw ( udpInDatagrams udpNoPorts udpInErrors
                 udpOutDatagrams udpTable
                 udpEntry udpLocalAddress udpLocalPort ) ],
        );

our $VERSION       = 0.01;

# All TCP/IP OID's start with this string.
use constant MIB_II              => '1.3.6.1.2.1.';

# The 'system' group re: SNMPv1 and RFC 1213.
use constant sysDescr            => MIB_II . '1.1.0';
use constant sysObjectID         => MIB_II . '1.2.0';
use constant sysUpTime           => MIB_II . '1.3.0';
use constant sysContact          => MIB_II . '1.4.0';
use constant sysName             => MIB_II . '1.5.0';
use constant sysLocation         => MIB_II . '1.6.0';
use constant sysServices         => MIB_II . '1.7.0';
# Additions to 'system' group re: SNMPv2 and RFC 1907.
use constant sysORLastChange     => MIB_II . '1.8.0';
use constant sysORTable          => MIB_II . '1.9';

# The 'interfaces' group re: SNMPv1 and RFC 1213.
use constant ifNumber            => MIB_II . '2.1.0';
use constant ifTable             => MIB_II . '2.2';
```

```
use constant ifEntry           => MIB_II . '2.2.1';
use constant ifIndex           => MIB_II . '2.2.1.1';
use constant ifDescr           => MIB_II . '2.2.1.2';
use constant ifType            => MIB_II . '2.2.1.3';
use constant ifMtu             => MIB_II . '2.2.1.4';
use constant ifSpeed           => MIB_II . '2.2.1.5';
use constant ifPhysAddress     => MIB_II . '2.2.1.6';
use constant ifAdminStatus     => MIB_II . '2.2.1.7';
use constant ifOperStatus      => MIB_II . '2.2.1.8';
use constant ifLastChange      => MIB_II . '2.2.1.9';
use constant ifInOctets        => MIB_II . '2.2.1.10';
use constant ifInUcastPkts     => MIB_II . '2.2.1.11';
use constant ifInNUcastPkts    => MIB_II . '2.2.1.12';
use constant ifInDiscards      => MIB_II . '2.2.1.13';
use constant ifInErrors        => MIB_II . '2.2.1.14';
use constant ifInUnknownProtos => MIB_II . '2.2.1.15';
use constant ifOutOctets       => MIB_II . '2.2.1.16';
use constant ifOutUcastPkts    => MIB_II . '2.2.1.17';
use constant ifOutNUcastPkts   => MIB_II . '2.2.1.18';
use constant ifOutDiscards     => MIB_II . '2.2.1.19';
use constant ifOutErrors       => MIB_II . '2.2.1.20';
use constant ifOutQLen         => MIB_II . '2.2.1.21';
use constant ifSpecific        => MIB_II . '2.2.1.22';

# The 'at' group re: RFC 1156.  Use of this group is deprecated.
use constant atTable           => MIB_II . '3.1';
use constant atEntry           => MIB_II . '3.1.1';
use constant atIfIndex         => '.1';
use constant atPhysAddress     => '.2';
use constant atNetAddress      => '.3';

# The 'ip' group re: RFC 1213.
use constant ipForwarding      => MIB_II . '4.1.0';
use constant ipDefaultTTL      => MIB_II . '4.2.0';
use constant ipInReceives      => MIB_II . '4.3.0';
use constant ipInHdrErrors     => MIB_II . '4.4.0';
use constant ipInAddrErrors    => MIB_II . '4.5.0';
use constant ipForwDatagrams   => MIB_II . '4.6.0';
use constant ipInUnknownProtos => MIB_II . '4.7.0';
use constant ipInDiscards      => MIB_II . '4.8.0';
use constant ipInDelivers      => MIB_II . '4.9.0';
use constant ipOutRequests     => MIB_II . '4.10.0';
use constant ipOutOutDiscards  => MIB_II . '4.11.0';
use constant ipOutNoRoutes     => MIB_II . '4.12.0';
use constant ipReasmTimeOut    => MIB_II . '4.13.0';
use constant ipReasmReqds      => MIB_II . '4.14.0';
use constant ipReasmOKs        => MIB_II . '4.15.0';
use constant ipReasmFails      => MIB_II . '4.16.0';
use constant ipFragOKs         => MIB_II . '4.17.0';
use constant ipFragFails       => MIB_II . '4.18.0';
use constant ipFragCreates     => MIB_II . '4.19.0';
use constant ipAddrTable       => MIB_II . '4.20';
use constant ipRouteTable      => MIB_II . '4.21';
use constant ipRouteEntry      => MIB_II . '4.21.1';
use constant ipRouteDest       => MIB_II . '4.21.1.1';
use constant ipRouteIfIndex    => MIB_II . '4.21.1.2';
use constant ipRouteMetric1    => MIB_II . '4.21.1.3';
```

```
use constant ipRouteMetric2    => MIB_II . '4.21.1.4';
use constant ipRouteMetric3    => MIB_II . '4.21.1.5';
use constant ipRouteMetric4    => MIB_II . '4.21.1.6';
use constant ipRouteNextHop    => MIB_II . '4.21.1.7';
use constant ipRouteType       => MIB_II . '4.21.1.8';
use constant ipRouteProto      => MIB_II . '4.21.1.9';
use constant ipRouteAge        => MIB_II . '4.21.1.10';
use constant ipRouteMask       => MIB_II . '4.21.1.11';
use constant ipRouteMetric5    => MIB_II . '4.21.1.12';
use constant ipRouteInfo       => MIB_II . '4.21.1.13';
use constant ipNetToMediaTable => MIB_II . '4.22';
use constant ipRoutingDiscards => MIB_II . '4.23.0';
# An addition to the 'ip' group from RFC 1354.
use constant ipForward         => MIB_II . '4.24';
use constant ipForwardNumber   => MIB_II . '4.24.1.0';
use constant ipForwardTable    => MIB_II . '4.24.2.0';
use constant ipForwardEntry    => MIB_II . '4.24.2.1';


# The 'icmp' group re: SNMPv1 and RFC 1213.
use constant icmpInMsgs            => MIB_II . '5.1.0';
use constant icmpInErrors          => MIB_II . '5.2.0';
use constant icmpInDestUnreachs    => MIB_II . '5.3.0';
use constant icmpInTimeExcds       => MIB_II . '5.4.0';
use constant icmpInParmProbs       => MIB_II . '5.5.0';
use constant icmpInSrcQuenches     => MIB_II . '5.6.0';
use constant icmpInRedirects       => MIB_II . '5.7.0';
use constant icmpInEchos           => MIB_II . '5.8.0';
use constant icmpInEchoReps        => MIB_II . '5.9.0';
use constant icmpInTimestamps      => MIB_II . '5.10.0';
use constant icmpInTimestampsReps  => MIB_II . '5.11.0';
use constant icmpInAddrMasks       => MIB_II . '5.12.0';
use constant icmpInAddrMaskReps    => MIB_II . '5.13.0';
use constant icmpOutMsgs           => MIB_II . '5.14.0';
use constant icmpOutErrors         => MIB_II . '5.15.0';
use constant icmpOutDestUnreachs   => MIB_II . '5.16.0';
use constant icmpOutTimeExcds      => MIB_II . '5.17.0';
use constant icmpOutParmProbs      => MIB_II . '5.18.0';
use constant icmpOutSrcQuenches    => MIB_II . '5.19.0';
use constant icmpOutRedirects      => MIB_II . '5.20.0';
use constant icmpOutEchos          => MIB_II . '5.21.0';
use constant icmpOutEchoReps       => MIB_II . '5.22.0';
use constant icmpOutTimestamps     => MIB_II . '5.23.0';
use constant icmpOutTimestampReps  => MIB_II . '5.24.0';
use constant icmpOutAddrMasks      => MIB_II . '5.25.0';
use constant icmpOutAddrMaskReps   => MIB_II . '5.26.0';


# The 'tcp' group from RFC 1213.
use constant tcpRtoAlgorithm    => MIB_II . '6.1.0';
use constant tcpRtoMin          => MIB_II . '6.2.0';
use constant tcpRtoMax          => MIB_II . '6.3.0';
use constant tcpMaxConn         => MIB_II . '6.4.0';
use constant tcpActiveOpens     => MIB_II . '6.5.0';
use constant tcpPassiveOpens    => MIB_II . '6.6.0';
use constant tcpAttemptFails    => MIB_II . '6.7.0';
use constant tcpEstabResets     => MIB_II . '6.8.0';
use constant tcpCurrEstab       => MIB_II . '6.9.0';
use constant tcpInSegs          => MIB_II . '6.10.0';
```

```
use constant tcpOutSegs              => MIB_II . '6.11.0';
use constant tcpRetransSegs          => MIB_II . '6.12.0';
use constant tcpConnTable            => MIB_II . '6.13';
use constant tcpInErrs               => MIB_II . '6.14.0';
use constant tcpOutRsts              => MIB_II . '6.15.0';

# The 'udp' group from RFC 1213.
use constant udpInDatagrams          => MIB_II . '7.1.0';
use constant udpNoPorts              => MIB_II . '7.2.0';
use constant udpInErrors             => MIB_II . '7.3.0';
use constant udpOutDatagrams         => MIB_II . '7.4.0';
use constant udpTable                => MIB_II . '7.5';
use constant udpEntry                => MIB_II . '7.5.1';
use constant udpLocalAddress         => MIB_II . '7.5.1.1';
use constant udpLocalPort            => MIB_II . '7.5.1.2';

# Not included: the 'egp', 'cmot', 'transmission', and 'snmp' group.

1;
```

Index